New Perspectives on
Microsoft®
Visual Basic 4.0
for Windows®

INTRODUCTORY

The New Perspectives Series

The New Perspectives Series consists of texts and technology that teach computer concepts and the programs listed below. Both Windows 3.1 and Windows 95 versions of these programs are available. You can order these New Perspectives texts in many different lengths, software releases, custom-bound combinations, CourseKits™ and Custom Editions®. Contact your CTI sales representative or customer service representative for the most up-to-date details.

The New Perspectives Series

Computer Concepts

dBASE®

Internet Using Netscape Navigator™ Software

Lotus® 1-2-3®

Microsoft® Access

Microsoft® Excel

Microsoft® Office Professional

Microsoft® PowerPoint®

Microsoft® Visual Basic®

Microsoft® Windows® 3.1

Microsoft® Windows® 95

Microsoft® Word

Microsoft® Works

Corel Perfect Office™

Paradox®

Presentations™

Quattro Pro®

WordPerfect®

New Perspectives on
Microsoft®
Visual Basic 4.0
for Windows®

I N T R O D U C T O R Y

Michael V. Ekedahl

William A. Newman
University of Nevada – Las Vegas

COURSE
TECHNOLOGY

ONE MAIN STREET, CAMBRIDGE, MA 02142

an International Thomson Publishing company I(T)P®

Cambridge • Albany • Bonn • Boston • Cincinnati • London • Madrid • Melbourne • Mexico City
New York • Paris • San Francisco • Singapore • Tokyo • Toronto • Washington

New Perspectives on Microsoft Visual Basic 4.0 for Windows—Introductory is published by Course Technology.

Managing Editor	Mac Mendelsohn
Series Consulting Editor	Susan Solomon
Senior Editor	Kristen Duerr
Product Manager	Mark Reimold
Project Manager	Cindy Johnson
Developmental Editor	Kathleen Habib
Associate Product Manager	Jennifer Normandin
Editorial Assistant	Rachel Crapser
Production Editor	Christine Spillett
Text and Cover Designer	Ella Hanna
Cover Illustrator	Nancy Nash

© 1997 by Course Technology.
A Division of Course Technology – I(T)P®

For more information contact:

Course Technology
One Main Street
Cambridge, MA 02142

International Thomson Editores
Campos Eliseos 385, Piso 7
Col. Polanco
11560 Mexico D.F. Mexico

International Thomson Publishing Europe
Berkshire House 168-173
High Holborn
London WCIV 7AA
England

International Thomson Publishing GmbH
Königswinterer Strasse 418
53227 Bonn
Germany

Thomas Nelson Australia
102 Dodds Street
South Melbourne, 3205
Victoria, Australia

International Thomson Publishing Asia
211 Henderson Road
#05-10 Henderson Building
Singapore 0315

Nelson Canada
1120 Birchmount Road
Scarborough, Ontario
Canada M1K 5G4

International Thomson Publishing Japan
Hirakawacho Kyowa Building, 3F
2-2-1 Hirakawacho
Chiyoda-ku, Tokyo 102
Japan

ISBN 0-7600-4587-9

Printed in the United States of America

10 9 8 7 6 5 4 3

At Course Technology we have one foot in education and the other in technology. We believe that technology is transforming the way people teach and learn, and we are excited about providing instructors and students with materials that use technology to teach about technology.

Our development process is unparalleled in the higher education publishing industry. Every product we create goes through an exacting process of design, development, review, and testing.

Reviewers give us direction and insight that shape our manuscripts and bring them up to the latest standards. Every manuscript is quality tested. Students whose backgrounds match the intended audience work through every keystroke, carefully checking for clarity and pointing out errors in logic and sequence. Together with our own technical reviewers, these testers help us ensure that everything that carries our name is error-free and easy to use.

We show both how and why technology is critical to solving problems in college and in whatever field you choose to teach or pursue. Our time-tested, step-by-step instructions provide unparalleled clarity. Examples and applications are chosen and crafted to motivate students.

As the New Perspectives Series team at Course Technology, our goal is to produce the most timely, accurate, creative, and technologically sound product in the entire college publishing industry. We strive for consistent high quality. This takes a lot of communication, coordination, and hard work. But we love what we do. We are determined to be the best. Write us and let us know what you think. You can also e-mail us at info@course.com.

The New Perspectives Series Team

Joseph J. Adamski	Kathy Finnegan	Dan Oja
Judy Adamski	Robin Geller	June Parsons
Roy Ageloff	Kate Habib	Sandra Poindexter
David Auer	Roger Hayen	Mark Reimold
Rachel Bunin	Charles Hommel	Ann Shaffer
Joan Carey	Cindy Johnson	Susan Solomon
Patrick Carey	Chris Kelly	Christine Spillett
Barbara Clemens	Mary Kemper	Susanne Walker
Rachel Crasper	Terry Ann Kremer	John Zeanchock
Kim Crowley	Nancy Ludlow	Beverly Zimmerman
Kristen Duerr	Mac Mendelsohn	Scott Zimmerman
Jessica Evans	Jennifer Normandin	

Preface The New Perspectives Series

What is the New Perspectives Series?

CTI's **New Perspectives Series** is an integrated system of instruction that combines text and technology products to teach computer concepts and microcomputer applications. Users consistently praise this series for innovative pedagogy, creativity, supportive and engaging style, accuracy, and use of interactive technology. The first New Perspectives text was published in January of 1993. Since then, the series has grown to more than 40 titles and has become the best-selling series on computer concepts and microcomputer applications. Others have imitated the New Perspectives features, design, and technologies, but none have replicated its quality and its ability to consistently anticipate and meet the needs of instructors and students.

What is the Integrated System of Instruction?

You hold in your hands a textbook that is one component of an Integrated System of Instruction: text, graphics, video, sound, animation, and simulations that are linked and that provide a flexible, unified, and interactive system to help you teach and help your students learn. Specifically, the *New Perspectives Integrated System of Instruction* consists of five components: a CTI textbook, Course Labs, Course Online, Course Presenter, and Course Test Manager. These components—shown in the graphic on the back cover of this book—have been developed to work together to provide a complete, integrative teaching and learning experience.

How is the New Perspectives Series different from other microcomputer concepts and applications series?

The **New Perspectives Series** distinguishes itself from other series in at least four substantial ways: sound instructional design, consistent quality, innovative technology, and proven pedagogy. The applications texts in this series consist of two or more tutorials, which are based on sound instructional design. Each tutorial is motivated by a realistic case that is meaningful to students. Rather than learn a laundry list of features, students learn the features in the context of solving a problem. This process motivates all concepts and skills by demonstrating to students *why* they would want to know them.

Instructors and students have come to rely on the high quality of the **New Perspectives Series** and to consistently praise its accuracy. This accuracy is a result of CTI's unique multi-step quality assurance process that incorporates student testing at three stages of development, using hardware and software configurations appropriate to the product. All solutions, test questions, and other CourseTools (discussed later in this preface) are tested using similar procedures. Instructors who adopt this series report that students can work through the tutorials independently, with a minimum of intervention or "damage control" by instructors or staff. This consistent quality has meant that if instructors are pleased with one product from the series, they can rely on the same quality with any other New Perspectives product.

The **New Perspectives Series** also distinguishes itself by its innovative technology. This series innovated Course Labs, truly interactive learning applications. These have set the standard for *interactive* learning.

How do I know that the New Perspectives Series will work?

Some instructors who use this series report a significant difference between how much their students learn and retain with this series as compared to other series. With other series, instructors often find that students can work through the book and do well on homework and tests, but still not demonstrate competency when asked to perform particular tasks outside the context of the text's sample case or project. With the **New Perspectives Series**, however, instructors report that students have a complete, integrative learning experience that stays with them. They credit this high retention and competency to the fact that this series incorporates critical thinking and problem solving with computer skills mastery.

How does this book I'm holding fit into the New Perspectives Series?

New Perspectives microcomputer concepts and applications books are available in the following categories:

Brief books are about 100 pages long and are intended to teach only the essentials. They contain 2 to 4 chapters or tutorials.

Introductory books are about 300 pages long and consist of 6 or 7 chapters or tutorials. An Introductory book is designed for a short course or for a one-term course, used in combination with other Introductory books. The book you are holding is an Introductory book.

Comprehensive books are about 600 pages long and consist of all of the chapters or tutorials in the Introductory book, plus 3 or 4 more Intermediate chapters or tutorials covering higher-level topics. Comprehensive applications texts include Brief Windows tutorials, the Introductory and Intermediate tutorials, 3 or 4 Additional Cases, and a Reference Section.

Advanced applications books cover topics similar to those in the Comprehensive books, but in more depth. Advanced books present the most high-level coverage in the series.

Custom Books The New Perspectives Series offers you two ways to customize a New Perspectives text to fit your course exactly: *CourseKits*, 2 or more texts packaged together in a box, and *Custom Editions*, your choice of books bound together. Custom Editions offer you unparalleled flexibility in designing your concepts and applications courses. You can build your own book by ordering a combination of titles bound together to cover only the topics you want. Your students save because they buy only the materials they need. There is no minimum order, and books are spiral bound. Both CourseKits and Custom Editions offer significant price discounts. Contact your CTI sales representative for more information.

New Perspectives Series Concepts and Applications				
■ Brief Titles or Modules	■ Introductory Titles or Modules	■ Intermediate Modules	■ Advanced Titles or Modules	□ Other Modules □ Individual Concepts Chapters
Brief	**Introductory**	**Comprehensive**	**Advanced Applications**	**Custom Editions**
Concepts and Applications				
2 to 4 tutorials or chapters	Brief + 4 or 5 more tutorials or chapters	1 Introductory + 3 or 4 Intermediate tutorials or chapters. Applications have Brief Windows, Additional Cases and Reference section.	Quick Review of basics + in-depth, high-level coverage	Choose from any of the above to build your own Custom Editions® or CourseKits®

In what kind of course could I use this book?

This book can be used in any course in which you want students to learn all the most important topics of Visual Basic 4.0 for Windows, including working with data from another file or database. Students learn how to plan, program, and debug their Visual Basic applications using modern programming techniques and practicing good graphical user interface design. This text is suited for a three-credit introductory Visual Basic course for students with little or no programming background. It assumes that students have learned basic Windows 95 navigation and file management skills from Course Technology's *New Perspectives on Microsoft Windows 95 Brief* or an *equivalent* book.

How do the Windows 95 editions differ from the Windows 3.1 editions?

Larger Page Size   If you've used a New Perspectives text before, you'll immediately notice that the book you're holding is larger than the Windows 3.1 series books. We've responded to user requests for a larger page with larger screen shots and associated labels. Look on page VB 28 for an example of how we've made the screen shots easier to read.

SESSION 1.2

Sessions   We've divided the tutorials into sessions. Each session is designed to be completed in about 45 minutes to an hour (depending, of course, upon student needs and the speed of your lab equipment). With sessions, learning is broken up into more easily-assimilated chunks. You can more accurately allocate time in your syllabus. Students can better manage the available lab time. Each session begins with a "session box," which quickly describes the skills students will learn in the session. Furthermore, each session is numbered, which makes it easier for you and your students to navigate and communicate about the tutorial. Look on page VB 5 for the session box that opens Session 1.1.

Quick Check

Quick Checks   Each session concludes with Quick Checks, meaningful, conceptual questions that test students' understanding of what they learned in the session. Answers to all of the Quick Check questions are at the back of the book preceding the Index. You can find examples of Quick Checks on pages VB 20 and VB 39.

New Design   We have retained the best of the old design to help students differentiate between what they are to *do* and what they are to *read*. The steps are clearly identified by their shaded background and numbered steps. Furthermore, this new design presents steps and screen shots in a larger, easier to read format. Some good examples of our new design are pages VB 24 and VB 25.

What features are retained in the Windows 95 editions of the New Perspectives Series?

"Read This Before You Begin" Pages   This page is consistent with CTI's unequaled commitment to helping instructors introduce technology into the classroom. Technical considerations and assumptions about software are listed to help instructors save time and eliminate unnecessary aggravation. The "Read This Before You Begin" page for this book is on page VB 2.

Tutorial Case   Each tutorial begins with a problem presented in a case that is meaningful to students. The problem turns the task of learning how to use an application into a problem-solving process. The problems increase in complexity with each tutorial, and within each tutorial. These cases touch on multicultural, international, and ethical issues—so important to today's business curriculum. See page VB 3 for the case that begins Tutorial 1.

Step-by-Step Methodology   This unique CTI methodology keeps students on track. They enter data, click buttons, or press keys always within the context of solving the problem posed in the tutorial case. The text constantly guides students, letting them know where they are in the course of solving the problem. In addition, the numerous screen shots include labels that direct students' attention to what they should look at on the screen. On almost every page in this book, you can find an example of how steps, screen shots, and labels work together.

TROUBLE?

TROUBLE? Paragraphs   These paragraphs anticipate the mistakes or problems that students are likely to have and help them recover and continue with the tutorial. By putting these paragraphs in the book, rather than in the Instructor's Manual, we facilitate independent learning and free the instructor to focus on substantive conceptual issues rather than on common procedural errors. Two representative examples of TROUBLE? are on pages VB 61 and VB 71.

REFERENCE window

Reference Windows   Reference Windows appear throughout the text. They are succinct summaries of the most important tasks covered in the tutorials. Reference Windows are specially designed and written so students can refer to them when doing the Tutorial Assignments and Case Problems, and after completing the course. Page VB 35 contains the Reference Window for Adding an Image to a Form.

Task Reference   The Task Reference is a summary of how to perform common tasks using the most efficient method, as well as references to pages where the task is discussed in more detail. It appears as a table at the end of the book. In this book the Task Reference is on pages VB 289 to VB 296.

Tutorial Assignments, Case Problems, and Lab Assignments   Each tutorial concludes with Tutorial Assignments, which provide students with additional hands-on practice of the skills they learned in the tutorial. The Tutorial Assignments are followed by four Case Problems that have approximately the same scope as the tutorial case. In the Windows 95 applications texts, there is always one Case Problem in the book and one in the Instructor's Manual that require students to solve the problem independently, either "from scratch" or with minimum guidance. Finally, if a Course Lab (see next page) accompanies the tutorial, Lab Assignments are included. Look on page VB 40 for the Tutorial Assignments for Tutorial 1. See page VB 41 for examples of Case Problems. The Lab Assignment for Tutorial 1 is on page VB 45.

Exploration Exercises   The Windows environment allows students to learn by exploring and discovering what they can do. Exploration Exercises can be Tutorial Assignments or Case Problems that challenge students, encourage them to explore the capabilities of the program they are using, and extend their knowledge using the online Help facility and other reference materials. Page VB 87 contains Exploration Exercises for Tutorial 2.

The New Perspectives Series is known for using technology to help instructors teach and administer, and to help students learn. What CourseTools are available with CTI textbooks?

All of the teaching and learning materials available with the New Perspectives Series are known as CourseTools.

Course Labs: Now, Concepts Come to Life   Computer skills and concepts come to life with the New Perspectives Course Labs—highly interactive tutorials that combine illustrations, animation, digital images, and simulations. The Labs guide students step-by-step, present them with Quick Check questions, let them explore on their own, test their comprehension, and provide printed feedback. Lab Assignments are included at the end of each relevant chapter or tutorial in the text book. The Lab available with this book and the tutorial in which it appears is:

Visual Programming
Tutorial 1

Course Online: A Website Dedicated to Keeping You and Your Students Up-To-Date   When you use a New Perspectives product, you can access CTI's faculty and student sites on the World Wide Web. You can browse the password-protected Faculty Online Companion to obtain all the materials you need to prepare for class, including online Instructors Manuals, Solutions Files, and Student Files. Please see your Instructor's Manual or call your CTI customer service representative for more information. Students may access their Online Companion in the Student Center using the URL **http://coursetools.com**.

Course Test Manager: Testing and Practice at the Computer or on Paper
Course Test Manager is cutting-edge Windows-based testing software that helps instructors design and administer pretests, practice tests, and actual examinations. This full-featured program allows students to randomly generate practice tests that provide immediate on-screen feedback and detailed study guides for questions incorrectly answered. On-screen pretests help instructors assess student skills and plan instruction. Instructors can also use Course Test Manager to produce printed tests. Also, students can take tests at the computer that can be automatically graded and can generate statistical information on students' individual and group performance.

What other supplements are available with CTI textbooks?

Instructor's Manual   New Perspectives Series Instructor's Manuals are available in printed form and through the CTI Faculty Online Companion on the World Wide Web. (Call your customer service representative for the URL and your password.) Each Instructor's Manual contains the following items:
- *Instructor's Notes* containing an overview, an outline, technical notes, lecture notes, and an extra case problem for each tutorial.
- *Printed solutions* to all of the Tutorial Assignments, Case Problems, Additional Cases and Lab Assignments.

Solutions Files Solution Files contain every file students are asked to create or modify in the tutorials, Tutorial Assignments, Case Problems and Additional Cases.

Student Files Student Files, containing all of the data that students will use for the tutorials, Tutorial Assignments, Case Problems and Additional Cases, are provided through CTI's online companions, as well as on disk. A Readme file includes technical tips for lab management. See the inside covers of this book and the "Read This Before You Begin" page before Tutorial 1 for more information on Student Files.

Most of the CourseTools and supplements are supplied in a package called an Instructor's Resource Kit. Which CourseTools and supplements are included in the Instructor's Resource Kit for this text book?

You will receive the following items in the Instructor's Resource Kit:
- Instructor's Manual
- Solution Files
- Student Files
- Course Labs
- Course Test Manager Engine and Test Bank

To obtain a copy of the Course Presenter for this textbook, contact your CTI Customer Service Representative.

Acknowledgments

Our appreciation goes to each of the reviewers whose suggestions and comments helped create this book, and to Mr. Clark Hu, Ph. D. student in the College of Hotel Administration, University of Nevada—Las Vegas, for his work on the test bank. We would also like to thank all the members of the New Perspectives team who helped guide the book's development and production. We would like to thank the staff at Gex and the quality assurance staff for their fine work.

Special thanks to Kate Habib for her valuable suggestions and tireless efforts as developmental editor, and to Cindy Johnson for her efforts. We would also like to thank Kristen Duerr for her coordination of the project.

Michael V. Ekedahl thanks his wife Katrina for her patience while he completed his work. He would also like to thank his dogs Rio and Binky for their constant support and companionship.

William A. Newman thanks his wife Anthea, mother Irene and mother-in-law Annette Karnas, for their encouragement and support. Special thanks go to his two dogs Sasha and Sabrina Spot for their companionship.

Michael V. Ekedahl
William A. Newman

Table of **Contents**

TUTORIAL 3

Objects and the Events They Generate

Developing an Event-Driven Cash Register Program for Master Burger   **VB 91**

Reference Windows

Microsoft®
Visual Basic 4
for Windows®

INTRODUCTORY

TUTORIALS

Read This **Before You Begin**

TO THE STUDENT

STUDENT DISKS

To complete the Introductory tutorials, Tutorial Assignments, and Case Problems in this book, you need Student Disks. Your instructor will either provide you with Student Disks or ask you to make your own.

If you are supposed to make your own Student Disks, you will need two blank, formatted high-density disks. You will need to copy a set of folders from a file server or standalone computer onto your disks. Your instructor will tell you which computer, drive letter, and folders contain the files you need. The following table shows you which folders go on each of your disks, so that you will have enough disk space to complete all the tutorials, Tutorial Assignments, and Case Problems:

Student Disk	Write this on the disk label	Put these folders on the disk
1	Introductory Tutorials 1–4	Tutorial.01, Tutorial.02, Tutorial.03, Tutorial.04
2	Introductory Tutorials 5	Tutorial.05
3	Introductory Tutorial 6, Appendix A	Tutorial.06, Appendix.A

When you begin each tutorial, be sure you are using the correct Student Disk. See the inside front or inside back cover of this book for more information on Student Disk files, or ask your instructor or technical support person for assistance.

COURSE LABS

The Introductory tutorials features an interactive Course Lab to help you understand visual programming concepts. There is one Lab Assignment at the end of Tutorial 1 that relates to this Lab. To start the Lab, click the **Start** button on the Windows 95 Taskbar, point to **Programs**, point to **Course Labs**, point to **New Perspectives Applications**, and click **Visual Programming**. (This path may have changed by the time you read this, please refer to the README file for the lab or consult your instructor if you encounter difficulties.)

USING YOUR OWN COMPUTER

If you are going to work through this book using your own computer, you need:

■ **Computer System** Microsoft Windows 95 Windows NT 4.0, or later and Microsoft Visual Basic 4.0 (or Microsoft Visual Basic 4.0 Working Model) must be installed on your computer. This book assumes a complete installation of Visual Basic. The screens captured for this text show Visual Basic 4.0 Working Model.

■ **Student Disks** Ask your instructor or lab manager for details on how to get the Student Disks. You will not be able to complete the tutorials or exercises in this book using your own computer until you have Student Disks. The student files may also be obtained electronically over the Internet. See the inside front or inside back cover of this book for more details.

■ **Course Lab** See your instructor or technical support person to obtain the Course Lab software for use on your own computer.

VISIT OUR WORLD WIDE WEB SITE

Additional materials designed especially for you are available on the World Wide Web. Go to **http://coursetools.com**.

TO THE INSTRUCTOR

To complete the tutorials in this book, your students must use a set of student files. These files are included in the Instructor's Resource Kit, and they may also be obtained electronically over the Internet. See the inside front or inside back cover of this book for more details. Follow the instructions in the Readme file to copy them to your server or standalone computer. You can view the Readme file using WordPad.

Once the files are copied, you can make Student Disks for the students yourself, or tell students where to find the files so they can make their own Student Disks. Make sure the files get correctly copied onto the Student Disks by following the instructions in the Student Disks section above, which will ensure that students have enough disk space to complete all the tutorials, Tutorial Assignments, and Case Problems.

VISUAL BASIC 4.0 WORKING MODEL CD-ROM

This text is available with and without Microsoft's Visual Basic 4.0 Working Model CD-ROM. The tutorials in this book can be completed using only the Working Model if you so desire.

COURSE LAB SOFTWARE

Introductory Tutorial 1 features an online, interactive Course Lab that introduces visual programming concepts. The Course Lab software is distributed on a CD-ROM included in the Instructor's Resource Kit. To install the Course Lab software, follow the setup instructions in the Readme file on the CD-ROM. Refer also to the Readme file for essential technical notes related to running the Labs in a multi-user environment. Once you have installed the Course Lab software, your students can start the Lab from the Windows 95 desktop by clicking Start, pointing to Programs/Course Labs/New Perspectives Applications, and clicking Visual Programming.

CTI COURSE LAB SOFTWARE AND STUDENT FILES

You are granted a license to copy the Student Files and Course Lab to any computer or computer network used by students who have purchased this book.

Getting Started with Visual Basic

Running and Creating a Program for the Dunn Financial Group

LAB
Visual Programming

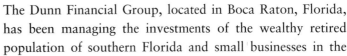

CASE

Dunn Financial Group

The Dunn Financial Group, located in Boca Raton, Florida, has been managing the investments of the wealthy retired population of southern Florida and small businesses in the area for over five years. The company was started by Gerrold Campbell, who retired from a large investment firm in New York City. This year he decided to computerize many of the company's operations so that the Dunn Financial Group could be more responsive to the needs of its clients.

Mark Fisk is the chief computer programmer/analyst for the Dunn Financial Group. Based on Mark's recommendations, the company is beginning to use Visual Basic 4.0 for Windows 95 as its standard programming language. Mark believes that the Dunn Financial Group should use Visual Basic for all its programs for several reasons:

■ The company uses many other Windows 95 programs, and Visual Basic programs can include buttons, menus, and other Windows 95 features that users are accustomed to already.

■ Programs can be written quickly in Visual Basic because of the many tools supplied to the programmer.

■ Visual Basic can work effectively with business data.

The first program Gerrold asked Mark to create was a program to list the names and addresses of all the company's clients. Each account manager at Dunn Financial maintains a separate client list in an address book, but the company had no consolidated list of clients. Mark has already written the program to manage the client list and, so that you can become familiar with Visual Basic, he would like you to use the program to enter the information for a new client and change the information for an existing client. In this tutorial, you will run the program that Mark has written, then you'll write your first Visual Basic program.

Using the Tutorials Effectively

These tutorials will help you learn about Visual Basic 4.0 for Windows 95. The tutorials are designed to be used at a computer. Each tutorial is divided into sessions. Watch for the session headings, such as Session 1.1 and Session 1.2. Each session is designed to be completed in about 45 minutes, but take as much time as you need. It's also a good idea to take a break between sessions.

Before you begin, read the following questions and answers. They are designed to help you use the tutorials effectively.

Where do I start?

Each tutorial begins with a case, which sets the scene for the tutorial and gives you background information to help you understand what you will be doing in the tutorial. Read the case before you go to the lab. In the lab, begin with the first session of a tutorial.

How do I know what to do on the computer?

Each session contains steps that you will perform on the computer to learn how to use Visual Basic 4.0 for Windows 95. Read the text that introduces each series of steps. The steps you need to do at a computer are numbered and are set against a colored background. Read each step carefully and completely before you try it.

How do I know if I did the step correctly?

As you work, compare your computer screen with the corresponding figure in the tutorial. Don't worry if your screen display is somewhat different from the figure. The important parts of the screen display are labeled in each figure. Check to make sure these parts are on your screen.

What if I make a mistake?

Don't worry about making mistakes—they are part of the learning process. Paragraphs labeled "TROUBLE?" identify common problems and explain how to get back on track. Follow the steps in a TROUBLE? paragraph *only* if you are having the problem described. If you run into other problems:

- Carefully consider the current state of your system, the position of the pointer, and any messages on the screen.

- Complete the sentence, "Now I want to..." Be specific, because you are identifying your goal.

- Develop a plan for accomplishing your goal, and put your plan into action.

How do I use the Reference Windows?

Reference Windows summarize the procedures you learn in the tutorial steps. Do not complete the actions in the Reference Windows when you are working through the tutorial. Instead, refer to the Reference Windows while you are working on the assignments at the end of the tutorial.

How can I test my understanding of the material I learned in the tutorial?

At the end of each session, you can answer the Quick Check questions. The answers for the Quick Checks are at the end of the book.

After you have completed the entire tutorial, you should complete the Tutorial Assignments and Case Problems. They are carefully structured so that you will review what you have learned and then apply your knowledge to new situations.

What if I can't remember how to do something?

You should refer to the Task Reference at the end of the book; it summarizes how to accomplish tasks using the most efficient method. The Notes column includes shortcuts or additional information.

Before you begin the tutorials, you should know how to use the menus, dialog boxes, Help facility, and My Computer in Windows 95. Course Technology publishes two excellent texts for learning Windows 95: *New Perspectives on Microsoft Windows 95—Brief* and *New Perspectives on Microsoft Windows 95—Introductory*.

Now that you have seen how to use the tutorials effectively, you are ready to begin.

SESSION

1.1

In this session you will learn about the different windows and components of the Visual Basic system and how to use them. You will learn how to start Visual Basic, use the online Help, open a Visual Basic project, run a program, stop a program, print a form image, and exit Visual Basic.

What Is Visual Basic?

Visual Basic 4.0 for Windows 95, or simply Visual Basic, is a computer programming language you use to create programs that perform specific tasks. **Computer programming** is the process of writing a set of organized statements using a language such as Visual Basic. For example, Mark created a program to maintain a list of Dunn Financial's clients. The program contains the Visual Basic statements needed to display a client's name and address on the screen, locate a client's name and address, add the information for new clients, update existing client information, and delete the information for obsolete clients.

When you write a computer program in Visual Basic, you use various tools to design the **user interface**, which is a term that describes what a user of the program sees on the screen and how the user interacts with the program. The screen that the user sees is called a **form.** You use different tools to create items on the form, such as buttons the user can click and boxes that can display text or pictures. Some tools are designed to reflect how you fill out a paper form. For example, there are tools that allow the user to check a box or choose one item from a list of items.

In Visual Basic, these tools are called **controls**. Each kind of control has a different appearance and behaves differently. For example, a TextBox control consists of a box with a cursor so the user can enter text in the box. A CommandButton control consists of a button and the button's caption, which describes the purpose of the button. The user clicks the button to perform the action indicated by its caption. You add a control to a form by drawing a copy of the control on the form. Each control you place on a form is called an **object**. Figure 1-1 shows a sample of Visual Basic controls and their purpose.

Figure 1-1 ◀
Sample of
Visual Basic
controls

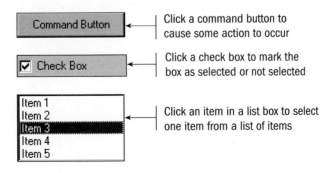

Click a command button to cause some action to occur

Click a check box to mark the box as selected or not selected

Click an item in a list box to select one item from a list of items

The design of some programs requires multiple forms. For example, an inventory program might include one form describing inventory on hand and another to process orders. In Visual Basic, the design specifications for all of the forms used by a program are stored in a file called a **project**. A project lists each form in the program along with information about the tools used in the program. The project helps you manage all the different components of your program. Figure 1-2 shows the relationship between a project file and its forms.

Figure 1-2 ◀
Visual Basic
files

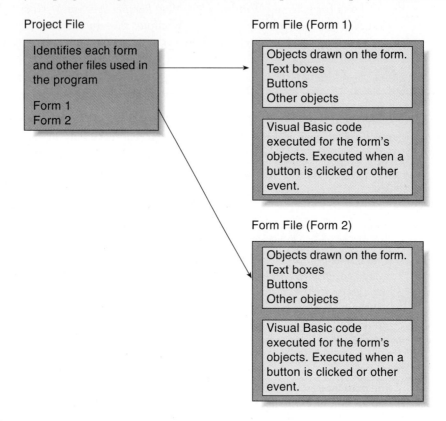

Each program has a single project file that lists the components of the program. One of these components is the form module. The form module contains all of the objects on the form, and all of the code for those objects.

Visual Basic is an **event-driven** programming language, which means that objects—pictures, words, and buttons on the screen—cause events to occur when a user activates the objects. The objects are activated, for example, when the user clicks a button or types information in the program. These events execute the program's instructions to perform a specified task.

With Visual Basic, programming is a three-step process. First, you create the user interface, then you write the statements to perform each of the tasks required by the program. The third step is a loop; you test the program, correct any errors, and test the program again. Figure 1-3 shows the steps you take to write a program.

Figure 1-3 ◀
Steps for
writing a
program

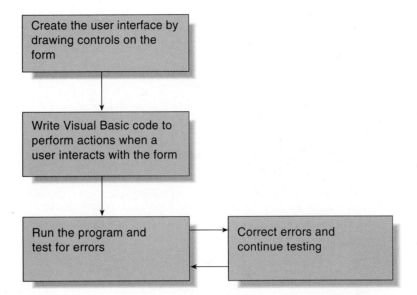

After drawing the boxes, buttons, and other objects on the form, you need to write the Visual Basic statements that are executed when a user enters text, clicks a button, or selects a menu option. These statements will perform the tasks needed to solve the problem. For example, Dunn Financial needed a consolidated list of its clients. Therefore, Mark wrote a program that contains statements to add, change, and delete client information when a user clicks the appropriate button. The set of statements written for a program is called the program's **code**.

As you write code to accomplish specific tasks, you will want to test the code to make sure it works correctly. Any errors in the code, including typographical errors, will prevent the program from running. A reader can usually understand the meaning of a sentence written in English even when words are misspelled or punctuation is not correct. In Visual Basic, however, the statements you type must be exactly correct. As you type statements, Visual Basic checks them for correctness and informs you of any syntax errors. A **syntax error** is an error that violates the rules of the Visual Basic language. For example, you might have accidentally typed the word "Pirnt" instead of "Print."

After correcting any syntax errors, you need to run the program to test that the results are correct. A program can encounter another kind of error when it is running. Although the syntax of a statement is correct, the statement might be impossible to carry out, and a run-time error is generated. A **run-time error** occurs when the program is running and it tries to do something impossible. For example, if a program tries to read a file from the disk drive, and no disk has been inserted in the drive, it is impossible for the program to read the file. You will learn more about run-time errors later in this text.

Starting Visual Basic

To run and work with the program Mark created, you first need to start Visual Basic. You can start Visual Basic using the Start button on the taskbar or a shortcut icon on the Windows 95 desktop, if an icon has been defined for Visual Basic on the computer you're using. Your instructor will tell you how to start Visual Basic in your particular environment.

To start Visual Basic using the Start button:

1. Make sure your computer is on and that the Windows 95 desktop is displayed on your screen.

2. Find the Start button, which is usually located at the bottom-left corner of the screen on the taskbar.

3. Click the **Start** button to display the Start menu, then move the mouse pointer to the item labeled **Programs**.

When the Programs item is highlighted, another menu appears listing the programs available on your computer.

4. Move the mouse pointer to the item labeled **Visual Basic 4.0**. Another menu appears listing the options available in the Visual Basic system. See Figure 1-4.

Figure 1-4 ◀
Starting Visual
Basic

Visual Basic 4.0
Working Model
shortcut icon

Windows 95
Start button

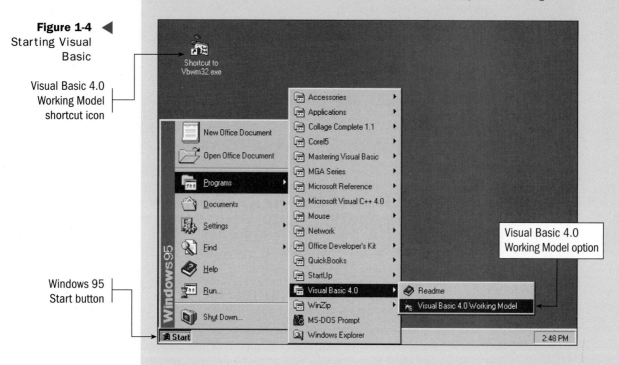

The Start menu options on your screen might be different from those in Figure 1-4, depending on the software you have on your computer.

TROUBLE? If the Visual Basic 4.0 option is not listed on your Programs menu, check to see if a shortcut icon for Visual Basic appears on the desktop, then double-click the icon to start Visual Basic. If you cannot locate Visual Basic anywhere on your computer, ask your instructor or lab staff for assistance.

5. Click **Visual Basic 4.0 Working Model**.

The introductory Visual Basic screen appears while the rest of the Visual Basic system is loaded into the computer's memory. Once Visual Basic is loaded, your screen should look similar to Figure 1-5.

Figure 1-5 ◀
Visual Basic
windows

menu bar —

toolbar —

toolbox —

Form window —

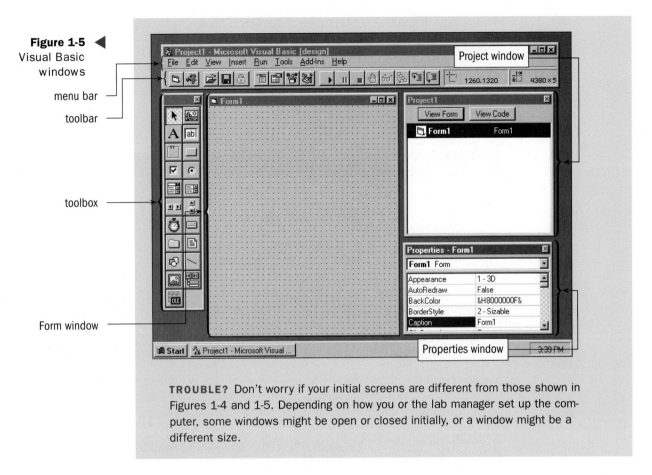

TROUBLE? Don't worry if your initial screens are different from those shown in Figures 1-4 and 1-5. Depending on how you or the lab manager set up the computer, some windows might be open or closed initially, or a window might be a different size.

When you start Visual Basic and open different project files, the size and location of the windows on the screen will vary. You can change the size and position of most Visual Basic windows to suit your own preferences, just as you can resize or move other windows in Windows 95.

When you start Visual Basic, be sure the Visual Basic startup screen contains the text Visual Basic Working Model 4.0, Visual Basic Standard Edition 4.0, or Visual Basic Professional Edition 4.0. There are several operating differences between Version 4.0 and older versions. You must be using Version 4.0 of Visual Basic to complete these tutorials.

The Visual Basic Environment

As shown in Figure 1-5, the main Visual Basic screen contains common Windows components, such as the menu bar and toolbar, plus application-specific components such as the Project window, Form window, Properties window, and toolbox. Together, these components allow you to design, create, edit, run, and test programs.

The menu bar provides the commands you use to create and run Visual Basic programs. The menu bar functions like the menu bar in any other Windows 95 program.

The toolbar provides buttons for many of the commands available from the menu bar. Clicking a toolbar button is a faster way of choosing a command than using the menu bar. As in other Windows 95 applications, you can display a ToolTip for a button on the Visual Basic toolbar by positioning the mouse pointer on the button. The ToolTip that appears shows the name of the button.

To practice displaying a ToolTip for a toolbar button:

1. Position the mouse pointer over the **Open Project** button 🖼 on the toolbar. After a few seconds, the ToolTip appears and displays the button name, Open Project.

2. Move the mouse pointer off the button.

Project Window

The **Project window** shows all of the components of the program. You use the Project window to manage the program components. (The project is the same as the program.) A project usually consists of at least one form, which is referred to as a **form module**. Other types of modules, a standard module and a class module, can also be a part of a project. The buttons View Form and View Code allow you to display the forms and code associated with the project. The item "Form1" is an empty form Visual Basic creates for you so that you can start a new project. Visual Basic operates on one project at a time. If you open another project, Visual Basic closes the existing project and opens the other project.

Form Window

The **Form window** is the window in which you design the user interface for the program. When a user runs the program, the user communicates with the program using the objects on the form. You interact with the objects in the Form window as you create and run programs.

Properties Window

The **Properties window** provides options you use to manage the appearance of each object on a form. A **property** is a characteristic of an object, such as the object's color, caption, screen location, or size. You will use the Properties window in the next session when you write your first program.

Toolbox

The **toolbox** contains all of the tools necessary to create a program. You use the icons in the toolbox to place controls on a form. As noted earlier, a control is an object, such as a box, button, or label, that you draw on a form to allow users of the form to interact with it. You can also add controls simply to enhance the visual appeal of a form. When you create your first program in the next session, you will use the toolbox to draw controls on your form.

Before you open and run the program Mark created, he suggests that you use the online Help system to learn more about specific Visual Basic terms and concepts.

Getting Help

Visual Basic has an extensive **Help system** that provides on-screen information about Visual Basic components, features, commands, and so on. For example, you can look up how to write Visual Basic statements or how to use any of the financial and mathematical functions built into Visual Basic. The Help system is based on the idea of hypertext, which means that you can navigate through the system by looking at definitions of terms you do not understand or related topics without having to search for the information. Most of the Help screens contain examples that you can copy and paste into actual Visual Basic code.

You can get Help at any time by pressing the F1 key or by selecting an option from the Help menu. Figure 1-6 describes the options available on the Help menu.

Figure 1-6 ◄
Help menu
options

Option	Description
Contents	Displays the Help window, which provides a list of avail-able Help topics from which to choose and also allows you to search for a particular topic
Search For Help On	Displays the Index tab of the Help window, where you can search for a particular topic for which you want to see Help information
Obtaining Technical Support	Displays the Contents tab of the Help window, where you can search for different ways to get support for Visual Basic
Learning Microsoft Visual Basic	Provides computer-assisted lessons that help you learn about Visual Basic
About Microsoft Visual Basic	Displays a screen telling you the version of Visual Basic you are using

Depending on whether you are running Visual Basic Working Model, Standard, or Professional edition, your Help menu options might differ from those in Figure 1-6.

Using the Index Tab

The **Index tab** of the Help window displays an alphabetical list of topics, just like a typical index in the back of a book. You can either select a topic from the list or type a topic to find information about it.

Mark suggests that you use the Index tab to find Help information about the Project window.

To use the Index tab to find information about the Project window:

1. Click **Help** on the menu bar, then click **Search For Help On**.

2. Make sure the Index tab is selected in the Help window, as shown in Figure 1-7.

Figure 1-7 ◄
Index tab of the
Help window

type text into
this text box

matching entries
are displayed in
this list box

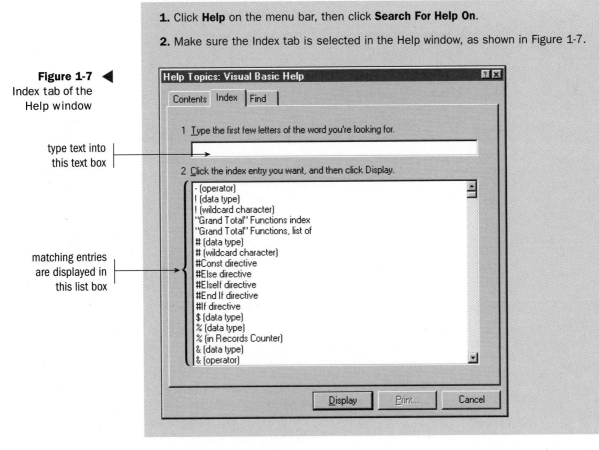

Notice that a flashing cursor appears in the text box at the top of the window. In this text box, you need to type the word or words for which you want Help information.

3. In the text box, type **project window**. As you type, the box listing available Help topics changes to match the text you are typing.

4. In the list box, make sure the topic **Project window** is highlighted, then click the **Display** button. The Topics Found dialog box opens. See Figure 1-8.

Figure 1-8 ◄
Topics Found
dialog box

click this topic ──────→

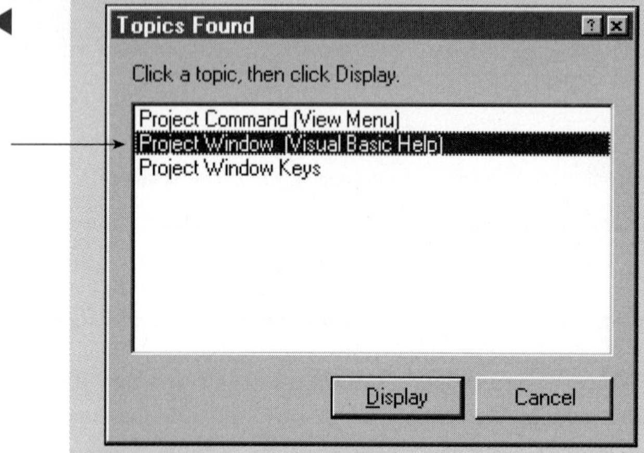

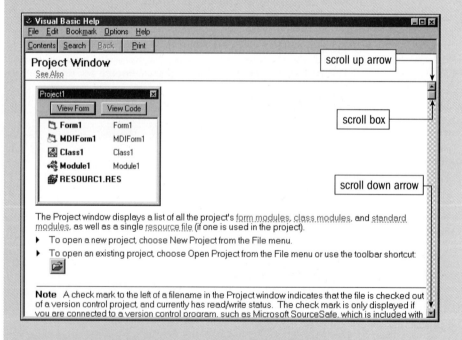

5. Click the topic **Project Window (Visual Basic Help)** then click the **Display** button. The Help system displays information about the Project window. See Figure 1-9.

Figure 1-9 ◄
Help
information
about the
Project window

Depending on the settings of your system, the size and shape of your Help window might differ from the window in Figure 1-9.

6. Read the displayed information, using the up and down scroll arrows or the scroll box to move through the screen. Note that you can open an existing project using either the Open Project command on the File menu or the Open Project button on the toolbar.

7. When you are finished reading the information, scroll back up to the top of the screen. Note that some terms are displayed in a different color and underlined with dashes. You can click these terms to display additional Help information.

8. Click the highlighted text **form modules**, read the displayed definition of this term, then click anywhere on the screen to close the definition window.

   Note the text "See Also" at the top of the screen. You can click this text to display a list of related Help topics.

9. Click **See Also**, look at the displayed list of related topics, then press the **Esc** key to close the window.

   As an alternative to pressing the Esc key, you can click anywhere on the screen to close the windows.

10. Click the **Close** button ☒ on the Help window title bar to close the window and exit the Help system.

Using the Table of Contents

The **Contents tab** of the Help system displays a set of books, each of which contains a particular category of information. You click a book to open it and display the topics in that category; then you can choose a particular topic to view. You will use the Contents tab to view information about the Project window.

To use the Contents tab to find information about the Project window:

1. Click **Help** on the menu bar, then click **Contents**.

2. If necessary, click the **Contents** tab to make it the active tab. Your screen should look like Figure 1-10.

Figure 1-10 ◀
Contents tab of the Help window

open this book ⟶

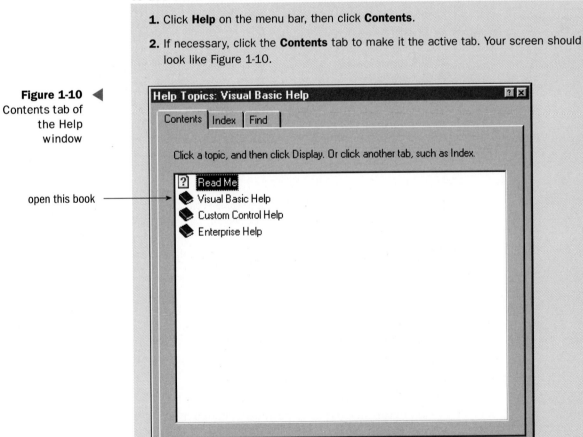

Depending on whether you are running Visual Basic Working Model, Standard, or Professional edition, the items listed in the Contents tab might differ from those shown in Figure 1-10.

3. Click the book labeled **Visual Basic Help**.

4. Click the **Open** button to open the book. The icon changes from a closed book to an open book and several other options appear, as shown in Figure 1-11.

Figure 1-11 ◀
Contents tab
with an
open book

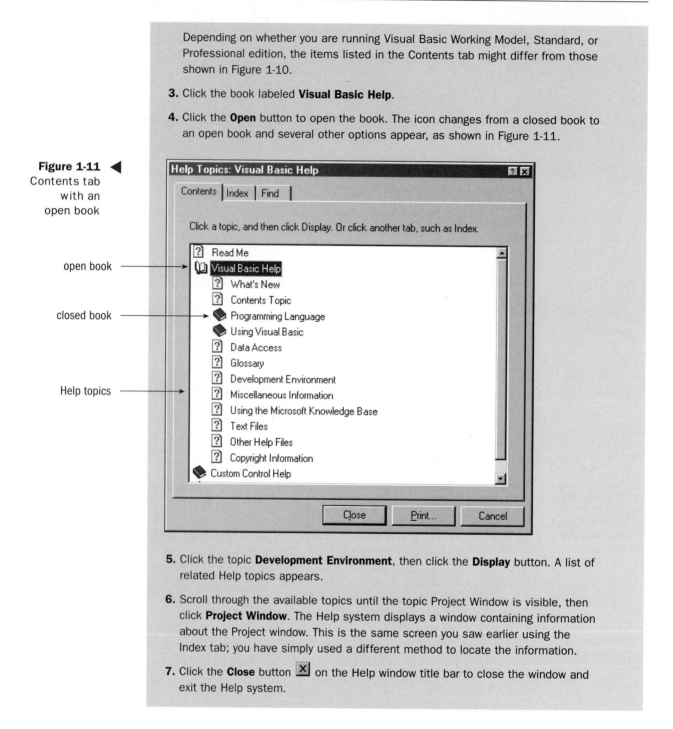

open book

closed book

Help topics

5. Click the topic **Development Environment**, then click the **Display** button. A list of related Help topics appears.

6. Scroll through the available topics until the topic Project Window is visible, then click **Project Window**. The Help system displays a window containing information about the Project window. This is the same screen you saw earlier using the Index tab; you have simply used a different method to locate the information.

7. Click the **Close** button ☒ on the Help window title bar to close the window and exit the Help system.

Now that you have learned how to use the Help system and viewed information on opening a project, you are ready to open the project Mark wants you to view and run.

Opening a Project

When you want to run an existing or partially completed Visual Basic program, you begin by opening the program's project file.

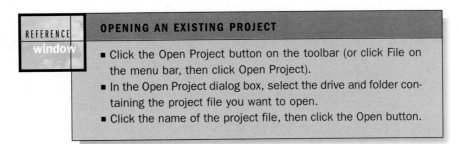

REFERENCE
window

OPENING AN EXISTING PROJECT

- Click the Open Project button on the toolbar (or click File on the menu bar, then click Open Project).
- In the Open Project dialog box, select the drive and folder containing the project file you want to open.
- Click the name of the project file, then click the Open button.

Mark created a program that stores name and address information for each of Dunn Financial's clients. The account managers and other employees use the program to look up addresses. Ultimately, the information will also be used to print a mailing list for company newsletters. The program stores the information in a database file. A **database** file allows you to add, change, delete, and organize information stored in the database. A database file is not stored as part of the project or the form. Rather, it is stored as a separate file that can be accessed by many programs. The ability to manage data in this way is another benefit of using Visual Basic in the business environment.

Mark wants you to open the project he created. The project file, which is named Dunn, is located on your Student Disk.

To open the Dunn project:

1. Place your Student Disk in the appropriate disk drive (either A or B).

    TROUBLE? If you don't have a Student Disk, you need to get one before you can proceed. Your instructor will either give you one or ask you to make your own. See your instructor for information.

2. Click the **Open Project** button 🖼 on the toolbar. The Open Project dialog box opens. See Figure 1-12.

Figure 1-12 ◀
Open Project
dialog box

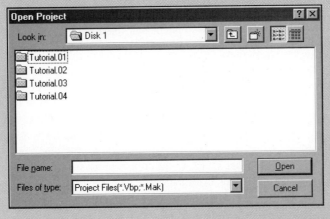

    TROUBLE? If you see a message box asking if you want to save the changes to Form1, click the No to All button to close the box without saving any changes.

3. Click the **Look in** list arrow to display the list of available drives and folders on your computer, then click the name of the drive in which you placed your Student Disk.

4. In the list of folders, click **Tutorial.01** then click the **Open** button. The list of files in the selected folder appears.

5. Click the file named **Dunn.vbp** then click the **Open** button to open the project. Note that the filename extension ".vbp" identifies the file as a Visual Basic project.

6. Move and resize the Properties and Project windows so that your screen looks like Figure 1-13.

Figure 1-13 ◀
Windows for
the open
project

project name in
Project window
title bar

filename of form

form name

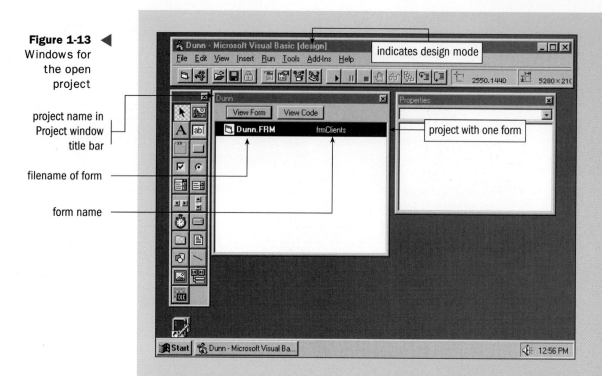

Notice that the name of the project, Dunn, now appears in the title bar of the Project window. Also, notice the notation "[design]" in the Visual Basic title bar; this indicates that Visual Basic is in design mode. You learn more about the different Visual Basic operating modes later in this session.

TROUBLE? If your screen doesn't include all the windows or components shown in Figure 1-13, you can display the missing window or component using the View menu. For example, if the toolbox is not displayed on your screen, click View on the menu bar, then click Toolbox. A check mark next to an item on the View menu means that the item is currently displayed on the screen.

The Project window lists the forms included in a program. Because the client program contains only one form, only one item is listed in the Project window. The filename for the form is Dunn.FRM. This is the name of the file stored on the disk. The name of the form is frmClients. You will use the form name when you write Visual Basic statements that reference the form. Form names should always begin with the prefix "frm" followed by a name that describes the form's purpose. A caption is also displayed on the form's title bar. The caption provides the user with a visual clue to the form's purpose. To see the form and each of the objects drawn on it, you need to view the form.

7. Click the **View Form** button in the Dunn Project window. The Form window shown in Figure 1-14 opens. The title of the form "Dunn Clients," is displayed in the form's title bar. The form title, or caption, is specified by the form's Caption property.

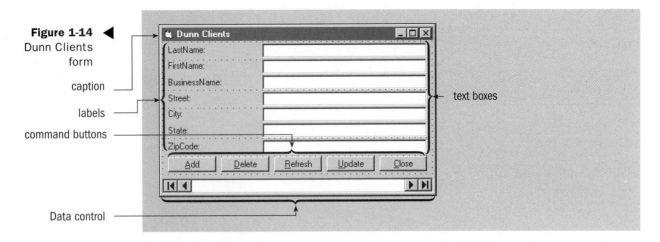

Figure 1-14
Dunn Clients
form

caption

labels

command buttons

text boxes

Data control

You will work with the program using three different types of objects placed on the form:

- Text boxes store pertinent information about a client in the database. The complete information for a client is called the **record** for that client.

- Command buttons allow you to add information for new clients, change or delete information for existing clients, and close the program.

- The Data control allows you to locate different client records in the database.

The labels on the form describe the contents of the different text boxes. However, you do not interact with labels, they are used only to display information and make the user interface easier to understand.

Running a Program

Now that the form is visible on the screen, you can run the program and begin to interact with the different objects on the form. By using some of the different Visual Basic controls, you will begin to see how they function before creating your own program.

When you run a program, Visual Basic loads the **startup**, or first, form and displays all the objects drawn on the form. Because the Dunn program contains only one form, it was identified as the startup form by Visual Basic. The program then waits for you to interact with it. When you click a button, you generate an event, and Visual Basic executes the code written to respond to the event. For example, when you click the Add button on the form, Visual Basic executes the statements to create a new client record. After executing all of the statements for the Add button, Visual Basic waits for your next action.

While you are running a program, the toolbox and Properties window are not displayed. You cannot use these components while the program is running, so Visual Basic hides them. You will also notice that many toolbar buttons and menu commands are "grayed out," or dimmed. You cannot use any dimmed commands while a program is running.

Mark wants you to run the client list program to become more familiar with Visual Basic. He also wants you to add a new client record to the database and update the record of an existing client.

To run the Dunn project and add the new record to the database:

1. Click the **Start** button on the toolbar. The first client record in the database is displayed. See Figure 1-15.

   Notice that another window, the Debug window, appears on the screen. This window helps you fix any problems with your program.

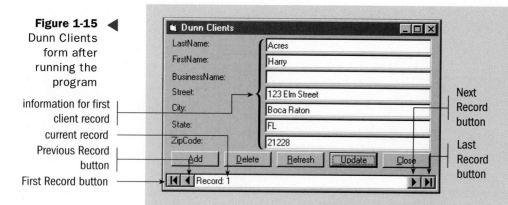

Figure 1-15 ◀
Dunn Clients
form after
running the
program

information for first
client record

current record

Previous Record
button

First Record button

Next
Record
button

Last
Record
button

The navigation buttons in the Data control allow you to move between the client records.

2. Click the **Add** button to create a new, empty record in the database.

3. Click the first text box and enter the name and address of the following new client into the appropriate boxes on the form. (Leave the BusinessName text box blank.) To move forward to the next text box, press the **Tab** key. To move back to the previous text box, hold down the **Shift** key and press the **Tab** key at the same time.

**Mary Faiers
1031 Palm Street
Ft. Lauderdale, FL 34118**

4. When you have finished filling in the boxes, click the **Update** button on the form to record the changes to the database. Until you click the Update button, your changes are not saved to the database file.

In addition to adding records to the database, you can change the information in existing records and delete records entirely. Next, Mark asks you to update the information for an existing client, which recently changed its business name.

To change the record in the database:

1. Click the **Previous Record** button at the bottom of the form to display the record for John Smith.

2. Click the BusinessName text box to position the cursor.

3. Change the BusinessName to **Varity Enterprises**.

4. Click the **Update** button on the form to record the change to the database record.

Operating Modes

Visual Basic always operates in either run mode, design mode, or break mode. The title bar at the top of the screen indicates the current mode. In this case, because you are in the process of running a program, the screen indicates run mode. Activities you complete in design mode include creating and saving projects, designing forms, setting properties, and writing code. You will learn more about design mode in Session 1.2 when you create a program. You will learn about break mode in later tutorials.

Stopping a Program

You have finished working with the Dunn program, so you can now stop running it. When you stop a program from running, you change the operating mode from run mode to design mode. There are two ways to stop running a program—using the End button on the toolbar or the End command on the Run menu.

To stop running the Dunn program:

1. Click the **End** button ▣ on the toolbar. Visual Basic stops running the program and returns to design mode. Note that the form no longer contains information and the title bar displays the notation "design." Also, the Properties window and toolbox are again displayed.

Next, Mark asks you to print the Dunn Clients form. He wants to bring the printed copy of the form to a meeting in which he and other Dunn Financial employees will review the design of different forms.

Printing an Image of the Form

Often, you will need a printed copy of the form or forms in your programs. For example, many organizations require program documentation to include all of the screen images used in a program. In this case, Mark needs a printed form to bring to his design review meeting.

To print an image of the Dunn Clients:

1. Click **File** on the menu bar, then click **Print**. The Print dialog box opens. See Figure 1-16.

Figure 1-16 ◀
Print dialog box

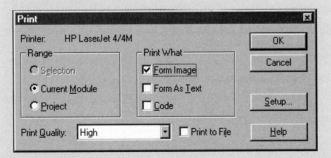

Note that the entry next to Printer will vary based on the printer you're using.

2. If necessary, click **Current Module** to select it. A bullet appears next to the Current Module option when it is selected. This causes the form module you have been working with to be printed.

3. Click **Form Image**. A check mark appears next to the Form Image option when it is selected.

4. Click the **OK** button to print the form image.

Exiting Visual Basic

Now that you have run the Dunn program and printed the form image, you can exit Visual Basic. Because you have not made any changes to the program, you do not have to save it before exiting. Remember that when you added the new record to the database and changed the existing record, the changes were saved to the database file when you clicked the Update button.

You can exit Visual Basic either by clicking the Close button on the Visual Basic title bar or choosing the Exit command from the File menu. When you exit Visual Basic, it checks to see if you have made any changes to your program that need to be saved. If there are unsaved changes, Visual Basic displays a message asking if you want to save the information. Before exiting, Visual Basic closes all open forms and the project file.

To exit Visual Basic:

1. Click the **Close** button  on the Visual Basic title bar.

> **TROUBLE?** If you resized the form or made any other changes to it, Visual Basic will ask if you want to save the changes. Click the No to All button.

> Visual Basic closes any open forms, then closes the project file before exiting.

Quick Check

1. Describe the steps to create a program.

2. What is a project?

3. What is a form?

4. What is the difference between using the Index tab and the Contents tab on the Help window to locate specific information?

5. Describe the resulting actions when you click the following buttons:

6. How do you print an image of a form?

SESSION

1.1

In this session, you will create your first Visual Basic program. You will learn how to set the form's properties, add controls to a form, set properties for the objects on a form, write a Visual Basic statement, and run the completed program to test it.

Planning a Program

You should always carefully consider the problem you are trying to solve and the best solution to the problem before you begin writing the program. You should also design the form before creating objects on the form. This will make the programming process easier and less error prone.

Before you begin to create your form, Mark shows you the layout of the form including the controls you will add. The layout of the form is shown in Figure 1-17.

Figure 1-17
Layout of
the form

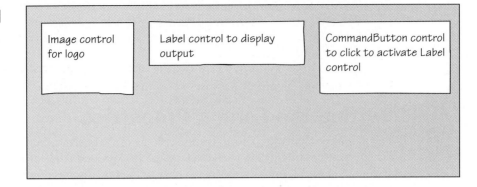

The form contains an Image object that will display the Dunn Financial logo. The command button, when clicked, will display a line of text in the Label control. Mark suggests that you use the Help system to learn more about the specific controls you will be adding to your form.

To learn more about the Label control:

1. Start Visual Basic and place your Student Disk in the disk drive.

2. Click the **Label** control ▯ on the toolbox.

3. Press the **F1** key to display Help information about the control.

4. Read the text in the displayed window, using the scroll arrows and scroll box to move through the text.

   Because you will be using the Label control when you create your program, you will print a copy of the Help information for reference later on.

5. Click the **Print** button on the Help window, then click the **OK** button in the Print dialog box.

6. Click the **Close** button ▯ on the Help window title bar to close the window and exit Help.

In addition to the Label control, your program will also include a CommandButton control and an Image control. So, you will display and print Help information about these two controls.

To obtain Help for the CommandButton and Image controls:

1. Click the **CommandButton** control ▯ on the toolbox.

2. Press the **F1** key to display Help information for the CommandButton control.

3. Click the **Print** button on the Help window, then click the **OK** button in the Print dialog box to print the information.

4. Repeat Steps 1 through 3 for the **Image** control 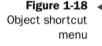.

5. Click the **Close** button ☒ on the Help window title bar to close the window and exit Help.

Now you're ready to begin creating the form. First, you need to set the properties of the form itself.

Setting the Form's Properties

The first step in creating a form is to set the form's properties. In this case, you need to set the size and position of the form, change the background color of the form to light green, and set the form's Caption property to change the text displayed in the form's title bar.

To set or change any property, you first need to display the Properties window for the selected object (in this case, the form).

To display the Properties window for the form using the shortcut menu:

1. Move the pointer into the Form window.

2. Click the right mouse button to display the shortcut menu shown in Figure 1-18.

Figure 1-18 ◀
Object shortcut menu

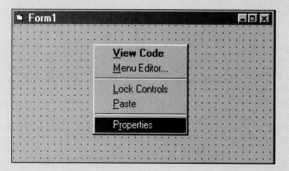

3. Click **Properties** on the shortcut menu. The Properties window becomes the active window and displays the properties for the selected object, in this case, the form. See Figure 1-19.

Figure 1-19 ◀
Properties window components

title bar

object box

property names

property values

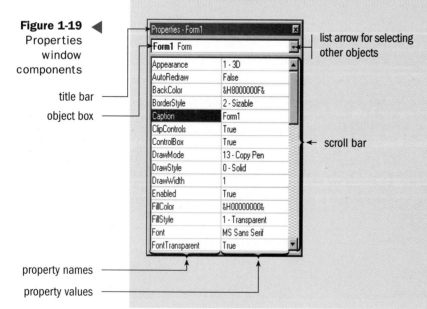

list arrow for selecting other objects

← scroll bar

The Properties window title bar identifies the current form object, in this case, Form1, which is the default Name property assigned to a new form. The object box identifies the selected object, which is also Form1. The list arrow at the right side of the object box allows you to select another object and display its properties. The left column in the window lists the properties available for the selected object, and the right column lists the current value for each property. If all the properties will not fit in the window, you can use the displayed scroll bar to scroll through the properties list. Note that properties are always listed in alphabetical order.

4. Use the scroll bar to move through the list of properties to see which properties you can set for a form.

Setting the Size and Position of a Form

The needs of a particular program determine the size of each form. The program you are creating will contain only a few controls; therefore, the form can be relatively small. You can create the form to be about two inches tall and four inches wide. All Visual Basic dimensions are measured in twips. A **twip** is a unit of screen measurement specifying about 1440 twips per inch. So, to create a two-inch by four-inch form, you would set the Height and Width properties to 2880 and 5760, respectively. The size indicator on the far right of the toolbar tells you the height and width of the current object in twips.

You can also specify where on the screen the form should be displayed by setting the Top and Left properties. If you set both the Top and Left properties of a form to 0, the form would be displayed in the upper-left corner of the screen. The position indicator on the right of the toolbar tells you the position of the current object. If the object is a form, the position is relative to the upper-left corner of the screen. If the object is an instance of a control you drew on the form, the position is relative to the upper-left corner of the form.

REFERENCE window	**SETTING THE SIZE AND POSITION OF A FORM**
	■ If the Properties window is not displayed, place the pointer in an empty area of the form, click the right mouse button to display the shortcut menu, then click Properties.
	■ Click the value for the Height property and type in the new value for the height.
	■ Click the value for the Width property, and type the new value for the width.
	■ Click the values for the Top and Left properties, and type the new value for each.

To change the size and location of the form relative to the screen, you need to change four properties: Height, Width, Top, and Left. Mark has asked that you create a two-inch by four-inch form, located about one and a half inches from the upper-left corner of the screen. Remember that one inch equals approximately 1440 twips, so the height of the form will be 2880, the width of the form will be 5760, and the top and left dimensions will be 2100 each.

To set the size and position of the form:

1. Locate the Height property, click the property value to select it, then type **2880**.

2. Locate the Width property, click the property value to select it, then type **5760**.

3. Locate the Top property, click the property value to select it, then type **2100**.

4. Locate the Left property, click the property value to select it, then type **2100**.

The size and location of the form change as you enter each value.

Setting the Background Color of a Form

Color selection is an important consideration when you design a form. It's best to avoid using too many colors on a form, because they can make the form confusing and distracting. If your form contains several objects that perform similar functions, you should use the same color for each of the objects. For example, all labels should be the same color. Also, you should carefully consider the foreground and background color of each object; if there is not enough contrast, the information might be hard to read.

The selection of individual colors is also important. Colors like gray, blue, and green tend to work well because they are soft. Colors like red and yellow stand out and could bother the eyes; therefore, they should be used in limited situations for emphasis.

REFERENCE window	**CHANGING THE BACKGROUND COLOR OF A FORM**
	■ If the Properties window is not displayed, place the pointer in an empty area of the form, click the right mouse button to display the shortcut menu, then click Properties.
	■ Click the default value for the BackColor property to display the list arrow for the property.
	■ Click the list arrow to display the color palette for the BackColor property.
	■ Click the color you want for the form.

To set the background color of a form, you need to change the form's BackColor property. You need to set the background color to light green. Mark suggested this color because it will provide a good contrast with the form objects, particularly the logo.

To change the background color of the form:

1. Locate the property named BackColor, then click its default property value. A list arrow appears. You can click the list arrow to display the options available for this property.

2. Click the list arrow for the BackColor property. The color palette appears. See Figure 1-20.

Figure 1-20 ◀
Color palette

click this color

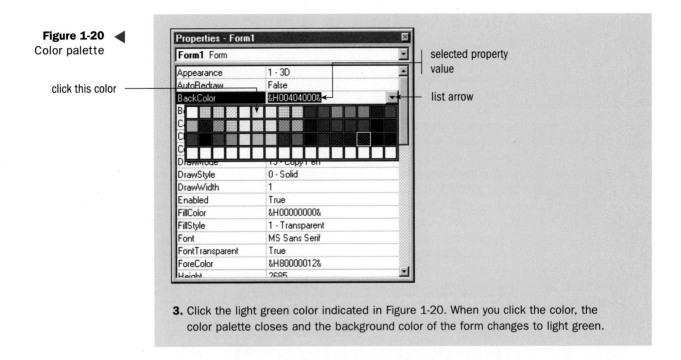

selected property
value

list arrow

3. Click the light green color indicated in Figure 1-20. When you click the color, the color palette closes and the background color of the form changes to light green.

Setting the Caption for a Form

Like any window in Windows 95, a Visual Basic form contains text in the title bar to identify the purpose of the form. You specify this text by setting the form's Caption property. A caption can include spaces and punctuation characters. Although the caption can contain any number of characters, it should fit in the title bar of the form.

Mark suggests that you use the caption "Dunn - My First Program" for the practice form you are creating.

To set the caption for the form:

1. Locate the property named Caption, then double-click its default property value, **Form1** to highlight the value. The text you type next will replace the highlighted default value.

2. Type **Dunn - My First Program**. The caption in the form's title bar changes to the new value. See Figure 1-21.

Figure 1-21 ◀
Setting the
form's caption

caption in the form's
title bar

> 🎙 Dunn - My First Program

Now that you have set the properties for the form, you're ready to add the necessary controls to the form. Then you can set the properties for each control.

Adding Controls to a Form

When you place a control on a form, the control is called an **object**. The form itself is also an object. You can have multiple occurrences of the same type of object on a form; each occurrence of the object is called an **instance**. For example, if you wanted to include three command buttons on your form, you would use the CommandButton control on the tool-box to place three CommandButton objects on the form. Each instance of the CommandButton object would perform a different task.

The controls available on the toolbox depend on both the version of Visual Basic you are using and whether or not any third-party add-in controls have been added to the tool-box. A **third-party add-in control** is a control created by another vendor and sold for use with the standard Visual Basic controls. Such add-in controls can provide added functionality, such as spell checking, or they might simply provide ways to make your programs more visually appealing.

As shown, in the completed form in Figure 1-22, you need to add three controls to the form: a Label control, a CommandButton control, and an Image control.

Figure 1-22 ◀
Completed
form

Image control —

Label control —

CommandButton
control

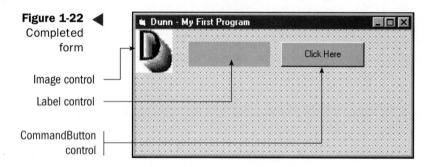

You will begin by adding a Label control to display a line of text. Remember, you use the controls on the toolbox to add objects to a form. After you place an object on the form, you can manipulate it; for example, you can reposition, resize, or delete any object you create.

Adding a Label Control

The **Label** control allows you to display text on your form. For example, you might want a label to include text that identifies another object on the form. Another use of the label is to display the results of some computation. For example, you might have a program that adds sales numbers and displays a number representing total sales. You can display such a value in a label. Remember, labels are for display purposes only; a user cannot interact with a label.

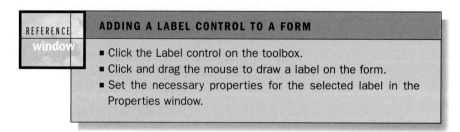

REFERENCE
window

ADDING A LABEL CONTROL TO A FORM

- Click the Label control on the toolbox.
- Click and drag the mouse to draw a label on the form.
- Set the necessary properties for the selected label in the Properties window.

In this case, the label you will add to the form will display the text "I have a working program." This text will appear in the label after you click the command button on the form. (You'll create the CommandButton control later in this session.) You specify the text for the label using the Caption property for the Label object.

To add the Label control to your form:

1. Click the **Label** control 🅰 on the toolbox.

2. Place the pointer in the left side of the Form window, which is where you want the upper-left corner of the Label object to be located. See Figure 1-22 for the location of the label control. The pointer changes to +.

3. Click and hold the left mouse button down, then drag the pointer down and to the right to create an outline of the Label object.

   Notice that while you are in design mode the form includes a grid of dots. When you draw objects on the form, the grid helps you align the objects.

4. When the size of the object is similar to the size of the Label object shown in Figure 1-23, release the mouse button. The object appears on the form.

Figure 1-23 ◄
Creating a label

default name for object

sizing handles

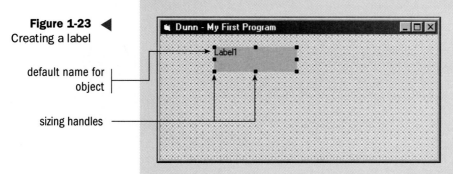

TROUBLE? Don't worry if the Label object on your screen isn't in exactly the same location or isn't the same size as the object shown in the figure. You will learn how to reposition and resize objects later.

Note that Visual Basic assigns a name to the object, in this case, Label1. Each object on a form must have a unique name. Therefore, if you place a second instance of the Label object on the form without changing the name of the first label, Visual Basic would assign the name Label2 to the second Label object. Also, notice the eight small, black boxes that appear around the border of the label. These boxes are called **sizing handles** and they identify the active object. You can use the handles to resize the object, as you will learn later in this session. Because the label is the active object, the Properties window shows the properties for this object.

Setting an Object's Properties

Each object on a form has attributes known as properties. The properties of an object can determine the appearance of the object (for example, its color), the font of the object's text (if any), the position of the object on the screen, and whether or not the object is visible on the screen. Some properties, such as color and screen location, are common to most types of objects. However, other properties are unique and define the specific attributes of a particular object type. As an analogy, consider two objects—an automobile and an airplane. Both an automobile and an airplane have similar properties, such as color, weight, and engine size. This does not necessarily mean that they have the same color, just that each has a color. However, some properties are meaningful only to the airplane; for example, only an airplane has a wing size.

Next, you need to set the properties for the Label object. Although you can set properties at any time, it is best to set them immediately after creating the object so that you do not forget to set the necessary properties. Here you need to clear the initial Caption property for the Label object so that it will be ready to display a line of text when a user clicks the command button next to the label. (You will create the CommandButton object and Visual Basic statements to display the line of text later.) When you run a program, the values set in the Properties window will be the initial properties.

To set the Caption property of the Label object:

1. Make sure the Label object is still selected (that is, handles appear on the object).

2. In the Properties window, double-click the default Caption property value **Label1** to highlight the value.

   The Caption property for the Label object must be blank when the program is run so that it can display a line of text when a user clicks the CommandButton object next to the label.

3. Press the **Delete** key to delete the highlighted Caption property value. The Label object now contains no text. See Figure 1-24.

Figure 1-24 ◄
Setting the Caption property

empty Label object ────

blank Caption property

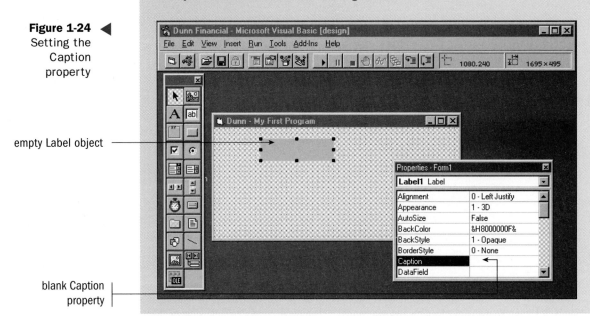

Moving an Object

When you create an object on the form, you will often need to change the location of the object—perhaps because a design specification has changed or because the objects on the form are not visually balanced. You can move any object on a form by first clicking the object to select it then using the pointer to drag the object to a new location. You will practice moving the Label object on your form.

To move the Label object:

1. Make sure the Label object is still selected.

2. Place the pointer anywhere within the Label object, but not on a handle.

3. Click and hold down the left mouse button, then move the mouse to drag the object to a different location. An outline of the object appears on the form and moves to show the new object position as you move the mouse. See Figure 1-25.

Figure 1-25 ◀
Moving the
label

outline of object —————

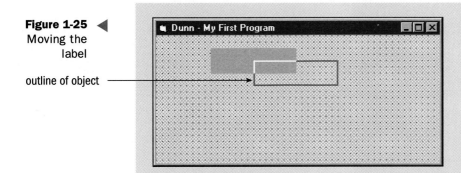

Note that the position indicator on the toolbar shows the position of the active object, the label.

4. Release the mouse button when the object is in the location you want.

5. Use the mouse to move the Label object back to the location shown in Figure 1-23.

6. To deselect the Label object, click anywhere in a blank area of the Form window. The Form window now becomes the selected object, and its properties are displayed in the Properties window.

Resizing an Object

In addition to moving an object, you can also change an object's size by modifying the object's width or height. Again, this might be necessary because of changes in design specifications or to improve or correct the appearance of objects on the form. For example, if you create a Label object that is too small to hold the label's Caption property value, you would need to increase the size of the object.

To resize the Label object:

1. Click the Label object to select it and display the sizing handles.

  TROUBLE? If you accidentally double-clicked the object, the Code window will be activated. (You will learn more about the Code window later in this session.) Click the Close button ☒ on the Code window title bar to close the window, then repeat Step 1.

2. Position the pointer on the handle in the lower-right corner of the object. The pointer changes to ↖. When you use one of the four corner sizing handles to resize an object, the object will be resized both horizontally and vertically. When you use one of the center sizing handles, the object will be resized in one direction only, depending on the handle you're using.

3. Click and hold down the left mouse button, then move the pointer down and to the right to increase the size of the object, as shown in Figure 1-26.

Figure 1-26 ◀
Resizing the
label

outline shows the
resized object ⟶

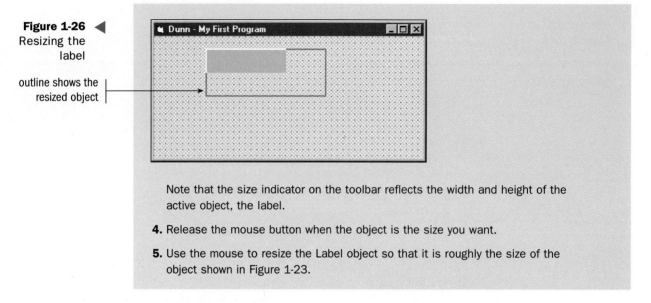

Note that the size indicator on the toolbar reflects the width and height of the active object, the label.

4. Release the mouse button when the object is the size you want.

5. Use the mouse to resize the Label object so that it is roughly the size of the object shown in Figure 1-23.

Just as you set the size and position of the form by setting the Height, Width, Top, and Left properties of the form, you can set the properties of an object in the same way. The only difference is that the Top and Left properties of an object are relative to the form, not the entire screen.

To set the size and position of the label using the Properties window:

1. Set the following properties for the Label object in the Properties window:
Height = **495**; Left = **1080**; Top = **240**; Width = **1695**.

Deleting an Object

Occasionally you will need to delete an object from a form, perhaps because you created the object by mistake or the object is no longer used in the program. To delete an object you simply select the object then press the Delete key. Because you will be using the Label object in your program, there is no need to delete it.

Now that you have created the label and set its properties, you can create the next object on the form—the command button.

Creating a Command Button

The **CommandButton** control on the toolbox allows you to create a button that a user of your program clicks to carry out an action. Remember, Visual Basic is an event-driven programming language, which means that objects such as command buttons cause events to occur when the objects are activated by a user.

When a user clicks a command button, Visual Basic executes the code written for the button's Click event. Like other objects, a command button has properties that control its appearance. The Caption property, for example, defines the text displayed in the object.

CREATING A COMMAND BUTTON

- Click the CommandButton control on the toolbox.
- Click and drag the mouse to draw the CommandButton object on the form.
- Set the necessary properties for the selected command button in the Properties window.
- Use the Code window to enter the necessary Visual Basic code for the button's Click event.

For the form you are creating, the action of the command button will be to display the text "I have a working program." in the label you created earlier. You need to create the button and set its size and caption.

To create the command button and set its properties:

1. Click the **CommandButton** control on the toolbox.

2. Position the pointer in the Form window, to the right of the Label object, at the upper-left corner of where you want to include the CommandButton object.

3. Click and hold down the left mouse button, then drag the pointer down and to the right. An outline of the object appears as you draw it.

4. When the object is about the size you want, release the mouse button.

   Now you can set the properties for the command button so that it is positioned correctly. You want the command button to be the same size as the label and in the same position as the label, relative to the top of the form. Therefore, you'll use the same Height, Width, and Top properties for the command button as you did for the label; only the Left property will be different.

5. Set the Height property to **495**, the Left property to **3000**, the Top property to **240**, and the Width property to **1695**.

   Next, you need to add the text "Click Here" to the command button, so you need to set the Caption property for the object.

6. Select the Caption property value in the Properties window, then type **Click Here,** as shown in Figure 1-27. Note that the caption on the command button is updated with the new text.

Figure 1-27 ◀
Setting the
Caption
property
for the
command
button

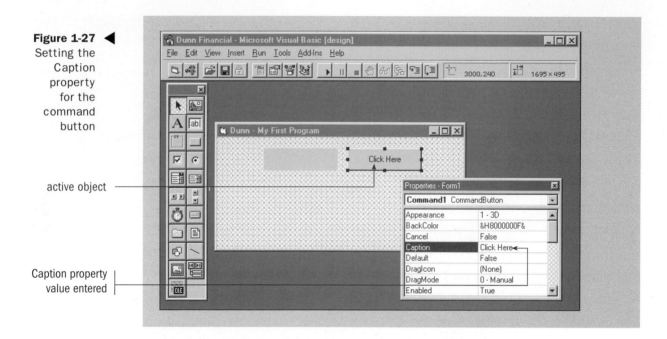

active object ────

Caption property
value entered

In addition to setting the properties for the command button, you also need to create the Visual Basic code that will run when a user clicks the button.

The Code Window

To create the Visual Basic code you must define the actions taken when the event (clicking the button) occurs. These actions consist of Visual Basic code contained in event procedures. An **event procedure** is a set of Visual Basic statements that are executed when a user performs an action on an object, such as clicking a command button. An object can have several different event procedures. Some objects can execute one series of statements when the user clicks the mouse button and another series of statements when the user double-clicks the mouse button. This is because these are two different events, and an object can execute different event procedures in response to different events.

You write all Visual Basic language statements using a text editor called the **Code window**. After you type a line of code and press the Enter key, Visual Basic will format the line and check the syntax of the statement to make sure it is correct. If you enter a statement that Visual Basic cannot understand, it will display a dialog box describing the error.

The code you need to enter for the command button on your form will cause the Caption property of the Label object to change when a user clicks the command button. The text "I have a working program." will be displayed in the label when a user clicks the command button. When complete, the code for the CommandButton object will contain the following program statements:

```
'This is a comment in my first program
Private Sub Command1_Click()
     Label1.Caption = "I have a working program."
End Sub
```

Before you enter the code in the Code window, take a moment to first examine each statement separately and see what it does.

```
'This is a comment in my first program
```

This statement is known as a program comment. You include **program comments** in code to explain the purpose of the program and describe what it accomplishes. A program comment always begins with the apostrophe character ('). Visual Basic ignores all program comments and does not try to execute them.

```
Private Sub Command1_Click()
```

This statement defines a procedure that can contain Visual Basic code. The procedure named Command1_Click() will be executed when a user clicks the CommandButton object named Command1, which is the command button you created earlier. You will learn more about the significance of these names in later tutorials. The line begins with the words Private and Sub. The word Private tells Visual Basic that this event procedure can only be used inside this form. The word Sub tells Visual Basic that the procedure will not send information back to other procedures. All event procedures are designated as Private Sub procedures by default. Visual Basic will create the Private Sub statement automatically when you open the Code window for the object.

```
Label1.Caption = "I have a working program."
```

This line in the program contains a statement that is executed by Visual Basic. The text enclosed in quotation marks is stored in the Caption property of the Label1 object, which is the label you created earlier. The text within quotation marks will be displayed in the label when a user clicks the command button. This statement is shown indented in the code. Statements between the Private Sub and End Sub statements are usually indented so that the start and end of a procedure can be easily recognized. Indenting statements is solely for the benefit of the programmer. Visual Basic ignores all leading spaces and tab characters that you use to indent statements.

```
End Sub
```

This statement signifies the end of the event procedure, telling Visual Basic that there are no more statements in the procedure. Visual Basic will create the End Sub statement automatically when you open the Code window.

Now that you understand the code you need to write, you're ready to enter the code in the Code window.

Entering the Code for the Command Button

To create the code for the command button, you need to open the Code window and enter the necessary statement. You open the Code window by choosing the View Code command from the shortcut menu for the selected CommandButton object.

To open the Code window and write the code for the CommandButton object:

1. Make sure the CommandButton object is selected.

2. Click the right mouse button to display the shortcut menu, then click **View Code**. The Code window opens. See Figure 1-28.

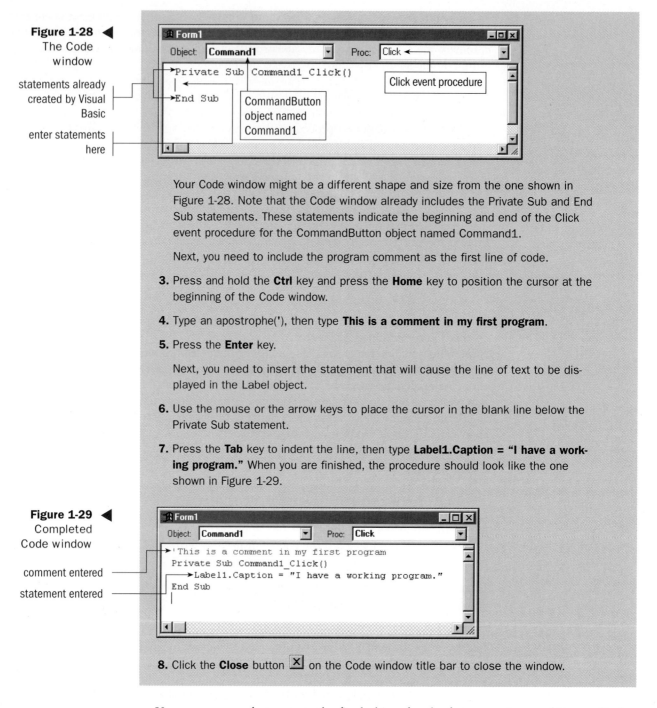

Figure 1-28 ◀
The Code window

statements already created by Visual Basic

enter statements here

Your Code window might be a different shape and size from the one shown in Figure 1-28. Note that the Code window already includes the Private Sub and End Sub statements. These statements indicate the beginning and end of the Click event procedure for the CommandButton object named Command1.

Next, you need to include the program comment as the first line of code.

3. Press and hold the **Ctrl** key and press the **Home** key to position the cursor at the beginning of the Code window.

4. Type an apostrophe('), then type **This is a comment in my first program**.

5. Press the **Enter** key.

Next, you need to insert the statement that will cause the line of text to be displayed in the Label object.

6. Use the mouse or the arrow keys to place the cursor in the blank line below the Private Sub statement.

7. Press the **Tab** key to indent the line, then type **Label1.Caption = "I have a working program."** When you are finished, the procedure should look like the one shown in Figure 1-29.

Figure 1-29 ◀
Completed Code window

comment entered

statement entered

8. Click the **Close** button ⊠ on the Code window title bar to close the window.

You are now ready to create the final object for the form—an Image object to display the Dunn Financial logo.

Adding an Image Control to a Form

To add visual interest to your program, you can include graphic images or pictures on a form. Graphic images are stored in many different formats. In this case the image of the Dunn Financial logo is stored as a Windows bitmap file. Bitmap files have the extension .bmp.

The **Image** control allows you to display graphic images on a form. Be careful not to include too many large images in your program. In addition to taking up a lot of space on the disk, these images are stored as part of the form, so opening and saving the form will take longer and cause your program to appear sluggish to the user.

By default, a picture you insert into an Image object has a fixed size and may differ from the size and shape of the Image object. So, if you create a one-inch by one-inch Image control on your form and insert a picture that is two-inches by two-inches, the picture will appear as two-inches by two-inches. Setting the Image object's Stretch property to True causes the picture to be the size of the Image object. Whether or not you should set the Stretch property to True depends on the particular picture you're placing in the form. For example, if the shape of the picture is significantly different from the shape of the Image object, and the Stretch property is set to True, the picture will be scaled to fill the Image object and could appear distorted.

REFERENCE window

ADDING AN IMAGE CONTROL TO A FORM

- Click the Image control on the toolbox.
- Click and drag the mouse to draw the Image object on the form.
- Set the necessary properties for the selected Image object in the Properties window. For example, to cause the picture placed inside the Image object to be stretched to the size of the object, set the Stretch property to True.
- Click the button in the property value for the Picture property to open the Load Picture dialog box.
- Click the name of the file containing the image you want, then click the Open button.

Mark is considering including the Dunn Financial logo on all forms, so he asks you to include it on your practice form to see how it looks. The picture file is called DunnLogo and it is stored in the Tutorial.01 folder on your Student Disk. First, you need to create an Image object to hold the picture, then you'll set the Picture property to load the picture file into the object.

To create the Image object:

1. Click the **Image** control 🖼 on the toolbox.

2. Position the pointer in the upper-left corner of the form.

3. Hold down the left mouse button and move the mouse down and to the right. An outline of the Image object is displayed.

You have defined the region for the picture. Next, you need to set the Stretch property to True so that the picture will be adjusted to fit inside the object you just drew on the form. Then you must include the picture in your program by setting the value of the Picture property to the filename of the picture.

To set the properties for the Image control:

1. Make sure the Image object is selected.

2. In the Properties window, set the Height property to **750**, the Left property to **0**, the Top property to **0**, and the Width property to **750**.

3. Locate the Stretch property in the Properties window, then click its property value to display the list arrow. Your Properties window should look like Figure 1-30.

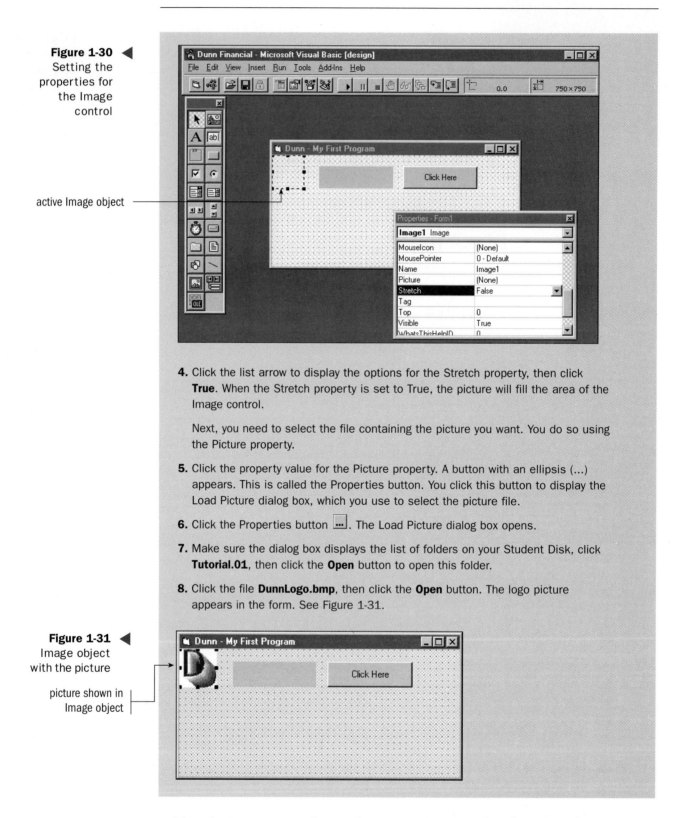

Figure 1-30 ◄
Setting the
properties for
the Image
control

active Image object ─────

4. Click the list arrow to display the options for the Stretch property, then click **True**. When the Stretch property is set to True, the picture will fill the area of the Image control.

   Next, you need to select the file containing the picture you want. You do so using the Picture property.

5. Click the property value for the Picture property. A button with an ellipsis (...) appears. This is called the Properties button. You click this button to display the Load Picture dialog box, which you use to select the picture file.

6. Click the Properties button ⬚. The Load Picture dialog box opens.

7. Make sure the dialog box displays the list of folders on your Student Disk, click **Tutorial.01**, then click the **Open** button to open this folder.

8. Click the file **DunnLogo.bmp**, then click the **Open** button. The logo picture appears in the form. See Figure 1-31.

Figure 1-31 ◄
Image object
with the picture

picture shown in
Image object

Now that your program is complete, you can run it and see how it works.

Running the Completed Program

To run a program, you simply click the Start button on the toolbar. Remember, any time you run a program, Visual Basic switches from design mode to run mode, activates the startup form, and waits for user input. You can stop a program at any time by clicking the End button on the toolbar.

To run and test the program:

1. Click the **Start** button on the toolbar.

   Your form appears on the screen; Visual Basic has loaded all the form's objects and their associated code.

2. Test the program by clicking the command button with the caption "Click Here." The text "I have a working program." appears in the Label object. See Figure 1-32.

Figure 1-32 ◀
Running and testing the program

text appears in the Label object

click the CommandButton object

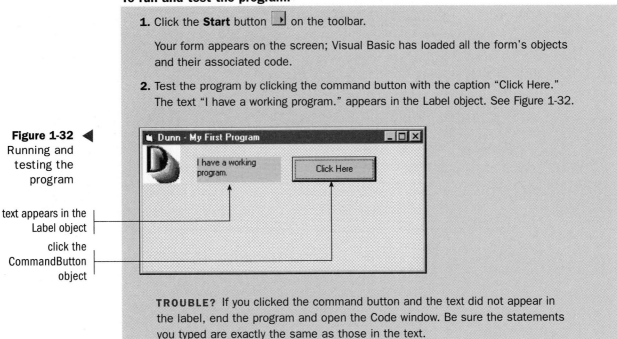

TROUBLE? If you clicked the command button and the text did not appear in the label, end the program and open the Code window. Be sure the statements you typed are exactly the same as those in the text.

You have finished creating and running your program. Now you need to save the form and the project.

Saving the Form and Project

To save a form or project, Visual Basic must be in design mode. So, you first need to stop the program, then save the form and project to your Student Disk. Because the form and the project are stored in separate files, you can save them using different Visual Basic commands. The form file contains all the objects and code for the form. The project file contains all the forms used by the program.

Mark would like every filename to begin with the word "Dunn." The rest of the filename should reflect the contents of the file. So, you'll name both the form file and the project file "Dunn Test Logo."

To stop the program and save the form file:

1. Click the **End** button on the toolbar. The program stops running and the screen returns to design mode.

2. Click **File** on the menu bar, then click **Save File As**. The Save File As dialog box opens, allowing you to specify the disk drive, directory, and filename in which to save the form file.

3. Click the **Tutorial.01** folder then click the **Open** button to open the folder.

4. Type **Dunn Test Logo.frm** in the File name text box. See Figure 1-33.

Figure 1-33 ◀
Saving the form

filename for form ——

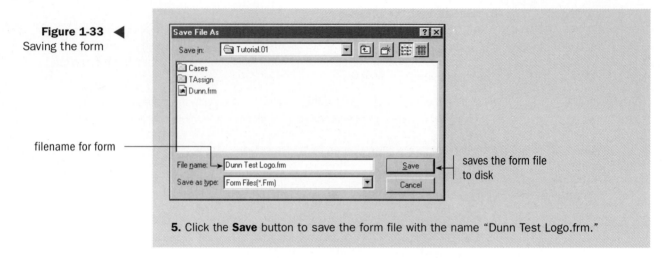

saves the form file
to disk

5. Click the **Save** button to save the form file with the name "Dunn Test Logo.frm."

The form definition and all the objects you created are saved in the form file. Additionally, each of the properties you set is stored in the form file. Note that when you selected the Picture property for the Image object, the picture of the Dunn Financial logo was imported into the form file.

Now that you have saved the form file, you can save the project file.

To save the project file:

1. Click **File** on the menu bar, then click **Save Project As**. The Save Project As dialog box opens.

2. Be sure that **Tutorial.01** is the current folder.

3. Type **Dunn Test Logo.vbp** in the File name text box. See Figure 1-34.

Figure 1-34 ◀
Saving the
project

filename for project ——

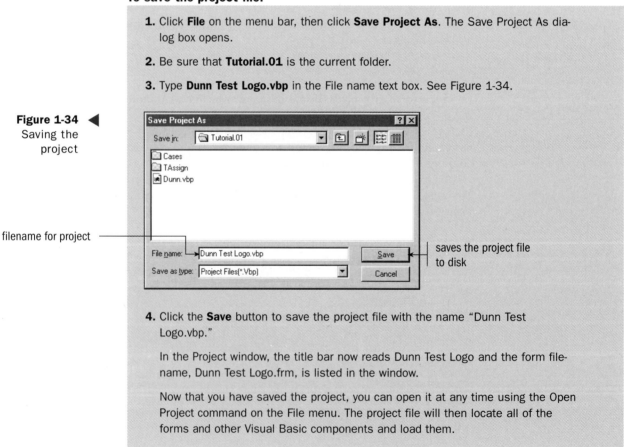

saves the project file
to disk

4. Click the **Save** button to save the project file with the name "Dunn Test Logo.vbp."

In the Project window, the title bar now reads Dunn Test Logo and the form filename, Dunn Test Logo.frm, is listed in the window.

Now that you have saved the project, you can open it at any time using the Open Project command on the File menu. The project file will then locate all of the forms and other Visual Basic components and load them.

Mark would like to copy the form to show to Gerrold, so he asks you to print the form image.

To print an image of the form:

1. Click **File** on the menu bar, then click **Print**. The Print dialog box opens.

2. If necessary, click **Current Module** to select it. This causes the form module to be printed.

3. Click **Form Image** to select it.

4. Click the **OK** button to print the form image.

   Now that you've printed the form, you can exit Visual Basic.

5. Click **File** on the menu bar, then click **Exit** to exit Visual Basic.

Congratulations, you have completed the task of writing your first Visual Basic program. Mark is pleased with the results and is certain that you are ready to create more challenging programs.

Quick Check

1. What is the Properties window used for?
2. What is the purpose of the Label control?
3. How do you resize, move, and delete objects?
4. What is the purpose of the CommandButton control?
5. What is the purpose of the Image control?
6. What is the purpose of the Code window?
7. How do you save a form and a project?

Figure 1-35 lists and defines the new terms presented in this tutorial.

Figure 1-35 ◀
New terms

Term	Description
Code	A Visual Basic statement or statements to accomplish a particular task.
Control	A control is a tool used to perform some task in Visual Basic. Every control has a set of characteristics known as properties. A control can recognize different events such as a mouse click or a keystroke.
Event Procedure	A set of Visual Basic statements that are executed in response to an action like clicking the mouse.
Event	An event is an action that occurs because of some user or program activity. A program can respond to events such as clicking a mouse button or typing a keystroke.
Form	A form is a window in which you design a user interface. When a user runs a program, the user communicates with the program using the objects on the form. Forms are stored on the disk with the extension .frm. Forms are stored in the program's project file.
Module	A part of your program stored as a file on the disk. All the parts of a form are stored in a single file, called a form module
Object	An object is an instance (occurrence) of a control drawn on a form. An object might be a label or a command button.
Program	A program is a set of statements written in a computer language to accomplish a specific task. The task can be as simple as adding two numbers together or as complex as computing the payroll for a large corporation.
Project	A project is the collection of files that make up a Visual Basic program. A project file is stored on the disk with the extension .vbp. A project file contains a list of the forms and other parts of a program.
Property	A property is a characteristic of an object, such as the object's color, caption, screen location, or size. Properties also determine whether an object is visible or not.
Syntax	Syntax is the set of rules that determine the order and punctuation for the statements you write in a program.
Twip	A device independent unit of measurement used to position objects on the screen. There are about 1440 twips per inch.

Tutorial Assignments

Amy DuBrava, an account manager at the Dunn Financial Group, reviewed the practice program you created that displayed the Dunn Financial logo. Amy had designed another potential logo for Dunn Financial, and she would like you to create a program to display this logo. You will also add a CommandButton object to exit the program. When you finished creating the program, you will run it then print the form image.

1. Make sure your Student Disk is in the disk drive, then start Visual Basic.
2. Draw an Image control in the upper-left corner of the form. Refer to Figure 1-36 for placement and sizing.
3. Set the necessary property for the Image object so that the picture you place in it will fill the Image object.
4. Load the picture from the file **DunnLogo.bmp**, which is located on your Student Disk in the TAssign folder of the Tutorial.01.
5. Draw a CommandButton object on the bottom of the form.
6. Specify the caption **Exit** for the CommandButton object.
7. Open the Code window for the CommandButton object.

8. Type the following program comment as the first line of code: **'This code will end my Logo program.**
9. Enter the word **End** between the Private Sub and End Sub statements; this will make the program stop running when you click the command button. Close the Code window when the code is complete. Your screen looks like Figure 1-36.

Figure 1-36 ◀

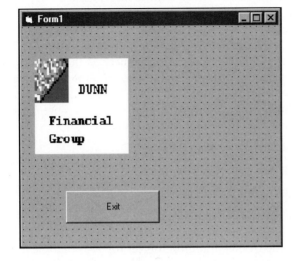

10. Run the program.
11. When you have finished reviewing the Logo program, use the Exit button to stop the program from running.
12. Save the form file as **Dunn Logo.frm** in the TAssign folder of the Tutorial.01 folder on your Student Disk.
13. Save the project file as **Dunn Logo.vbp** in the TAssign folder of the Tutorial.01 folder on your Student Disk.
14. Print the image of the form you created.
15. Exit Visual Basic.

Case Problems

1. Mountaintop College Mountaintop College is a small, private two-year college in the Sierra Nevada mountains. The chairperson of the computer department, Mary Gorden, would like an organization chart of the department, but she does not have a computer application specifically designed for drawing organization charts. You'll use Visual Basic to create the organization chart. The top box of the chart will contain the name of the department chairperson (Mary Gorden). Two middle-level boxes will contain the names of the two computer instructors, Judie Kindschi and Tom Galvez. One bottom-level box will contain your name. After creating the form for the organization chart, you'll run the program to test it.

1. Make sure your Student Disk is in the disk drive, then start Visual Basic.
2. Draw a Label object at the top of the form in the center. Refer to Figure 1-37 for placement and sizing.
3. Draw two more Label objects in the middle of the form side-by-side, below the first Label object.
4. Draw one more Label object below the two Label objects.
5. Change the BorderStyle property of all four labels to **1-Fixed Single.**

6. Look up "Line control" in the online Help system and read the Help information. Then, using the Line control, draw lines showing the departmental relationship between the labels.
7. Draw a CommandButton object on the bottom-left side of the form.
8. Specify the caption **Exit** for the CommandButton object.

9. Open the Code window for the CommandButton object.
10. Enter the word **End** between the Private Sub and End Sub statements; this will make the program stop running when you click the command button. Close the Code window when the code is complete.
11. Draw another CommandButton object on the bottom-right side of the form.
12. Specify the caption **Click Here To Insert Names** for the CommandButton object. If the entire caption doesn't fit in the command button, increase the size of the button.
13. Open the Code window for the CommandButton object you just created.

14. Type the following program comment as the first line of code: **'This code will place each department member's name in the appropriate label.**
15. Type the following lines of Visual Basic code between the Private Sub and End Sub lines. Substitute your name for the reference Your Name. Close the Code window after you enter all the code.

   Label1.Caption = "Mary Gorden"

   Label2.Caption = "Judie Kindschi"

   Label3.Caption = "Tom Galvez"

   Label4.Caption = "Your Name"

16. Run the program.
17. Click the CommandButton object for inserting the names. Your screen looks like Figure 1-37. If any names do not fit correctly in the label, click the Exit button and resize the label. Repeat this step as necessary until all the names are fully displayed in the labels.

Figure 1-37 ◀

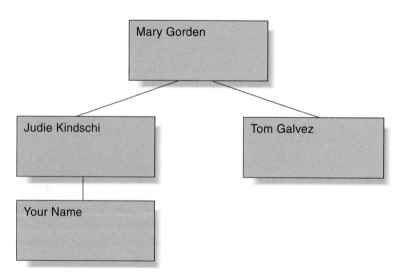

18. Use the Exit button to stop the program from running.

19. Open the Code window for the Exit CommandButton object, then type the code **PrintForm** before code you wrote to end the program. This PrintForm statement will cause the form image to be printed when you click the Exit command button.
20. Run the program again and test the operation of both command buttons.
21. Save the form file as **Mountaintop Chart.frm** in the Cases folder of the Tutorial.01 folder on your Student Disk.
22. Save the project file as **Mountaintop Chart.vbp** in the Cases folder of the Tutorial.01 folder on your Student Disk.
23. Exit Visual Basic.

2. Advance Computer Graphics Advance Computer Graphics uses a large number of graphic images in the Visual Basic programs created throughout the company. The owners of Advanced Computer Graphics know that Windows 95 contains a large number of bitmap (bmp) graphics files and they would like to use the Image control to display them on their forms. But they are unsure about how the Stretch property works. You will create a program that has two Image objects to display various bitmap files and a CommandButton object to exit the program. One of these Image objects will have the Stretch property set to True, and one will have the Stretch property set to False. This will illustrate to the owners how the Stretch property controls the size of Image objects.

1. Make sure your Student Disk is in the disk drive, then start Visual Basic.
2. Draw two Image objects on the form, one on the right side of the form and one on the left. Make both objects fairly large, but leave room for the CommandButton object.
3. Change the Stretch property of the left Image object to **True**.
4. Load any picture contained in the Windows folder (on drive C). This folder contains a variety of bitmap graphics files, such as Thatch and Castle.
5. Select the right-hand Image object, then load any other picture contained in the Windows folder (on drive C) in this object, without changing its Stretch property.
6. Draw a CommandButton object on the form.
7. Specify the caption **Exit** for the CommandButton object.
8. Open the Code window for the CommandButton object.
9. Type the following program comment as the first line of code: **'This code will end my Stretch program.**
10. Enter the word **End** between the Private Sub and End Sub statements; this will make the program stop running when you click the command button. Close the Code window when the code is complete. Your screen looks like Figure 1-38, but your bitmap graphics files may differ.

Figure 1-38 ◀

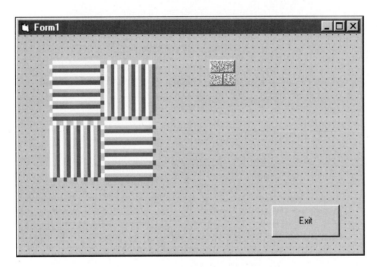

11. Run the program and notice the different results for the two Image objects.
12. Use the Exit button to stop the program from running.
13. Print the image of the form you created.
14. Save the form as **Advance Stretch.frm** in the Cases folder of the Tutorial.01 folder on your Student Disk.
15. Save the project as **Advance Stretch.vbp** in the Cases folder of the Tutorial.01 folder on your Student Disk.
16. Exit Visual Basic.

3. Atlantic Beverages Atlantic Beverages is a wholesale supplier of soft drinks specializing in the hotel industry. The delivery manager, Sam Levinson, would like a program to produce a list that will be used by the company's drivers. The program you create will move a variety of standard text items to different parts of the completed shipping document. You'll create a sample form to demonstrate how text can be moved to different parts of the form. The form you need to create will include three labels and three command buttons.

1. Make sure your Student Disk is in the disk drive, then start Visual Basic.
2. Draw three Label objects of approximately the same size in the upper half of the form.

3. Draw three CommandButton objects of approximately the same size in the lower half of the form.
4. Open the Code window for the first command button.
5. Type the following program comment as the first line of code: **'This code will show the movement of text to Label1 and Label2.**

6. Type the following lines of Visual Basic code between the Private Sub and End Sub lines. Close the Code window after you enter all the code.
   Label1.Caption = "This text is going to Label1"
   Label2.Caption = "This text is going to Label2"
7. Open the Code window for the second command button.
8. Type the following program comment as the first line of code:
   'This code will show the movement of text to Label3.
9. Type the following line of code between the Private Sub and End Sub lines. Close the Code window after you enter the code.
   Label3.Caption = "This text is going to Label3"
10. Specify the caption Exit for the third command button.
11. Open the code window for the Exit CommandButton object
12. Type the following program comment as the first line of code:
    'This code will end my Label move text program.
13. Enter the word **End** between the Private Sub and End Sub statements; this will make the program stop running when you click the Exit command button. Close the Code window when the code is complete. Your screen looks like Figure 1-39.

Figure 1-39 ◀

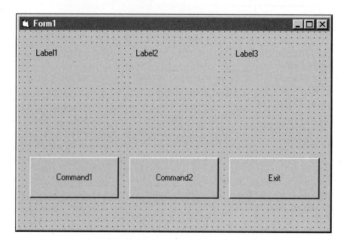

14. Run the program and test the operation of each of the command buttons.
15. Use the Exit button to stop the program from running.
16. Save the form as **Atlantic Beverages.frm** in the Cases folder of the Tutorial.01 folder on your Student Disk.
17. Save the project as **Atlantic Beverages.vbp** in the Cases folder of the Tutorial.01 folder on your Student Disk.
18. Print the image of the form you created.
19. Exit Visual Basic.

4. Kate's Printing Kate's Printing prints unique greeting cards for the general public. When customers come into the shop they typically see a variety of fonts, styles, colors, etc. to help them choose their cards. Kate Liu, the owner of the shop, wants to know if a Visual Basic program could be used to demonstrate the various printing options to customers by changing different properties of a label, command button, line, and image. You will look at a number of properties for each of these controls. Consult the Visual Basic Help system for additional information about the different properties.
1. Start Visual Basic.
2. Starting from the top middle of the form and working down, draw a Label object, a CommandButton object, a Line object, and an Image object.

3. Select the Label objects then select at least five properties that you have not seen before and use them to modify the characteristics of the Label object. Make sure that the Properties window does not obscure the Label object. In particular, change the various Font properties and observe the results. Write down what occurs when you change each property. The following is a list of some commonly used label properties:

Font (choose a variety of sizes and types)
BackColor (choose a variety of colors from the palette)
ForeColor (choose a variety of colors from the palette)
BorderStyle (cycle through the options)
Height (choose various sizes)
Left (choose various sizes)
Width (choose various sizes)

4. Repeat Step 3 for each of the other objects. If you do not see an obvious change to make to the object, consult the Help system for that property.
5. Print the Form Image.
6. Exit Visual Basic but do not save the program.

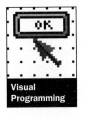

Visual Programming

Visual Programming Lab

This Lab Assignment is designed to accompany the interactive CourseLab called Visual Programming. To start the Visual Programming Lab, click the Start button on the Windows 95 taskbar, point to Programs, point to CourseLabs, point to New Perspectives Applications, and click Visual Programming. If you do not see CourseLabs on your Programs menu, see your instructor or lab manager.

In the Visual Programming Lab, you use an event-driven, object-oriented programming environment to create simple programs. This Lab provides a "taste" of what it would be like to program in a visual language such as Visual Basic.

1. Click the Steps button to learn how to create a graphical user interface containing buttons, labels, and text boxes. As you work through the Steps, answer all of the Quick Check questions. After you complete the Steps, you will see a Summary Report of your answers. Follow the directions on the screen to print this report.
2. In Explore, create a program to calculate the total cost of carpeting a room. Test your program, then print it showing the cost of $12.99/square yard carpeting for a 10 × 14 foot room.
   Assume that the room is rectangular. The known information is the length and width of the room, and the price of a square yard of carpet. You must calculate:

   ■ the square feet of carpet needed (length * width of room)
   ■ the square yard of carpet needed (square feet/9)
   ■ total price of carpet (price per square yard * the square yards needed)

   Your user interface should look like the following screen.

Figure 1-40 ◀

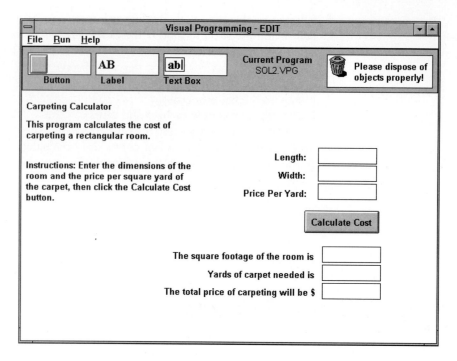

3. Suppose you like to shop from catalogs. Your favorite catalog is having a sale—selected merchandise is discounted 10%, 20%, 30%, or 40%. You want to know how much you'll save if you buy some of the merchandise you want. In Explore, create a program to calculate savings. Test your program, then print it showing the savings for an $863 item at a 30% discount.

   Assume that the items you purchase will be discounted and that there is no additional charge for shipping. The known information is the original price of the item and its discount—10%, 20%, 30%, or 40%. Calculate how much you will save (for example, for a 10% discount, multiply the original cost by .10.) Your user interface should look like the following screen.

Figure 1-41 ◀

```
┌──────────────────────────────────────────────────────────────┐
│ ─              Visual Programming - EDIT              ▼ ▲      │
├──────────────────────────────────────────────────────────────┤
│  File   Run   Help                                            │
├──────────────────────────────────────────────────────────────┤
│  ┌────┐   ┌──────┐   ┌──────┐   Current Program  🗑 Please dispose of │
│  │    │   │  AB  │   │ ab│  │     SOL3.VPG          objects properly! │
│  └────┘   └──────┘   └──────┘                                 │
│   Button    Label     Text Box                                │
├──────────────────────────────────────────────────────────────┤
│  DISCOUNT SHOPPER              Product price:                  │
│                                                               │
│  This program helps you        ┌──────────┐                   │
│  calculate how much money      │          │                   │
│  you save when you shop!       └──────────┘                   │
│                                                               │
│  Instructions:  Enter the price                               │
│  of the product, then click                                   │
│  the appropriate discount    [10%][20%][30%][40%]             │
│  button.                                                      │
│                              You save $ ┌──────────┐          │
│                                         └──────────┘          │
│                                                               │
└──────────────────────────────────────────────────────────────┘
```

4. In your recording studio, studio musicians are paid by the hour, but your sound technicians are salaried. You started to make a program to calculate weekly paychecks, but it doesn't seem to work. Your assumption is that some

employees are salaried and some are hourly. You know the salaries for the salaried employees. You know the hourly wage and the hours worked each pay period for the hourly employees. You want to calculate the weekly pay for salaried employees (Wages/52) and the weekly pay for hourly employees (Wages * Hours).

In Explore, open the program pay.vpg and test it.

Enter 32240 in the Wages box, then click the Salaried button. The output should be 620. Next enter 8 in the Wages box and 40 in the Hours box. Click the Hourly button. The output should be 320. Find what's wrong with this program and correct it. Print your solution.

Understanding Code and Variables

Designing and Writing a Financial Calculator Program for the Dunn Financial Group

OBJECTIVES

In this tutorial you will:

- Design a Visual Basic program

- Create multiple instances of the TextBox, CommandButton and Label objects, and use more of their properties

- Modify the tab order of objects on a form

- Declare and use variables

- Create expressions

- Use Visual Basic functions to convert data, format data, and compute financial values

- Write code inside a form module

- Fix syntax and run-time errors

- Print various parts of a program

Dunn Financial Group (Continued)

CASE

As part of the Dunn Financial Group's everyday business practices, analysts forecast their clients' investment growth over time. The analysts use this information to estimate cash flow and income and to prepare the necessary financial statements. Often, clients use these statements to consider the effects of different interest rates on their income. To streamline the forecasting process, the management team has asked Mark Fisk, the senior computer programmer/analyst, to create a Visual Basic program that will compute the necessary information.

Before creating the program, Mark spent time designing it so that it would meet the needs of the financial analysts who will use it. Once his design was complete, he began to create many of the objects on the form. He still needs to create the remaining objects, then run and test the program to make sure it works properly. After reviewing Mark's design specifications, you will help him complete the program to calculate the future value of investments made by Dunn Financial's clients.

In this session you will learn how to write pseudocode, which describes what a program will do; design the screens for a program; define the tasks, objects, and events for a program; create a program's objects and set their properties; and set the tab order of objects on a form.

Designing a Computer Program

Mark has been a programmer for many years, and he realizes that creating programs involves more than simply sitting down at a computer, designing the interface, and writing the code. In fact, to ensure a quality product, Dunn Financial has strict guidelines specifying that an adequate amount of time be spent understanding the problem and finding the best solution before programming can begin. The company also established a standard set of steps, known as a **methodology**, for designing programs. The methodology requires that each step be completed in sequence before moving on to the next step. The four steps to design a computer program are as follows:

1. Completely understand the problem and what data you need to solve it.

2. Write out the program steps in simple, non-technical terms. This is known as pseudocode.

3. Sketch a picture of the user interface design for each computer screen in the program.

4. Break down the pseudocode and user interface design into the tasks the program needs to accomplish, the objects needed for entering and displaying information, and how the objects will respond to different events. This is called a Task Object Event (TOE) chart.

After these steps are accomplished, you can begin creating the actual user interface and writing program code. Although it might seem more efficient to avoid the design steps and immediately start to code your program, the opposite is true. Computer programs look and work better with some forethought to the final product and where it will fit into other programs. You would not think of starting to build a house without a set of plans and some thought given to the materials and time involved. The same is true for programming. A little time spent in planning will save you many hours of work debugging a program or correcting design flaws.

Understanding the Problem

Of all the steps involved in creating a program, understanding what you want to accomplish might be the most difficult. Most problems are not originally structured or given in the terms that you need in order to set them up on a computer. Also, some problems might require that you break them down into multiple programs with multiple tasks for each program. For example, the analysts at Dunn Financial would like a set of tools to help them simplify the work of estimating their clients' investment performance. This is an example of a macro (large) problem that must be further investigated and broken down into the actual tasks that the analysts perform in their day-to-day work. As you try to understand the scope of a problem, you might find that simply redoing manual tasks on a computer is not the best way to accomplish the overall goal. In some cases, a complete change in the way the activity is done, while taking advantage of the computer, can provide the best solution to the problem.

The IPO Model

To understand a problem and its computer solution, it is often useful to first consider the problem in terms of the Input-Processing-Output (IPO) model. Most programs start with some type of input data. The program takes the **input** data, **processes** it in some way, and then creates the required **output**. Figure 2-1 illustrates the IPO model.

Figure 2-1 ◀
The IPO model

Input   Processing   Output

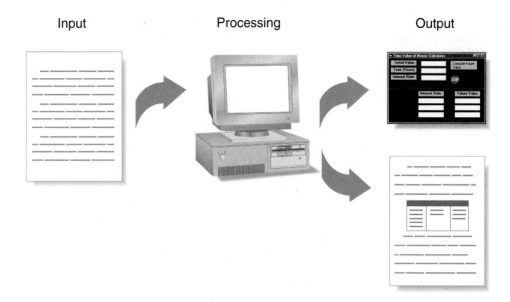

You must understand what data is required to solve the problem and what processes need to be performed on the data to complete the output. In the case of Dunn Financial, the analysts need a program to calculate the future value of a client's investments. The program must take the initial value of an investment, the term, and the rate of interest, then calculate the future value of the investment at different interest rates and display the results. The input consists of three data items: the initial value of the investment, the length of time that interest accrues (the term), and the interest rate. The processing required is to calculate the future value of the investment at three different interest rates: an initial rate plus two different rates, each one increasing by 1%. The output consists of the three different interest rates and the corresponding future value of the investment for each interest rate.

Writing the Pseudocode for the Program

After identifying the problem and determining the input data, processing requirements, and output for the program, the next step is to write the pseudocode for the program. As noted earlier, **pseudocode** uses simple, non-technical terms to describe the program steps. You can write the pseudocode either on a piece of paper or using any word processor, such as Notepad, which is available in the Accessories folder of Windows 95.

Mark already wrote the pseudocode for the calculator program using Notepad. You now need to review the pseudocode.

To view and print the pseudocode Mark wrote:

1. From the Windows 95 desktop, click the **Start** button on the task bar.

2. Point to **Programs**, point to **Accessories**, then click **Notepad** to start the Notepad program.

   You can also use any other word processing program to view and print the pseudocode.

3. Open the file named **Dunn_PC.txt** located in the Tutorial.02 folder on your Student Disk.

4. Print the file. The printed psuedocode is shown in Figure 2-2.

Figure 2-2 ◀
Pseudocode for
Dunn
Financial's
calculator
program

Input Section

     Get the initial value of the investment

     Get the term of the investment

     Get the annual interest rate

Processing Section

     Use the Future Value function to calculate the
     future value of the investment for the specified
     term at the annual interest rate

     Use the Future Value function two more times
     to calculate the future value of the investment
     at interest rates that increase by 1% each time

Output Section

     Wait for the user to click either the Compute
     Future Value button or the Stop button

     If the user clicks the Compute Future Value button,
     display each of the amounts calculated with the Future
     Value function

     If the user clicks the stop sign image, stop the program
     from processing

Note that the input data consists of three items: the initial value of the investment, the length of time for which the program will compute interest (the term), and the annual interest rate. The user will need to enter these three items before the program processes the input.

After a user enters the necessary input data, the program can calculate the value of the investment at some future time period. The analysts need to estimate the effects of different interest rates on the investment so that each client can evaluate these effects. The calculator program must compute the investment return using three different interest rates: the initial interest rate specified by the analyst, an interest rate 1% greater than the rate specified, and an interest rate 2% greater. Visual Basic contains a Future Value function (FV) that will perform these computations for you.

The pseudocode in the Output Section describes the steps the program takes after processing the input data. The program will display the results of the calculations for the three different interest rates if the user clicks the Compute Future Value button, which is a command button. Or, the user can click the Image object showing a stop sign to stop the program from processing.

Designing the User Interface for the Program

Designing a user interface requires a bit of an artistic eye and adherence to several design elements. Figure 2-3 describes the elements of good user interface design.

Figure 2-3 ◀
Elements of
good user
interface design

Design Element	Description
Control	The user should always control the program, not the other way around.
User friendliness	The interface should help the user accomplish tasks and not call attention to itself. Too many different fonts, lines, or images tend to distract the user from the task at hand.
Intuitiveness	The interface should follow a direct style that proceeds logically. So, if a user needs to complete different steps to accomplish an activity, the steps should be grouped together.
Consistency/Clarity	The interface should be conceptually, linguistically, visually, and functionally consistent. Visual elements should be readily comprehensible.
Feedback	The interface should provide immediate and clear feedback to the user. For example, if a user adds a record to a file, the interface should inform the user that the record was added. Likewise, if a user makes an error when entering data, the interface should communicate the cause of the error and possible solutions to the user.
Graphics	The interface should not be cluttered with graphics that serve no useful purpose. Graphics cause a program to run more slowly and they can detract from the objects that are most important to complete the task. Logos, icons, and pictures are frequently included to guide the user. For example, an icon of a stop sign is an intuitive metaphor to use as a button to end the program.
Fonts	The font style used should be consistent throughout the interface. Avoid using more than two or three different fonts on a form. Too many fonts can cause the user interface to appear cluttered and unbalanced.
Input	The interface should minimize instances in which the user needs to switch input modes from the mouse to the keyboard and back. This will allow the user to complete tasks more quickly and efficiently.

Adapted from *Code Complete*, Steve McConnell, Microsoft Press, 1993.

Mark has already completed the design of the user interface for the calculator program, as shown in Figure 2-4.

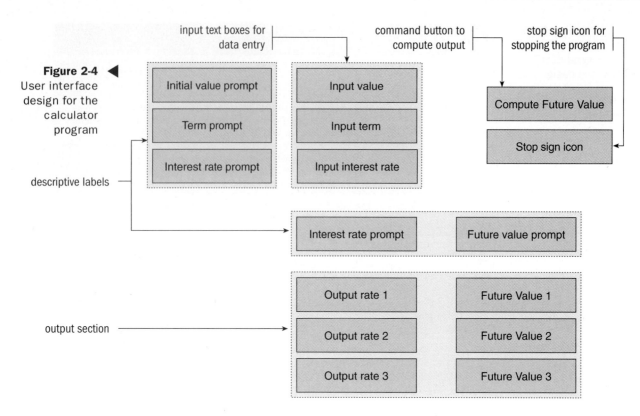

Figure 2-4 ◀
User interface
design for the
calculator
program

input text boxes for data entry

command button to compute output

stop sign icon for stopping the program

descriptive labels

output section

As shown in Figure 2-4, the interface will provide three text boxes for the user to input the necessary data—the initial value of the investment, the term, and the interest rate. Note that the design includes descriptive labels (prompts) to the left of these three text boxes so that the user will know what data to enter in them. The interface also contains labels for the three different interest rates and the corresponding future values of the investment. Finally, the form will include a command button to compute the output and a stop sign image to stop the program.

Creating the TOE Chart for the Program

The last step in designing a program is to create a TOE (Task Object Event) chart. A **TOE chart** is a three-column table that breaks down the necessary tasks in the program. The first column contains a description of each program task; the second column lists the object that will accomplish each task; and the third column contains the type of event that will trigger the object into performing its task. Because labels are used only to describe the input and output of the program and do not respond to events, the third column will not contain entries for any Label objects.

Mark already created the TOE chart for the calculator program using Notepad. Next, you will open the Notepad file to view and print the chart.

To view and print the TOE chart for the calculator program:

1. In Notepad or any word processing program, open the file named **Dunn_TOE.txt**, which is located in the Tutorial.02 folder on your Student Disk.

2. Print the file.

3. Exit Notepad (or your word processing program). The printed TOE chart is shown in Figure 2-5.

Figure 2-5 ◀
TOE Chart for
Dunn
Financial's
calculator
program

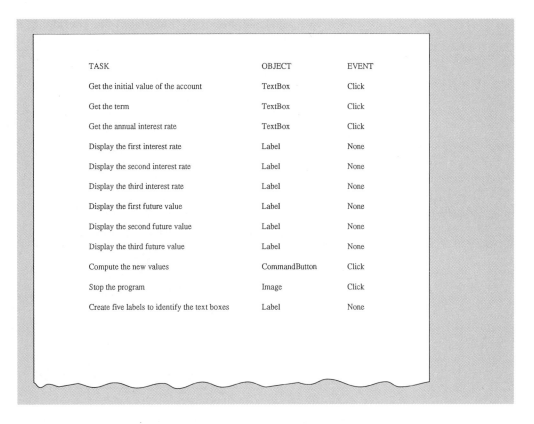

TASK	OBJECT	EVENT
Get the initial value of the account	TextBox	Click
Get the term	TextBox	Click
Get the annual interest rate	TextBox	Click
Display the first interest rate	Label	None
Display the second interest rate	Label	None
Display the third interest rate	Label	None
Display the first future value	Label	None
Display the second future value	Label	None
Display the third future value	Label	None
Compute the new values	CommandButton	Click
Stop the program	Image	Click
Create five labels to identify the text boxes	Label	None

After completing all the necessary steps for designing the calculator program, Mark started to work on the form for the program and entered some of the objects on it. Now he wants you to open the form and complete it for him.

Creating the Calculator Program

According to Mark's design specifications for the calculator program, a user will supply input values representing an initial value, term, and interest rate. When the user clicks the Compute Future Value button, the program will process and display the three future value results along with the interest rates, based on the input values. The finished form for the calculator program will look like Figure 2-6.

Figure 2-6 ◀
Completed
calculator form

labels identifying
input

text boxes

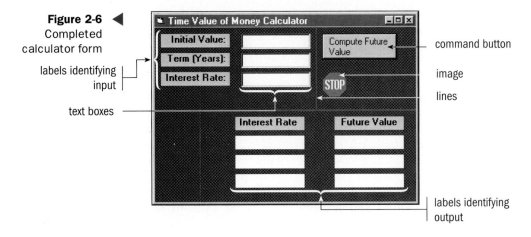

command button

image

lines

labels identifying
output

You will begin by opening the project file that contains the partially completed calculator form.

To start Visual Basic and open the project file containing the calculator form:

1. Be sure your Student Disk is in the disk drive.

2. Start Visual Basic then open the project file named **Dunn_Cal.vbp** located in the Tutorial.02 folder on your Student Disk.

   Mark already created the form for the program and added some objects to it. You need to open and look at the form.

3. Click the **View Form** button in the Project window. The Form window opens and displays the partially completed form. See Figure 2-7.

Figure 2-7 ◀
Calculator form with some objects entered

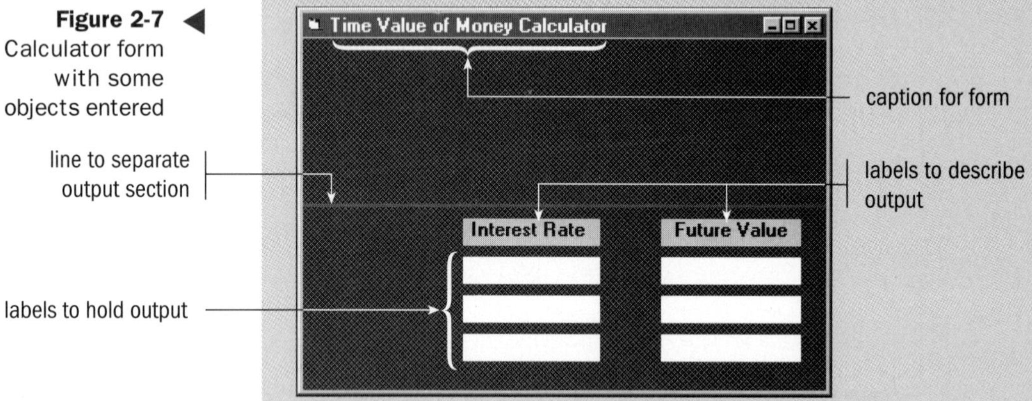

line to separate output section

labels to hold output

caption for form

labels to describe output

TROUBLE? If the Project window is not open on your screen, click View on the menu bar then click Project to open the window.

Before working on the form, you will save it with a different name, then save the project file with a different name. Doing so will keep the original files intact, allowing you to start over if you make a serious mistake.

4. Click **File** on the menu bar, then click **Save File As.**

5. Select the Tutorial.02 folder on your Student Disk, change the entry in the File name text box to **Dunn Calculator.frm**, then click the **Save** button to save the form with the new name.

6. Click **File** on the menu bar, then click **Save Project As**.

7. Select the Tutorial.02 folder on your Student Disk, change the entry in the File name text box to **Dunn Calculator.vbp**, then click the **Save** button to save the project file with the new name.

As you perform the steps to write the program, you will save your work frequently. If you make an error you cannot correct, you can load the most recently saved copies of the form and project files and continue your work from that point.

Note the objects that Mark has already created. The two labels containing the text, Interest Rate and Future Value, identify the output areas for the program. The text boxes will hold the output data after the program processes it. Additionally, Mark drew a line on the form to visually separate the output section from the rest of the form. Finally, Mark set the form's Caption property to "Time Value of Money Calculator"; this text appears in the title bar of the form.

Fundamentals of Visual Basic Project Files

Every Visual Basic program is composed of a number of files called modules. Whether or not a program uses all the types of modules depends on the needs of the program. When you create and save a form, all of its information is stored in a Form module. This module is stored on the disk as a file with the extension .frm.

Every Visual Basic program contains a project file with the extension .vbp. The project file defines all of the files used by the program. Project files are usually stored on the disk in the same folder as the other module files related to a program.

One of the elements in a project file is a form. Most projects generally contain many forms. The following entry from the project file identifies the form used in your program stored on the disk as Form1.frm.

```
Form=Form1.frm
```

If the project file cannot locate all the files in the program, you might need to edit the project file. The instructions in this text ask you to save all your project and form files to your Student Disk. However, you might inadvertently save a project or form to the hard disk on your computer instead of to your Student Disk. The most common instance of this is when your form file is on the hard disk while your project file is on the Student Disk. The project file contains a number of items related to your program including where to find and load the form or forms for the project. If you open a saved project from your Student Disk, and Visual Basic displays the message "File not found: Continue Loading Project?" the project file cannot locate one or more of its form files.

To fix the problem, you need to find the missing form file and copy it to your Student Disk in the same folder as the project file. Or, you need to open and edit the project file using Notepad or any other word processing program, because the file is saved as a text file. After you open the project file, you will see each form in the program listed on a separate line such as FORM=FORM1.frm. If you want the project file to look for a form file in a particular location, such as on your Student Disk, you need to tell Visual Basic the drive on which the form is stored. To do this, simply change the FORM=FORM1.frm line to FORM=A:\folder\FORM1.frm, where A: (or B:) is the drive and "folder" is the folder on your disk where the form is stored. Be sure to save the project file as a text file if you are using a word processing program other than Notepad.

Creating the Label Objects

As you learned in Tutorial 1, you add objects to a form then set their properties. You will use the Label control to add labels that will display both descriptive text and the results of the calculations on the screen. The user will not change the text in the labels or interact with them in any way. You can refer to Mark's plan of the user interface (Figure 2-4) to help you determine where to place the labels on the form.

To place the Initial Value label on the form:

1. Click the **Label** control A on the toolbox.

2. Move the pointer to the upper-left corner of the form.

3. Click and hold down the left mouse button, then move the mouse down and to the right. An outline of the object is displayed as you move the pointer.

4. When the size of the object approximates the size of the object in Figure 2-8, release the mouse button.

5. To ensure an exact size and placement, set the Height property of the label to **255**, the Width property to **1335**, the Left property to **120**, and the Top property to **120**.

Figure 2-8
Figure 2-8 ◀
Creating the
Label object

Label object ——

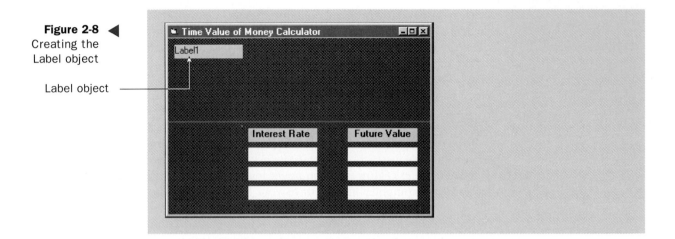

Setting the Properties for the Label Object

Now you need to change the appearance of the label you just created. Mark wants the text in each of the labels to be bold so they will stand out more from the rest of the form, and he wants the labels to be right-justified so that the alignment will be the same as the alignment of text in the corresponding text box objects. Also, he asks you to give each label a meaningful caption.

To set the properties for the label object:

1. Be sure the label you just created is selected, that is, the handles appear around the label.

   TROUBLE? If the object is not selected, click the label so that the handles appear.

2. In the Properties window for the label, click the value for the Alignment property.

3. Click the Properties button for the Alignment property, then click **1 - Right Justify**. This selection will cause the text of the label to be aligned on the right of the Label object.

4. Locate the Caption property, double-click the existing text (Label1) to select it, then type **Initial Value:**.

   Note that as you type text in the Properties window, the same text appears in the Label object in the Form window, and the text is right-justified. See Figure 2-9.

Figure 2-9 ◀
Setting the
label's
properties

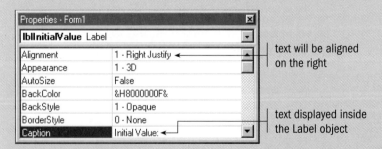

text will be aligned
on the right

text displayed inside
the Label object

Next you need to set the font for the label to bold.

5. Click the value for the Font property to display the Properties button ⊡, then click the Properties button. The Font dialog box opens.

6. Click **Bold** in the Font style list box, then click the **OK** button. The text in the label now appears in the bold font. See Figure 2-10.

Figure 2-10 ◀
Font dialog box

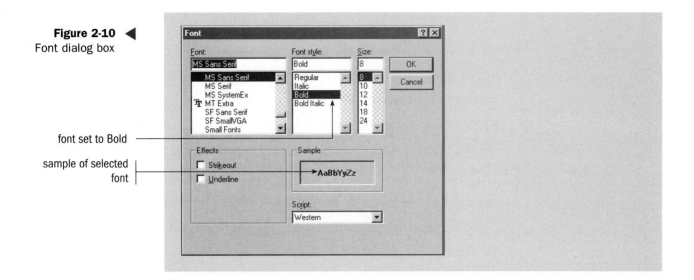

font set to Bold ————

sample of selected
font ————

Naming the Label Object

The initial name of the Label object you created is Label1. Visual Basic assigns a unique name to every toolbox object you create. You can change the name to a more meaningful one by setting the Name property. Note that the Name and Caption properties are different. You use the Name property to identify the object and to refer to it when writing Visual Basic statements; you use the Caption property to display text inside the object. You will change the Name property for most objects so that the code in your program will be easier to understand. When this small program is complete, it will contain about 20 objects. As your programs become more complicated, they will contain hundreds, perhaps thousands, of objects. Imagine trying to keep track of all these objects if you did not use names that reflect the purpose of each object.

As is the case when setting other properties, you should set the Name property for an object immediately after creating it. Object names should begin with a consistent prefix, so that you can easily identify the type of object by its name. Figure 2-11 identifies the standard prefixes for the toolbox controls used in this tutorial. As new controls are introduced later in this text, the standard prefix for the control will be shown.

Figure 2-11 ◀
Standard pre-
fixes for Visual
Basic object
names

Object	Prefix	Examples
Form	frm	frmMain frmCustomer
CommandButton	cmd	cmdPrint cmdComputeFutureValue
Image	img	imgEnd imgRun
Label	lbl	lblAppName lblInitialValue
Line	lin	linTop linBottom
TextBox	txt	txtInput1 txtInterestRate

The following is a list of rules for naming an object in Visual Basic:

- The first character of the name must be a letter.

- The following characters can be letters, numbers, or the underscore character.

- A name must be fewer than 255 characters in length.

- A name cannot include special characters such as symbols or spaces.

The label you just created identifies the initial value of the investment, so you will name it lblInitialValue.

To set the Name property for the Label object:

1. In the Properties window for the Label object, locate the Name property.

2. Select the default value (Label1), then type **lblInitialValue.**

Creating Multiple Instances of Objects

So far, you have created only one instance of an object on your form. You could create additional instances of the Label object by following the same steps you just completed. However, each new object you create would assume the default (standard) properties of the control, and you would have to change them all individually. To save time and effort, Mark suggests that you use the copy and paste features to make copies of the Label object already on the form and preserve the properties you set in the initial object.

As you create additional instances of an object, Visual Basic assigns unique names to them. For example, if you create two labels, they will be named Label1 and Label2, respectively. You will need to change these names to conform to the prefixes listed in Figure 2-11.

You are now ready to create the labels to prompt the user for the term of the investment in years and the interest rate.

To create the additional Label objects:

1. If necessary, click the **Initial Value** label to select it.

2. Click **Edit** on the menu bar, then click **Copy** to copy the object into the Windows Clipboard.

3. Click **Edit** on the menu bar, then click **Paste** to paste a copy of the object from the Clipboard onto the form.

   Visual Basic displays a message asking if you want to create a control array. Control arrays are used to manipulate objects as a group and are discussed in later tutorials. For now, you do not want to create a control array.

4. Click the **No** button to close the message box.

   TROUBLE? If you clicked the Yes button by mistake, a control array was created. To delete the control array, delete both the object you just pasted and the original object you copied into the Clipboard. Then recreate the objects.

   The copy of the Label object appears in the upper-left corner of the form.

5. Click and hold the mouse button on the object, then move the object by dragging it below the first label you created. Your screen should look like Figure 2-12.

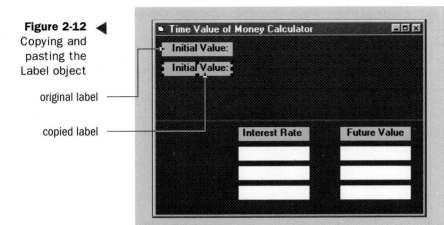

Figure 2-12 ◀
Copying and
pasting the
Label object

original label ────

copied label ────

Note that the copied label already has the correct property values for right-justified alignment and bold font. The only properties you need to set are the Caption and Name properties.

6. Set the Caption property for the copied label to **Term (Years):** and the Name property to **lblTermYears**.

7. Activate the Form window by clicking its title bar, click **Edit** on the menu bar, then click **Paste** to make another copy of the label from the Clipboard. Respond "No" to the message box asking if you want to create a control array.

   TROUBLE? If a new copy of the object did not appear in the upper-left corner of the form, either the Form window was not active or the contents of the Clipboard were cleared. Make sure the Form window is active; if it is, then the Clipboard was cleared. Click one of the labels you created, click Edit on the menu bar, then click Copy. Then repeat Step 7.

8. Move the new label below the second label you created.

9. Set the Caption property for the third label to **Interest Rate:** and the Name property to **lblInterestRate**. Your form should look like Figure 2-13.

Figure 2-13 ◀
Descriptive
labels on
the form

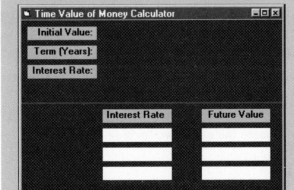

Next, you need to create text boxes to the right of each label prompt.

Creating a TextBox Object

A TextBox object is similar to a label in that it also displays textual information. However, only Visual Basic code can change the contents of a label while the program is running, because a user cannot type information into it. A text box allows a user to type in values so that those values can be used in the program.

Like a label, a TextBox object has properties, such as Alignment and Font, that you can set so that the text a user enters in the text box appears the way you want it to. The text displayed in a label is controlled by the Caption property, whereas the text displayed in a text box is controlled by the Text property.

REFERENCE
window

CREATING A TEXTBOX OBJECT

- Click the TextBox control on the toolbox, then use the mouse to draw a TextBox object on the form.
- Set the necessary properties for the TextBox object, such as Alignment, BorderStyle, and Font, in the Properties window.
- If you want the text to appear on multiple lines, set the MultiLine property to True.

Now you will create the three text boxes in which a user will enter the necessary input data for the initial value, term, and interest rate. These boxes will appear to the right of the labels that you created to identify the text boxes. The first text box is used to enter the initial value for the investment. Because the prefix for a TextBox object is txt, Mark suggests you name the object txtInitialValue. Generally, numeric information is right-justified in a column. So, you will set the Alignment property to right-justified.

To create the first TextBox object for the calculator program:

1. Click the **TextBox** control [abl] on the toolbox, then use the mouse to draw a text box on the form to the right of the Initial Value label. The text box should be the same size as the adjacent label.

2. Set the Name property for the text box to **txtInitialValue**.

   Next you need to set the Text property, which determines what text, if any, is initially displayed in the text box when a user runs the program. Mark wants the text boxes to be empty so that a user can immediately type the input data into them. So, you need to delete the default value for the Text property.

3. Select the default value (Text1) for the Text property, then press the **Delete** key.

4. Set the Alignment property for the text box to **1 - Right Justify**.

You can now create the remaining TextBox objects by copying and pasting the text box you just created.

To copy and paste the other two textbox objects:

1. Make sure the text box you just created is selected and the Form window is active.

2. Click **Edit** on the menu bar, then click **Copy**. A copy of the TextBox object is placed on the Clipboard, overwriting the current contents of the Clipboard.

3. Click **Edit** on the menu bar, then click **Paste**. When the message box appears for creating a control array, click the **No** button. A copy of the text box is pasted on the form.

4. Move the new text box to the right of the Term (Years) label.

5. Set the Name property for the new text box to **txtTermYears**.

6. Activate the Form window, click **Edit** on the menu bar, then click **Paste** to paste another copy of the text box on the form. Be sure not to create a control array.

7. Move the new text box to the right of the Interest Rate label.

8. Set the Name property for the new text box to **txtInterestRate**. Your form should look like Figure 2-14.

Figure 2-14 ◀
Form after
creating the
TextBox
objects

txtInterestRate

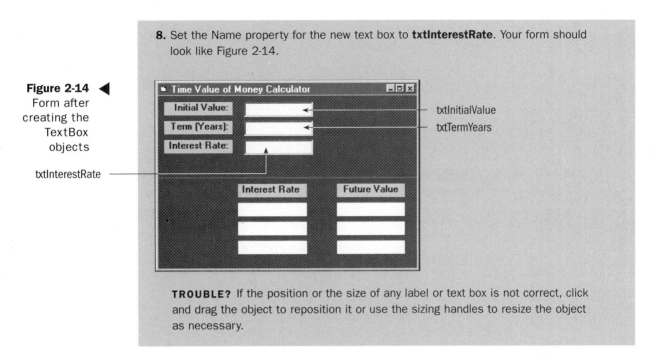

txtInitialValue
txtTermYears

TROUBLE? If the position or the size of any label or text box is not correct, click and drag the object to reposition it or use the sizing handles to resize the object as necessary.

Next you need to create the CommandButton object on the form so that a user can click this button to calculate the future values for the three different interest rates.

Creating a CommandButton Object

In Tutorial 1 you created a CommandButton object that, when clicked, caused a line of text to appear in a Label object. You will use the same procedure here to create the command button for the calculator program. When a user runs the calculator program and clicks the command button, the program will calculate the different interest rates and future values.

The CommandButton control has a Default property that, when set to True, allows a user to press the Enter key as an alternative to clicking the button to activate the button's Click event procedure. Only one CommandButton object on a form can be the default object, that is, have its Default property set to True. It would not make sense to try to have two default objects that would both try to respond to the Enter key being pressed. Setting the Default property of a command button can improve the user interface of a form, because it allows the user to press the Enter key to execute the most commonly used button. It is important to minimize the transitions between the keyboard and mouse whenever possible in the user interface.

Now you will create the CommandButton object for the calculator program. According to Mark's design, the button will include the caption "Compute Future Value" to identify its function. Like the other objects you just created, the command button should have a descriptive name identifying the purpose of the object. Because the prefix of a command button is cmd, and the button's purpose is to compute a future value, Mark suggests you name the object "cmdComputeFutureValue".

To create the CommandButton object and set its properties:

1. Click the **CommandButton** control ⬛ on the toolbox, then use the mouse to draw the CommandButton object on the form, to the right of the top-most text box.

2. Set the Height property of the command button to **495**, the Width property to **1455**, the Left property to **3240**, and the Top property to **120**.

3. Set the Caption property of the command button to **Compute Future Value**.

TROUBLE? If the caption does not fit inside the command button you created, resize the object to make it wider or taller, as necessary.

4. Set the Name property of the command button to **cmdComputeFutureValue**.

Next, you need to set the Default property for the command button to True so that a user can press the Enter key to activate the button. This will make it easier for a user to complete the form by typing the input data then pressing the Enter key to calculate the results.

5. Click the value for the Default property, click the Properties button ⬚, then click **True**. With this setting, a user can either press the Enter key or click the command button to activate it. See Figure 2-15.

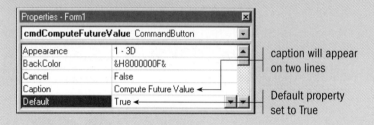

Figure 2-15 ◀
Setting the command button properties

caption will appear on two lines

Default property set to True

The next object you need to create is an Image object that will contain a stop sign icon. Mark wants a user to be able to click the icon to stop the program from running.

Creating an Image Object

In Tutorial 1, you used the Image control on the toolbox to create an Image object that contained the Dunn Financial logo. You can also create an Image object that will respond to different events, so that a user can click the Image and execute the code for its Click event, just like a command button. Because the standard prefix for an Image object is img, and the statement to stop running a program is "end," a good name for the object is imgEnd. As you saw in Tutorial 1, part of creating an Image is to load a picture into the Image object by setting its Picture property. The Image control can display icons, bitmaps, and Windows metafiles. The Image chosen by Mark is a stop sign that is stored as an icon file on your Student Disk.

To create the Image object, set its properties, and write its code:

1. Click the **Image** control ⬚ on the toolbox, then use the mouse to draw the Image object below the command button on the form.

2. Click the Properties button ⬚ for the Stretch property, then click **True**. This setting will cause the picture to fit the Image object you created.

3. Click the value for the Picture property to display the Properties button ⬚, then click it. The Picture dialog box opens.

4. Make sure Tutorial.02 is the displayed folder, click **stop.ico**, then click the **Open** button. The stop sign icon appears in the Image object. See Figure 2-16.

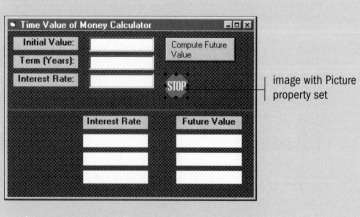

Figure 2-16 ◀
Creating the Image object

image with Picture property set

5. Set the Name property for the Image to **imgEnd**.

Setting the Tab Order

Every form has only one active object at a time. When you type text into a TextBox object, for example, you are using the active object. This object is said to have the **focus**. When using a program, you generally change the focus between one object and another by pressing the Tab key or clicking an object.

The TabIndex property for an object determines the order in which the object receives the focus when a user presses the Tab key. This order is called the **tab order**. The tab order is determined initially by the order in which you created objects on the form, but you can change the tab order by changing the value of the TabIndex property. When you change the TabIndex property of an object, the TabIndex properties of the other objects are adjusted accordingly. The TabIndex property begins by counting from 0 and incrementing each object by 1. So, the first object has a TabIndex property of 0, the second a TabIndex property of 1, the third a TabIndex property of 2, and so on. You do not have to set the tab order for objects such as labels, because they never receive the focus.

Setting the appropriate tab order for the objects on the form is important; you want to make sure that it follows a logical sequence each time the user presses the Tab key. When a user types information into the objects on a form, the information should be completed from top to bottom or left to right, depending on the program.

The analysts at Dunn Financial will type information into the three text boxes you created on the form. The objects are arranged in a column, so the tab order should move from top to bottom. Initially, the tab order will be the order in which the objects were created on the form. The order should be set so that the first text box in the column (txtInitialValue) receives the focus first, then the next text box, and so on. So, the first text box needs a TabIndex property setting of 0, the second a TabIndex of 1, and the third a TabIndex of 2. After typing information in all the TextBox objects the user will want to activate the Compute Future Value button, so its TabIndex property setting will be 3.

To set the TabIndex property of the objects used for input:

1. Click the TextBox object to the right of the Initial Value label to select it.

2. Change the TabIndex property value for the text box to **0**. A TabIndex property of 0 indicates that this object will be the active object (first object to receive the focus) when a user runs the program.

3. Click the TextBox object to the right of the Term(Years) label, then set its TabIndex property to **1**. When a user presses the Tab key after entering the initial value of the investment, this text box will receive the focus and the user can enter the term.

4. Click the TextBox object to the right of the Interest Rate label, then set its TabIndex property to **2**. After a user enters the term and presses the Tab key, the text box for Interest Rate will have the focus and the user can enter the interest rate.

5. Click the CommandButton object, then set its TabIndex property to **3**. After a user enters the interest rate and presses the Tab key, the command button will have the focus and the user can calculate the future values.

You only need to set the tab order for those objects in which a user will enter the input data, so you do not have to change the TabIndex property for any other objects on the form.

Next you need to add the final object to the form—a line to separate the command button and stop sign Image from the rest of the form. This will help to visually separate the input section from the buttons used for processing.

Creating a Line Object

You can draw lines and other shapes on a form to identify different sections of the form or to draw attention to a particular form area. You use the Line control on the toolbox to draw lines on a form. You can draw lines in any direction and choose different thicknesses and colors for lines.

REFERENCE window	**CREATING A LINE OBJECT**
	▪ Click the Line tool on the toolbox, then use the mouse to draw a line on the form. ▪ To define the color of the line, change the BorderColor property. ▪ To change the type of line, set the BorderStyle property. For example, the style could be dashed or solid. ▪ To change the thickness of the line, set the BorderWidth property.

In the calculator program, Mark already drew a horizontal line to separate the output section from the rest of the form. Now that the form contains the input and processing sections, he wants you to include a vertical line to separate these sections as well, which will improve the user interface by segmenting the different areas. The color and thickness of the vertical line should be the same as those of the line Mark already created.

To create a vertical line on the form:

1. Click the existing horizontal line on the form to make it active. In the Properties window, look at the settings for the BorderColor and BorderWidth properties. (To see the BorderColor property, you will need to click the Properties button […]).

   Now you will create a vertical line and set the same property values as the values of the existing line.

2. Click the **Line** control ⌐ on the toolbox, then use the mouse to draw a vertical line between the input section (labels and text boxes) and the processing section (command button and stop sign). Release the mouse button when the bottom of the vertical line meets the horizontal line already on the form. See Figure 2-17.

Figure 2-17 ◀
Creating the
Line object

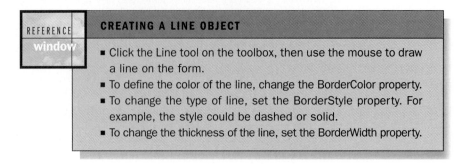

3. Click the value of the BorderColor property.

4. Click the Properties button […] to open the color palette.

5. Set the BorderColor property to **light green** to match the other line on the form. See Figure 2-18.

Figure 2-18 ◄
Setting the
BorderColor
property

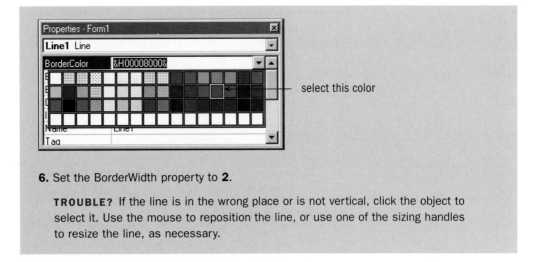

6. Set the BorderWidth property to **2**.

TROUBLE? If the line is in the wrong place or is not vertical, click the object to select it. Use the mouse to reposition the line, or use one of the sizing handles to resize the line, as necessary.

The form now contains all the necessary objects as shown in Mark's plan. This is a good time to save the form and project files.

To save the form and project files:

1. Make sure the Form window is active.

2. Click the **Save Project** button 🖫 on the toolbar.

Quick Check

1. Explain why it is necessary to plan a program before you begin to write the code for the program.

2. List the four steps that are necessary to design a program.

3. What does the term IPO stand for and what is the purpose of the IPO model?

4. What is pseudocode? Give a short example of pseudocode for balancing a checkbook.

5. What does TOE stand for and what is the purpose of the TOE chart?

6. Describe the differences between a Label control and a TextBox control.

7. Why is a Line control useful?

Now that you have completed Session 2.1, you can exit Visual Basic or you can continue to the next session.

SESSION

2.2

In this session, you will set properties using Visual Basic code, declare form-level and local variables, use the Val, Format, and Future Value functions, handle errors, and print various parts of a program.

Setting Properties Using Visual Basic Code

Until now, you have set an object's properties by changing values in the Properties window when you created the objects. You can also write Visual Basic statements that allow you to view and change properties while a program is running. You can perform many tasks, such as changing the font of text in a text box for emphasis while a user is entering text.

As you have seen, you can use the Properties window to set the Font property of a label or the Caption property of a command button. You can also set these properties at run time using Visual Basic code. When to set properties depends on the needs of your program. Properties that do not change, such as a command button's caption, should be set at design time using the Properties window. When the appearance of an object needs to change while the program is running, you must change the property by writing Visual Basic code. In fact, you cannot use the Properties window while the program is running. For example, you might set the initial font and type style of a text box using the Properties window. Then, when the object is active while the program is running, the font can change to emphasize the object to the user.

To set the properties of an object while the program is running, you use the following syntax for the code you enter in the Code window:

ObjectName.PropertyName = value

- *ObjectName* is the name you assigned to the object's Name property when you created it. Remember, Visual Basic always assigns a name to an object. You should set the Name property to change the name to something meaningful to your program.

- *PropertyName* is the name of the object's property you want to change while the program is running.

- The *value* is the new value for the property. You must be careful to assign only valid values to properties. For example, properties such as Caption can contain any text value, whereas properties such as FontBold, which you use to make text appear in bold type, can contain only the values True or False.

To improve the user interface, Mark wants to emphasize the active text box by displaying the text in a bold type while the user is entering the text. When the user presses the Tab key to move to a different object, the text in the newly selected object should appear in bold type and the text in the previously selected object should no longer be bold. To accomplish this task, you need to learn about two new events. You have already learned how to write the code for the Click event, which occurs when a command button is clicked.

Objects can respond to events other than just the Click event, and different objects can respond to different events. A TextBox object can respond to several events, including GotFocus and LostFocus. The **GotFocus** event occurs when a text box receives the focus, and the **LostFocus** event occurs when a text box loses focus. You can write code for these events that provides visual help to the user, such as displaying a message in a status bar or changing the type style of text. In your program, you need to use the GotFocus and LostFocus events to change the type style of text in the active object to bold.

Before you can write the code for the GotFocus and LostFocus events, you need to learn how to use the Code window to select an object and the appropriate event procedure. The Code window contains two list boxes. The Object list box shows all the objects in your program. After you select an object, you can select an event procedure from the Proc list box. The events shown in the Proc list box depend on the type of object you selected, because different objects respond to different events. When you select an object, Visual Basic sets the Proc list box to the most commonly used event for that object.

You will begin by opening the Code window and selecting the first text box, txtInitialValue, and its GotFocus event.

To select the object and event in the Code window, then write the code for the event:

1. Click **View** on the menu bar, then click **Code**. The Code window opens.

2. Click the **Object** list arrow, then click **txtInitialValue**, as shown in Figure 2-19.

Figure 2-19 ◀
Selecting an
object in the
Code window

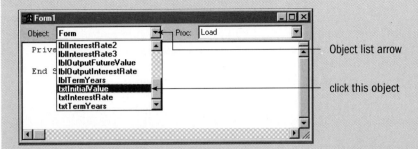

Object list arrow

click this object

TROUBLE? The size and shape of your Code window might differ from the window in Figure 2-19. You can resize your Code window to suit your preferences. The initial entries in the Object and Proc list boxes might also differ from those in the figure, depending on the currently selected object.

Next, you need to specify the correct event procedure for the selected object. Mark wants the text user types in the text box to be bold when the TextBox object has the focus. So, you need to select the GotFocus event.

3. Click the **Proc** list arrow, then click **GotFocus**. The code you will enter for the event will be executed when the TextBox object gets the focus. See Figure 2-20.

Figure 2-20 ◀
Selecting the
event for the
object

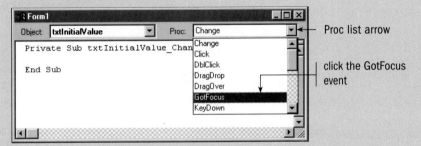

Proc list arrow

click the GotFocus event

The TextBox object supports 17 different events. In addition to getting and losing focus, a Change event occurs when the contents of a text box change. This is useful if you want to verify that the user entered valid information in the text box. Each time a user types a character into a text box, a KeyPress event is generated, allowing you to validate user input after every keystroke. Even though Visual Basic generates these events while your program is running, you do not need to write code to respond to them. Thus, if you do not want to validate keystrokes, you would not write any code for the KeyPress. Understanding the different events supported by an object and when they occur is an important part of Visual Basic programming.

Now that you have selected the object and the event procedure, you can write the code for the event so that text typed in the object will be bold while the user is typing it. The FontBold property, when set to True, causes the text to appear in bold type.

4. In the blank line between the beginning and ending lines of code, enter the code shown in Figure 2-21. To indent the line, press the Tab key before entering the code.

Figure 2-21 ◀

enter this code

```
Form1
Object:  txtInitialValue        Proc:  GotFocus

Private Sub txtInitialValue_GotFocus()
    txtInitialValue.FontBold = True
End Sub
```

Next you need to write the code for the LostFocus event for the Initial Value text box. This code will cause the text entered in the text box to return to normal style after the user presses the Tab key or clicks a different object. A setting of False for the FontBold property causes text to not appear in bold type.

To write code for the LostFocus event:

1. Click the **Proc** list arrow, then click **LostFocus**. When you select the new event, the Code window displays the beginning and ending lines of code for the new event, and the code you wrote for the previous event procedure is no longer displayed in the Code window.

2. Enter the following code for the LostFocus event procedure:

```
Private Sub txtInitialValue_LostFocus()

    txtInitialValue.FontBold = False

End Sub
```

The code you entered for the Initial Value text box will change the text to bold when the text box is active, that is, when the GotFocus event occurs for the object. The font will change to a normal type style when the text box is no longer active, that is, when the LostFocus event occurs for the object. You now need to enter the same code for the other two text boxes. To do so, you first need to select the txtTermYears text box using the Object list arrow in the Code window. Then you can write the code for the object's GotFocus and LostFocus events.

To write the code for the other two TextBox objects:

1. Click the **Object** list arrow, then click **txtTermYears**.

2. Click the **Proc** list arrow, then click **GotFocus**.

3. Enter the following code for the GotFocus event procedure:

```
Private Sub txtTermYears_GotFocus

    txtTermYears.FontBold = True

End Sub
```

4. Select the **LostFocus** event, then enter the following code for the LostFocus event procedure:

```
Private Sub txtTermYears_LostFocus

   txtTermYears.FontBold = False

End Sub
```

5. Repeat Steps 1 through 4 for the **txtInterestRate** text box.

Before you continue, Mark suggests that you run the program to determine if the code you just entered is correct, then save your work. As you develop programs, it is a good idea to test your work frequently so that you can discover and correct mistakes as you make them. After testing, you should save your work in case you make an error, the computer crashes, or the power goes out.

To test the code for the GotFocus and LostFocus event procedures:

1. Click the **Close** button ☒ on the Code window title bar to close the window.

2. Run the program by clicking the **Start** button ▶ on the toolbar. Notice that the cursor (a flashing vertical line) appears in the Initial Value text box, because you set its TabIndex property to 0, making it the first active object in the form when the program is running.

3. Type any number in each of the three text boxes, pressing the Tab key to move from one TextBox to the next. Check to see that the text you type is displayed in bold when a text box object has the focus and a regular type style when the object loses focus.

4. Click the **End** button ■ on the toolbar to stop running the program. Because you have not yet written the code for the stop sign icon, you cannot use it to stop running the program.

TROUBLE? If the text in any of the text boxes did not appear bold when you were typing it, open the Code window and select the GotFocus event for the appropriate text box. Make sure that your code is correct by checking it against the code shown earlier in the steps. If the text does not return to a normal type style when you leave the object, check the code for the appropriate LostFocus event. Make any necessary corrections, then repeat Steps 1 through 4.

5. Click the **Save Project** button 🖫 on the toolbar.

When you want to stop running a program, you can always click the End button on the toolbar, as you did in the preceding steps. However, a user of your program might not be familiar with this button; therefore, the program should include a button or image that the user can click to stop the program from running. This button or image should respond to the Click event that executes the End statement, which works in the same way as the End button on the toolbar.

In your program, Mark wants a user to be able to click the stop sign image to stop the program from running. So, you need to write the code for the Image object's Click event procedure.

To write the code for the Image object:

1. Open the Code window and select the **imgEnd** object.

2. Click the **Proc** list arrow, then click the **Click** event.

To include the End statement in a procedure, you simply type the word "End" before the last statement in the Code window.

3. Type the word **End** in the line above the End Sub statement.

4. Click the **Close** button ☒ on the Code window title bar to close the window.

Variables

In addition to receiving user input with text boxes and displaying information with labels, a program generally needs to perform computations on the input to produce the output. The calculator program you are writing for Mark needs to compute two interest rates based on the annual interest rate entered into the Interest Rate text box. The program must compute the future value of an investment based on the different interest rates. To store the results of the computations while the program is running, you use variables. A **variable** is a programming element used to store a value temporarily. Like an object, every variable you create has a name.

Every variable also has a data type that determines the kind of information the variable can store. A variable type can store either textual information or numbers, but not both. There are specific data types to store whole numbers, numbers containing decimal points, and dates. Other data types store values like True or False. Unlike objects, a variable does not have properties nor does it respond to events. It simply stores information while the program is running.

When you create a variable, you must assign it a name that adheres to the following naming conventions:

- A variable name must begin with a letter.

- A variable name cannot contain a period.

- The length of the name must not exceed 255 characters.

- The name must be unique.

Figure 2-22 contains examples of valid and invalid variable names.

Figure 2-22 ◄
Variable names

Valid Variable Name	Invalid Variable Name
ValidVariable1	1InvalidVariable
Valid_Number	Invalid.Number

Declaring a Variable

The process of creating a variable is known as declaring a variable. To declare a variable, you use the Visual Basic **Dim** statement, which has the following syntax:

Dim *Varname* [**As** *Type*]

- *Varname* is the name you want to assign to the variable.

- *Type* is the data type of the variable. The data type can be one of the Visual Basic data types identified in Figure 2-23 or any user-defined data type. In some cases the program can create its own data types.

Every declared variable consumes physical space in computer memory. Variables of different types consume a different amount of space and store different kinds of values. Figure 2-23 lists some of the Visual Basic data types, their storage sizes in bytes, and some possible values for each type.

Figure 2-23 ◄
Partial list of
Visual Basic
data types

Data Type	Storage Size	Possible Values
integer	2 bytes	Positive and negative whole numbers between -32768 and 32767. A number such as 84 or -1715 can be stored as an integer.
Single	4 bytes	A number with a decimal point, such as 3.14, -10034.388, or 0.113.
String	1 byte per character	Can store up to about 2 billion characters for variable-length strings. Text entries such as "John Doe" or "Pacific Ocean" are stored as strings.

Choosing the correct data type for a variable is important. For example, if a variable will contain only whole numbers (numbers without a decimal point), you should choose the Integer data type instead of Single. Although a program usually works with either data type, operations on floating point values (numbers with a decimal point) take considerably longer to perform. Also the Single type variable consumes more memory than an Integer type variable. Although you will not declare any string variables in this program, the information stored in a TextBox object is always considered a string in Visual Basic. When you want to perform a calculation on a string, you must convert it to a number.

When you use the Dim statement to declare a variable, you are *explicitly* declaring the variable, but there is another way to create variables. If you use a variable name in any Visual Basic statement without first explicitly declaring the variable with the Dim statement, Visual Basic will create the variable for you. This is referred to as implicit declaration, and is strongly discouraged. For example, if you intended to use a variable named InterestRate in a statement but you made a typographical error, Visual Basic would assume you wanted to create a new variable. Although the program would run, the variable would not contain the correct information. So, the results would be wrong when you use the variable in a computation.

You can prohibit Visual Basic from implicitly creating variables by using the Option Explicit statement, which has the following syntax:

Option Explicit

■ This statement forces variable names to be explicitly defined with the Dim statement. If you try to use a variable that was not declared with the Dim statement, Visual Basic will display a dialog box telling you the variable is not defined. The Option Explicit statement also helps you identify incorrectly spelled variables that would create other errors, called logic errors, which are more difficult to detect. All programs you create in this book will contain the Option Explicit statement.

Local and Form-Level Variables

Now that you know how to declare variables, you need to know where to declare them. If you declare variables inside a procedure (between the Private Sub and End Sub statements), you can use the variable inside that procedure only. A variable declared inside a procedure exists only while the procedure is running, and is called a **local variable**. If you declare a variable outside a procedure, the variable can be used by all the different procedures in your form. The variable and its value exist whenever the program is running; this type of variable is called a **form-level variable**.

Each form has an object called (General) and a procedure called (declarations), which you access using the Code window. This is known as the general declarations section, and you use it to declare form-level variables.

Now you need to open the Code window and select the general declarations section so that you can enter the form-level variables for your program.

To open the general declarations section of the Code window:

1. Click **View** on the menu bar, then click **Code** to open the Code window.

2. Click the **Object** list arrow then click **(General)**.

3. Click the **Proc** list arrow then click **(declarations)**.

Declaring Form-Level Variables

Some of the variables in the calculator program need to be used by different event procedures, so you must declare them as form-level variables. Specifically, although a user will enter the annual interest rate, the program must compute the monthly interest rate, because the compounding of interest occurs monthly rather than annually. The program will compute three different interest rates, so you need three variables to store the three monthly interest rates. Just as you choose a name for an object that reflects the purpose of the object, you should choose a variable name that describes the purpose of the variable. Mark suggests you use MonthRate1, MonthRate2, and MonthRate3 as the names for the three variables to hold the monthly interest rates. Also, because interest rates are expressed with a decimal point, (for example 7% is expressed as 0.07), you will use the Single data type for the variables.

Now you are ready to declare the three form-level variables for your program.

To declare the variables for the three monthly interest rates:

1. Make sure the Code window shows **(General)** as the selected object and **(declarations)** as the selected procedure.

2. Enter the code shown in Figure 2-24.

Figure 2-24 ◄
Declaring
form-level
variables

each comment line
starts with the '
character

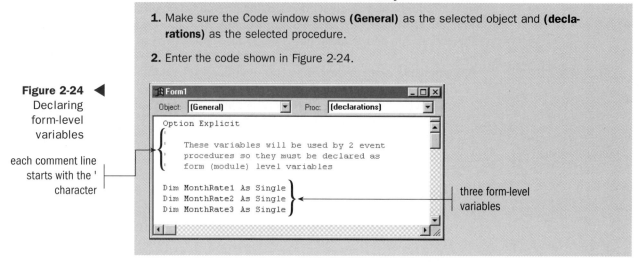

three form-level
variables

The first statement (Option Explicit) tells Visual Basic you must declare all variables before using them. The next lines are comment lines, so they each must start with the apostrophe character. The blank line below the comments, known as whitespace, is ignored by Visual Basic. Inserting whitespace in your code between the declaration of groups of related variables or between other related statements can improve the readability of the code. Including the apostrophe on a blank line is optional. The last three lines declare three different form-level variables of the Single data type to store the three monthly interest rates.

When you type the statements into the Code window, Visual Basic capitalizes the first character of all reserved words. **Reserved words** are words that are part of the Visual Basic language. Option Explicit, Dim, As, and Single are all reserved words.

Declaring Local Variables

In addition to declaring form-level variables, you need to declare local variables that will be used only inside the Click event procedure for the command button. These variables will hold the three future values of the investment and the input data entered by the user. There is a significant difference between local variables, declared inside a procedure, and form-level variables, declared in the general declarations section. The storage space in computer memory is allocated for form-level variables when the program starts. Storage space for local variables is allocated only when a procedure is executed, and the space is deallocated when the procedure finishes. So, by declaring local variables you can reduce the total amount of memory used by variables. By decreasing the amount of memory your program uses, it will generally run faster and leave more memory for other Windows 95 programs to run.

You can now declare the variables that will hold the results of the future value computations and the variables that will hold the input data entered by the user. These local variables will exist only while the command button's Click event procedure is running.

To declare the local variables for the command button's Click event:

1. Make sure the Code window is active.

2. Click the **Object** list arrow, then click **cmdComputeFutureValue**.

3. Enter the code shown in Figure 2-25. Be sure that the Proc list box is set to the Click event.

Figure 2-25 ◄
Declaring local
variables for
the command
button

```
Private Sub cmdComputeFutureValue_Click()
'
'    These variables are used only by this proceudre.
'    Since they are declared inside the procedure,
'    they cannot be used by other procedures in the
'    form.
     Dim TempFutureValue1 As Single
     Dim TempFutureValue2 As Single
     Dim TempFutureValue3 As Single

     Dim NumInterestRate As Single
     Dim NumInitialValue As Single
     Dim MonthTerm As Single

End Sub
```

statements indented
to improve
readability

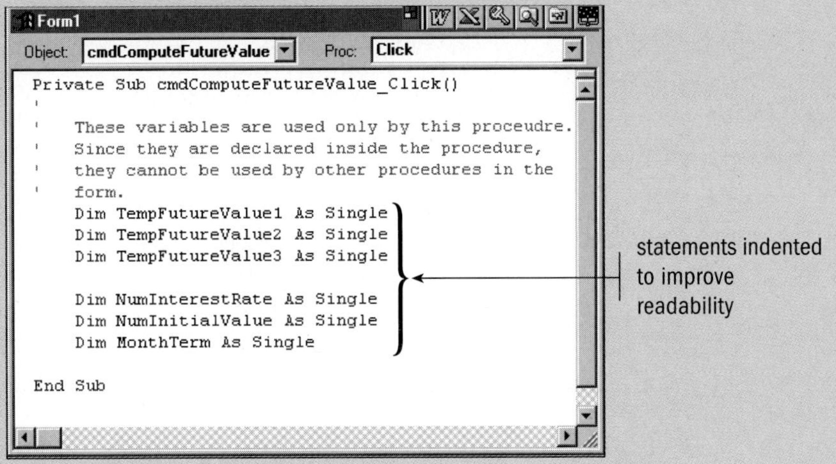

The variable names TempFutureValue1, TempFutureValue2, and TempFutureValue3 indicate that the variables will be used to temporarily store the results of the three future value computations while the procedure is executing. Also, because they will contain numbers with decimal points, such as 1233.48, the variables have been declared with the Single data type. When you perform arithmetic computations on variables that contain a decimal point, you must use a numeric data type like Single.

Whenever you declare local variables inside a procedure, it should be indented so that the beginning and end of the procedure are clearly identifiable. This will be especially important as your procedures become large enough that they cannot be completely displayed in the Code window.

Using Expressions and Operators to Manipulate Variables

Now that all the variables for your program have been declared, you can store information in them and use them to compute the output for your program. For example, you need to take the annual interest rate entered by the user and divide it by 12 to get the monthly interest rate. The result of this computation will be stored in the form-level variable MonthRate1, which you declared earlier.

You use **expressions**, which consist of variables, **operators** (+, – , and so on), and constants, in statements to perform calculations and store the results in other variables. Constants are like variables in that they can hold values, but their values cannot be changed. Operators fall into three categories; arithmetic, comparison, and logical. The simple expressions in Figure 2-27 through Figure 2-29 later in this section use the addition (arithmetic) operator and the division (arithmetic) operator to perform computations and store the results in other variables.

When you write expressions using operators and variables, you need to understand the concept of precedence. **Precedence** is a term used to explain the standard order of execution in which arithmetic operations are performed with operators like + – / ^ and *. The concept of precedence was formulated to allow an expression to be written as one continuous statement to a computer. To do this, the computer scans the formula from left to right, looking for an operation that has the highest level of precedence. The highest level of precedence is to raise a number to a power. If the computer does not find any operations at that level, it goes to the next level, multiplication and division, and looks for those operations. If the computer finds an operator at the proper level, the computer executes that operation. If the computer finds more than one operator at the same level, it performs the leftmost operation first.

Figure 2-26 lists the Visual Basic operators that work with numeric data in the order of their precedence and gives an example of each.

Operators in Order of Precedence	Description	Example
^	Raises a number to the power of an exponent	2 ^ 3 is equal to 8
*,/	Multiplication and division	2 * 3 is equal to 6 8 / 4 is equal to 2
\	Integer division	10 \ 3 is equal to 3 5 \ 2 is equal to 2
Mod	Modulo Arithmetic; returns the integer remainder of a division operation	10 mod 3 is equal to 1
+,–	Addition and subtraction	2 + 3 is equal to 5 2 – 3 is equal to –1

Often, you need to change the standard order of operations to ensure that the correct sequence of operations is performed. You can do so by using one or more matched pairs of parentheses. By enclosing an operation within parentheses, that operation takes precedence over the levels in the standard order. For example, in the formula (Var1 + Var2) ^ Var3, the addition would take place first rather than the exponentiation, because the addition operator is enclosed in parentheses. In the formula ((Var1 + Var2) – (Var3 + Var4)) ^ Var5, the parentheses are **nested**, which means that the innermost and leftmost operation Var1 + Var2 would occur first, (Var3 + Var4) would occur second, the result of ((Var1 + Var2) – (Var3 + Var4)) would occur next, and finally the result would be raised to the power Var5. Consider the formula shown in Figure 2-27.

Figure 2-27 ◀
Algebraic
formula

$$\left(\frac{Var1 + Var2}{Var3 - Var4} \right) Var5^{Var6}$$

In Figure 2-27, the order of operations is clearly shown by the way the formula is presented. If you transformed this formula directly into a computer-readable expression, it would look like the formula in Figure 2-28.

Figure 2-28 ◀
Computer-
readable
expression

$$Var1 + Var2 / Var3 - Var4 * Var5 ^ Var6$$

Without using parentheses, the order of operations would follow the standard order of evaluation, but adding parentheses will change the results. Figure 2-29 shows the different order evaluation with and without parentheses.

Figure 2-29 ◀
Evaluating
expressions

Standard order of evaluation

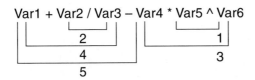

Order of evaluation with parentheses

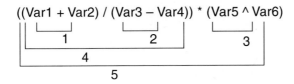

Additional parentheses can also improve the readability of your program, so you should use them liberally. Including parentheses around the sub-expression (Var5 ^ Var6) in Figure 2-29 does not change the order of the expression, but it does enhance the readability by clarifying the order in which you want the computer to evaluate the expression.

In addition to writing expressions containing arithmetic operators, you can also write expressions that use operators to perform comparisons. Comparisons are useful to evaluate such situations as whether or not two numbers are equal or two text strings are the same. Furthermore, you can also use logical operators to connect expressions together. You will learn about comparison and logical operators later in this text.

Using Visual Basic Functions

Visual Basic includes financial and mathematical functions, which are **intrinsic functions** built into the programming language. Functions are procedures. Like an event procedure, a function procedure contains one or more Visual Basic statements that are executed when a user performs an action. Function procedures differ from event procedures in that you have to explicitly write a Visual Basic statement to use them. This is referred to as calling a procedure. In your program, you will use three function procedures: the Val function, the Format function, and the Future Value (FV) function. You can look up how to use other intrinsic functions in Visual Basic online Help.

Converting Data Using the Val Function

Although the values entered by the user in the three TextBox objects will contain only digits (0-9) and possibly a decimal point, Visual Basic stores each of these values as a string of characters rather than a number. Visual Basic does not know how you intend to use the information in a TextBox object, so it always stores the value as a string of characters. When the program tries to perform an arithmetic operation on the text in the text box, Visual Basic tries to convert the value from a string of characters to a number. However, if the user entered a letter instead of a number in one of the TextBox objects, Visual Basic cannot properly convert the value into a number, and a run-time error will occur.

The **Val** function converts a string of characters (a value assigned the String data type) to a number, which is necessary if you want the data to be used in a calculation. To use a number in a calculation, you need to convert the information into a numeric value and store the result in a variable specifically created as a numeric value. The Val function performs this task automatically. If the string contains letters, the Val function stops scanning the string and returns the value of the digits already scanned.

You use the following syntax for the Val function:

result = **Val**(*string*)

- When you use a function like Val, you provide information to it using an argument. Variables in your program can be used as arguments. The Val function accepts one argument, a *string*, and attempts to convert the *string* into a numeric value. The converted value is stored in *result*, a variable or object property.

Figure 2-30 shows how the Val function would convert several different strings.

Figure 2-26 ◀
Arithmetic
operators

Expression	Result
Val(123.4a)	123.4
Val("")	0
Val(aaa)	0
Val(23aa34)	23

Notice the string named "" in Figure 2-30. This is known as an empty string. If you want to delete text from the Caption property of a label or the Text property of a text box, you must assign an empty string to the property.

The next step in creating your program is to write the code for the event procedure to update the three labels containing interest rate values whenever a user changes the Text property for the interest rate text box. Just as you wrote code to change the type style when an object becomes active (GotFocus) or becomes inactive (LostFocus), you now need to write code to display the different interest rates in the output section, whenever the value of the Interest Rate text box changes. The Change event occurs whenever the contents of a text box change.

The future value of the investment should compound interest monthly, so you need to compute the value of the variables for the three monthly interest rates. The future value is computed using the variables MonthRate1, MonthRate2, and MonthRate3 when the user clicks the Compute Future Value command button.

To write the code for the Interest Rate TextBox object's Change event:

1. Select the **txtInterestRate** object and the **Change** procedure in the Code window.

2. Enter the following code (shown in bold):

```
Private Sub txtInterestRate_Change()

    Dim NumInterestRate As Single
    NumInterestRate = Val(txtInterestRate.Text)
    MonthRate1 = NumInterestRate / 12
    MonthRate2 = (NumInterestRate + 0.01) / 12
    MonthRate3 = (NumInterestRate + 0.02) / 12

End Sub
```

Before you proceed, you need to examine the code in more detail. First, notice that the procedure is named "txtInterestRate_Change()." This name indicates that the program will respond to a Change event generated by the object named txtInterestRate. Whenever a user types information into the Interest Rate text box, the statements in this Change event procedure will be executed.

```
Dim NumInterestRate As Single
```

This statement creates a local variable named NumInterestRate. The variable is local because you declared it inside the event procedure txtInterestRate_Change and, therefore, it can be used inside this procedure only. This variable will store the numeric representation of the annual interest rate contained in the TextBox object.

```
NumInterestRate = Val(txtInterestRate.Text)
```

This statement uses the Val function to convert the text a user enters in the Interest Rate text box into a numeric value so it can be used in the necessary calculations. Even though a user will enter a number into this text box, Visual Basic will store the entry as a string of characters rather than a numeric value. This Val statement converts the string representation of the number and transfers it into the numeric variable, NumInterestRate. The number will then be available for use in the calculations that will compute the future values of the investment.

```
MonthRate1 = NumInterestRate / 12
MonthRate2 = (NumInterestRate + 0.01) / 12
MonthRate3 = (NumInterestRate + 0.02) / 12
```

Recall that you declared the variables MonthRate1, MonthRate2, and MonthRate3 in the general declarations section, so they are form-level variables and can be used by this or any event procedure. The user will enter an annual interest rate value. However, because the interest on an investment is compounded every month, these statements divide the annual rate by 12, the number of months in a year. Then the statements compute different interest rates by adding 1% to the annual rate. Note that parentheses are needed to override the default precedence rules, so that the addition is completed before the division.

Formatting a Numeric Value

The code you just wrote computes the monthly interest rate for the three form-level variables. These variables will be used in the Click event procedure for the command button to compute the future value of the investment. So, now you have all the information needed to compute and display the three interest rates in the output labels. Remember from Tutorial 1 that you displayed text in a label by setting its Caption property. You will use the Caption property again to display information. However, this time, you will display numbers instead of text. Dunn Financial requires that interest rate values always appear with a leading 0 and two decimal places. You can change the way numbers are displayed using the Format function, which has the following syntax:

Format(*expression*[,*format*])

- The **Format** function reads the numeric value contained in the *expression* and converts it to a string. The function allows you to control the appearance of the string by placing information in the *format* argument. Unlike the Val function, the Format function requires two arguments.

- You can specify a format argument in one of two ways. You can select from a list of named formats that have already been defined for you, or you can use special symbols to control, in more detail, the appearance of the text. One of the most common named formats, the fixed format, displays information with two decimal places and a leading 0 if the value is less than 1. Another format, currency, displays information with a leading dollar sign and two decimal places. Use Help on the Format function to look at all the options for named formats.

When you use functions like Format or write complicated statements, the code containing the function or statement might not fit on a single line in the Code window. You can break up a line using the underscore (_) character at the end of a line to tell Visual Basic that the next line is a continuation of the statement on the current line. If a statement is very long, you can include the underscore character at the end of multiple lines. Generally you indent continuation lines so they stand out in the code. You can insert a continuation character only between words; you cannot break up a word. Also, you must always precede the continuation character with a space.

Next, you will enter the statements that format the different interest rates; these statements are split over two lines to improve the readability of the code.

To display the formatted values in the interest rate Label objects:

> **1.** Add the following code to the end of the Change event procedure for the Interest Rate text box. Be sure to enter the code before the End Sub statement.
>
> ```
> lblInterestRate1.Caption = Format(NumInterestRate, _
>     "fixed")
> lblInterestRate2.Caption = Format(NumInterestRate + _
>     0.01, "fixed")
> lblInterestRate3.Caption = Format(NumInterestRate + _
>     0.02, "fixed")
> ```

The statements include the Format function so that each numeric value will appear with a leading 0 and two decimal places, as specified by the named format, fixed.

There are many different formats supported by the Format function. For more information start the Help system and select Format function.

Next, you need to write the code for the CommandButton object that will compute the future value of the initial investment at different interest rates.

Using the Future Value Function

The **Future Value (FV)** function returns the future value of a fixed amount of money based on a constant interest rate. The FV function has the following syntax:

FV (*rate,periods,payment*[,*present-value*][,*type*]])

- The *rate* represents the interest rate per period, and *periods* represents the number of periods.

- If regular payments are made, they are identified in *payment*. So, if you are computing the future value of a fixed amount, which does not involve regular payments, the value of *payment* would be 0. You can think of a regular payment as making a deposit into the investment account each period.

- The next two arguments are optional, which is why they are enclosed in brackets. When computing the future value of an amount, the *present* or (*current*) *value* of the sum is listed. The *type* argument is used to describe when payments are made. If payments are made at the end of the period, the value for type is 0. If payments are made at the beginning of a period, the value for type is 1. Because the statements containing the FV function are too long to fit on a line, you will use the continuation character to break statements across two lines.

Your program will use the FV function to compute the three future values of an investment made by a Dunn Financial client.

To create the code necessary to compute the future values:

> **1.** Select the **cmdComputeFutureValue** object and the Click procedure in the Code window. Note that the window already contains the Dim statements, which you entered earlier.
>
> **2.** Enter the following code after the Dim statements:
>
> ```
> MonthTerm = Val(txtTermYears.Text) * 12
>
> NumInitialValue = Val(txtInitialValue.Text)
>
> TempFutureValue1 = FV(MonthRate1, MonthTerm, 0, _
>     -NumInitialValue)
> ```

```
TempFutureValue2 = FV(MonthRate2, MonthTerm, 0, _
    -NumInitialValue)
TempFutureValue3 = FV(MonthRate3, MonthTerm, 0, _
    -NumInitialValue)
lblFutureValue1.Caption = Format(TempFutureValue1, _
    "currency")
lblFutureValue2.Caption = Format(TempFutureValue2, _
    "currency")
lblFutureValue3.Caption = Format(TempFutureValue3, _
    "currency")
```

Before proceeding, take a minute to examine the code you just entered in more detail.

```
MonthTerm = Val(txtTermYears.Text) * 12
```

Earlier, when defining the Change event procedure for the txtInterest Rate object, you set the variables for the three monthly interest rates, which you will use to compute the future value of the investment. But, you need to compute the term of the investment expressed in months. To do so, this statement multiplies the term of the investment expressed in years by 12 and stores the result in the variable MonthTerm. Because the information in the text box is a string of characters, the statment includes the Val function to convert the string to a number before performing the multiplication.

```
NumInitialValue = Val(txtInitialValue.Text)
```

This statement includes the Val function to convert the initial value of the investment, which is stored as a string of characters in the Initial Value text box, into a numeric value.

```
TempFutureValue1 = FV(MonthRate1, MonthTerm, 0, _
    -NumInitialValue)

TempFutureValue2 = FV(MonthRate2, MonthTerm, 0, _
    -NumInitialValue)

TempFutureValue3 = FV(MonthRate3, MonthTerm, 0, _
    -NumInitialValue)
```

These three statements use the FV function to compute the future value of the investment using three different interest rates. You already set the value for the first argument, MonthRate1, when you defined the Change event procedure for the txtInterestRate object. Remember the three monthly rate variables are form-level variables declared in the general declarations section, so they can be used by any procedure in your program. The second argument, MonthTerm, is the term of the investment, which you defined earlier in this event. Both the rate and term are expressed in months. Because there are no additional deposits for the investment, the third argument representing the payment is 0.

For all arguments, payments are represented by negative numbers. Because the variable NumInitialValue represents the initial payment, the number should be negative.

```
lblFutureValue1.Caption = Format(TempFutureValue1, _
    "currency")

lblFutureValue2.Caption = Format(TempFutureValue2, _
    "currency")

lblFutureValue3.Caption = Format(TempFutureValue3, _
    "currency")
```

These three statements display the results in the appropriate Label objects. The statements include the currency format so that numbers will be displayed with a leading dollar sign and two decimal places. Again, this will improve the appearance of the information for the user.

You have now completed all the code to compute the future values of the investment, format the future values with a leading dollar sign, and display the output in the appropriate labels. You are now ready to test your program and run the code you have just written. Mark suggests that you use an initial investment amount of $1500.00, an interest rate of .05, and a term of 10 years.

To run the program and enter the test values:

1. Close the Code window.

2. Click the **Start** button ▣ on the toolbar to run the program. Your form should look like Figure 2-31.

Figure 2-31 ◀
Running the completed calculator program

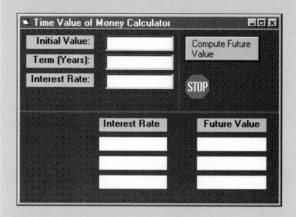

3. Enter the values shown in the text boxes in Figure 2-32, pressing the Tab key to move from one text box to the next.

4. Press the **Enter** key to activate the Compute Future Value button. The program calculates the results for the three interest rates and the corresponding future values. See Figure 2-32.

Figure 2-32 ◀
Testing the calculator program

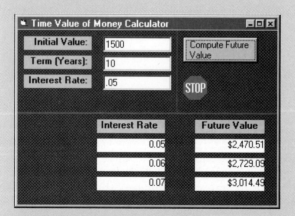

TROUBLE? If your results differ from those in Figure 2-32, there is probably an error in the code for either the CommandButton object's Click event procedure or the txtInterestRate object's Change event procedure. Check the event procedures in your program first for code accuracy against the code shown in the tutorial figures. Also, refer to the next section, "Handling Errors," for help in identifying and correcting errors. Make any necessary corrections, then run and test the program again.

5. Click the **stop sign** image to stop the program from running.

6. Click the **Save Project** button ▣ on the toolbar to save your work.

Because you set the Default property of the command button to True, you can press the Enter key to activate the command button, and execute its Click event procedure. This causes the code you wrote to multiply the annual term of the investment by 12 to derive the term expressed in months. The monthly interest rates were computed in the Change event procedure for the txtInterestRate object. This information was supplied as arguments to the FV function to compute the future value. You did not have to worry about exactly how Visual Basic computed the future value. The intrinsic function did this for you. The output was then displayed according to the settings specified by the Format function.

Handling Errors

Errors are divided into three types: syntax errors, run-time errors, and logic errors. As you learned in Tutorial 1, syntax errors occur when a statement you have written violates the rules of the Visual Basic language. Typographical errors, mismatched parentheses, omitting the comment character as the first character on a comment line, are all examples of syntax errors. Visual Basic identifies some syntax errors while you are writing code in the Code window. After you type each line, Visual Basic scans the line for correctness.

Many errors are not discovered until you run a program. These are run-time errors, and they occur when you enter a valid statement that is impossible to carry out for some reason.

Logic errors occur when your program contains a design problem that causes the program to produce incorrect results. For example, you might have added two variables together rather than multiplied them. Logic errors are not found by Visual Basic; you must identify and correct them.

Fixing Syntax Errors

When a syntax error occurs, Visual Basic displays the message box shown in Figure 2-33.

Figure 2-33 ◄
Syntax error
message box

To correct a syntax error:

1. Click the **OK** button in the message box. Visual Basic activates the Code window and highlights the statement containing the error.

2. Analyze the statement and make the necessary corrections.

3. Continue running the program by clicking the **Start** button on the toolbar.

Fixing Run-time Errors

A common run-time error occurs when the program tries to store too large a number in a variable. This is called **numeric overflow**. For example, if you try to enter too large a number in a text box in your calculator program, a numeric overflow will occur. Run-time errors also occur when you try to store the wrong kind of information in a variable and when you try to perform arithmetic operation, such as multiplication, on variables that do not contain numbers. The latter is called a **type mismatch,** because when you perform the arithmetic operation, Visual Basic expects the variables to contain numbers, not text.

To practice fixing a run-time error, you will purposely generate an error by entering values that are too large for the text boxes in the input section.

To purposely generate a run-time error:

1. Click the **Start** button � on the toolbar to run the program.

2. Enter the value **1000000** for the Initial Value, **100000** for the term, and **100000** for the Interest Rate, then press the **Enter** key to activate the Compute Future Value button. Visual Basic displays the run-time error message box indicating numeric overflow. See Figure 2-34.

Figure 2-34 ◀
Run-time error message

error description ──────

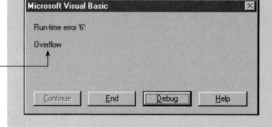

3. Click the **End** button in the message box to stop the program. You return to design mode.

Printing Your Program

As you develop a program, it is often helpful to print the code you have written, the object properties you changed using the Properties window, or an Image of the form itself. Furthermore, as your programs become larger and more complex, it is helpful to have a printed copy of all the code available for reference.

Now that your program is complete, Mark asks you to print various parts of the program so he can keep them for later reference.

To print the elements of the calculator program:

1. Click **File** on the menu bar, then click **Print**. The Print dialog box opens. See Figure 2-35.

Figure 2-35 ◀
Print dialog box

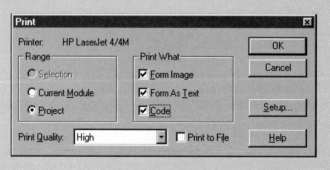

2. Click the **Project** option in Range section.

3. Select the **Form Image**, **Form As Text**, and **Code** options in the Print What section of the dialog box, then click the **OK** button.

As you learned in Tutorial 1, the Form Image option prints an Image of the form as it appears on the screen. The Form As Text option prints all of the objects you created on the form and the properties you changed. For each object, all the properties you set using the Properties window are displayed. If you did not change a property it will not be printed. The Code option prints the contents of the general declarations section then each of the procedures you have written for the form. When you select multiple objects in the Print What section, Visual Basic will print the Code first, the Form As Text next, and finally the Form Image.

Now examine the information you just printed. Your output consists of three parts. The Code contains all the code in your program. First, the statements in the general declarations section are printed. Then each of the event procedures is printed in alphabetical order.

Look at the selected output from the Form As Text section, the second part you printed.

```
VERSION 4.00
```

The first line lists the version of Visual Basic.

```
Begin VB.Form Form1
      BackColor          =      &H00404000&
      Caption            =      "Time Value of Money Calculator"
      ClientHeight       =      2880
      ClientLeft         =      2316
      ClientTop          =      1596

      ...
```

These lines define the form itself, identifying the name of the form and the properties set for the form, including all the non-default values on the form such as the background color. Remember, the Caption property was set for you already. The ClientHeight, ClientLeft, and ClientTop properties determine the form's position on the screen. You did not set these properties explicitly—Visual Basic set them when you created the form. Depending on the location of your form on your screen, these property values might differ from those in your printout.

```
      Begin VB.CommandButton cmdComputeFutureValue
            Caption        =      "Compute Future Value"
            Default        =      -1 'True
            Height         =      495
            Left           =      3240
            TabIndex       =      3
            Top            =      120
            Width          =      1445
      End
```

These lines identify the properties you set for the CommandButton object. As with the form, the Caption and position of the object are defined, but two new properties—Default and TabIndex—are also listed. You set the Default property so that the Click event occurs when a user presses the Enter key. You also set the TabIndex property, which determines the order in which objects are selected when a user presses the Tab key. Finally, the definition is terminated by the End statement.

The output includes a final End statement that signifies the end of the form definition.

Your calculator is now complete. Mark plans on showing the analysts how to use the program so that they can begin testing it. After they are confident that it is producing correct results, Mark plans on making the program available to the analysts so that they can use it to forecast investments.

Quick Check

1. How does a Label object differ from a TextBox object?

2. What is the purpose of the Dim statement?

3. Describe the difference between the GotFocus, LostFocus, Click, and Change events and when they occur.

4. Put the following operators in their correct order of precedence: MOD, +, -, \, ^, *, /.

5 What is the difference between syntax errors, run-time errors, and logic errors?

6 List the three options for printing a program and describe the output that each option produces.

Figure 2-36 lists and defines the new terms presented in this tutorial.

Figure 2-36 ◀
New terms

Term	Description
Expression	An expression consists of operators that perform tasks, such as addition, on operands, which are numbers or variables. Expressions produce some type of result, such as adding two numbers together.
Focus	Only one object on a form is active at one time. For example, if a TextBox object is active, the user can type information into it. The active object is said to have the focus.
Intrinsic function	Intrinsic functions perform many mathematical, financial, or other operations using code already written and built into the Visual Basic system.
IPO model	The Input-Processing-Output (IPO) model is a design tool that helps you identify the input to your program, the processing that is to occur, and the output produced.
Operators	Operators are used in expressions to perform computations and comparisons. Examples of operators are $+$, $-$, $*$, $/$ and $^$.
Precedence	Precedence is the predetermined order in which arithmetic operators are evaluated.
Procedure	A procedure is a sequence of statements treated as a unit used to accomplish a specific task. Computer programs are usually broken down into procedures to improve readability and simplify development.
Pseudocode	Pseudocode is a way to express the actions of a program in general, non-technical terms. An example of a pseudocode is "Get the input data."
Statement	A statement is a complete Visual Basic language unit used to express an action declaration or definition. A statement is much like a sentence written in English.
TOE chart	The Task Object Event (TOE) chart is used with event-driven programs to help you identify the tasks that need to be performed in your program, the objects related to those tasks, and the events that will cause the objects to perform the tasks.
Variables	Variables are named locations in the computer's random access memory used to temporarily store information such as numbers or textual data.

Tutorial Assignments

In addition to investment services, the Dunn Financial Group provides taxation services for its clients. Mark has asked you to create a program that will compute straight-line depreciation of an asset for a single period. The program should provide an interface that allows the user to input the initial cost of an asset, the value of an asset at the end of its useful life, and the life of the asset. To create the program, you will use the SLN function, which is an intrinsic financial function like the FV function.

1. Make sure your Student Disk is in the disk drive, then start Visual Basic.
2. Change the Caption property of the form to **Straight-Line Depreciation**. Change the Name property to **frmDepreciation.**
3. Draw four Label objects in a column on the left side of the form.

4. Change the Caption property of these labels to **Cost**, **Salvage**, **Life**, and **Depreciation** starting from the top label.

5. Change the Font properties of the labels to make them more attractive. Consult the Visual Basic online Help for more information on the Font property.

6. Draw four TextBox objects next to the labels. Change the Name property of the text boxes to **txtCost**, **txtSalvage**, **txtLife**, and **txtDepreciation** (in order). Change the Text property for each text box to blank.

7. Draw a CommandButton object on the top right of the form. Change its Name property to **cmdCalculate**. Change its Caption property to **Calculate Depreciation**.

8. Draw a CommandButton object on the middle right of the form. Change its Name property to **cmdClear**. Change its Caption property to **Clear**.

9. Draw a CommandButton object on the bottom right of the form. Change its Name property to **cmdExit**. Change its Caption property to **Exit**. Your form should look similar to Figure 2-37.

Figure 2-37 ◀

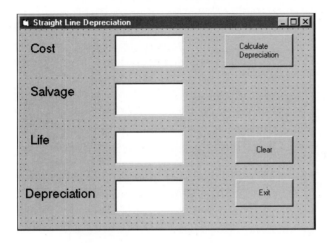

10. Open the Code window for the cmdClear object's Click event procedure and enter code that will set to blank the Text property of the four TexBox objects. Remember to include a comment about what the procedure does. Consult the Visual Basic online Help for more information on the Text property.

11. Open the Code window for the cmdExit object's Click event procedure, then enter the code that will exit the running program when this button is clicked.

12. Consult Visual Basic online Help for information on financial functions. Open the Help window for the SLN function. Print the Help topic to guide you through creating the rest of this program.

13. Open the Code window for the cmdCalculate object's Click event procedure. Type the code that will set the txtDepreciation object's Text property to the straight-line depreciation of txtCost, txtSalvage, and txtLife. Format the result as currency. Enter the following comment to describe what this procedure does: **'This SLN function will calculate the straight-line depreciation.** Type the line **txtDepreciation.Text=Format(SLN(txtCost.Text, txtSalvage.Text,txtLife.Text),"currency")** between the Private Sub and End Sub lines. Close the Code window.

14. Test your program by entering **100000** as the asset cost, **50000** as the salvage value, and **5** for the asset life in years. Click the Calculate Depreciation button to cause the depreciation function to execute. The result should be $10,000.00 as the depreciation amount for each year.

15. Test the Clear button.

16. Continue to run and test the program with numbers of your choice in the Cost, Salvage, and Life text boxes.

17. Print the form image.

18. In the TAssign folder of the Tutorial.02 folder on your Student Disk save the project as **Dunn SL Depreciation** in the Tutorial.02 TAssign folder on your Student Disk. Answer **Yes** to save the form automatically as **frmDepreciation**.

19. Exit Visual Basic.

Case Problems

1. Perfect Printing Perfect Printing is a business that specializes in unique printing products for industrial applications. The owner, Roger Kringle, would like to have a program that can display a variety of fonts, sizes, and colors on a computer screen after a user types in some text. Roger asks you to write a program for Perfect Printing that tests different fonts in an output object using a text box for input.

1. Make sure your Student Disk is in the disk drive, then start Visual Basic.
2. Change the Name property of the form to **frmLabel**. Change the **Caption property** of the form to **Label Testing**.
3. Draw a TextBox object on the form. Change its Name property to **txtInput**. Delete the value of the Text property to clear it.
4. Draw a CommandButton object on the form. Change its Caption property to **Exit**. Change its Name property to **cmdExit**. Open the Code window for the cmdExit object's Click event procedure, then type the code that will exit the running program when this button is clicked.
5. Draw a Label object on the form about the same size as the TextBox object. Change its Name property to **lblOutput**. Change its Caption property to **Empty Label**. Your form should look similar to Figure 2-38.

Figure 2-38 ◀

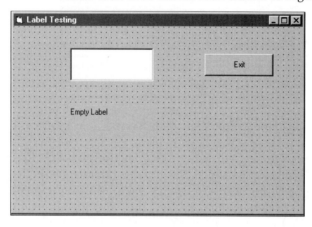

6. Open the Code window for the TextBox object and select its Change event procedure. Type the code that will set the Caption property of the label to anything typed in the text box (that is, the Text property of the text box). Consult the Visual Basic online Help for more information on the Label object's Caption property and the TextBox object's Change event. Remember to add a comment that describes what this procedure does.
7. Run the program.
8. Type anything you want in the text box, and note the results displayed in the label.
9. Test the Exit button.
10. Open the Properties window for the Label object and change the Font, Font Style, and Size properties to any setting you choose. Change the BackColor and ForeColor to any combination that you think looks the best.
11. Run and test the program.
12. Repeat steps 10 and 11, changing the properties until you are satisfied with the results.
13. Change the MultiLine property of the text box to **True**. Then run the program again and type multiple lines in the text box. How does the label react?
14. Print the form image.
15. Save the form as **frmLabel** and the project as **Perfect Printing** in the Cases folder of the Tutorial.02 folder on your Student Disk. Exit Visual Basic.

2. Timberline Ltd. Timberline Ltd. is an engineering firm that constructs planning models in Visual Basic of various ecosystems around the world. Because so much of the work at Timberline Ltd. is based on using proper formulas in their calculations, it is important for the model formulas to be correct. You will work on one of these models to test your ability to convert algebraic formulas to their proper computational form. Specifically, you will build a program to convert and test the following formulas:

1. $\dfrac{(Var1 + Var2)}{(Var3)}$

2. $\dfrac{(Var1)^{Var5}}{(Var2)(Var4)}$

3. $\dfrac{(Var1-Var2)^{Var3}}{(Var4)}$

4. $\dfrac{(Var4-Var2)(Var3)}{(Var5)^{Var2}}$

5. $\left(\dfrac{\frac{Var2}{Var1}}{\frac{Var4}{Var5}}\right)^{Var2}$

6. $\dfrac{\left(\frac{Var1}{Var2}\right)\left(\frac{Var3}{Var4}\right)}{(Var5)^{Var1}}$

1. Make sure your Student Disk is in the disk drive, then start Visual Basic.
2. Change the Name property of the form to **frmTest**. Change the Caption property of the form to **Testing Formulas**.

3. Open the general declarations section of the Code window and type the code that requires variables to be declared in the program. Then declare five Integer type variables—Var1, Var2, Var3, Var4, and Var5. Consult the Visual Basic online Help for more information on declaring Integer type variables.
4. In the Code window for the form's Load event procedure, assign numerical values to each of the variables as follows: **Var1 = 1, Var2 = 2, Var3 = 3, Var4 = 4**, and **Var5 = 5**. Consult the Visual Basic online Help for more information on assigning a value to a variable. Close the Code window for the form.

5. Draw a CommandButton object on the lower right of the form. Change its Caption property to **Exit**. Change its Name property to **cmdExit**. Open the Code window for the object's Click event procedure, then type the code that will exit the running program when this button is clicked.
6. Draw six Label objects on the form, three on the top half and three on the bottom half. Change the Name property for the objects to lblAnswer1, lblAnswer2, lblAnswer3, lblAnswer4, lblAnswer5, and lblAnswer6. Change the Caption property for the objects to Click for Answer1, Click for Answer 2, etc. (*Hint*: The copy and paste operations also work within the Properties window.)
7. Open the Code window for lblAnswer1_Click, then enter the expression that is the converted algebraic form of the first formula listed at the beginning of this Case problem. The expression should contain the Name and Caption property of the label followed by an equal sign and the converted formula.
8. In the remaining five Label objects, enter the proper formula conversion for the formulas (2 through 6) listed at the beginning of this Case Problem. Close the Code window.
9. Save the project as **Timberline** in the Cases folder of the Tutorial.02 folder on your Student Disk. Answer **Yes** to save the form automatically as **frmTest**.

10. Run the program and click each label. The following answers should be displayed in the labels:

    lblAnswer1.Caption = 1
    lblAnswer2.Caption = 0.125
    lblAnswer3.Caption = –0.25
    lblAnswer4.Caption = 0.24
    lblAnswer5.Caption = 6.25
    lblAnswer6.Caption = 0.075

    If any of your answers do not match the answers shown, you have made a mistake converting a formula. Click the Exit button. Fix each incorrect expression by changing the code in the Code window for the appropriate label. Run the program until you have fixed all errors.

11. Test the Exit button.

12. Print the form image and the code.

13. Save the project again if you made any corrections after your last save, then exit Visual Basic.

3. Ms. Phillips Grading Program. One of your former instructors at school, Ms. Phillips, would like you to design and build a Visual Basic program that will take the name of a student and the student's three test grades for the term, then compute the average for the tests and display a letter grade. To build a good program for Ms. Phillips, you first need to start with a good design. Refer to the topic "Designing a Computer Program" in Session 2.1, then create the necessary pseudocode, sample user interface, and TOE chart for the grading program.

4. Summit Banking. Summit Banking has asked you to modify some of the customer reports used at the bank. The bank purchased a set of add-on financial controls from a vendor and installed them in your copy of Visual Basic. These controls have no errors but they all seem to require forms of formatted output of Single data types with which you are not familiar. Using the online Help to learn about the Format function, create a test program according to the following steps:

1. Draw a text box. Name the text box with a valid name. Clear the Text property.
2. Draw four empty labels. Name the labels with valid names of your choice. Clear their captions.
3. Draw a working Exit command button.
4. Draw a command button with a valid name and the caption **Move Number**.
5. Declare a Single data type variable in the general declarations section of the Code window with a valid name. Be sure to use the Option Explicit statement.
6. Write a statement in the Move Number command button to move the Text property value to the Single data type variable you declared, using the Val function, when clicked.

7. Write code for the Move Number command button to move the Single data type variable to the first Label with no formatting.
8. Write code for the Move Number command button to move the number to the remaining three labels with the following formats: currency, fixed, and $$$$#,###.##.
9. Draw descriptive labels for the text box and output labels.
10. Save the project as Summit Banking and save the form as **frmLabelTest** in the Cases folder of the Tutorial.02 folder on your Student Disk.
11. Test your program with a variety of numbers, both integer and decimal, using the text box to enter a number, then clicking Move Number. Do not use any special characters such as $ with the numbers or the Val function will not perform the conversion operation.
12. When you are finished, save the form and project again if you have made any changes since your last save.
13. Print the form image, the code, and the form as text.
14. Exit Visual Basic.

Objects and the Events They Generate

Developing an Event-Driven Cash Register Program for Master Burger

OBJECTIVES

In this tutorial you will:

- Create instances of several new controls including shapes, scroll bars, check boxes, frames, and option buttons

- Insert existing code into a program

- Write statements that make decisions based on an object's status

- Execute code conditionally using the If and Select Case statements

- Write code for event procedures that will generate other events

- Create a control array

- Examine program components in the Object Browser dialog box and the Debug window

- Create a message box by calling the MsgBox function

CASE

Master Burger Company

Master Burger Company is a fast-food franchise business with headquarters in Lemming, California. Currently it operates more than 270 stores in the United States and Europe, and is planning to expand into New Zealand and Australia. The company's mission has always been to provide fresh food and exceptionally fast service, so it maintains a very simple menu of food items to avoid any spoiled or stale food. Gill Clark, the information services manager, wants you to use Visual Basic to develop a prototype for a point-of-sale cash register program to be used in each Master Burger restaurant. Ultimately, the company will use this cash register program to perform tasks not supported by ordinary cash registers, such as tracking inventory and using a touch screen for input.

For the prototype program, the mouse will be the only input device. However, the program will eventually be used on a computer with a touch screen for all user input. So, the program must include Visual Basic controls that do not require keyboard input. You can use a box for each menu item that, when checked, indicates that the item has been ordered. You can also use scroll bars to change the quantity ordered for each menu item. When an item is selected or the quantity ordered for an item changes, the program must compute the extended price of the item, the sales tax for the order, and the order total. The extended price is the price of the item multiplied by the quantity ordered.

SESSION 3.1

In this session you will learn how to use the Shape, ScrollBar, and CheckBox controls to create a cash register program that will receive input only from a mouse. You will also create event procedures that can generate other events.

Designing the Program

The program you will create is a prototype of the complete cash register program that Gill will show to senior management before putting the final program in the company's 270 stores. The following are some of the significant design criteria for the program:

- The user must be able to select menu items and specify the quantity ordered for each menu item using objects displayed on the screen.

- All input to the program must be supplied by the mouse. No keystrokes can be used.

- The program must update extended prices for each item when the quantity ordered changes. The extended price is computed by multiplying the quantity ordered by the unit price.

- Whenever the extended price for an item changes, the sales tax and order total must be recomputed and displayed.

Gill has already written the pseudocode and the TOE chart for the program. You can look at this design documentation to help you create the program.

To view and print the pseudocode and TOE chart for the cash register program:

1. Start Notepad or any word processing program.

2. Click **File** on the menu bar, then click **Open** and select the file **MB_TOE1.txt** from the **Tutorial.03** folder on your Student Disk.

3. Click **File** on the menu bar, then click **Print** to print the pseudocode and TOE chart.

4. Close Notepad or the word processing program.

It is helpful to keep the pseudocode and TOE chart next to you as you create the program. Gill has already designed the user interface screen, as shown in Figure 3-1.

Figure 3-1 ◀
Screen design for the cash register

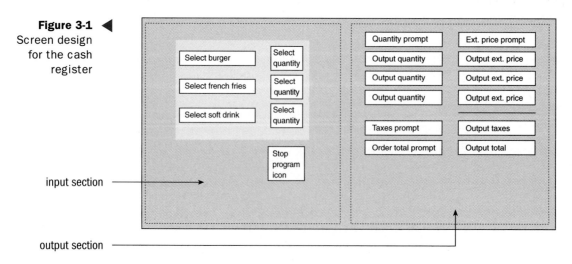

input section ⟶

output section ⟶

The user interface design visually identifies the objects used for input by enclosing them in a lighter-colored box. These input objects will be used to select an item and to select the quantity ordered. The Stop program icon will be used to exit the program. The output section contains several Label objects that display and describe the output.

Adding a Shape Object to the Form

A well-designed user interface often includes color to differentiate input areas from output areas. The cash register program will be enhanced if you set off the menu items section, or input area, with a colored rectangle. To do this, you will add a Shape object to the form. A **Shape** object visually identifies objects on a form by grouping them together.

REFERENCE
window

ADDING A SHAPE OBJECT TO A FORM

- Click the Shape control on the toolbox.
- Click and drag the mouse to draw a shape on the form.
- Set the necessary properties for the Shape object in the Properties window.

Gill has already started to create the form. He created all of the Label objects used for output, programmed the Stop icon, and visually separated the regions of the form with lines. Gill wants to use contrasting shades of blue for the form and highlight the input section to bring attention to that region. To do this, you will add a rectangle Shape object to the form.

To add a shape to the cash register program:

1. Start Visual Basic and make sure your Student Disk is in the disk drive.

2. Open the project file named **Burger1.vbp** in the Tutorial.03 folder on your Student Disk. If necessary, click the **View Form** button in the Project window to display the form.

   Before adding objects to the form, you will save it and the project file with different names to keep the original files intact.

3. Click **File** on the menu bar, then click **Save File As** and save the form as **Burger 1.frm**. Click **File** on the menu bar, then click **Save Project As** and save the project as **Burger 1.vbp**.

4. Click the **Shape** control 🔲 on the toolbox.

5. Move the pointer to the form and draw an outline of the shape so that it looks like the shape shown in Figure 3-2. By default, the Shape control draws a rectangle.

Figure 3-2 ◄
Creating a
Shape object

region of the Shape
object

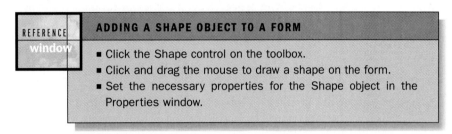

existing descriptive
labels

existing labels for
output

A Shape object has several properties to define its size, pattern, color, border, and shape. The **BackColor** and **BackStyle** properties work together to define the shape's background. When the BackStyle property is set to its default, 0-Transparent, the BackColor setting is ignored.

The **FillStyle** property lets you draw a pattern on the shape's background. You can identify the valid values for the different patterns in the Properties window for the shape. The **FillColor** property works with the FillStyle property to set the color of the shape. When the FillStyle property is set to its default, 1-Transparent, the FillColor setting is ignored. When you set the color of a shape, be sure you choose colors that provide enough contrast between different items so that they are easy to see. You should generally avoid colors like red because bright colors tend to be distracting and irritating.

The **BorderStyle** property defines the appearance of the border surrounding the shape. This property can assume any of the values listed in the Properties window for the shape or on the BorderStyle property Help screen.

The thickness of the shape's border is set using the **BorderWidth** property. A BorderWidth setting of 0 indicates that no border will be drawn for the shape.

The **Visible** property of a shape can be set to True or False. A shape can be seen at run time only when its Visible property is set to True.

The appearance of the Shape control is set using the **Shape** property (not to be confused with the Shape control). This is the Shape property of the Shape control. The valid values for the Shape property are Rectangle, Square, Oval, Circle, Rounded Rectangle, and Rounded Square.

For more information about the properties for a Shape object, or how to set them at run time by writing code, look at the online Help for the specific property.

The cash register program will include a rounded rectangle shape. Rounding the corners of the rectangle softens the corners and makes the shape more appealing.

To set the properties for the Shape object:

1. Activate the Properties window for the Shape object.

2. Click the default property value for the Shape property. Click the Properties button ⏷, then click **4 - Rounded Rectangle**.

3. Set the BorderWidth property to **2**.

4. Set the BackStyle property to **1 - Opaque**. This setting will fill the region inside the shape with the default BackColor.

5. Set the BackColor property to **light blue**, to emphasize the menu items against the background of the form.

   TROUBLE? If the color of the shape does not change to light blue, the BackStyle property is probably set to 0 - Transparent. Change the BackStyle property setting to 1 - Opaque.

The shape is now ready for you to place the menu items on it.

Adding a CheckBox Object to the Form

The cash register program needs three objects to represent the menu items for a hamburger, french fries, and soft drink, so that a clerk can click the items as the customer orders them. Visual Basic provides several ways to indicate an item has been ordered. You could add a TextBox object and have the user type in the number of items ordered, but that would require input from the keyboard. This would violate the design specifications. In this case, a **CheckBox** is the best control for the task because a user can click a check box to mark an item that has been ordered.

To create the order menu check list, you will create multiple instances of the CheckBox control, one for each menu item. This is the first task in the TOE chart—to create three check boxes so a clerk can click one or more of them.

A CheckBox object has three valid values. If it is not checked (default) the Value property is 0-Unchecked. When a check box is checked, the Value property is 1-Checked. Finally, if a check box is dimmed, the Value property is 2-Grayed. A CheckBox object that is dimmed has a gray check mark in it; it is neither checked nor unchecked. If you click a dimmed check box once, it becomes unchecked; if you click it twice, it becomes checked. You can use a dimmed check box so that the user can tell that the box is neither checked nor unchecked and that input needs to be provided.

REFERENCE window	**ADDING A CHECKBOX OBJECT TO A FORM**
	▪ Click the CheckBox control on the toolbox.
	▪ Click and drag the mouse to draw a check box on the form.
	▪ Set the Caption property to describe the object's purpose.
	▪ Set other properties for the check box in the Properties window as needed.

In the cash register program, different check boxes will indicate whether a customer ordered a hamburger, french fries, and/or a soft drink. Remember that each object name should start with the appropriate prefix to improve the readability of a program. The names of all CheckBox objects should begin with the prefix "chk."

To create the CheckBox objects for the menu items:

1. Click the **CheckBox** control ☑ on the toolbox.

2. Draw a check box inside the Shape object, as shown in Figure 3-3.

Figure 3-3 ◄
Creating a
CheckBox
object

new check box ———

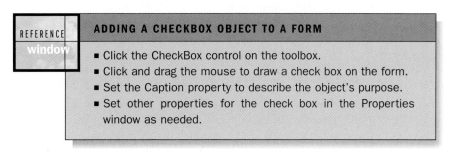

3. Set the Caption property for the check box to **Burger** and the Name property to **chkBurger**.

4. Create the second check box and position it directly below the first check box.

5. Set the Caption property for the second check box to **French Fries** and the Name property to **chkFrenchFries**.

6. Create the third check box and position it directly below the second check box.

7. Set the Caption property for the third check box to **Soft Drink** and the Name property to **chkSoftDrink**. Your form should look like Figure 3-4.

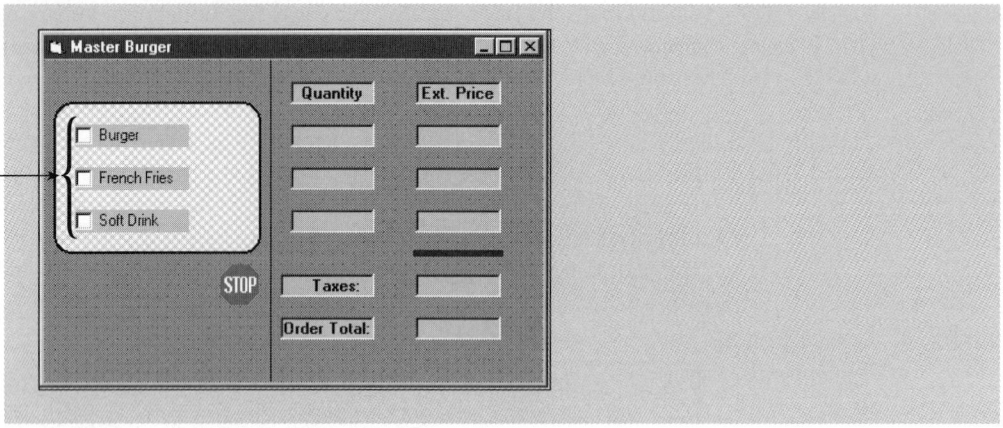

Figure 3-4 ◀
Completed
CheckBox
objects

new check boxes ───────

Adding Scroll Bars to the Form

After clicking a check box, a Master Burger clerk must be able to specify the quantity of the item the customer wants. The user interface for the cash register program must permit a clerk to use only a mouse or touch screen to enter the quantity. For example, if a customer orders three hamburgers, the clerk will click the Burger check box to indicate the item has been ordered, but the clerk also needs to indicate that the customer wants three hamburgers. Because the mouse or touch screen is the only means of input, the clerk cannot type in the number of hamburgers ordered using a control such as a text box.

You could create two Image objects or CommandButton object's for each item. One command button would contain code in the Click event procedure to increment a variable representing the quantity ordered, and the other command button would decrement the variable. Although this approach would work, you would have to write several lines of code, so it is not the most efficient solution. Visual Basic provides a control called a **scroll bar** that will increment and decrement the quantity ordered of an item without requiring you to write any code. Determining the correct control for a particular task makes the programming task more efficient and makes the program easier to use.

Visual Basic provides vertical and horizontal scroll bars, which work in the same way as the scroll bars in most Windows 95 programs. The two types of scroll bars share the same properties. The choice of which one to use depends on the requirements of the user interface. Horizontal scroll bars are well suited for measures of distance, such as inches, because the metaphor of a ruler on a map tends to be a left-to-right sliding scale. Because you would think of an order quantity going up or down rather than left to right, the vertical scroll bar is the better choice for the cash register program. In circumstances where the type of scroll bar is irrelevant, consider using the one that will balance the layout of the screen. The prefix for a vertical scroll bar, or VScrollBar control, is "vsb," and the prefix for a horizontal scroll bar, or HScrollBar control, is "hsb."

The **Value** property of a scroll bar is an integer that contains the current value of the scroll bar. The range of valid values is controlled by the **Max** and **Min** properties. Figure 3-5 shows the two regions of a vertical scroll bar. When a user clicks the arrows, the Value property increases or decreases by the value contained in the **SmallChange** property. When a user clicks the region between the arrows, the Value property changes by the value of the **LargeChange** property. Both properties have a default value of 1.

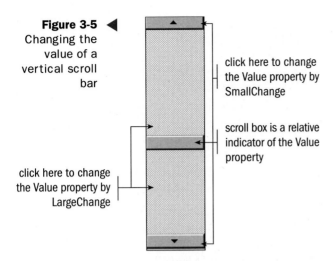

Figure 3-5 ◀
Changing the
value of a
vertical scroll
bar

click here to change
the Value property by
SmallChange

scroll box is a relative
indicator of the Value
property

click here to change
the Value property by
LargeChange

By default, the value of a vertical scroll bar grows as the bar moves downward. If you set the Min property to 0 and the Max property to 25, clicking the up arrow would cause the value to decrease, and clicking the down arrow would cause the value to increase. Think of using a scroll bar to scroll down through a document; the down arrow moves you from line 1 of the document to the next line. The line number continues to increase as you move down the document, as illustrated in Figure 3-6.

Figure 3-6 ◀
Setting the
Max and Min
properties

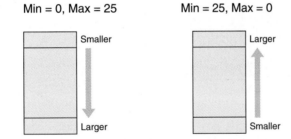

Min = 0, Max = 25

Smaller

Larger

Min = 25, Max = 0

Larger

Smaller

REFERENCE
window

ADDING A SCROLLBAR OBJECT TO A FORM

- Click the VScrollBar or HScrollBar control on the toolbox.
- Click and drag the mouse to draw a scroll bar on the form.
- In the Properties window, set the SmallChange property for the scroll bar to the value by which the scroll bar will change when either arrow is clicked.
- Set the LargeChange property for the scroll bar to the value by which the scroll bar will change when any gray area of the scroll bar is clicked.
- Set the Min and Max property values for the scroll bar to define the range for the scroll bar.

For the cash register program, you will create vertical scroll bars that can be used to specify the quantity ordered for each of the three products on the menu. This is the second task in the TOE chart—to change the quantity of each menu item using a scroll bar. When a clerk clicks the vertical scroll bar's up arrow, the order quantity for the specific item must increase by 1. When a clerk clicks the scroll bar's down arrow, the order quantity must decrease by 1.

By setting the Max property to 0 and the Min property to the expected value of the largest order, the value of a scroll bar will increase when its up arrow is clicked. Gill thinks it is reasonable to set 25 as the expected value of the largest order.

To create the vertical scroll bars on the form and set their Min and Max properties:

1. Click the **VScrollBar** control ⬚ on the toolbox.

2. Draw a scroll bar between the Burger check box and its quantity ordered label. Refer to Figure 3-7 for the placement of the scroll bars.

3. Activate the Properties window for the scroll bar and set its Name property to **vsbBurger**.

4. Set the value of the Max property to **0** and the Min property to **25**.

5. Draw a second vertical scroll bar between the French Fries check box and its quantity ordered label. Set its Name property to **vsbFrenchFries**, its Max property to **0**, and its Min property to **25**.

6. Draw the third vertical scroll bar between the Soft Drink check box and its quantity ordered label. Set its Name property to **vsbSoftDrink**, its Max property to **0**, and its Min property to **25**. Your screen should look like Figure 3-7.

Figure 3-7 ◀
Completed
ScrollBar
objects

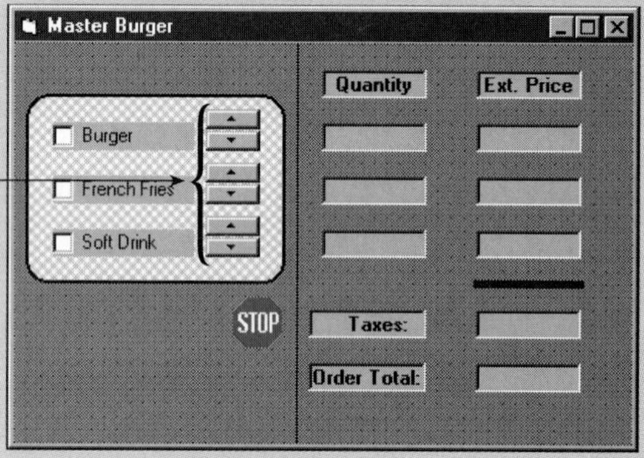

new scroll bars —

The three scroll bars are now in place. A Master Burger clerk will use them to indicate the quantity of each menu item ordered. When the value of the scroll bar changes, you want the value of the corresponding quantity ordered label to change. Recall that in Tutorial 2 you used the Change event procedure to compute different interest rates whenever the contents of a text box changed. In this program, you need to know when the numeric value of a scroll bar changes, so that the program can update the quantity ordered and extended price of an item and display the information in the corresponding Label objects. Whenever a user clicks part of a scroll bar and changes its value, the program generates a Change event, which you use with the Value property in a computation to update the values of the necessary labels.

To write the code that will place the value of the Burger scroll bar into its quantity ordered label:

1. Open the Code window for the vsbBurger_Change event and enter the following code:

```
Private Sub vsbBurger_Change()
     lblQtyBurger.Caption = vsbBurger.Value
End Sub
```

When one of the scroll arrows is clicked, the program generates a Change event for the vsbBurger object. The code in this Change event procedure copies the Value property of vsbBurger to the Caption property of lblQtyBurger.

You now need to create the code for the scroll bars for the French Fries and Soft Drink items. You will create the same code for these items as you did for the Burger scroll bar.

To write the code for the two remaining scroll bars:

1. Activate the Code window for the vsbFrenchFries_Change event and enter the following code:

```
Private Sub vsbFrenchFries_Change()
    lblQtyFrenchFries.Caption = vsbFrenchFries.Value
End Sub
```

2. Repeat Step 1 for the vsbSoftDrink_Change event, using the names **lblQtySoftDrink** and **vsbSoftDrink**.

3. Close the Code window.

Whenever a clerk clicks a scroll bar, the caption of the corresponding label will display the quantity ordered for the item, as indicated by the value of the scroll bar.

Gill suggests that you test the program to see whether or not the quantity ordered labels are updated correctly when a scroll bar is clicked. Testing the program will also give you an opportunity to see how the Change event works for a scroll bar. Because you have set the Max and Min properties, you cannot set the Value property outside the specified range. The scroll bar that has the focus is shown with a blinking cursor in the scroll button.

To test the scroll bars and their corresponding quantity ordered labels:

1. Click the **Start** button on the toolbar to start the program.

2. Click the Burger check box.

3. Click the Burger scroll bar's up arrow. The corresponding label displays the value 1.

4. Click the Burger scroll bar's down arrow. The label displays the value 0. Because you did not change the SmallChange property from the default value of 1, the value of the scroll bar changes by 1 each time you click one of its arrows.

5. Repeat Steps 2, 3, and 4 to test the French Fries and Soft Drink scroll bars.

6. End the program by clicking the stop sign to test the Image object.

   TROUBLE? If any quantity ordered label did not change, end the program and open the Code window for the corresponding scroll bar. Check the code and make sure that the Caption property is set for the correct Label object.

   If the value of an item incremented or decremented incorrectly, check the Min and Max properties of the corresponding scroll bar; Min should be 25 and Max should be 0. Make any necessary corrections, then repeat Steps 1 through 5.

7. Click the **Save Project** button on the toolbar to save the form and project.

Note that when you click one of the scroll arrows for a menu item, the value of its scroll bar changes. This means that a Change event is generated for the scroll bar. For example, the code in the vsbSoftDrink_Change event procedure sets the caption for lblQtySoftDrink which, in turn, generates a Change event for that object as well. This process is illustrated in Figure 3-8.

Figure 3-8 ◀
Events causing
other events

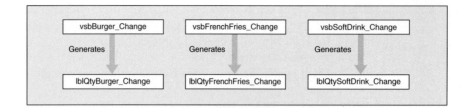

Using Boolean Variables to Improve the User Interface

To help a Master Burger clerk visually identify when an item has been ordered, Gill wants each scroll bar and its corresponding quantity ordered and extended price labels to be visible only when the item's check box has been clicked. The scroll bar and labels should be invisible when an item's check box has not been clicked. You can accomplish this by setting the Visible property of the scroll bar and labels to True or False.

True and False are the valid values for Boolean variables. A **Boolean variable** operates like an on/off switch; True signifies on and False signifies off. You cannot assign any value other than True or False to a Boolean variable.

The Visible property for an object determines whether or not the object appears on the screen when the program is running. As with other properties, you can set the Visible property for an object at design time using the Properties window, or by coding an event procedure that will be called at run time.

When the cash register program starts, no scroll bars or labels should appear on the form until a clerk clicks the corresponding check box. You could set the Visible property for each object individually, but this would be time consuming. Visual Basic allows you to select different types of objects and display only the properties common to all of the objects in the Properties window. You can then set any of the common properties of all the selected objects at once. In this case, you need to change the Visible property for two different types of objects: scroll bars and labels. To select more than one object, you click the first object to display its handles, which indicate that the object is active; then you press and hold down the Shift key and click the additional objects. When you select and work with multiple objects, the Properties window does not display an object name.

To set the Visible property for the scroll bars and labels:

1. Press and hold down the **Shift** key as you click each scroll bar and each label for quantity ordered and extended price. As you activate an object, it is marked with gray handles. See Figure 3-9.

Figure 3-9 ◀
Selecting
multiple
objects

marked objects
appear with gray
handles

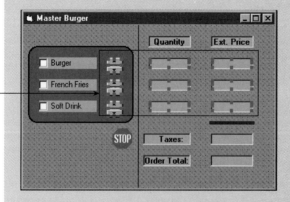

2. Set the Visible property for the selected objects to **False**. As shown in Figure 3-10, the Properties window displays only those properties that are common to both a label and a vertical scroll bar.

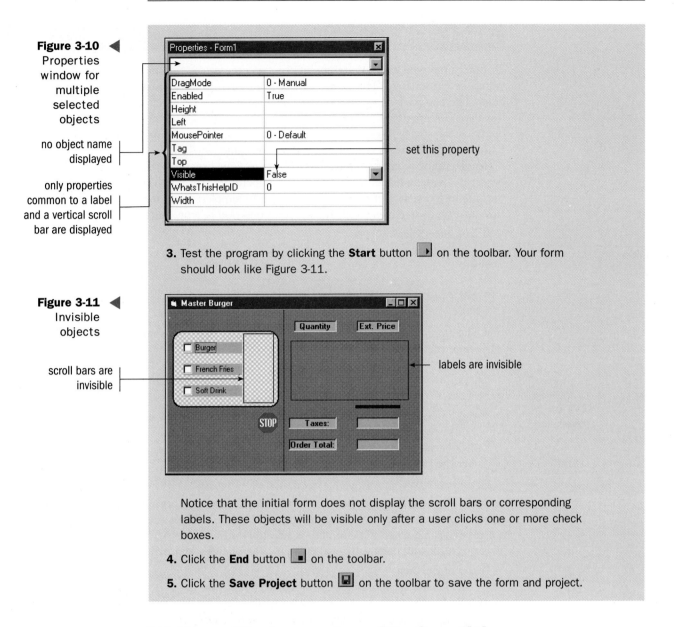

Figure 3-10 ◀
Properties window for multiple selected objects

no object name displayed

only properties common to a label and a vertical scroll bar are displayed

set this property

3. Test the program by clicking the **Start** button ▶ on the toolbar. Your form should look like Figure 3-11.

Figure 3-11 ◀
Invisible objects

scroll bars are invisible

labels are invisible

Notice that the initial form does not display the scroll bars or corresponding labels. These objects will be visible only after a user clicks one or more check boxes.

4. Click the **End** button ■ on the toolbar.

5. Click the **Save Project** button 🖫 on the toolbar to save the form and project.

Writing Statements with Conditions

Now that your program starts running with the scroll bars and labels invisible, you need to write the code that will cause these objects to become visible if a corresponding check box is checked. You want the scroll bars and labels to remain invisible, or become invisible again, if the corresponding check box is not checked.

The programs you have developed until now have all executed statements sequentially in the order they appear in the procedure, until the procedure reaches the End Sub statement. This is fine for simple tasks, but most programs need the capability to execute one set of statements in certain circumstances and another set of statements in different circumstances. Visual Basic allows you to write statements to address different conditions. Fox example, you can write a statement such as "If a menu item check box is checked, then make its corresponding scroll bar and labels visible; otherwise, keep these objects invisible." The following pseudocode shows the statement in generic form.

If some expression is true then
    execute one group of statements.
Otherwise
    execute a different group of statements.
End of If statement

Using Comparison Operators

To determine which set of statements to execute, you use comparison operators on two values or expressions. The values can be compared in many ways using **comparison operators**. The comparison operators used by Visual Basic are equal to (=), not equal to (<>), less than (<), greater than (>), less than or equal to (<=), greater than or equal to (>=), or contains the string (**Like**). The result of a conditional operation is always either True or False and, therefore, is considered a Boolean value.

To determine which statements to execute in your program, you will use the comparison operator = with an If statement. Comparison operators are seldom used by themselves. Rather, they are included as part of some statement. The simplest form of an **If** statement, which will execute a set of statements only if a specific condition is True, has the following syntax:

If *condition* **Then**
    statement(s)
End If

- The *condition* part of an **If** statement must evaluate to a Boolean value of True or False.

- The *statement(s)* part can be any valid Visual Basic statement, which is executed when the *condition* is True.

The following pseudocode describes a simple If statement that will execute statements if the French Fries check box is checked.

If the French Fries check box is checked then
    Make the corresponding scroll bar visible
    Make the corresponding label visible
    Set the value of the scroll bar to 1
End of If statement

This statement is useful, but it does not account for situations in which a different activity needs to be executed when a condition is False. Here, is the program must make the scroll bar visible when a menu item is selected and invisible when the item is not selected. This type of If statement, often called an **If...Then...Else** statement, has the following syntax:

If *condition* **Then**
    statements executed when the condition is **True**
Else
    statements executed when the condition is **False**
End If

- The only difference between this statement and the simpler form of the If statement is that it allows for one action if the condition is True and for another action if the condition is False.

This If...Then...Else statement is represented with the following pseudocode:

If the French Fries check box is checked then
    Make the corresponding scroll bar visible
    Make the corresponding label in visible
    Set the value of the scroll bar to 1
Otherwise execute the following statements
    Make the corresponding scroll bar invisible
    Make the corresponding label invisible
    Set the value of the scroll bar to 0
End of If statement

You will write an If...Then...Else statement to make visible or invisible the scroll bars and the quantity ordered and extended price labels for each menu item when its corresponding check box is checked. For example, when the chkBurger object is checked, the Visible property for the lblQtyBurger and lblExtBurger should be set to True; otherwise it should remain set to False.

To make the user interface as intuitive and easy to use as possible, Gill wants the program to set the value of the corresponding scroll bar and quantity ordered label when the value of the check box changes. When the box is first checked, the quantity ordered label must be set to 1, the most likely quantity that will be ordered. You can do this by setting the Value property of the scroll bar to 1 when you set its Visible property to True.

Occasionally, a customer will decide not to order a product that has already been checked. When a check box is unchecked, the scroll bar and the labels for quantity ordered and extended price need to be set to 0 and become invisible again.

Looking Up Intrinsic Constants with the Object Browser

Recall that a check box can assume three valid Value properties. A value of 0 indicates that the check box is not checked; a value of 1 indicates that it is checked; and a value of 2 indicates that it is dimmed. These check box values are constants. Constants are similar to variables, but their values do not change while the program is running. There are two types of constants: intrinsic constants and user-defined constants. **intrinsic constants** are defined by Visual Basic. **User-defined constants** are defined by you, the programmer, in a Visual Basic statement.

Using a tool called the Object Browser, you will see how to express the check box values as intrinsic constants. For the CheckBox object, the intrinsic constants reference the same Value property you set using the Properties window. Visual Basic has defined several intrinsic constants you can use in a program to make it more readable and intuitive.

The **Object Browser**, which is available only at design time, allows you to look at the intrinsic constants defined by Visual Basic that relate to the properties of all the objects you create, as well as the modules and procedures you have defined for your project. Many of these constants are also listed in the Help system.

To make your program more readable, you will use intrinsic constants in the If statements to determine whether or not a particular check box is checked. Before you can use these constants, you need to find out their names. You can look up intrinsic constants using the Object Browser. The names of all Visual Basic constants begin with the prefix "vb."

To use the Object Browser to examine the intrinsic constants applicable to a check box:

1. Click the **Object Browser** button 🔲 on the toolbar. The Object Browser dialog box opens.

2. Click the **Libraries/Projects** list arrow, then click **VB - Visual Basic objects and procedures**.

3. Click **CheckBoxConstants** in the Classes/Modules section of the Object Browser dialog box.

   The Methods/Properties section contains three constants—vbChecked, vbGrayed, and vbUnchecked, as shown in Figure 3-12.

Figure 3-12 ◄
Object Browser
dialog box

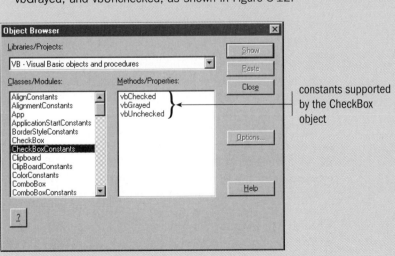

4. Click **vbChecked**. Notice that the value of the constant, 1, is displayed at the bottom of the dialog box.

5. Click **vbGrayed** and notice the value of the constant is 2.

6. Click **vbUnchecked** and notice the value of the constant is 0.

7. Click the **Close** button ⊠ on the Object Browser title bar to close the dialog box.

When you use intrinsic constant names in a program, Visual Basic converts the names into their respective values when the program is run, which makes the program more readable and reliable. For example, if you needed to set the Value property to unchecked, the following two statements would accomplish this; however, the statement containing the constant makes it clearer that you want the value to be unchecked:

```
chkBurger.Value = 0
chkBurger.Value = vbUnchecked
```

You will use intrinsic constants to write the code to make the scroll bars and labels visible when a clerk checks a check box.

To set the Visible property for the scroll bars and labels based on the check box values:

1. Open the Code window for the chkBurger_Click event procedure and enter the following code:

```
'Make visible the scroll bar, quantity ordered label, and
'extended price label when the check box is checked.
'Make the objects invisible when the check box is not checked.
'Initialize the order quantity.
Private Sub chkBurger_Click()
    If (chkBurger.Value = vbChecked) Then
        vsbBurger.Visible = True
        vsbBurger.Value = 1
        lblQtyBurger.Visible = True
        lblExtBurger.Visible = True
    Else
        vsbBurger.Visible = False
        vsbBurger.Value = 0
        lblQtyBurger.Visible = False
        lblExtBurger.Visible = False
    End If
End Sub
```

2. Repeat Step 1 for the chkFrenchFries_Click event procedure. Be sure you use the object names **vsbFrenchFries**, **lblQtyFrenchFries**, and **lblExtFrenchFries**.

3. Repeat Step 1 for the chkSoftDrink_Click event procedure. Be sure you use the object names **vsbSoftDrink**, **lblQtySoftDrink**, and **lblExtSoftDrink**.

You have now written the code to make the scroll bars and labels visible when the value of a corresponding check box is 1 (vbChecked), and to set the Value property of the scroll bar to 1 when its box is first checked. This code will also reset the Visible and Value properties to False and 0, respectively, when the check box Value property is 0 (vbUnchecked).

Because you already wrote the code to set the value of the corresponding label whenever the scroll bar changes, you do not need to explicitly set the initial value of the label. Rather, when the Value property of the scroll bar is set, the Change event happens to the scroll bar and the Caption of the label is set in the VScrollBar_Change event. Figure 3-13 shows how each event causes the next event.

Figure 3-13 ◀
Relationship
between
events (1)

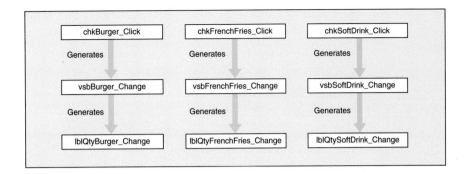

Now that the event code for each check box is complete, you have reached a milestone in your program. It is a good time to test your program, correct any errors, and save your work.

To test the check boxes:

1. Start the program.

2. Click the **Burger** check box. The corresponding scroll bar, vsbBurger, and the labels, lblQtyBurger and lblExtBurger, become visible. The caption for lblQtyBurger is 1.

3. Click the **Burger** check box again. The objects are invisible again.

4. Repeat Steps 2 and 3 for the **French Fries** and **Soft Drink** check boxes.

   TROUBLE? If the visibility of an object does not change in response to a click in the corresponding check box, end the program, then open the Code window for the CheckBox object's Click event procedure and verify that your code is identical to the code shown in the tutorial steps. Make any necessary corrections, then repeat Steps 1 through 4.

5. End the program.

6. Click the **Save Project** button 🖫 on the toolbar.

The cash register program now accepts all the input data that a Master Burger clerk will enter. You are ready to begin programming the output objects.

Creating User-Defined Constants

You still must create the code to compute and display the labels for the extended prices, as described in the pseudocode Gill wrote for the program. The extended price is computed by multiplying the quantity ordered by the price of the item. Before you can compute the extended price, you need to include the price of each item in the program. You could declare variables and assign values to them as you did in Tutorial 2. However, in this case, the price of an item will not change while the program is running, so a constant is more suitable for storing the prices. You used an intrinsic constant in the If statement you wrote to determine if a check box is checked. You can also create user-defined constants by using the **Const** statement. The syntax for a user-defined constant is:

[**Public** | **Private**] **Const** *constantname* [**As** *type*] = *expression*

- The **Public** keyword is used at the form level to declare constants that can be used by all procedures in all forms. You need this keyword only if you have more than one form in your project. The **Private** keyword is used at the form level to declare a constant that can be used only by procedures in the form where the constant is declared. Constants are Private if you omit the Public or Private keyword.

- You can declare constants only in the general declarations section of the Code window; you cannot declare constants inside a procedure.

- The *constantname* assigned to a user-defined constant is usually declared in all uppercase characters so that it is easily recognized as a constant.

- Constants can represent any of the Visual Basic data types by using the **As** *type* clause.

- The *expression* represents a valid Visual Basic expression that becomes the value of the constant. The expression is often a simple value, such as a price, but it can also consist of other constants and operators. See the Visual Basic online Help for more information on the Const statement.

You will define the price constants in the general declarations section of the Code window so that they can be used by all the form's procedures. Because the constants in your program need to be visible only to the form in which they are declared, you will declare them as Private. Each constant will be declared as a Single data type, because the prices contain a decimal point. Also, you will include the Option Explicit statement in the general declarations section so that typographical errors in constant and variable names, which might otherwise be hard to find, will cause syntax errors, which are easier to detect.

The constants will be used in various expressions throughout the program to compute the extended prices of products ordered. Including constants makes the program more readable and easier to maintain. Furthermore, if the price of an item changes, you only need to change the constant once rather than searching for each occurrence of the price used in the program.

Next, you will declare the prices as constants in the general declarations section of the Code window so they will be available to all the procedures in the form.

To create the constants in the cash register program:

1. Open the general declarations section of the Code window for the form.

2. Type the following code:

```
Option Explicit
Private Const PRICEBURGER As Single = 1.44
Private Const PRICEFRENCHFRIES As Single = 0.74
Private Const PRICESOFTDRINK As Single = 0.66
Private Const PERCENTTAX As Single = 0.07
```

This code declares three constants for the item prices and another constant for the sales tax rate. The code also sets the value for each constant.

Next, you must create the code to calculate the extended price and place it in the caption of the corresponding extended price label. The extended prices are computed by multiplying the quantity ordered by the price constant you defined for each item in the general declarations section and storing the intermediate result in a variable. Then, the intermediate result (the variable) is placed into the label. The variable is necessary so that the program can use the value of the Label object to compute the order total. Because the contents of each label are formatted with a leading dollar sign, you would need to remove the dollar sign, and then call the Val function to convert the label caption back to a number and calculate the order total. By creating the intermediate variable now, you will be able to use the variable to compute the order total.

To declare the variables for the extended prices:

1. In the general declarations section of the Code window, type the following three lines below the constants you just defined:

```
Dim TmpExtBurger As Single
Dim TmpExtFrenchFries As Single
Dim TmpExtSoftDrink As Single
```

Each of these variables will store temporary information for the extended price of an item. Because these variables are temporary, the prefix Tmp is used. Note that the first character is capitalized to indicate that this is a variable. If the letter is not capitalized, it denotes an object name.

For each of the three different products, when either arrow of the scroll bar is clicked, the code you previously wrote executes in response to the VScrollBar_Change event and updates the caption of the corresponding quantity ordered label. When the label representing the quantity ordered of an item changes, the extended price also needs to change. Figure 3-14 shows how these events occur.

Figure 3-14 ◀
Relationship between events (2)

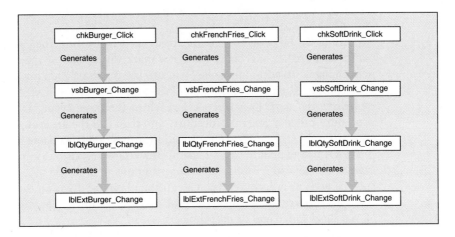

Now that you have declared the necessary variables, you can use them to write the code that will calculate the extended prices.

To write the code that will calculate and display the extended prices:

1. Activate the Code window for the Change event associated with the object named lblQtyBurger. Make sure that you activate the Change event, not the Click event.

2. Enter the following code:

```
Private Sub lblQtyBurger_Change()
    TmpExtBurger = lblQtyBurger.Caption * PRICEBURGER
    lblExtBurger.Caption = TmpExtBurger
End Sub
```

3. Repeat Steps 1 and 2 for the lblQtyFrenchFries_Change event procedure. Be sure to substitute **lblQtyFrenchFries** for lblQtyBurger, **TmpExtFrenchFries** for TmpExtBurger, **PRICEFRENCHFRIES** for PRICEBURGER, and **lblExtFrenchFries** for lblExtBurger.

4. Repeat Steps 1 and 2 for the lblQtySoftDrink_Change event procedure. Be sure to substitute **lblQtySoftDrink** for lblQtyBurger, **TmpExtSoftDrink** for TmpExtBurger, **PRICESOFTDRINK** for PRICEBURGER, and **lblExtSoftDrink** for lblExtBurger.

You have now written all the code to update the extended price of each item when the quantity ordered changes. This is a good time to test your program, correct any errors, and save the form and project files.

To test the extended prices:

1. Start the program.

2. Click each of the three check boxes. The extended prices are computed.

    TROUBLE? If an extended price is not computed correctly, end the program and activate the Code window for the Change event procedure of the corresponding quantity ordered Label object. Be sure that the code is the same as the code shown in the previous set of steps. Make any necessary corrections, then repeat Steps 1 and 2.

3. End the program.

4. Click the **Save Project** button on the toolbar.

Creating a General Procedure

According to the program specifications written by Gill, the cash register program must compute the taxes and order total automatically whenever the extended price of a menu item changes. To accomplish this, you can use the same code for all three event procedures, lblExtBurger_Change, lblExtFrenchFries_Change, and lblExtSoftDrink_Change. Instead of writing the same lines of code in each of the three event procedures, you can create a procedure called a general procedure, and then call the general procedure with one line of code from the individual event procedures. A **general procedure** is like an event procedure, but you must explicitly call a general procedure because it does not respond to an event. One of the keys to writing successful programs is to divide tasks into logical components, such as general procedures, which can then be reused within the same program or in one or more different programs. General procedures are either intrinsic (provided with the Visual Basic language) or user-defined.

When you create a general procedure to compute the taxes and totals, you must specify the procedure name, type, and scope. Visual Basic will help you by creating a template for the procedure with the Insert Procedure dialog box.

To open the Insert Procedure dialog box for the form:

1. Open the Code window for the Form object.

2. Click **Insert** on the menu bar, then click **Procedure**. The Insert Procedure dialog box opens. See Figure 3-15.

Figure 3-15 ◀
Insert
Procedure
dialog box

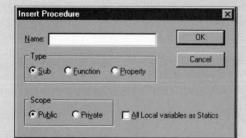

    TROUBLE? If the Procedure option is dimmed in the Insert menu, be sure the Visual Basic title bar displays [design], and that the Code window is the active window.

The Insert Procedure dialog box consists of three sections—Name, Type, and Scope. In the **Name** text box you type a name for the general procedure.

The **Type** identifies whether the procedure is a Subroutine (Sub) procedure, Function procedure, or Property procedure. **Sub** procedures communicate information to other parts of the program by setting form-level variables, but do not return values to the procedures from which they were called. **Function** procedures return values to the procedures from which they were called. **Property** procedures allow you to create your own objects.

Public and Private are the keywords that describe the **Scope** of the procedure. If a procedure is **Private**, it can be called only from the form in which it is declared. If it is **Public**, the procedure can be called from anywhere in the project. Public procedures are useful only when a program contains several different form modules or other modules.

You will use the Insert Procedure dialog box to create the general procedure that will calculate the taxes and order total when any extended price changes. Because you will use the general procedure to set the values of the form-level variables TmpTaxes and TmpTotal, and you do not need any value to be returned to the procedure, you will create a Sub procedure. Also, you will declare the general procedure as Private, because all the code for your program is contained in the same form.

To write the general procedure to compute the taxes and order total:

1. Type **ComputeTotals** in the Name text box.

2. In the Type section, click the **Sub** radio button.

3. In the Scope section, click the **Private** radio button.

4. Click the **OK** button.

   The Code window will activate the ComputeTotals procedure inside the General object. The General object indicates that the procedure is not executed when an event occurs to a specific object, but is general to the form module, and can be called by any event procedure.

5. Enter the code shown in Figure 3-16 into the procedure:

Figure 3-16 ◀
Creating a
general
procedure

procedure is in the
General object

procedure name

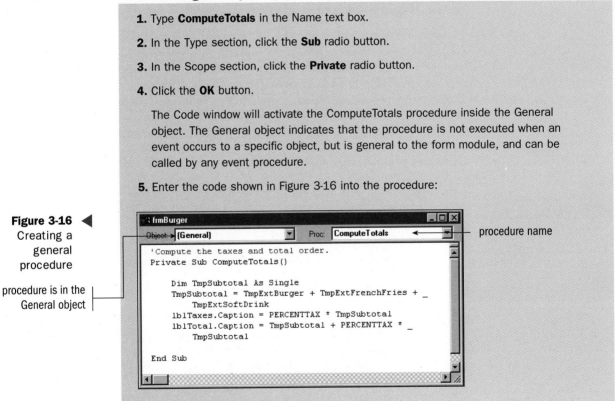

As shown in Figure 3-16, the ComputeTotals procedure is in the General object. This means that it is a general procedure rather than an object-specific event procedure. Now you can examine each line of the code in more detail.

```
Dim TmpSubtotal As Single
```

The variable TmpSubtotal is declared inside the ComputeTotals general procedure. You only need this variable when the taxes and order total are being updated. This variable is considered local to the procedure, and other event or general procedures are not able to reference it. Furthermore, the memory for the variable is allocated only when the procedure is called, and then it is released when the procedure terminates. In other words, the variable exists only while the procedure is executing.

```
TmpSubtotal = TmpExtBurger + TmpExtFrenchFries + _
    TmpExtSoftDrink
```

This statement computes a subtotal by adding together the extended prices for each item. Remember that you declared the variables TmpExtBurger, TmpExtFrenchFries, and TmpExtSoftDrink in the general declarations section of the Code window. Because the statements are too long to fit on a line, you need to use the statement continuation character (_), as you did in Tutorial 2.

```
lblTaxes.Caption = PERCENTTAX * TmpSubtotal
```

To compute the taxes, this statement multiplies the TmpSubtotal by the user-defined constant PERCENTTAX, which you declared in the general declarations section of the Code window.

```
lblTotal.Caption = TmpSubtotal + PERCENTTAX * _
    TmpSubtotal
```

This statement computes the taxes again and adds the result to the subtotal of the items ordered.

Calling the General Procedure

Once you have created a general procedure, you need to call it either from another general procedure or an event procedure. Gill's design for the cash register program specifies that when the extended price of an item changes, the taxes and order total must recompute automatically. So, the ComputeTotals general procedure should be called in the Change event procedure for each extended price label. You need to call the Compute-Totals general procedure by typing its name in the appropriate event or general procedure. You will also format each extended price label as currency.

To call the general procedure to compute the taxes and order total:

1. Activate the Code window for the lblExtBurger_Change event procedure and enter the following code:

```
Private Sub lblExtBurger_Change()
    ComputeTotals
    lblExtBurger.Caption = Format(lblExtBurger.Caption, _
        "currency")
End Sub
```

Placing the ComputeTotals general procedure call in the Change event for this extended price label ensures that when the extended price changes, the taxes and order total will be updated. The Format statement sets the output format as currency, with a leading dollar sign and two decimal places. After being formatted with a leading dollar sign, this extended price label cannot be used by the Val function, as the Val function requires an argument to begin with a number (not a dollar sign). This is why you used intermediate variables to calculate the order total in the general procedure.

2. Repeat Step 1 for the lblExtFrenchFries_Change event procedure. Be sure you use the object name **lblExtFrenchFries** for lblExtBurger.

3. Repeat Step 1 for the lblExtSoftDrink_Change event procedure. Be sure you use the object name **lblExtSoftDrink** for lblExtBurger.

Now you will run the program to test it.

4. Start the program.

5. Enter an order and make sure that each extended price is formatted correctly and that the taxes and order total are computed correctly. Note that the taxes and order total have not yet been formatted.

   TROUBLE? If an extended price is not formatted as currency, check that you wrote the correct Format statement in the corresponding extended price object. If the totals do not change, be sure that each extended price object is calling the ComputeTotals general procedure.

6. End the program.

7. Click the **Save Project** button 🖫 on the toolbar.

Each of the three Change event procedures computes and displays the sales tax and order total, then formats the extended price label in which it is called. The objects for the taxes and order total are not yet formatted as currency. You can accomplish this by placing a Format statement in the Change event procedure for each of the objects.

To format the taxes and order total as currency:

1. Open the Code window for the lblTaxes_Change event procedure and enter the following code:

```
Private Sub lblTaxes_Change()
    lblTaxes.Caption = Format(lblTaxes.Caption, _
          "currency")
End Sub
```

2. Repeat Step 1 for the lblTotal_Change event procedure. Be sure you use the object name **lblTotal** instead of lblTaxes.

Now that you have written all the code for the event procedures and the general procedure, you should examine the relationship between the events in the program. Figure 3-17 illustrates these relationships.

Figure 3-17 ◀
Event diagram
for the cash
register
program

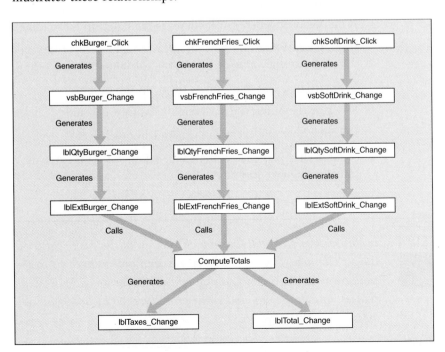

When a clerk clicks one of the check boxes, the value of the corresponding scroll bar is changed by the code in the Click event procedure for the check box. The code for the Change event in the scroll bar then updates the quantity ordered. The Change event for the quantity ordered, in turn, updates the extended price. The Change event for each extended price label calls the ComputeTotals general procedure, which updates the taxes and order total labels. The Change events for the taxes and order total labels format their values as currency. Understanding the relationship between multiple objects and the different events that occur is critical to writing Visual Basic programs.

Gill wants to make sure that the program runs properly, that the extended prices are computed and formatted correctly, and that the taxes and order total are correct. He asks you to test the program.

To test the program:

   1. Start the program.

   2. Click each of the CheckBox objects. The labels for the quantity ordered, extended price, taxes, and order total are updated and formatted as you click each check box.

   3. Use the scroll up arrows to change the quantity ordered for each item to **2**. The labels are updated and formatted as you change each order quantity.

   4. End the program.

   5. Save the project.

Quick Check

1 Define the following scroll bar properties: Min, Max, LargeChange, SmallChange, and Value.

2 What is a Boolean value?

3 What is the function of a check box?

4 What values can a check box contain?

5 Write the code for the following pseudocode statements:

If the Visible property of lblTaxes is equal to True, then set the caption to 33.

If the Visible property of lblTaxes is not equal to False, then set the value to 0.

If the January sales (lblJan) are greater than the February sales (lblFeb), then add 1 to the value of the caption of January sales.

If yesterday is less than today, then end the program.

6 Describe the difference between a Change event and a Click event.

7 Describe how one event can generate another event.

Now that you have completed Session 3.1, you can exit Visual Basic or you can continue to the next session.

SESSION

3.2

In this session, you will improve the design of the cash register program for Master Burger Company. You will add frames and option buttons to the form, create a control array, use the Select Case statement to execute code depending on the circumstances, update general and event procedures to include new objects, and display a message in a message box.

Cash Register Program Design Changes

After reviewing the cash register program, Gill identified some shortcomings in its design. Since Master Burger charges $1.50 for delivery, the program should include option buttons for this activity. A clerk can click to specify the type of order and trigger a delivery charge if the order is delivered. Also, Master Burger has recently added seating to its restaurants and, as an incentive, offers a 50¢ discount if the order is consumed in the restaurant. The same group of option buttons should include a button to trigger this discount. Finally, when a clerk clicks the stop sign image, Gill wants the program to display a message before exiting to make sure that the clerk did not click the image by accident.

Gill revised the pseudocode and TOE chart for the program to reflect these design changes. You can look at this information to help you modify the program.

To view and print the revised pseudocode and TOE chart for the cash register program:

1. Use Notepad or any word processing program to open and print the pseudocode and TOE chart in the file **MB_TOE2.txt**, which is located in the **Tutorial.03** folder on your Student Disk.

To implement the design changes, you need to add some new controls and write the necessary code. Gill has completed the revised screen design for the cash register program, as shown in Figure 3-18.

Figure 3-18 ◀
Revised screen design for the cash register program

input section

option buttons to specify location for order

output section

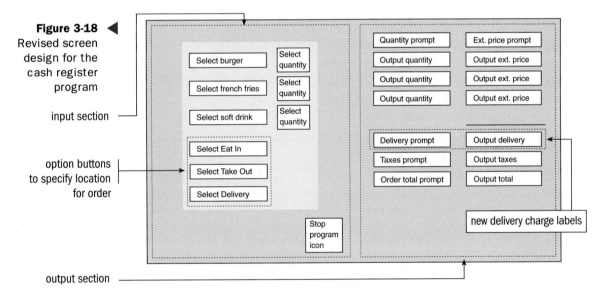

To make a copy of the existing form and project:

1. Start Visual Basic, if necessary.

2. Open the project named **Burger 1.vbp** that you created in Session 3.1. Make a copy of the form and project, saving them as **Burger 2.frm** and **Burger 2.vbp**, respectively.

3. Click the **View Form** button if needed.

Notice that the order location information needs to appear below the soft drink check box. Because you need to fit more information on the form, and more objects in the shape that defines the input area, you need to increase the height of both the form and the shape.

To resize the form and the shape:

1. Move the mouse to the bottom of the form until the pointer changes to ↕, then click and drag the mouse downward to make the form taller. Your form should look like Figure 3-19.

2. Select the stop sign image. Repeat Step 1 to move the object to the lower edge of the form.

3. Select the Shape object. Be sure that the handles appear around the object.

4. Repeat Step 1 to resize the Shape object. The form and shape should look like those in Figure 3-19.

Figure 3-19 ◀
Resizing the
form and shape

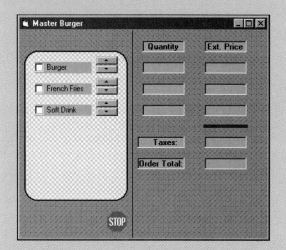

TROUBLE? Don't worry if the size of the Shape object does not match the figure exactly; you can change the size again, if necessary, later in the session.

Using Objects as a Group Within a Container

In Session 3.1, you used the CheckBox object to determine whether or not an item was ordered. You will now learn how to use another control, the OptionButton control, to allow a clerk to select only one item from a group of items. In this case the clerk must select whether the food will be delivered, taken out, or eaten in the restaurant. The Check-Box control would not be appropriate because it would not ensure that the clerk marked only one selection in the group. Also, because the mouse must be the only means of input, a TextBox control is not a possibility either. The **OptionButton** control allows you to create a group of items from which a user can select only one item.

OptionButton objects are usually positioned and operate as a group inside another object known as a **Frame**. When you draw a Frame object on a form and place option buttons inside the frame, only one of the OptionButton objects in the frame can be selected at a time.

To implement Gill's design changes to the cash register program, you need to specify whether an order will be eaten in the restaurant, taken out, or delivered. To do so, you will add a frame and three option buttons to the form. When a clerk clicks one of the three option buttons, the other two option buttons in the group will be unselected automatically.

When you create a frame that will be used to group other controls, you must draw the frame first, then draw the controls inside the frame. This enables you to move the frame and the objects in it together. If you draw an object outside a frame and then try to move the object inside, it will sit on top of the frame and you will have to move the frame and the object separately; they will not function as a group.

When you draw an option button directly on a form or inside a frame, the option button is considered to be **contained by** the form or frame. Whether an option button is contained by a form or frame is stored in the Container property of the option button.

Most of the objects you draw on a form have a **Container** property, which is used to group objects together. Such objects are contained by the form—that is, the Container property for the objects is set to the Name property of the form. The Container property is a **run-time property,** which means that it is available only while the program is running; therefore, the property is not listed in the Properties window for an object. For more information about the Container property, refer to the Help system.

Figure 3-20 shows how option buttons can be contained by a frame, which, in turn, is contained by the form. The figure also shows how option buttons can be contained by the form itself.

Figure 3-20 ◀
Containers

frame 1 and frame 2
contained by the form

contained by
frame 1

contained by
frame 2

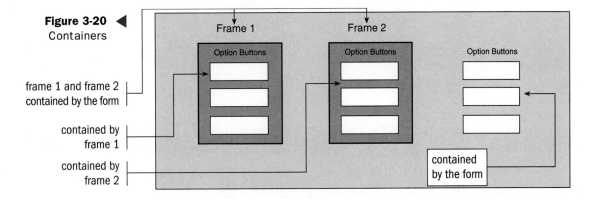

Creating a Frame

You create a Frame object in the same way that you created a Shape object earlier in the tutorial. The size of the frame you draw must be large enough to hold the objects that you will place in it. Like other objects, a frame can be resized as needed. The standard prefix for Frame object is "fra."

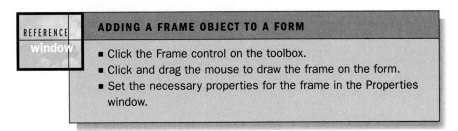

REFERENCE
window

ADDING A FRAME OBJECT TO A FORM

- Click the Frame control on the toolbox.
- Click and drag the mouse to draw the frame on the form.
- Set the necessary properties for the frame in the Properties window.

You will create a Frame object, named fraLocation, that will contain three option buttons indicating whether the order will be eaten in the restaurant, taken out, or delivered.

To add the Frame object to the form:

1. Click the **Frame** control ▥ on the toolbox, then draw a rectangular frame on the form below the CheckBox objects.

2. Set the Caption property of the frame to **Location** and the Name property to **fraLocation**. See Figure 3-21.

Figure 3-21 ◀
Creating a
Frame object

new Frame object —

caption —

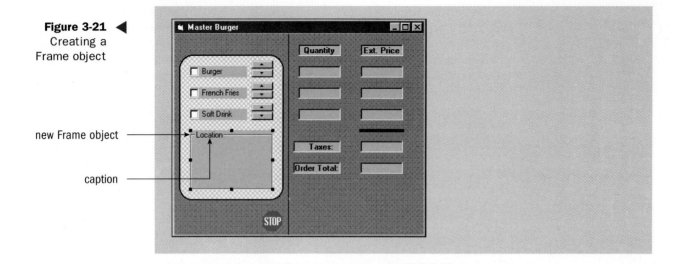

Creating Option Buttons

When you create OptionButton objects, you are interested in finding out which single button is clicked from a group of buttons contained inside a frame. This group of buttons is called an **option group**. Visual Basic automatically sets the same Container property value button for each option button in an option group. The standard prefix for naming OptionButton objects is "opt."

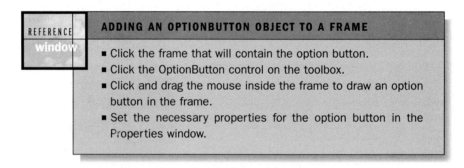

REFERENCE
window

ADDING AN OPTIONBUTTON OBJECT TO A FRAME

- Click the frame that will contain the option button.
- Click the OptionButton control on the toolbox.
- Click and drag the mouse inside the frame to draw an option button in the frame.
- Set the necessary properties for the option button in the Properties window.

You will create three option buttons, one for each possible location where an order will be eaten. These option buttons make up an option group.

To add the first option button to the Frame object:

1. Make sure the Frame object is active.

2. Click the **OptionButton** control 🄲 on the toolbox.

3. Draw an option button inside the frame. Set the option button's Name property to **optLocation** and its Caption property to **Eat In.** Your form should look like Figure 3-22.

Figure 3-22 ◀
Creating an
OptionButton
object

new OptionButton
object

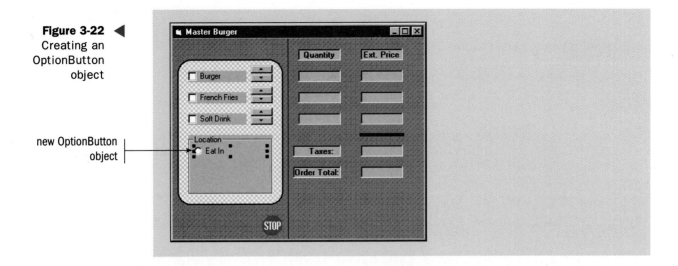

Viewing Run-time Properties

Gill asks you to verify that the Container property is set to the correct object. You can't use the Properties window to do so, because run-time properties are set only when the program is run. Gill suggests you use Visual Basic's debugging tools to examine the property.

Visual Basic allows you to enter statements to view the values of properties and the contents of variables while the program is in break mode. When in **break mode**, a program is temporarily suspended and another window, the Debug window, is displayed. You will use the Debug window here to look at the value of the Container property for the option button to make sure it is contained by the frame you previously created and, therefore, is part of the option group.

The Debug window allows you to use a statement called Print followed by variable names or object properties to look at their current values. You can use the Debug window only while in break mode. If the option buttons are not all contained by the correct object, the frame, a clerk could click more than one option button at a time, which would be incorrect. For more information about the Debug window, refer to Appendix A.

To see which container the option button belongs to:

1. Start the program.

2. Click the **Break** button ▭ on the toolbar to temporarily suspend the program. The Debug window becomes the active window. See Figure 3-23. The shape and size of your Debug window might differ from Figure 3-23.

Figure 3-23 ◀
The Debug
window

enter statements
here

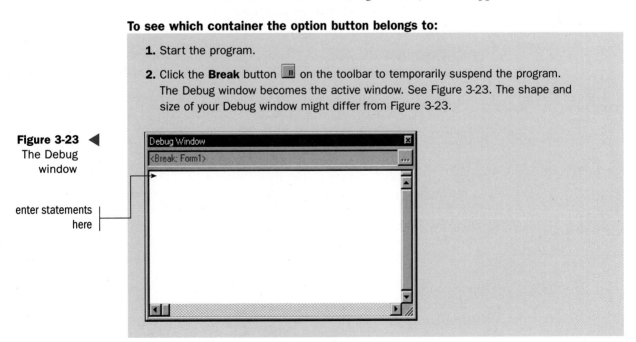

3. Type the following statements into the Debug window. (Note that your typed statements are bolded; the program's responses are not.)

```
print optLocation.Container.Name
fraLocation
print fraLocation.Container.Name
frmBurger
```

From this example, you can see that the option button (optLocation) is contained by the frame (fraLocation) you created. The frame is contained by the form (frmBurger). If you had mistakenly created the option button outside the frame, the object button would be contained by the form.

4. Click the **End** button on the toolbar.

Creating Objects with the Same Name

The next step in developing the program is to create the other two option buttons and to write the code for the option buttons to determine whether an order will be eaten in the restaurant, taken out by the customer, or delivered.

Until now, each object you have created on a form has had a unique name and a unique event procedure. It is possible to group objects together, using a control array, so that they all share the same name and event procedures. This process is particularly well suited to working with the option buttons contained within an option group, because you typically want to manipulate option buttons as a unit. A **control array** is a group of controls of the same type that share the same name and event procedures. Control arrays make a program more efficient. When you add an object, such as another option button, to a control array of option buttons, the new object shares all of the event procedures with the other option buttons in the same control array. Because the objects share event procedures, system memory is conserved. Control arrays also provide a way to overcome the programming limitations of Visual Basic controls. Although you will not write programs in these tutorials that are large enough to reach the limits of the Visual Basic language, you should be aware of these limits. You can specify up to 256 different control names on a form. Even this small cash register program contains 33 instances of various controls. If you need more than 256 controls, you can use control arrays. Each control array can contain a maximum of 32,767 objects.

Creating a Control Array

Depending on which option button is clicked, the program must charge for delivery if the order will be delivered, apply a discount if the order will be eaten in the restaurant, or take no action if the order will be taken out. You could create option buttons with three different names then write the code for each different event procedure. However, you can use a control array for the option buttons so that you only need to write one event procedure.

When you create objects in a control array, the objects share the same name; that is, they have the same value for the Name property. The **Index property** is an integer that Visual Basic uses with the Name property to uniquely identify each object in a control array. Event procedures for control arrays receive an argument, a variable named Index, that contains the value of the Index property for the selected object in the control. You can use the Index property to determine which option button is selected from a group of option buttons.

The easiest way to create a control array is to copy and paste one object to create multiple instances of the object.

CREATING A CONTROL ARRAY

- Create an instance of an object on the form, then activate the object.
- Copy the object to the Windows clipboard by pressing Ctrl+C.
- Click the Container object to activate it.
- Paste the copied object in the Container object by pressing Ctrl+V.
- Click the Yes button in the dialog box asking if you want to create a control array.
- Move the new object to the appropriate location.
- Paste and move each object you want to add to the control array.

You will copy the Eat In option button and paste it in the Location frame two times to create the Take Out and Delivery option buttons.

To create the remaining objects of the control array:

1. Click the **Eat In** option button to select it.

2. Press **Ctrl+C** to copy the OptionButton object to the Windows clipboard.

3. Click the Location frame to select it.

4. Press **Ctrl+V** to paste the copied option button into the frame.

   A dialog box opens and asks if you want to create a control array.

5. Click the **Yes** button. The copy of the object appears in the upper-left corner of the frame.

6. Drag the new object below the first instance of the Eat In option button, then set the Caption property of the new object to **Take Out**.

7. Repeat Steps 3 through 6 to create the third option button, and set its Caption property to **Delivery**. Your form should look like Figure 3-24.

Figure 3-24 ◀
Creating a control array of option buttons

option buttons in control array

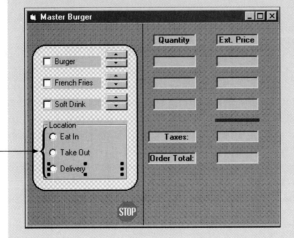

Most objects have an Index property, which contains an integer number that you use with a control array to distinctly identify each member of the control array. You will use the Index property to identify the three option buttons on your form.

To view the Index property values for the three option buttons:

1. Click the **Eat In** option button to select it. In the Properties window, note that the value of the Index property is 0. When you write the necessary code, you will reference this object with the name optLocation(0).

2. Repeat Step 1 for the other two option buttons and observe the Index property values of 1 and 2. You will reference these objects as optLocation(1) and optLocation(2), respectively.

You need to make sure that all the option buttons are in the correct container, fraLocation. Rather than using the Print method in the Debug window, you can simply run the program and click each button. If the buttons are correctly contained in the frame, only one button from the group will be active at a time.

To verify the option buttons' container:

1. Start the program.

2. Click each option button. When one button is selected, the other two buttons should be blank.

   TROUBLE? If you can click more than one option button at a time, the buttons are probably in a different container object from fraLocation. Click the Break button ▮▮ on the toolbar, then type the following statements into the Debug window.

   ```
   print optLocation(0).Container.Name
   print optLocation(1).Container.Name
   print optLocation(2).Container.Name
   ```

   In each case, the computer's response should be fraLocation.

   If any option button is not contained in fraLocation, delete that option button. Click one of the option buttons contained in the frame, then press Ctrl+C to copy it to the clipboard. Click the frame to select it, then press Ctrl+V to paste the copied button into the frame.

3. End the program, then save it.

Moving a Group of Controls

Gill wants the program to include additional Label objects to reflect delivery charges. Before creating these objects, you first need to relocate several objects already on the form, but you do not want the position of these objects, relative to each other, to change. Just as you selected several objects and set their properties as a group, you can move objects as a group. First you must select the object, either by clicking each object while holding down the Shift key, or using the mouse to draw a rectangle around the objects. Which selection method you use depends on where the objects are positioned on the screen, and on your personal preference.

You need to select and move the two Taxes labels and the two Order Total labels to make room for the labels relating to delivery charges.

To reposition the Taxes and Order Total labels:

1. Position the pointer above and to the left of the label with the caption Taxes.

2. Click and hold down the mouse button, then move the pointer down and to the right to draw a rectangle around the objects. When the rectangle encloses all four Label objects release the mouse button. Each selected object has gray handles. See Figure 3-25.

Figure 3-25 ◄
Selecting a
group of
objects

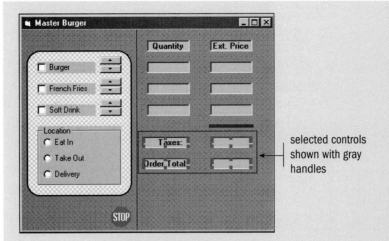

selected controls
shown with gray
handles

Now that the objects are selected, you can move all of them at the same time.

3. Click inside any one of the objects and hold down the mouse button.

4. Move the pointer toward the bottom of the form while holding the mouse button down. An outline of the object group moves as you move the mouse.

5. Release the mouse button when the object group is in the correct position, as shown in Figure 3-26.

Figure 3-26 ◄
Moving a group
of objects

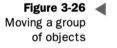
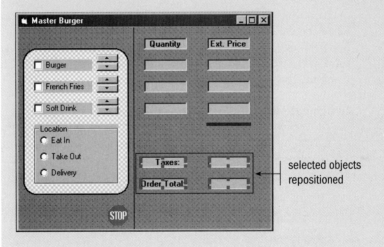

selected objects
repositioned

6. Click anywhere on the form to deselect the group of labels.

Now you have room on the form to create the additional labels to be used for delivery charges. The new labels should look like the Taxes and Order Total labels, so you will check the values for the Alignment, Font, and BorderStyle properties of the existing labels, then set the properties of the new labels to match them.

To add the new labels to the form:

1. Click the **Taxes** label. In the Properties window, note that the value for the Alignment property is set to 1 - Right Justify, the Font property is set to Bold, and the BorderStyle property is set to 1 - FixedSingle.

2. Click the **lblTaxes** object. In the Properties window, note that the value for the Alignment property is set to 1 - Right Justify and the BorderStyle property is set to 1 - FixedSingle.

3. Create a label above the Taxes label and change its Caption property to **Delivery:** Set its Alignment property to **1 - Right Justify**, its Font property to **Bold**, and its BorderStyle property to **1 - FixedSingle**.

4. Create a Label control above lblTaxes and change its Name to **lblDelivery**. Set its Alignment property to **1 - Right Justify**, its BorderStyle property **to 1 - FixedSingle**, and delete its Caption property value. Your form should look like Figure 3-27.

Figure 3-27 ◄
Delivery
objects

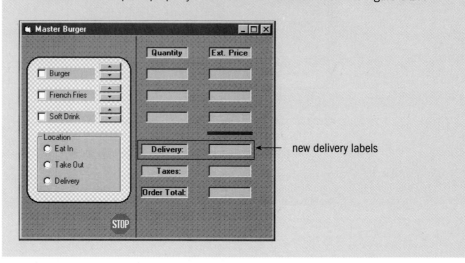

new delivery labels

According to Gill's design specifications, the taxes and order total must be updated when the value of lblDelivery changes. Recall that the ComputeTotals general procedure updates the taxes and total each time any extended price changes. To update the taxes and total when the delivery charge changes, the lblDelivery_Change event must call the ComputeTotals general procedure.

To compute the total when the delivery label changes:

1. Type the following code in the Code window for the lblDelivery_Change event procedure:

```
Private Sub lblDelivery_Change()
    ComputeTotals
End Sub
```

2. Close the Code window.

Now ComputeTotals will update the taxes and order total whenever the delivery charge changes. You are now ready to write the code for the option buttons.

Select Case Statements and Option Buttons

The option buttons on the cash register program should trigger a delivery charge if the order will be delivered or a discount if the order will be eaten in the restaurant. No surcharge or discount will be applied if the Take Out option button is clicked. The delivery charge is $1.50 for each delivery; the discount for orders eaten in the restaurant is 50¢ per order.

Earlier you used an If statement to test a condition and execute one set of statements when the condition was true and another set when the condition was false. Sometimes the decision to be made has more than two possible outcomes. For example, you now need to make a decision with three outcomes—an order will be eaten in the restaurant, taken out, or delivered. In a situation where the decision to be made requires three or more choices, you can use one of two different statements: an If statement or a Select Case statement.

The If statement for this situation has the following syntax:

If *condition1* **Then**
    statement-block1
ElseIf *condition2* **Then**
    statement-block2
ElseIf *condition-n* **Then**
    statement-block-n
[**Else**
    [*statements*]]
End If

- If *condition1* is True, the statements contained in *statement-block1* up to the ElseIf clause are executed, then the entire If statement exits whether or not any of the other *conditions* are True.

- If *condition2* is True, the statements contained in *statement-block2* up to the next ElseIf clause are executed. Again, the entire If statement exits whether or not any of the remaining *conditions* are True.

- The statement block following successive ElseIf clauses is executed depending on whether or not the condition is True or False.

- If none of the conditions are True, the statements inside the Else clause are executed, then the If statement terminates. The Else clause is optional.

Figure 3-28 illustrates how this type of If statement works by examining where an order will be eaten.

Figure 3-28 ◄
Analyzing the If statement

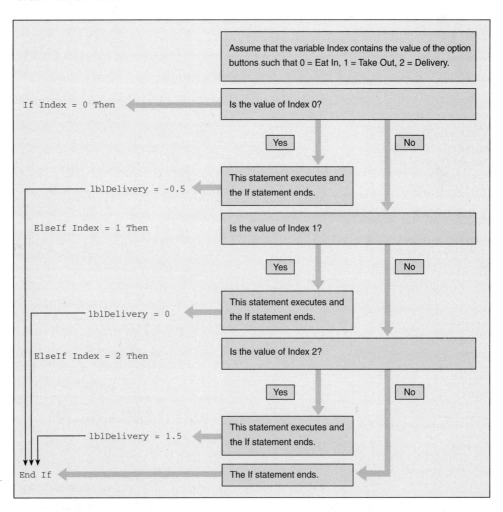

In circumstances where an ElseIf condition in an If statement uses the same expression and compares it to a different value, the Select Case decision structure can both simplify program logic and make a program more readable. **Select Case** statements are like If statements, but instead of testing multiple expressions, the Select Case statement tests only one expression and executes different statements based on the results of the expression. The following is the syntax of a Select Case statement:

Select Case *testexpression*
Case *expressionlist1*
     block1-statements
Case *expressionlist2*
     block2-statements
Case *expressionlist3*
     block3-statements
[**Case Else**
     [*else-block-statements*]]
End Select

- Visual Basic uses the Select Case statement by evaluating the *testexpression* when the Select Case statement first starts. It then compares the *expressionlist1* with the *testexpression*. If they are the same, the statements in *block1* are executed, then the entire statement terminates. If they are not the same, the *expressionlist2* is compared with the *testexpression*. This process is repeated until there are no more expressions to be tested.

- If no expression matches the *testexpression*, the statements in the Case Else clause are executed. The Case Else clause is optional.

- If more than one *expressionlist* is the same as the *testexpression,* only the statements in the first matching Case are executed.

- The *expressionlist* can be a list of values—such as 6,7,8—delimited with commas. It can also be a range of values separated by the word To, as in 5 To 10. Refer to Visual Basic online Help for more information on the Select Case statement.

Figure 3-29 shows the If statement from Figure 3-28 written as a Select Case statement.

Figure 3-29
Analyzing the
Select Case
statement

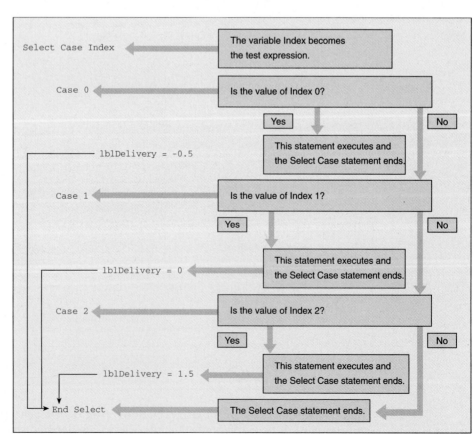

The code in Figure 3-29 will execute more quickly than the code in Figure 3-28, because Visual Basic only needs to check the Index once for the Select Case, rather than for each If and ElseIf. In addition, this Select Case statement will make your program easier to read than the longer If statement.

Using the Select Case Statement with a Control Arrays

You now need a way to check which option button is clicked and write a Select Case statement to update the delivery charges accordingly. In the option button control array, a specific option button is identified by its Index property. Visual Basic also uses the Index property with an argument in the event procedure to indicate which object in the control array is active. Instead of sending an argument from a procedure, as you have done when calling functions like Val, your event procedure will receive an argument, just as the Val procedure receives and processes arguments.

Like variables, an argument has a name and a data type, which are shown in the declaration for the argument. Figure 3-30 shows the argument for the optLocation_Click event procedure.

Figure 3-30 ◀
Argument in
the event
procedure

argument name

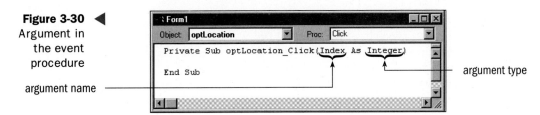

argument type

Notice that the syntax of the argument looks like a Dim statement. It contains a variable name, Index, and an As clause followed by a data type, Integer. Visual Basic stores the Index of the active option button as a local variable so that you can use it in the event procedure. If you have more than one option group on a form, each option group uses the same local variable, Index. This is the method of communicating information from one procedure to another or, in this situation, having the system communicate information to your procedure. If the Eat In option button is clicked, Visual Basic will set the Index property to 0; if the Take Out option button is clicked, Visual Basic will set the Index property to 1; and if the Delivery option button was clicked, Visual Basic will set the Index property to 2. This is how Visual Basic keeps track of and shares code among the control array's objects.

You will use this information to determine where an order will be eaten and to assign the delivery charge or restaurant discount by writing the necessary Select Case statement in the Code window for the control array's Click event.

To write the Select Case statement to assign the necessary discount or delivery charge:

1. Activate the Code window for the optLocation_Click event procedure and enter the following code:

```
Private Sub optLocation_Click(Index As Integer)
    Select Case Index
    'Eat In
    Case 0
        lblDelivery.Caption = -0.50
    'Take Out
    Case 1
        lblDelivery.Caption = 0
    'Delivery
    Case 2
        lblDelivery.Caption = 1.50
    End Select
End Sub
```

This sequence of statements works by first evaluating the value of Index, and then executing the statements for the respective case. So, if the value of Index is 0 (an eat-in order), then the caption of lblDelivery is set to -0.50 (the 50¢ promotional discount). If the value of Index is 1 (a takeout order), then the caption of lblDelivery is set to 0 (no discount or charge applied). If the value of Index is 2 (a delivered order) then the caption of lblDelivery is set to 1.50 (the delivery charge program).

The cash register program now calculates the extended prices for the Burger, French Fries, and Soft Drink items, calculates the taxes and order total in the ComputeTotals general procedure, and indicates a delivery charge or promotional discount for the order, if appropriate. The program must also include the delivery charge or promotional discount in the ComputeTotals general procedure so that each of these items is factored into the order total.

To update the ComputeTotals general procedure:

1. Activate the Code window for the ComputeTotals general procedure.

2. Change the line that computes the order total as shown (type the statements in bold):

```
lblTotal.Caption = TmpSubtotal + PERCENTTAX * _
    TmpSubtotal + Val(lblDelivery.Caption)
```

You have reached another milestone in your program. You should now check that the Location option buttons and Delivery and Order Total labels work correctly.

To test the Location option buttons and Delivery and Order Total labels:

1. Start the program.

2. Click each of the option buttons in the Location control array.

   The Delivery and Order Total labels change with each option button clicked.

3. End the program, then save it.

Displaying a Multiline Message in a Message Box

To prevent the program from ending if a clerk accidentally clicks the stop sign image, Gill wants the program to display a message in a message box asking the clerk to confirm ending the program. The message box will include a Yes button for ending the program and a No button for not ending it.

After the clerk clicks either button, the program can use an If or Select Case statement to test the value returned by the MsgBox intrinsic function and determine which button was clicked. Based on the returned value, the clerk can either continue using the cash register program or exit it. The **MsgBox** function accepts arguments to control the message displayed in the box (prompt), any icons that can be displayed (buttons), and the caption for the message box (title). The MsgBox function has the following syntax:

MsgBox(*prompt*[, *buttons*][, *title*])

- The *prompt* is a string expression that controls the text displayed in the message box. The maximum number of characters allowed in a prompt is 1024.

- The *buttons* argument is a numeric expression using intrinsic constants that define the behavior of the message box. You use these constants by adding one constant from each of three groups (decribed later in this section).

- The *title* appears in the title bar of the message box.

Gill suggests that you use the online Help system to learn more about the MsgBox function.

To view information about the MsgBox function using Help:

1. Click **Help** on the menu bar, then click **Search for Help On**.

2. Type **MsgBox function** in the top text box of the Help Topics dialog box.

3. Scroll down and look at the constants used for the button argument settings. Do not close the Help window.

The first group of constants, those with the values 0 through 5, determines how many buttons appear in the message box and the contents of those buttons.

Inside the message box, you can include one of several different icons to help communicate the importance of the message. The second group of constants, those with the values 16 through 64, describes the corresponding icons.

You can use one of three constants to define which button is the default. The button assigned as the default can be activated by pressing the Enter key as an alternative to clicking the button. These constants are named vbDefaultButton1, vbDefaultButton2, and vbDefaultButton3. They correspond to the first, second, and third buttons in the message box. If a default button does not make sense in your program, do not set this default value.

Finally, you can include a title for the message box, which works in the same way as the form's Caption property.

One of the capabilities of a message box is to display descriptive text in the region of the box itself. This text is sent to the MsgBox function as an argument. You can create the argument for the text using a string variable.

Creating a String Variable

Up until now, you have not created a variable to contain text. The data type for a variable that contains text is String. Just as you can perform arithmetic operations on numbers, you can also perform operations on text strings. For example, you can append the contents of one string to another. This process is called **concatenation**. You concatenate strings together using the ampersand (&) operator.

There are also several Visual Basic functions that operate on strings. The **StrComp** function compares two strings and returns a value indicating if the strings are the same or different. The **StrConv** function is used to make all of the letters in a string either uppercase or lowercase; this function can also capitalize the first letter of each word in a string.

All characters that you use have a numeric code associated with them. For example, the letter "a" is represented by one number, and the letter "A" is represented by a different number. There are also codes for characters that are not displayed on the screen. For example, a line feed character, represented by the number 10 causes the cursor to advance to the first column of the next line. You can use the line feed character to display a descriptive message as multiple lines of text.

To use these numbers as characters in a string, you must use the string function called **Chr**. For example, the following code declares a string variable Var1 that stores text in it.

```
Dim Var1 As String
Var1 = "You are about to exit the Cash Register." & _
    Chr(10) & "Are you sure you want to do this?"
```

Var1 is the variable of data type String. The next statement sets the value of the variable Var1. The sentence enclosed in the first set of quotation marks will appear first in the message box, then the concatenation character, &, adds the line feed character, Chr(10), to the string of text. The text within the second set of quotation marks will appear on a new line of text; this text is also joined by the concatenation operator.

Now you're ready to write the code for the message box that will appear when a clerk clicks the stop sign to exit the cash register program. The message box will ask for confirmation to exit the program.

To add a message box to the cash register program:

1. Close the Help window.

2. Open the Code window for the imgEnd_Click event procedure and enter the following code:

```
Private Sub imgEnd_Click()
    'Create arguments for MsgBox function.
    Dim Ans As Integer
    Dim Prompt As String
    Dim Attributes As Integer
    Dim Title As String

    'Set the values for the arguments.
    Prompt = "You are about to exit the cash register." & _
        Chr(10) & "Are you sure you want to do this?"
    Attributes = vbYesNo
    Title = "Master Burger"

    'Call the MsgBox function.
    Ans = MsgBox(Prompt, Attributes, Title)

    'Test which button the user clicked.
    If Ans = vbYes Then
        End
    End If
End Sub
```

The local variables will contain the returned value and arguments in preparation for calling the MsgBox function. Then the prompt value is the two-line text string, which includes the concatenation operator and the line feed character.

```
Attributes = vbYesNo
```

The Attributes argument creates a message box with a Yes button and a No button. The Title statement sets the title of the message box to Master Burger.

Finally, the MsgBox function is called and the returned value is tested to find out which button the user clicked.

You have now completed the development of the prototype cash register program. Gill asks you to test the program a final time to make sure the message box works properly.

To test the final cash register program:

1. Start the program.

2. Enter an order into the register.

3. End the program by clicking the stop sign image. The message box in Figure 3-31 opens.

Figure 3-31 ◀
Message box

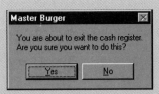

4. Click the **No** button. You return to the cash register program.

   TROUBLE? If the message box does not open, compare the code for the imgEnd object with the code in the previous steps. Make the necessary corrections, then repeat Steps 1 through 4.

5. End the program by clicking the stop sign image.

6. When the message box opens, click the **Yes** button.

7. Save the project to your Student Disk.

Now that you have completed the programming for the cash register, Gill will demonstrate the program to senior management. Once they have approved the program, it will be distributed throughout their 270 stores.

1 What is a frame?

2 What is the relationship between a frame and a group of option buttons?

3 What is the Debug window used for?

4 What is a control array?

5 How do you move a group of objects on a form as a single unit?

6 Describe how message boxes are used in a program.

Figure 3-32 lists and defines the new terms presented in this tutorial.

Figure 3-32 ◀
New Terms

Term	Description
Boolean variable	A Boolean variable is a variable that can have the value True or False.
Concatenation	Concatenation is the process of appending one string to another using the & operator.
Constant	A constant is just like a variable except that its contents cannot change while the program is running.
Container	A container is used to hold information describing objects that are grouped together.
Control array	A control array is a term used to describe multiple objects of the same type that have the same name and event procedure. You reference the members of a control array using the object's name and its Index property.
Debug window	The Debug window can be used in break mode to print the values of variables or the property values of objects in your programs.
General procedure	A general procedure, like an event procedure, contains statements to perform some task. However, unlike an event procedure, a general procedure is not called by the system in response to an event; rather, you must explicitly call a general procedure.
If statement	An If statement is a statement that will allow you to execute one set of statements given one set of circumstances and another set of statements when two circumstances are different.
Index	The Index property is used to reference individual members of a group of objects with the same name.
Message box	A message box is used to open a pop-up message window. The user can click one of several buttons. A message box is displayed on the screen when the MsgBox function is called.
Select Case statement	A Select Case statement is used to test a single condition. Depending upon the result of the test, you can conditionally execute different sets of statements.
String variable	A string variable is a data type that stores one or more characters.

Tutorial Assignments

Each Master Burger franchise has eight tables available for customers to eat their orders in the restaurant. In these Tutorial Assignments, you will create a seating chart program the clerks will use to assign tables to customers. When placing an eat-in order, the clerk assigns an available table to the customer and sets the table status to Occupied. A customer can also phone in to reserve a table. In this case, the clerk would set the table status to Reserved. The default table status is Not Occupied.

When changing a table's status, the clerk can also designate the type of table setting. At Master Burger, table settings include a standard setting, which includes all available condiments. The clerk can also indicate whether the table should be set with water.

In the seating chart program, each table will have a table number from 1 to 8 and will be part of a TextBox control array. The status and setting information will be displayed along with a customer name at each table, so the TextBox control array's MultiLine property will be set to True. Table numbers will be assigned with a vertical scroll bar and displayed in a text box. Finally, the program will include an Exit command button. Figure 3-33 shows the user interface design for the seating chart program.

Figure 3-33 ◀

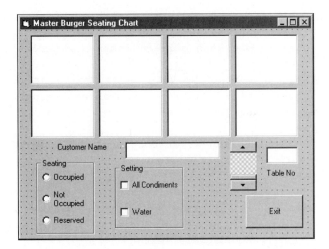

1. Make sure your Student Disk is in the disk drive, then start Visual Basic.
2. Change the form's caption to **Master Burger Seating Chart** and change its name to **frmSeating**.
3. Draw the first of eight text boxes for the Tables control array, then set its properties as follows: Text to **blank**, Name to **txtTable**, and MultiLine to **True**.
4. Copy and paste seven more text boxes for the control array on the form. Be sure that you answer **Yes** in the message box asking if you want to create a control array.
5. Draw a frame in the lower-left corner of the form to hold three option buttons, then set its properties as follows: Caption to **Seating** and Name to **fraSeating**.
6. Draw the first option button of the control array in the frame, then set its properties as follows: Name to **optOcc** and Caption to **Occupied**. Copy and paste the option button to create the remaining two option buttons in the control array. Remember to select the frame before you paste, or the object will be contained by the form rather than the frame. Change the Caption property of the two copied option buttons to **Not Occupied** and **Reserved**, respectively.
7. Draw a frame for the Setting section, then set its properties as follows: Name to **fraSetting** and Caption to **Setting**.
8. Draw a check box in the frame, then set its Caption property to **All Condiments**. Draw another check box in the frame, then set its Caption property to **Water**. Keep the Name property for the two check boxes set to Check1 and Check2, respectively.
9. Draw the text box for Customer Name, then set its properties as follows: Name to **txtCustName** and Text to **blank**.
10. Draw a label to the left of the Customer Name text box, then set its Caption property to **Customer Name**.
11. Draw a vertical scroll bar to the right of the Customer Name text box, then set its properties as follows: Name to **vsbTableNo**, Max to **1**, and Min to **8**, to represent the table number.
12. Draw a label to display the table number, then set its Name property to **lblTableNo**.
13. Draw a label below the Table Number label, then set its Caption property to **Table No.**
14. Draw a command button in the bottom-right corner of the form. Change its Caption property to **Exit**, then write the code for a typical program exit.
15. In Visual Basic Help, look up the SetFocus method. Review and print the topic.
16. Open the Code window for the optOcc_Click event and write the following code, which sets the correct table number and checks the option buttons and check boxes sending the information along with the customer's name to the proper table.

```
'Declare procedure level variable for the table text string
Dim TableString As String
'Clear table with correct index for tables 0-7 and make a
"string
txtTable(vsbTableNo.Value - 1).Text = ""
TableString = "Table " & vsbTableNo.Value
Select Case Index
Case 0
    TableString = TableString & " Occupied By " & _
        txtCustName.Text
Case 1
    TableString = TableString & " Not Occupied"
Case 2
    TableString = TableString & " Reserved By " & _
        txtCustName.Text
End Select
optOcc(Index).Value = False
If Check1.Value = 1 Then TableString = TableString & _
    " All Condiments "
If Check2.Value = 1 Then TableString = TableString & _
    " Water"
txtTable(vsbTableNo.Value - 1).Text = TableString
txtCustName.Text = ""
txtCustName.SetFocus
```

17. Activate the Code window for the vsbTableNo_Click Change event and write the necessary code to place the scroll bar setting in the Table Number label.

18. Test the program by typing a customer name, selecting a table number, selecting a setting, and selecting a seating. When you have corrected any errors and are satisfied that the program works correctly, exit the program using the Exit command button.

19. Examine the code in optOcc_Click. On a piece of paper, write down the purpose of each block of code and describe how it performs its function.

20. The Table Number label does not initially contain a table number. Why is this? Modify the program to display an initial value of 1 in the Table Number label. *Hint:* When does the code in the vsbTableNo_Change event execute?

21. Print the form and the code. Save the project as **Master Burger** in the TAssign folder of the Tutorial.03 folder on your Student Disk. Save the form as **frmSeating** in the same folder.

22. Exit Visual Basic.

Case Problems

1. Easy Carpet Emporium Easy Carpet Emporium stores specialize in low-cost home carpeting. The company would like a carpet selector program that its customers could use to preselect the type, quality, and size of carpeting after looking through the samples in the store. This system will allow Easy Carpet to have only one salesperson on the floor to process the order after it has been entered into the computer by the customer.

In response to a Click event, the carpet selector program will examine the option buttons the customer has checked and then place a text string describing the carpet in a label.

The pseudocode and TOE chart for the carpet selector program are stored on your Student Disk in the Cases folder of the Tutorial.03 folder. First you will print the design specifications and then create a sample program for Easy Carpet to use as a prototype in one of their stores. When you are finished, the program's user interface should look like Figure 3-34.

Figure 3-34 ◀

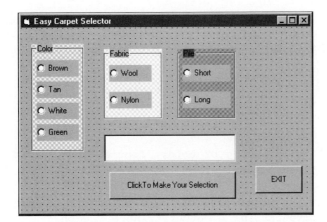

1. Use Notepad or any word processing program to print the pseudocode and the TOE chart stored in the file **Easydes.txt**, which is located in the Cases folder of the Tutorial.03 folder on your Student Disk.

2. Start Visual Basic and begin a new project (if necessary). Set the form's Name property to **frmCarpet** and its Caption property to **Easy Carpet Selector**.

3. Create a frame for the Color options, then set its properties as follows: Name to **fraColor**, Caption to **Color**, and BackColor to **light blue**.

4. Create a control array of four option buttons in the Color frame. Name the option buttons **optColor**, and set the Caption property of the option buttons to **Brown**, **Tan**, **White**, and **Green**, respectively. Make sure that you select the frame after you copy the first option button and before you paste each subsequent option button; otherwise the option buttons will be contained by the form and will not work correctly.

5. Create a frame for the Fabric options, then set its properties as follows: Name to **fraFabric**, Caption to **Fabric**, and BackColor to **light yellow**.

6. Create a control array of two option buttons in the Fabric frame. Name the option buttons **optFabric**, and set the Caption property of the option buttons to **Wool** and **Nylon**, respectively.

7. Create a frame for the Pile options, then set its properties as follows: Name to **fraPile**, Caption to **Pile**, and BackColor to **orange**.

8. In the Pile frame, create a control array of two option buttons. Name the option buttons **optPile**, and set the Caption property to **Short** and **Long**, respectively.

9. Create a text box in the middle of the form to display the customer's selection, then set its properties as follows: Name to **TxtCarpet**, Text to **blank**, and MultiLine to **True**.

10. Create a command button below the text box, then set its properties as follows: Name to **cmdChoice** and Caption to **Click To Make Your Selection**.

11. Draw a command button in the bottom-right hand corner of the form. Change its Caption property to **EXIT**, then write the code for a typical program exit.

12. In the general declarations section of the Code window, declare the variables that will preserve the local variable Index that is passed to each of the option button's procedures. Require that all variables be declared before they can be used in code. Type the following:

```
Option Explicit
Dim IndexColor as Integer
Dim IndexFabric as Integer
Dim IndexPile as Integer
```

13. Open the Code window for the OptColor_Click event and type the following statement, which will preserve the local optColor variable Index as a form-level variable:

```
IndexColor = Index
```

14. Repeat Step 13 for the other two option buttons, using their correct names as defined in the general declarations section.

15. Open the Code window for the cmdChoice_Click event and type the following code:

```
'Declare local string variable
Dim OutputString As String
'Clear TextBox
txtCarpet.Text = " "
'Build string of color, fabric, and pile with saved index of
'each control array
OutputString = "You have selected " _
    & optColor(IndexColor).Caption & " carpet"
OutputString = OutputString & " with " _
    & optFabric(IndexFabric).Caption & " Fabric"
OutputString = OutputString & " and " _
    & optPile(Indexpile).Caption & " pile"
'Move string to TextBox
TxtCarpet.Text= OutputString
```

16. Test the program by clicking the options in the frames and clicking the command buttons.

17. When you have corrected any errors and are satisfied that the program works correctly, click the Exit button. Print the form image and the code. Save the form and save the project as **Easy Carpet** in the Cases folder of the Tutorial.03 folder on your Student Disk.

18. If a customer wanted to select only one or two of the carpet options, how would you change this program? (*Hint:* You could set the options back to False using the form-level index variables. You would also need to change the OutputString code to check if an option was actually selected during the current customer selection.) Change the program to accomplish this, saving the form as **frmcarpet1** and the project as Easy Carpet 1 in the Cases folder of the Tutorial.03 folder on your Student Disk. Print the code and form image.

19. Exit Visual Basic.

2. Nutrition Foods 1 Nutrition Foods franchises allow one group manager to be in charge of up to four franchises. Each group manager receives a commission based on the overall sales of the franchises to which the manager is assigned. Nutrition Foods would like a calculator program to automatically compute the commission for each group manager.

The calculator program will include labels to identify and display the sales for each region, the commission, the total commission, and the total sales; scroll bars to enter the sales amounts in $100 increments; and a command button to exit the program.

The labels identifying and displaying the sales for each region will be in a control array, as will the scroll bars for entering the sales amounts.

Each time a VScrollBar_Change event occurs for any region, the program will automatically recalculate the total commission and the total sales amounts in the appropriate labels. The manager's commission is paid at the following rates:

- For sales < $5000, Commission = 0
- For sales >= $5,000 and ≤ $50,000, Commission = 1% of sales
- For sales > $50,000 and < $250,000, Commission = 2% of sales
- For sales >= $250,000, Commission = 3% of sales

Write the pseudocode, construct a TOE chart, and draw a sample user interface design. Save the pseudocode as **Nutrition Foods Calculator pseudocode**, and the TOE chart as **Nutrition Foods Calculator TOE chart** in the Cases folder of the Tutorial.03 folder on your Student Disk. Print the psuedocode and TOE chart. Label the sample user interface design as **Nutrition Foods Calculator interface design**.

3. Nutrition Foods 2 This Case Problem is an extension to Case Problem 2. For additional details on this program read Case Problem 2. You will now create the interface and write the code for the Nutrition Foods Calculator program.

1. Start a new Visual Basic project.
2. Set the form's Name to **frmGroupCalc** and its Caption to **Nutrition Foods Calculator** and set their properties as follows: Height = **4740**, Left = **1020**, Top = **1065**, and Width = **5895**.
3. Create four labels across the top of the form and set their properties as follows: Height = **288**, Top = **240**, Width = **780**, Caption = **Store 1**, **Store 2**, **Store 3**, and **Store 4**, respectively, and Alignment-**Center**.
4. Create a control array of four labels below the store number labels, and set its properties as follows: Height = **288**, Top = **960**, Width = **780**, Name = **lblRegion**, and Caption = **blank**.
5. Create a control array of four horizontal scroll bars below the label control array and set its properties as follows: Top = **1560**, Width = **780**, Name = **hsbRegion**, Min = **0**, and Max = **10000**. Recall that the Value property of a scroll bar cannot exceed about 32K. Later, you will multiply the scroll bar value by 100 to allow the display and use of larger numbers.
6. Create two identifying labels below the Store 3 column, and set their properties as follows: Left = **3120**, Width = **975**, Caption = **Total Commission** and **Total Sales**, respectively.
7. Create two output labels below the Store 4 column, and set their properties as follows: Left = **4560**, Width = **975**, Caption = **blank** for each, and Name = **lblTotalComm** and **lblTotalSales**, respectively.
8. Create an Exit command button with the appropriate code to end the program in the lower right corner of the form. Resize the form, if necessary.
9. Open the Code window for any hsbRegion object's Change event. Remember the HScrollBar objects share the same name and constitute a control array, so they are all programmed in one Code window. Type the following code:

```
'Define local variables for large number SubTotal and
'commission percent
Dim Subtotal As Long
Dim CommPercent As Single
'Display scroll values in multiples of 100 and sum
lblRegion(Index).Caption = _
    Format((Val(hsbRegion(Index).Value) * 100), "currency")
Subtotal = ((Val(hsbRegion(0).Value)) + _
    Val((hsbRegion(1).Value)) _
    + Val((hsbRegion(2).Value)) + (Val(hsbRegion(3).Value))
    * 100
'Calculate commission
If Subtotal >= 250000 Then
    CommPercent = 0.03
ElseIf Subtotal > 50000 Then
    CommPercent = 0.02
ElseIf Subtotal >= 5000 Then
    CommPercent = 0.01
Else
    CommPercent = 0
End If
lblTotalComm.Caption = Format(Subtotal * CommPercent, _
"currency")
lblTotalSales.Caption = Format(Subtotal, "currency")
```

10. Test the program by clicking each ScrollBar object and observing the results in the Total Commission and Total Sales labels. Verify with a calculator that the commission rules are being applied correctly to the Total Sales amount.

11. When you are satisfied that the program works correctly, click the Exit button. Print the form image and the code. Save the project as **Nutrition Foods** in the Cases folder of the Tutorial.03 folder on your Student Disk.

12. Change the If statement in the hsbRegion code to a Select Case statement. Test the program and save the form as **frmGroupCalc 1** and the project as **Nutrition Foods 1** in the Cases folder of the Tutorial.03 folder on your Student Disk. Print the form image and the code.

13. Exit Visual Basic.

4. Ms. Phillip's Grading Calculator Program. Case Problem 3 of Tutorial 2, discusses the design specifications for a grading calculator program for one of your former teachers, Ms. Phillip's. Ms. Phillip's wants a program that will take in the name of a student and the student's three test scores from the term. The program will then calculate the average score and assign a letter grade based on the following ranges: A >= 90, B = 79 to 89, C = 69 to 78, D = 59 to 68, F < 59. Create the calculator program using the Select Case statement to assign a letter grade based on the average. Display the result in a label in response to the Click event for a Calculate command button. Include a Print button to print the form using the PrintForm method. Use Visual Basic online Help for more information on the PrintForm method. Also include a Clear button to clear the text and captions of all the necessary objects before the input of data for another student, set the focus back to the student name, and code an Exit button. The code for the Exit button should display a Message Box asking Ms. Phillip's if she wants to exit the program. Check to ensure that your input objects have the correct tab order. Print the form image and the code. Save the form as **frmMs. Phillip's** and the project as **Ms. Phillip's** in the Cases folder of the Tutorial.03 folder on your Student Disk.

TUTORIAL 4

Creating a Program to Manage Data

Developing a Contact Management System for the
Atlantic Marketing Group

OBJECTIVES

In this tutorial you will:

- Set additional properties of controls so that they can interact with a database

- Write Visual Basic code to interact with a database

- Write Visual Basic code that will operate with existing menus

- Create different types of lists with the ComboBox and ListBox controls

- Locate records in a database using a search string

- Write Visual Basic code to detect errors that occur while a program is running

CASE

Atlantic Marketing Group

Atlantic Marketing Group, headquarterd in Egan, Minnesota, has been providing marketing services to all types of companies in the greater Minneapolis/St. Paul area since 1978.

The sales staff members of the Atlantic Marketing Group currently use a paper-based contact management system to keep track of basic information about current and prospective clients. For each client, the staff keeps a record of the interaction between the client and the sales force. The current contact management system consists of a paper form for each client. Each salesperson keeps these forms in a binder sorted by the client's last name, and writes notes on the form describing each interaction with the client. Because Atlantic Marketing now has more than 1000 clients and approximately 2500 prospective clients, the current paper-based system has become slow and burdensome.

Nina Valenza, a programmer for Atlantic Marketing, was asked to develop a program to automate the contact management system. Nina decided to use Visual Basic together with a Microsoft Access database to manage the information. A database makes any program that needs to manage data much simpler to write. The contact management system must be able to store each client's name, telephone number, the salesperson assigned to the client, the reason for adding the client, and the date added—all sorted by the client's last name. The system must operate with any number of clients and be able to find a specific client quickly and easily. A salesperson must be able to add client information, change existing client information, and remove obsolete client information. A salesperson must also be able to write brief notes about the client. Nina has already created the Access database and test data. You will help her complete the contact management system using Visual Basic.

SESSION

4.1

In this session, you will create an instance of the Data control to communicate with an Access database. You will learn how to set additional properties of TextBox objects so that they can display information from the database and store information into the database. You will also learn how to locate, add, update, and delete information in a database using the Data control and its Recordset property.

Viewing the TOE Chart and Pseudocode

Nina planned the contact management system based on the current paper form, which is shown in Figure 4-1.

Contact management form

Figure 4-1 ◀ Contact management form

> **Atlantic Marketing Group**
> **Contact Management Form**
>
> **Last Name:** Allen   **Salesperson Name:** Simone
>
> **First Name:** Mary   **Reason Added:** Referral
>
> **Telephone:** (208) 555-7986   **Date Added:** 3/22/98
>
> Notes:
>
> 3/22/98 Referred by John Alexander. Client sells sporting equipment to the upscale buyer. Looking for a comprehensive marketing program to increase sales to the midrange buyer.
>
> 4/7/98 First meeting with Mary. She wants a preliminary plan and proposal by 5/15.
>
> 5/13/98 Delivered and presented proposal. Will convene with senior management.

The paper form contains a client's name, telephone number, salesperson, reason added, and date added. There are several lines on the form to allow a salesperson to record the interaction between the client and salesperson. Nina has written both the pseudocode and the TOE chart for the contact management system. She suggests that you review the design specifications so that you can familiarize yourself with the project. The pseudocode and TOE chart are stored in the file AMG_TOE.txt on your Student Disk.

To view and print the pseudocode and TOE chart:

1. Start Notepad or any word processing program and make sure your Student Disk is in the disk drive.

2. Open the file named **AMG_TOE.txt** located in the Tutorial.04 folder on your Student Disk.

3. Print the file and exit Notepad or the word processing program.

Look at the pseudocode and TOE chart for the program. Notice that you will create command buttons to add, change, and delete client information in an Access database. To allow Visual Basic to interact with the database and locate records, you will use buttons on the Data control. Keep the pseudocode and TOE chart on hand for reference as you complete the program.

You are now ready to work on the program. You will begin by opening the project file Nina already created. This file is named AMG_CMS.vbp and is stored on your Student Disk.

To open the project file for the contact management system:

1. Start Visual Basic and open the project file named **AMG_CMS.vbp** in the Tutorial.04 folder on your Student Disk. If necessary, click the **View Form** button in the Project window to display the form.

2. Click **File** on the menu bar, then click **Save File As** and save the form as **Atlantic CMS.frm**.

3. Click **File** on the menu bar, then click **Save Project As** and save the project as **Atlantic CMS.vbp**.

As you look at the form, you can see that Nina created most of the Label and TextBox objects needed to display the information contained in the database. She also created a menu that appears at the top of the form. You will create the Salesperson Name, Reason Added, and Find objects in Session 4.2. The completed screen design is shown in Figure 4-2.

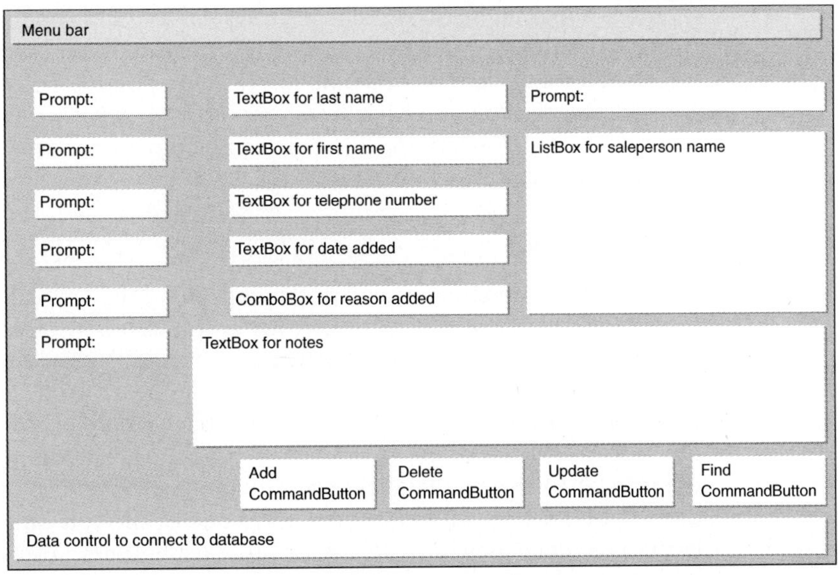

Figure 4-2 ◄
Completed
screen design

Understanding How Visual Basic Uses a Database

Before you can complete the program, you need to understand what a database is and how Visual Basic objects interact with a database. A **database** is a set of information related to a particular topic or purpose. Information is stored inside a database in a table. A **table** consists of rows and columns. The column defines a name for the information that is stored and the characteristics for the information. The columns in a table are called **fields**. In the database Nina created fields to hold the information. Last Name, First Name, Telephone Number, Date Added, and Notes are the fields in the Contacts table. The actual information in the table Nina created is stored in the rows. The rows in a table are called **records**. Figure 4-3 shows the six rows (records) and column names (fields) in the table. So that she could test the program, Nina entered six records as test data.

Figure 4-3 ◀
Database fields
and records

six records ──▶

four fields

Modern databases, or database management systems (DBMS), allow multiple users to access the information contained in the database at the same time. If two users add records at the same time, the DBMS keeps track of each request without causing an error or losing either user's information. When you are working in Visual Basic and Windows 95, the **Microsoft Jet database engine** is the DBMS that retrieves data from and stores data in an Access database. A database can organize and store information so that it can be viewed and retrieved based on the needs of a particular user. For example, the contact management system represents only part of the data that Atlantic Marketing needs to manage. Another component of the company's data is its billing system. If information about delinquent accounts could be accessed by the contact management system, a salesperson could discuss any payment problems with the client before agreeing to any future sales. Most databases in use today are **relational**; that is, information is contained in several tables that can be related together in different ways. In other words, billing transactions are stored in one table, and contact information is stored in another.

A relational database management system (RDBMS) allows you to define the relationships between different pieces of information. The use of an RDBMS to manage large volumes of data has become increasingly popular as the software technology has evolved and the computer hardware has become fast enough to run this complex software effectively. A relational database can be thought of as a set of tools to manage data on a computer.

Using the Data Control to Open a Database

Before you can communicate with the database Nina created, you need to connect your form to the database. There are two ways to interact with a database from a program. One way is to write Visual Basic statements that will access a database; the other is to use the **Data control** in the toolbox, which provides access to data stored in a database. The Data control enables you to move from record to record and to display information inside other controls created on the form. By setting the properties of the Data control you can use it to perform most database operations—retrieving data, changing data, adding new data, finding data—without writing any code at all. You cannot use the Data control to create new databases, only to connect to existing ones. You can create your own databases using Access or the Standard and Professional editions of Visual Basic.

You need to create a Data control to establish communication with the database Nina created. The standard prefix for a Data control is "dat."

To create the Data control:

1. Click the **Data** control 🔲 on the toolbox and draw an instance of the Data control across the bottom of the form. See Figure 4-4.

Figure 4-4 ◀
Creating the
Data control

caption ——————

Previous Record
button |

First Record button ——

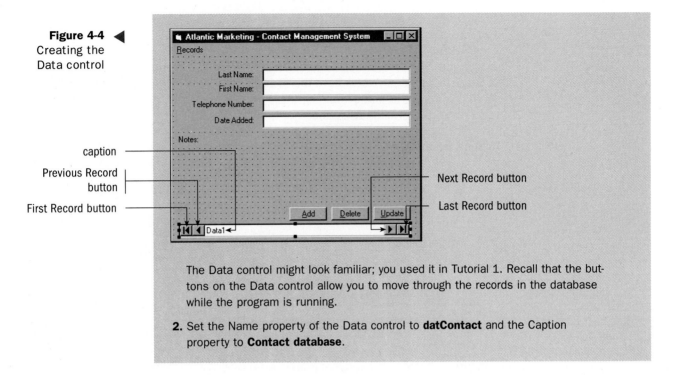

Next Record button

Last Record button

The Data control might look familiar; you used it in Tutorial 1. Recall that the buttons on the Data control allow you to move through the records in the database while the program is running.

2. Set the Name property of the Data control to **datContact** and the Caption property to **Contact database**.

The database Nina created contains the tables and other information you need to complete your program. Although the form now contains an instance of the Data control, it cannot store or display the information in the existing database until you set the necessary properties to connect the Data control to the database.

The properties of the Data control that allow you to communicate with the database are the DatabaseName, RecordSource, and Connect properties.

- The **DatabaseName property** identifies the name and location of the database file.

- The **RecordSource property** identifies the table of the database.

- The **Connect property** provides the information about the source of the database. The Data control can operate with Access, dBASE, FoxPro, and Paradox databases using the Connect property.

When you set these properties, the Data control creates the necessary objects to access the database at run time.

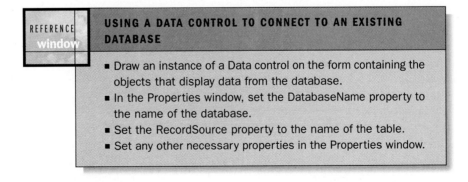

REFERENCE
window

USING A DATA CONTROL TO CONNECT TO AN EXISTING DATABASE

- Draw an instance of a Data control on the form containing the objects that display data from the database.
- In the Properties window, set the DatabaseName property to the name of the database.
- Set the RecordSource property to the name of the table.
- Set any other necessary properties in the Properties window.

The order in which you set the Data control properties is important. You must select the database (DatabaseName property) before you select the table (RecordSource property). Then, when you set the RecordSource property, Visual Basic connects to the database and shows you a list of its available tables. The Connect property is set to Access by default. Databases created in Access have the filename extension .mdb (Microsoft database). The file that contains the contact management test database is named AMG_CMS.mdb and is stored in the Tutorial.04 folder on your Student Disk.

To connect the Data control to the contact management database:

1. Open the Properties window for the Data control you just created.

2. Click the value column of the **DatabaseName** property.

3. Click the **Properties** button ⋯ and set the value to **A:\Tutorial.04\AMG_CMS.mdb**.

4. Make sure the value of the Connect property is **Access**. The Properties window should look like Figure 4-5.

Figure 4-5 ◀
Setting the
DatabaseName
and Connect
properties

Data control ──

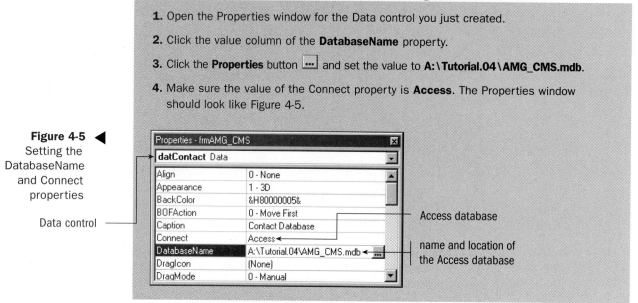

Now you have established a connection with the database for the contact management system. You have identified the database you want to use; now you need to identify the database table you want. To do so, you set the RecordSource property to a table that already exists. The RecordSource property Properties button displays a list of available tables in the database from which you can select the table you need. The table for the contact management system is named tblContact. Just like the other objects you have created, database objects have standard prefixes so that you can easily identify the type of object. The standard prefix for a table object is "tbl."

To view the available tables in the AMG_CMS database and set the RecordSource property:

1. Click the value column of the **RecordSource** property, then click the **Properties** button ▾ to display the list of tables, then click **tblContacts**. Your Properties window should look like Figure 4-6.

Figure 4-6 ◀
Setting
RecordSource
property

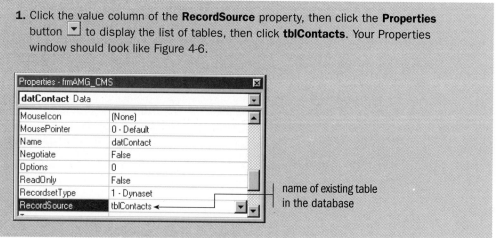

TROUBLE? If no information appears when you click the Properties button for the RecordSource property, then the database is not selected properly. Verify that the DatabaseName property is set to the correct path and filename, A:\Tutorial.04\AMG_CMS.mdb, and that the file exists on your Student Disk. Then repeat Step 1.

Note that the RecordsetType property has a default setting of 1-Dynaset.

2. Click the **Properties** button ⏷ for the RecordsetType property to see the other options this property.

You identified the database and the table to which the Data control will connect by setting the DatabaseName and RecordSource properties. If you run the program now, the TextBox objects on the form would be blank. Your next task is to specify which information you want to display in the text boxes.

The Data control uses the RecordsetType property to determine what operations can be performed on information from one or more tables. By default, the RecordsetType property is set to 1-Dynaset. A **dynaset** can be thought of as a dynamic view of the information contained in the database tables. You can create dynasets to view certain rows and columns from one or more tables, depending on the needs of the program.

The Data control indirectly sets the Recordset property. This property is not set at design time using the Properties window. Thus, it does not appear in the Properties window. Rather, the Data control uses the Connect, DatabaseName, RecordSource, and RecordsetType properties to set the Recordset property at run time. At run time, the Recordset object is stored in the Recordset property of the Data control. You use the Recordset object at run time to locate different records and to add, change, and delete records.

The Recordset Object

When you set the properties of the Data control, it uses that information to set the Recordset property to a Recordset object at run time. When the Connect, DatabaseName, RecordSource, and RecordsetType properties are set, a Database object and a Recordset object are indirectly created by the Data control. A **Database object** allows the program to communicate with the underlying database.

A **Recordset object** is a view of the data stored in the database. When you look at records stored in the Recordset object, only one record can be active at a time. The **current record pointer** indicates the active record in an open Recordset object. You do not access the current record pointer explicitly. Rather, you move the current record pointer indirectly using the Recordset object.

You can find out if the current record pointer is at the beginning or end of the database file using the BOF and EOF properties of the Recordset object. These two run-time properties can be either True or False. When the current record pointer is just before the first record, BOF is True. When the pointer is positioned just after the last record, EOF is True.

When you ran the clients database in Tutorial 1, you used the buttons on the Data control to move the current record pointer of the Recordset object. The buttons on the Data control call a procedure that acts on the Recordset object. A procedure that acts on an object is called a **method**. Figure 4-7 illustrates how a Recordset object is created and shows some of its properties and methods.

Figure 4-7 ◄
The Recordset
object

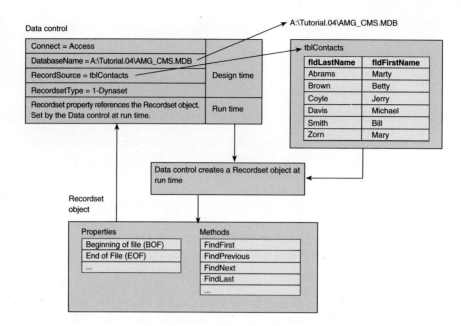

By setting the Connect, DatabaseName, RecordSource, and RecordsetType properties at design time, the Data control will be able to retrieve information from the table named tblContacts at run time. It does this by creating a Recordset object and storing the object in the Recordset property of the Data control at run time. Once the Recordset object is created, you can locate records and perform other operations.

Objects and Their Methods

An object is made up of properties, events, and methods. A method is a Visual Basic procedure that acts on a particular type of object. The methods of an object contain code that is built inside the object to accomplish a task. Consider a television's remote control as an object. The remote control is capable of a specific number of methods, or actions, such as changing a channel or adjusting the volume. You could use the ChannelUp and ChannelDown methods to set the CurrentChannel property. Likewise you can call the MovePrevious and MoveNext methods of the Recordset object to navigate through different records and set the current record pointer. Methods supply functionality to an object.

The Data control simplifies the process of working with a Recordset object, by providing buttons that navigate through the records of the Recordset object. The Data control also has methods that allow you to change the data in the Recordset object. However, there are limitations to the Data control. For example, it does not support a method to remove a record from a Recordset object. To do this you need to call the methods of the underlying Recordset object. Remember, this object is stored in the Recordset property of the Data control. You will now use the Data control's methods and the Recordset object's methods to navigate through the records in the database. Because several methods are built into the Data control, you can accomplish most tasks with just a few lines of Visual Basic code. Figure 4-8 compares some methods of the Data control with methods of the Recordset object, stored in the Recordset property of the Data control.

Figure 4-8 ◀
Data control
and Recordset
object methods

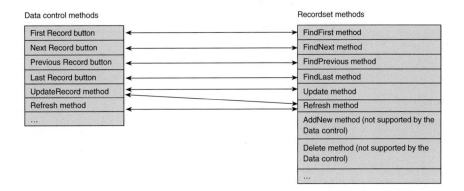

So that you can see the methods applicable to the Recordset object, Nina suggests that you look at the Help system.

To view the methods that pertain to the Recordset object and the Data control:

1. Click **Help** on the menu bar, then click **Search For Help On**.

2. Type **Recordset** in the first text box. Press the **Enter** key.

3. Click **Recordset Object**, **Recordsets Collection** in the Topics Found window. Click **Display**.

4. Click **Methods** at the top of the screen to view the applicable methods.

5. Repeat Steps 2 and 3 using the **Data** control as the Help entries.

6. Click **Methods** at the top of the screen to view the applicable methods.

The methods of the Recordset object operate on data in the database. For example, you can locate records in the database using the following four methods:

- The FindFirst method locates the first record in the Recordset object.

- The FindLast method locates the last record in the Recordset object.

- The FindNext method locates the next record in the Recordset object.

- The FindPrevious method locates the previous record in the Recordset object.

These four methods are not explicitly supported by the Data control. The Data control allows you to click buttons located on the control to perform the same tasks without writing any code. In essence, it calls the methods for you.

Using Bound Controls

If you run your program now, the text boxes will still be blank. You need to get the database information into the TextBox objects that Nina has already created on the form. No code needs to be written to accomplish the task. All you need to do is set some new properties for each TextBox object and they will display information from the database.

The TextBox objects on your form are similar to those you created in previous tutorials. However, the Text property of these TextBox objects will not be explicitly set in the Properties window or by the code you write in event procedures. Rather, each TextBox control will be **bound** to a specific field in the Recordset object. When a TextBox control is bound to a Recordset object, changes in the current record of the Recordset object are reflected in the TextBox control. Each bound TextBox control corresponds to a field in the Recordset object. Bound controls are often referred to as **data aware** controls.

Text boxes are not the only bound controls in Visual Basic. Other bound controls are the ComboBox and the ListBox. The process of binding a control requires setting properties you have not used yet; these properties are common to all bound controls. When you create a bound controls such as a text box, these properties are always blank; you must set them explicitly.

■ The **DataSource property** of a bound control is set to an instance of a Data control drawn on the same form. To see the list of available choices for this property, you click its Properties button. In the contact management program, this property will be set to datContact.

■ The **DataField property** is set to a field defined by the Recordset object used in the Data control. To see the list of available choices for this property, you click its Properties button. Database fields have the standard object prefix of "fld." By using this standard prefix, you can immediately determine the type of object you are working with.

Figure 4-9 shows the properties used to bind controls to interact with fields in a Recordset object.

Figure 4-9 ◀
Bound controls

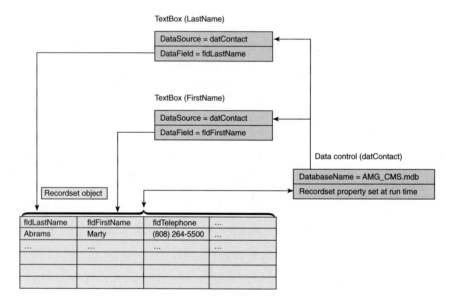

The Data control will establish a connection with a table in a database at run time and set its Recordset property to the Recordset object it created. You can reference the individual fields in the Recordset object by binding a text box to a Data control with the DataSource and DataField properties.

When you create bound controls and set their properties at design time, it is important that you set the properties of the Data control first. If the Data control does not currently reference an existing database and Recordset object, the bound TextBox objects will not be able to establish the connection to the appropriate fields in the database.

The Data control can use TextBox objects as part of a control array or as uniquely named objects. If you use a control array, you still need to set the DataSource and DataField properties for each object in the control array so that each object can communicate with the correct field in the Recordset object. Nina created all the text boxes as a control array to save the time it takes to name objects individually. This is a good practice only when you do not have to write code to reference the objects, or it is desirable for all the objects to share event procedures.

You will set the DataSource property for all the TextBox objects on your form as a group, because they all must be set to datContact, the only Data control on the form. Then you will set the DataField property for each TextBox object to its corresponding field in the Recordset object.

To set the properties for the TextBox objects:

1. Press and hold down the **Shift** key and click all four TextBox objects to select them. Your form should look like Figure 4-10.

Figure 4-10 ◀
Selecting
multiple
TextBox
objects

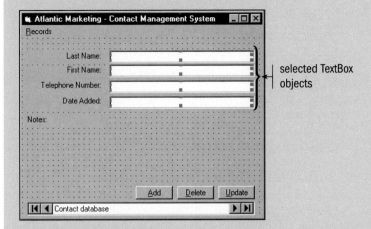

selected TextBox objects

2. In the Properties window, set the DataSource property to **datContact**, the name of the Data control. This is the only available option because there is only one Data control on the form. The Properties window should look like Figure 4-11.

Figure 4-11 ◀
Setting the
DataSource
property

no object displayed
when multiple objects
are selected

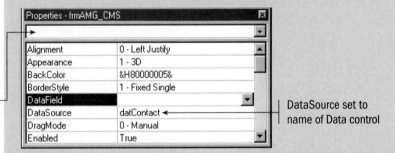

DataSource set to
name of Data control

Just as you have seen in previous tutorials, when you are setting properties for multiple objects, no object is displayed in the Properties window.

3. Click in any blank area of the form to deactivate the selected objects.

4. Click the text box for **Last Name**.

5. Click the Properties button ▼ for the DataField property. Your Properties window should look like Figure 4-12.

Figure 4-12 ◀
Setting the
DataField
property

available fields shown
in list box

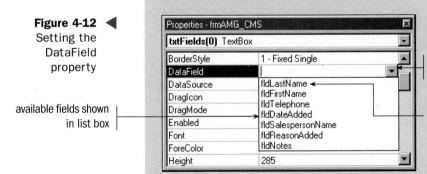

click the Properties
button to see the
fields in the table

click fldLastName

TROUBLE? If clicking the Properties button does not display the fields in the database, the DataSource property is not set correctly. Be sure the DataSource property is set to datContact. Also, be sure the instance of the Data control is connected to the correct database. Check that the DatabaseName property of the Data control is set to A:\Tutorial.04\AMG_CMS.mdb and that the database exists on your Student Disk.

6. In the displayed list of fields, click **fldLastName**.

The text box txtFields(0) is now connected to the field fldLastName in the table tblContacts. When you run your program, the information contained in this record will be displayed in the text box.

7. Click the **FirstName** text box, and then set its DataField property to **fldFirstName**.

8. Click the **Telephone Number** text box, and then set its DataField property to **fldTelephone**.

9. Click the **Date Added** text box, and then set its DataField property to **fldDateAdded**.

The program will now display the appropriate information from a database record in the text boxes when you run the program, and you can move from record to record using the buttons on the Data control. This is a good time to check that the program works, correct any errors, and save the project. When Nina created the database and the table containing the contacts, she designed it so that the table records would appear sorted by last name. So, when you run the program, the records will be displayed alphabetically by last name.

To run and test the program:

1. Start the program. The first record in the Recordset object is displayed. See Figure 4-13.

Figure 4-13 ◀
First record in
the Recordset
object

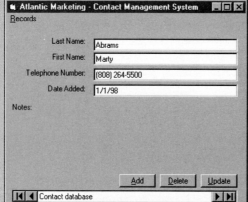

The record for Marty Abrams is displayed because Abrams is the first last name alphabetically in the database.

2. Click the **Next Record** button in the Data control. The form now displays the information for Betty Brown.

3. Click the **Previous Record** button ◀ in the Data control. The form displays the information for Marty Abrams again.

4. Click the **Last Record** button ▶❘ in the Data control. The form displays the information for Mary Zorn.

5. Click the **First Record** button ❘◀ in the Data control. The form displays the information for Marty Abrams again.

6. End the program and then click the **Save Project** button 🔲 on the toolbar to save the form and project files.

The form now connects to the database and displays name, phone number, and date added information in the text boxes. Nina also created a label for notes. The database includes such a Notes field, which contains notes the salesperson writes about interactions with the client. You need to create an object on your form that will hold the several lines of text in the Notes field of the database. You can create a text box to display multiple lines of text if you set three additional properties:

- The **MultiLine property** indicates whether a TextBox object can accept and display multiple lines of text. The default is False. If set to True, the MultiLine property can display multiple lines of text. You can set the MultiLine property only at design time.

- The **MaxLength property** indicates whether there is a maximum number of characters that can be entered in the TextBox object and, if so, specifies the maximum number. If the MaxLength property is set to 0 (the default), there is no maximum number of characters. If the value is not 0, the maximum number of characters is the MaxLength property value.

- The **ScrollBars property** sets a value indicating whether a TextBox control has horizontal or vertical scroll bars that will allow the user to scroll through the contents of the text box. If the property is 0-None (the default), no scroll bars will appear. If the property is set to 1-Horizontal, a horizontal scroll bar will appear across the bottom of the text box. A setting of 2-Vertical displays a vertical scroll bar across the right side of the text box. And, a setting of 3-Both displays vertical and horizontal scroll bars in the text box. You must also set the MultiLine property to True in order to use scroll bars.

Now you need to create a text box that can display multiple lines of text. In case all the text will still not fit in the object, you should also display the text box with scroll bars.

To create a text box to contain the information from the Notes field in the database:

1. Draw a large text box to the right of the Notes prompt on the form. (If necessary, refer back to Figure 4-2 to determine the size and placement of the text box.)

2. Set the Text property of the text box to blank. This setting will cause the text box to be empty initially.

3. Set the DataSource property of the text box to **datContact** and the DataField property to **fldNotes**. This binds the object to a field in the Recordset object.

4. Set the MultiLine property of the text box to **True**.

5. Set the ScrollBars property of the text box to **2 - Vertical**.

Setting these two properties will create a vertical scroll bar on the right side of the text box at run time. Because the Notes object is the fifth text box on the form, it should receive the focus just after the Date Added text box.

6. Set the TabIndex property of the text box to **5**.

All the TextBox objects on the form are now connected to fields in the database. The Notes text box displays information from the fldNotes field in the database, and you can use the vertical scroll bar in the text box to see all the information in that field. Nina suggests that you run the program to test the Notes text box.

To test the Notes text box you just added:

1. Start the program. The information from the first record in the database appears in the form. See Figure 4-14.

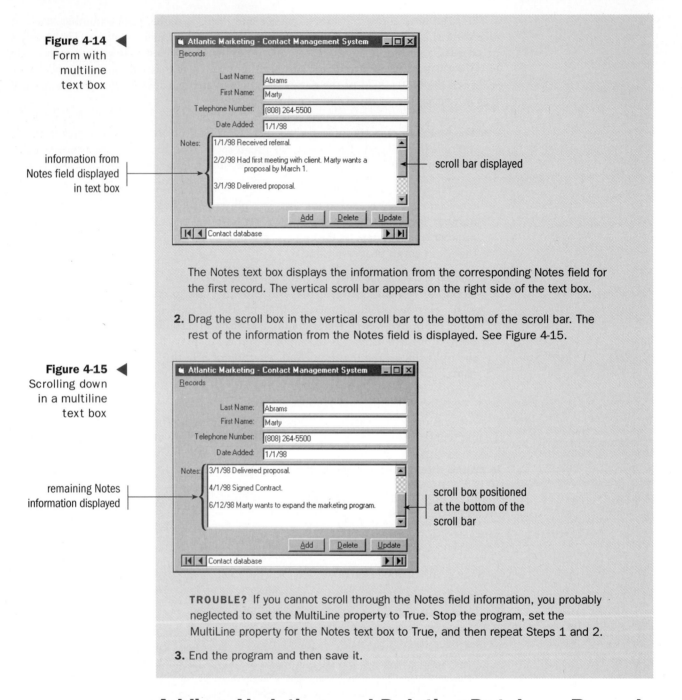

Figure 4-14 ◀
Form with
multiline
text box

information from
Notes field displayed
in text box

scroll bar displayed

The Notes text box displays the information from the corresponding Notes field for the first record. The vertical scroll bar appears on the right side of the text box.

2. Drag the scroll box in the vertical scroll bar to the bottom of the scroll bar. The rest of the information from the Notes field is displayed. See Figure 4-15.

Figure 4-15 ◀
Scrolling down
in a multiline
text box

remaining Notes
information displayed

scroll box positioned
at the bottom of the
scroll bar

TROUBLE? If you cannot scroll through the Notes field information, you probably neglected to set the MultiLine property to True. Stop the program, set the MultiLine property for the Notes text box to True, and then repeat Steps 1 and 2.

3. End the program and then save it.

Adding, Updating, and Deleting Database Records

Several methods that act on the Data control or the Recordset property of the Data control (the Recordset object) allow you to add, delete, and change the contents of the underlying database.

By creating objects on a form and setting the necessary properties, you have created a Visual Basic program that will operate with a database. So far you can only navigate through the records in the Recordset object created by the Data control. Now that your program and its objects are communicating with the database, you can proceed to the next phase of the program's development: providing add, update, and delete capabilities to the user of the program.

Nina has already created several CommandButton objects for these tasks. Notice that the "A" on the Add button, the "D" on the Delete button, and the "U" on the Update button are underlined. These underlined letters on command buttons represent shortcut keys. A **shortcut key** is a function key or key combination that executes a command, for example, pressing the key combination Alt+A will generate the cmdAdd_Click event. To set a shortcut key, you include an ampersand (&) character in the Caption property before the designated letter. The Caption property for the Add button is &Add. A shortcut key is also called a **hot key**. You need to write the necessary Visual Basic statements for each button's Click event procedure to add, update, and delete records in the Recordset object.

Adding Database Records

A Recordset object has methods that allow you to add records to a database. When the **AddNew method** is called, a new blank record is created, which you can then edit. After entering the information for the new record, you need to call the UpdateRecord method to store the record into the database. Updating a database is explained later in this section. The syntax for the Recordset object's AddNew method is:

Object.**AddNew**

- When you call an object's methods, you include a period (.) at the end of the object and then type the name of the method. The AddNew method acts on the Recordset property of the Data control (the Recordset object) and will create an empty database record to be edited.

The RecordsetType property of your Data control is set to Dynaset; therefore, a new record will be inserted at the end of the Recordset object, even if it was sorted. Remember that the Recordset object you are using represents the tblContacts table contained in the database. You need to write the code to add a new blank record to your database when the Add button is clicked.

To write the code to add new database records:

1. Open the Code window for the **cmdAdd** button's Click event procedure.

2. Enter the following code in the window:

```
Private Sub cmdAdd_Click()

    datContact.Recordset.AddNew

End Sub
```

The AddNew method operates on a Recordset object (in this case, the Recordset property of the datContact Data control). When the program calls the AddNew method, a new blank record is created in the Recordset object. A user can then enter data into each of the TextBox objects to identify the new contact for Atlantic Marketing.

Because the Recordset object exists only at run time, you cannot set the Recordset property from the Properties window at design time. Remember, the Data control uses its Recordset property to store the actual Recordset object. You can reference the Recordset object by using Visual Basic code.

Updating Database Records

When you change information in the current record, the contents of the database do not change immediately; instead, the changes are placed in a temporary storage area in the computer's memory called the **copy buffer**. By storing the changes in the copy buffer, you can choose not to update the database if you made an error. After making changes you can save them explicitly using the **UpdateRecord method** of the Data control. Also, if you click a button in the Data control to locate a different record, the Data control will automatically update the record for you. If you move from one record to another by explicitly calling the methods of the Recordset object, such as FindPrevious or FindNext, or if you close the Recordset object without calling the UpdateRecord method, your changes will be lost. Sometimes this is what you want to do. For example, if you make changes to the data and notice a mistake, you can leave the record without saving the changes. The syntax for the UpdateRecord method is:

*Object.***UpdateRecord**

- *Object* must be a valid instance of a Data control. The UpdateRecord method acts on the Data control and writes the changes of a record created by the AddNew method or an edited record to the database.

To put a new record in sorted order, you also need to use the **Refresh method** of the Data control. If you do not call the Refresh method, newly added records will always appear at the end of the Recordset object until the program is run again, causing the Recordset object to be refreshed. The syntax of the Refresh method is:

*Object.***Refresh**

- The Refresh method acts on a Data control or a Recordset object, and reloads the contents of the database information into the Recordset object. When the Refresh method is called, the current record pointer is set to the first record of the Recordset object.

You must include the UpdateRecord and Refresh methods together in the contact management program, because Nina wants each new record added to be stored alphabetically by last name.

To write the code to update and sort the database records:

1. Activate the Code window for the **cmdUpdate** button's Click event procedure.

2. Enter the following code in the window:

```
Private Sub cmdUpdate_Click()

    datContact.UpdateRecord
    datContact.Refresh

End Sub
```

Examine the code you wrote to update the database any time a user adds or changes a record.

```
datContact.UpdateRecord
```

The UpdateRecord method operates on an instance of a Data control (in this case, datContact). When the program calls the UpdateRecord method, the record stored in the copy buffer is saved to the end of the Recordset object and to the underlying table.

```
datContact.Refresh
```

The Refresh method causes the Recordset object to be reinitialized so that it will continue to be in sorted order.

Nina wants you to use the Add and Update buttons to add a new record to the test database to make sure the buttons work correctly.

To use the Add and Update buttons on your form to add a record to the database:

1. Start the program.

2. Click the **Add** button to create a new blank record.

3. Enter the information shown in Figure 4-16.

Figure 4-16 ◄
Adding a record
to the database

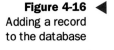

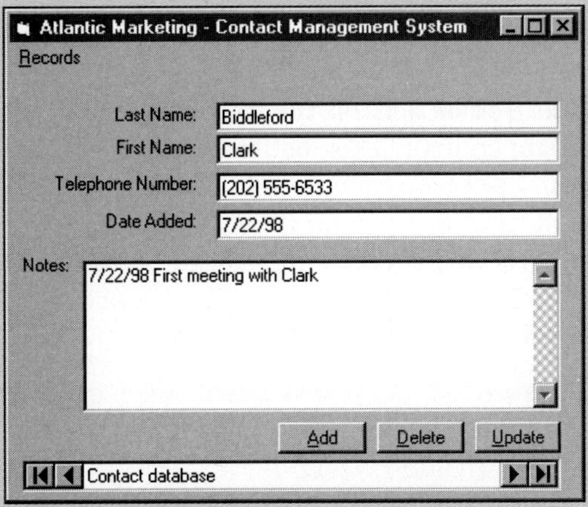

4. Click the **Update** button to save the new record to the database.

   TROUBLE? If you receive a run-time error, you probably tried to update the database without completing all the fields. End the program and then repeat Steps 1 through 4.

   The form displays the information for Marty Abrams again. Recall that the Refresh method sets the current record pointer to the first record in the Recordset object. The database is now in alphabetical order by last name.

5. Click the **Next Record** button in the Data control until you locate the record for Clark Biddleford.

   The new record was added between the records for Marty Abrams and Betty Brown.

6. End the program.

When the program calls the UpdateRecord method of the Data control, the changes are immediately stored in the tblContacts table in the database. This is one of the advantages of using a database rather than storing the information within your program. If the power goes out or the computer crashes, none of the changes made will be lost.

You are now ready to program the last button on the form. The Delete button will allow salespeople to remove obsolete records from the database.

Deleting Database Records

You need to write the necessary statement for the Click event procedure to delete an existing record from the database. To do this, you will use the **Delete method** of the Recordset object stored in the Recordset property of the Data control. Like the AddNew method, the Delete method applies to the Recordset object rather than the Data control itself. The syntax for the Delete method is:

*Object.***Delete**

■ The Delete method is used to delete the current record from a Recordset object, which removes the corresponding row from the underlying database table. When the program calls the Delete method on a Recordset object, a record must be currently displayed in the form.

After the Delete method removes the current record, the current record pointer moves to another record; otherwise, the deleted record will remain on the screen, even though it no longer exists and cannot be edited. Once the current record pointer moves to another record, the deleted record cannot be accessed again. So, when you write the code for the Delete button, you will call the MoveNext method of the Recordset object immediately after the Delete method to reposition the current record pointer to the next record in the database. The syntax for the MoveNext method is:

Object.**MoveNext**

- The **MoveNext method** acts on the Recordset object stored in the Recordset property of the Data control. This method is similar to the Next Record button in the Data control.

Now you will write the code for the Delete button's Click event procedure.

To write the code to delete database records:

1. Open the Code window for the **cmdDelete** button's Click event procedure.

2. Enter the following code in the window:

```
Private Sub cmdDelete_Click()
    datContact.Recordset.Delete
    datContact.Recordset.MoveNext
End Sub
```

The first statement calls the Delete method to delete the current record of the Recordset object. The second statement positions the current record pointer on the next record of the Recordset object. This action provides the user with a visual clue that the deleted record no longer exists.

You can now manipulate information in the database with Visual Basic in addition to navigating through the existing information. You are able to add, update, and delete information with a simple click of a command button. You have reached another milestone in the development of your program, so this is a good time to test the code you have written for the Delete button and save your completed work.

To test the code for the Delete button:

1. Start the program.

2. Click the **Next Record** button ▶ in the Data control once to locate the record for Clark Biddleford.

3. Click the **Delete** button to delete the record. After deleting the record, notice that the form displays the record for Betty Brown, the next record in the Recordset object.

   TROUBLE? If you receive a run-time error, you might have tried to delete a record when no record was displayed in the form. End the program and then repeat Steps 1 through 3.

4. End the program and then save it.

Quick Check

1 What properties does the Data control use to communicate with an existing Access database?

2 What is a bound control and what are the properties used to bind a control to data?

3 What is a Recordset object?

4 What are the properties and the settings for those property values needed to create a text box in which you can display and navigate through multiple lines of text?

5 Describe the methods to add, update, and delete information in a database. Be sure to identify which methods apply to the Data control and which apply to the Recordset object.

Now that you have completed Session 4.1, you can exit Visual Basic or you can continue to the next session.

SESSION

4.2

In this session, you will add commands to an existing menu and create two new bound controls: a ComboBox object and a ListBox object. You will also learn how to locate records using a search string, and how to prevent user errors from crashing a program.

Using a Menu to Mimic a Command Button

Nina knows from experience that a well-designed user interface gives users choices in the way they perform tasks, making users more comfortable with a program. Some users prefer to click buttons whereas others prefer to use menus. By giving users these choices, Nina thinks the program will be accepted more readily by the salespeople.

Nina wants the Records menu in the contact management system to mimic the functionality of the CommandButton objects. So, when a user clicks the Add, Update, and Delete commands on the menu, they should execute the same code as the equivalent command buttons. One way to achieve this would be to create a general procedure and have the equivalent command button and menu event procedures call the general procedure. However, you've already programmed the command buttons. Visual Basic allows you to explicitly call these event procedures, for example, cmdAdd_Click (the Add button's Click event procedure) in another event procedure, by setting the Value property of the command button to True.

You now need to write the statements that will execute when the user selects one of the commands on the Records menu.

To write the code necessary to mimic the command buttons:

1. Open the Code window for the **mnuAddItem** object's **Click** event procedure.

2. Enter the following code in the window:

```
Private Sub mnuAddItem_Click()
    cmdAdd.Value = True
End Sub
```

This statement will call the Click event procedure from the Add button, cmdAdd_Click, when a user selects the Add command on the Records menu.

3. Activate the Code window for the **mnuDeleteItem** object's **Click** event procedure and enter the following code in the window:

```
Private Sub mnuDeleteItem_Click()
    cmdDelete.Value = True
End Sub
```

This statement will call the Click event procedure from the Delete button, cmdDelete_Click, when a user selects the Delete command on the Records menu.

4. Activate the Code window for the **mnuUpdateItem** object's **Click** event procedure and enter the following code in the window:

```
Private Sub mnuUpdateItem_Click()
    cmdUpdate.Value = True
End Sub
```

This statement will call the Click event procedure for the Update button, cmdUpdate_Click, when a user selects the Update command on the Records menu.

The program now allows users to click buttons or menu selections to add, update, and delete records in the database. You should now test the code you just wrote to determine if the menu commands work correctly.

To test the code for the menus commands:

1. Start the program.

2. Click the **Records** menu, then click **Add** to create a new record.

3. Enter the information shown in Figure 4-17.

Figure 4-17 ◄
Add new record

4. Click the **Records** menu, then click **Update** to record the changes.

5. Locate the record for Clark Biddleford, click the **Records** menu, then click **Delete** to remove the record.

6. End the program and then save it.

Using a ComboBox Object to Look Up Information

Nina is faced with a problem. She wants users to enter information into a database table describing why a contact was added so that Atlantic Marketing can track the origin of its new business. There are a few common reasons for adding a contact, including a potential client contacting Atlantic Marketing, a referral from another client, or a call initiated by a salesperson. Because these common reasons account for more than 90 percent of the cases, it would save time if the salespeople did not have to type these reasons into a text box each time a record is added.

Nina considered using a group of option buttons, which would let users select one choice from several choices. But a group of option buttons would not provide a way for the user to enter a choice that is not in the group. The solution to the dilemma is a **ComboBox object**. One type of ComboBox object presents suggested choices to the user and, if none of the choices are appropriate, a user can enter a different choice.

There are three styles of ComboBox objects you can use by setting the object's Style property:

- A Dropdown ComboBox has a Style property setting of 0-Dropdown Combo. This type of combo box allows a user to either select an item from a list of suggested choice or type in a different item. The options do not appear until the user clicks the arrow to the right of the combo box. You will use a Dropdown ComboBox in the contact management system.

- A Dropdown List ComboBox works in the same way as a Dropdown ComboBox, except the user *must* select from the list of values. To create this type of combo box, set the Style property to 2-Dropdown List.

- A Simple ComboBox has a Style property setting of 1-Simple Combo. Instead of providing a drop-down list like the other combo boxes, a Simple ComboBox displays all the choices in the list at all times. Whenever the list will not fit inside the region of the object, a scroll bar is displayed. The user can specify a value for the combo box that is not in the list of suggested choices.

Figure 4-18 shows the different ComboBox objects.

Figure 4-18 ◀
Types of
ComboBox
objects

Dropdown and
Dropdown List
ComboBox objects

Simple ComboBox
object

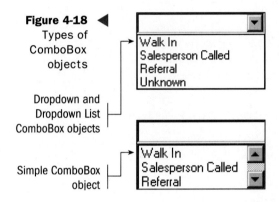

In addition to the Style property, other combo box properties determine how the combo box appears to the user:

- The **List property** specifies the items to be contained in the combo box.

- The **Text property** describes the initial text contained in the combo box when the program is run.

- If the items in the combo box should appear in alphabetical order, the **Sorted property** should be set to True.

- The combo box can be used as a bound control; that is, it can reference a record in a Recordset object by setting the **DataSource** and **DataField properties**. This is identical to the process you used to bind the TextBox objects to the database.

In your program, you will use the combo box only to write information to the database. Before you can add the combo box to your program, you will need to make room on your form.

To make room for new objects on the form:

1. Move the cursor to the lower right edge of the form. When the cursor becomes a ↖, click and drag the form's border down and to the right.

2. Select the Notes label, txtNotes, the three command buttons, and the Data control.

3. Click inside one of the selected objects and drag all the objects to the bottom edge of the form.

4. Click anywhere on the form to deselect all objects.

5. Enlarge txtNotes so that it fills the width of the form.

6. Move the three command buttons to the left.

Your form now has the space for you to add the new objects.

Just as you used the DataSource and DataField properties to bind the TextBox objects to the database, you will set those properties for the Reason Added ComboBox object. The prefix for a combo box is "cbo."

To create the Reason Added ComboBox object for your program:

1. Create a label below the Date Added label on the form and set its Caption property to **Reason Added:**. Set the Alignment property to **1 - Right Justify**.

2. Create a label on the form to the right of the Last Name text box. Set the Caption property of the label to **Salesperson Name:** and the Alignment property to **1 - Right Justify**.

3. Create a command button to the right of the other buttons on your form. Set its Name property to **cmdFind** and its Caption property to **F&ind**. The & character will set the Alt+I key combination as the hot key. That is, pressing Alt + I will have the same effect as clicking the button with the mouse.

4. Click the **ComboBox** control 🖩 on the toolbox and draw an instance of a combo box to the right of the Reason Added label. Set the Name property of the ComboBox object to **cboReasonAdded**. Your form should look like Figure 4-19.

5. Delete the value from the Text property so that the initial combo box will be empty when the program is run.

Figure 4-19 ◀
Creating a
ComboBox
object

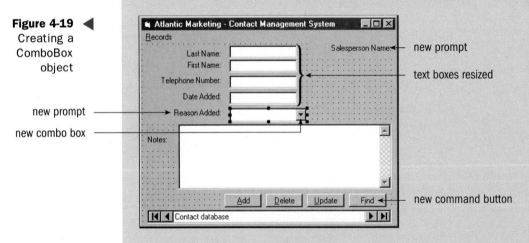

new prompt
new combo box
new prompt
text boxes resized
new command button

6. Set the DataSource property of the ComboBox object to **datContact** and the DataField property to **fldReasonAdded**.

7. Set the Sorted property to **True** so that the items in the combo box will be listed in alphabetical order.

8. Make sure the Style property is set to **0 - Dropdown Combo**.

If you know the list of choices for the combo box at design time, you can specify the items by setting the List property in the Properties window. If not, you can use a method of the combo box called AddItem to store information in the combo box at run time.

The AddItem Method

The **AddItem method** acts on a ComboBox object and is used to add an item to the list of choices for the combo box at run time. The AddItem method has the following syntax:

Object.**AddItem** *"text"*

- *Object* represents any valid combo box.

- The *text* represents the item to be added to the list, which will appear in the combo box when the program is running. So, if you wanted to add five different items to the list, you would call the AddItem method five times with different text strings.

Now that you have created the combo box and set its properties, you can specify the list of suggested reasons for adding a contact. Nina suggests that you use the AddItem method to create the list.

To create the list of choices for the combo box:

1. Open the Code window for the **Form_Load** event procedure.

2. Enter the following code in the window:

```
Private Sub Form_Load()
    cboReasonAdded.AddItem "Walk In"
    cboReasonAdded.AddItem "Salesperson Called"
    cboReasonAdded.AddItem "Referral"
    cboReasonAdded.AddItem "Unknown"

End Sub
```

Next you will run the program to test the ComboBox object.

3. Start the program.

4. Click the list arrow on the ComboBox object to display the choices. The choices are listed in alphabetical order.

5. End the program.

6. Save the form and project.

This code calls the AddItem method to load the four different reasons for adding a contact as separate lines in the combo box. Because you set the Sorted property to True, you can add the items in any order and they will appear alphabetically when the program is run.

The ListBox Control

Atlantic Marketing works on a bonus system. The salesperson whose clients contribute the greatest revenue to Atlantic Marketing receives a year-end bonus. Nina wants the program to keep track of which salesperson is assigned to each client, so that management can determine the bonus recipient. Like the reason added, the salesperson name should be selected from a list of choices. Nina would like all the names of the salespeople to be displayed on the form rather than having to click a list arrow to see the names, because the list is quite short. The user will never enter a name that is not on the list.

There is another control that is similar to a combo box called the **ListBox control**. They share almost the same properties. Instead of displaying items using a drop-down menu, the contents of a list box are always displayed. Also, the user cannot enter new items into a ListBox object. As is the case with a ComboBox object, you can create the list of choices for a ListBox object by setting properties in the Properties window at design time or by calling the AddItem method at run time. Unlike a ComboBox object, a ListBox object cannot take its list items from the database.

You will set the List property at design time, because the list will include the names of only five salespeople. In this case, you must enter the names in alphabetical order by last name. You cannot sort the items by setting the Sorted property to True, because that would sort the items by first name. The standard prefix for a list box is "lst."

To create the ListBox object containing the names of the salespeople:

1. Click the **ListBox** control 🖳 on the toolbox and draw an instance of a list box below the Salesperson Name label (refer to Figure 4-20 for the size of and placement of the list box). Set the Name property of the list box to **lstSalespersonName**.

2. Click the **Properties** button ⏷ to display the List property value, type **Bruce Brown**, then press the **Enter** key. The list closes when you press the Enter key; you need to click the Properties button to add each list item.

3. Repeat Step 2 for each of the following names:
   Cheryl Cantor
   Ray Duncan
   Luisa Simone
   Todd Spangler

   Your form should look like Figure 4-20.

Figure 4-20 ◀
Creating a
ListBox object

completed list box —————

4. Set the DataSource property of the list box to **datContact**.

5. Set the DataField property of the list box to **fldSalespersonName**.

6. Start the program to test the ListBox object.

   Notice that the ListBox object contains the names of all the salespeople, and that the object contains a vertical scroll bar for moving through the list of names. When a user adds a new record or changes an existing record, the user can select a salesperson's name from the list box and store it as part of the client record in the database.

7. End the program and save the form and project.

The program will now allow the user to enter the reason added, and will retrieve from the database and display the name of the salesperson assigned to the client. To make the interface more user-friendly, the program includes command buttons and a menu, allowing users to work with data in the way they prefer. Nina thinks that another way to make the interface more user-friendly is to provide a way for the user to find a record without scrolling through every client entry.

Searching for Records

Nina knows that moving from record to record using the buttons on the Data control is sufficient only when working with a small number of records. But the contact management system will ultimately contain the 3500 client records. The salespeople need to be able to locate a specific record quickly, without scrolling through several hundred or several thousand records to find the one they want.

You can use the **FindFirst method,** which acts on the Recordset object, to locate a specific record, without searching through the records. This is an easy way for the users of the program to find records, and it will be familiar to users because the current paper-based system is organized by last name. The syntax for the FindFirst method is:

*Object.***FindFirst** *criteria*

- The *Object* can be any valid Recordset object.

- The *criteria* defines which records in the database will be located. If several records match the criteria, the first record found will become the active record.

- You can use the **FindNext method** after the FindFirst method to locate subsequent occurrences of records matching the criteria. See the Help system for more information on the FindFirst and FindNext methods.

Locating a Record Using an Input Box

Nina wants the form to include a dialog box in which the user can enter a last name, and a corresponding command button that, when clicked, will locate and display the record with the specified last name. You can do this without placing any other objects on the form by using a window that will appear only when called. This approach is consistent with the Windows 95 user interface. When a user wants to locate a specific record, the user will click the Find command button and a temporary window, called an **input box,** will appear. An input box is similar to the message box you used in Tutorial 3; however, an input box can send a text string back to your program. To do this, the user can enter the last name of the client to search for and click a button in the input box. The input box will then close and the record will be displayed on the screen, if the record exists in the Recordset object.

To display an input box, you call the InputBox function, which has the following syntax:

InputBox(*prompt*[,*title*][,*default*])

- When the **InputBox** function is called it creates two buttons—OK and Cancel. If the user clicks the OK button, the contents of the input box are returned to the program and stored in a variable. If the user clicks the Cancel button, the InputBox function returns a string with no characters in it. This is known as a **zero-length string**. You can use an input box for any task that must prompt the user to enter a text string.

- You should specify a string (*prompt*) that clearly indicates what the user should do. The prompt contains descriptive text that will appear inside the input box.

- The *title* will appear in the title bar of the input box.

- If the *default* argument contains a value, that value is displayed in the input box when it appears. This value is then returned to the program when the user clicks the OK button. When there is a common response to the prompt in the input box, a *default* can save users time.

Figure 4-21 shows the parts of an input box.

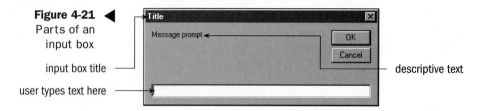

Figure 4-21
Parts of an
input box

input box title

user types text here

descriptive text

To improve your program further, you should write an If statement to determine whether or not the program should actually try to find a record in the database depending on whether the user clicked the Cancel or OK button in the input box. Remember, if the Cancel button was clicked, a zero-length string will be returned.

Now you will use the FindFirst method of the Recordset object and the InputBox function together to display the information for a specific record in the TextBox objects. To determine whether the user clicked the OK or Cancel button and to identify the value the user types, you need to declare a variable to hold this information. This variable will be named SearchString.

To write the code to display an input box and locate a specific record:

1. Open the Code window for the **cmdFind** object's **Click** event procedure.

2. Enter the following code in the window:

```
Private Sub cmdFind_Click()
    Dim SearchString As String
    SearchString = InputBox("Enter the Last Name: ", "Find")
    If SearchString <> "" Then
        datContact.Recordset.FindFirst "fldLastName =" & "'" _
            & SearchString & "'"
    End If
End Sub
```

Examine the procedure you just wrote. The code will execute in response to a Click event for the Find command button.

```
Dim SearchString As String
SearchString = InputBox("Enter the Last Name", "Find")
```

First, you declared a local variable named SearchString to hold the value returned by the InputBox function. Then you called the InputBox function using the prompt "Enter the Last Name:" and the title "Find" for the InputBox function. A default value would not be appropriate in this case, because each user will most likely search for a different record each time.

```
If SearchString <> "" Then
```

This statement provides the error checking for the procedure. In this case, you want the program to try to locate the record only if the user supplied a last name, so the program must test to make sure the SearchString is not blank. Remember that <> means "not equal to."

```
datContact.Recordset.FindFirst "fldLastName =" & "'" _
    & SearchString & "'"
        End If
```

This statement provides the functionality for the procedure. You need to tell the FindFirst method what to find by building a text string that will be processed by the FindFirst method. Remember the & character concatenates strings.

For example, if the variable SearchString contained the text "Smith," the string evaluates to:

```
FindFirst LastName = 'Smith'
```

Then, the If statement will exit and the screen will display the record with the last name Smith. This is a good time to test the Find button to see if it calls the InputBox function and FindFirst method correctly.

To test the code for the Find button:

1. Start the program.

2. Click the **Find** button. The Find input box appears.

3. Enter the last name **Zorn** in the Find input box as shown in Figure 4-22.

Figure 4-22 ◀
Find input box

enter the name to search for

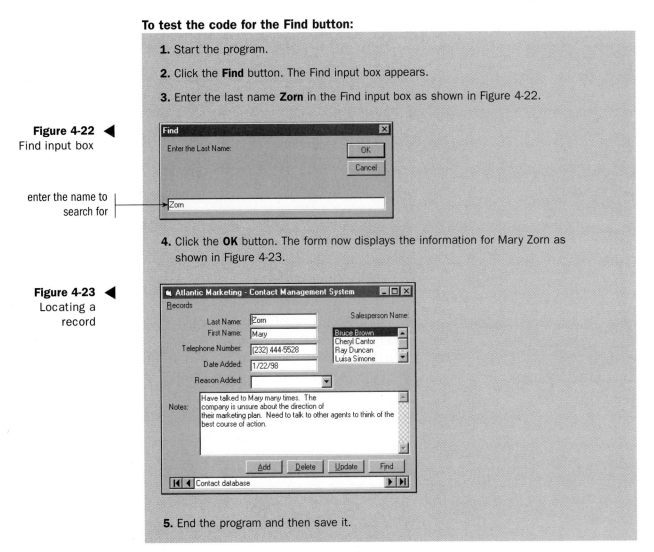

4. Click the **OK** button. The form now displays the information for Mary Zorn as shown in Figure 4-23.

Figure 4-23 ◀
Locating a record

5. End the program and then save it.

Developing an Error Handler

Because this program will be used by the entire sales force of Atlantic Marketing, Nina does not want the program to stop if a user tries to perform an impossible action, such as deleting a record that does not exist. If a user tried to delete a non-existent record, a run-time error would be generated by the program. Because she cannot prevent a user from entering incorrect data or trying to delete a non-existent record, Nina must find a different way to solve the problem.

The problem can be solved by writing Visual Basic statements that will execute when a run-time error occurs. This set of statements is collectively referred to as an **error handler**. Figure 4-24 describes the processing that takes place by a procedure's error handling routine.

Figure 4-24 ◀
Control flow of
an error handler

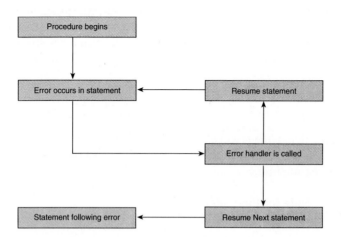

When a run-time error occurs in a statement, the error handler code is called. Depending on the cause and severity of the error, your error handler may display a message box describing the cause of the error to the user, or reset the variables. The error handler can then continue execution at the statement that caused the error or the statement following the statement that caused the error.

All error handling is performed at the procedure level. That is, if an event or general procedure should continue processing when run-time errors occur, the procedure can have one error handler. You create an error handler using the **On Error** statement. If a run-time error occurs while a procedure is executing an error handler, control will be returned to the calling procedure's error handler, if one exists. If you don't use an On Error statement to handle a run-time error, the program will stop executing and a run-time error dialog box will be displayed.

Trapping Errors Resulting from an UpdateRecord Statement

One of the problems that can occur when working with a database is when a user tries to update a record that contains no new information. Entering invalid data will also cause a run-time error. You need to create a means by which errors will not stop the program from running. Nina wants the program to tell the user what is wrong and allow the user to continue.

You can use the On Error statement combined with the Resume Next statement to identify errors and continue processing. The Resume Next statement, when executed, will cause execution to continue at the statement following the statement that caused the error. You can think of this as validating the correctness of a user's actions. The On Error statement has the following syntax.

On Error GoTo ErrorHandler
   statements
Exit Sub
ErrorHandler:
   statements
Resume Next

- The On Error statement tells Visual Basic that when a run-time error occurs in this procedure, the **ErrorHandler** will be called. You do not explicitly call the error handler. Rather, Visual Basic calls it when an error occurs. If an error occurs, Visual Basic uses the GoTo statement to determine the code that will be executed in response to the error.

- The name **ErrorHandler** is called a label, but it is not the same as a Label control. The label is used to define a location in your program. In this case, when the ErrorHandler is called, the next statement that will be executed is the statement followed by the line ErrorHandler:.

- After the statements have executed, the Resume Next statement is called. This tells Visual Basic to continue execution at the statement immediately following the statement that caused the error.

- Usually, a procedure exits when the last line of the procedure (End Sub) is reached, which means Visual Basic would continue execution of the procedure, causing the statements in the error handler to be executed even if there was no error. The Exit Sub statement can occur anywhere in a procedure. When the Exit Sub statement is reached, the procedure will exit. Because the error handler usually appears at the end of a procedure, the Exit Sub statement is necessary to exit a procedure when no error occurs. Otherwise, the error handler would execute every time the procedure was called.

When an error occurs in the contact management system, Nina wants the program to execute code in response to the error and display a message in a message box that explains the cause of the error to the user.

You can use the **Err object** and its properties to indicate the type of error that occurred. When a run-time error occurs, Visual Basic sets the properties of the Err object.

- The **Description property** contains a short description of the error.

- The **Number property** contains a numeric value representing the error.

- The **Source property** contains the name of the object or program that originally generated the error.

The error handler you create will give a specific message if a user tries to add a client record with no last name, and a general message for every other run-time error that occurs.

To display a message when a run-time error occurs and continue program execution:

1. Open the Code window for the **cmdUpdate** object's **Click** event procedure.

2. Enter the following code in the window:

```
Private Sub cmdUpdate_Click()

    On Error GoTo cmdUpdate_Error

    datContact.UpdateRecord
    datContact.Refresh

    'The Exit Sub causes the procedure to exit here unless
    'an error occurs.
    Exit Sub

    cmdUpdate_Error:
    If txtFields(0) = "" Then
        MsgBox "Cannot insert record without Last Name", _
            vbExclamation
    Else
        MsgBox "Cannot perform operation # " & Err.Number & _
            ": " & Err.Description, vbExclamation
    End If
    Resume Next

End Sub
```

Examine the code you just wrote. The code will be executed whenever clicking the Update button causes a run-time error. This will happen if a user tries to update a record without including a last name, or if a user has not typed anything new in the record. Recall that the Update menu item's Click event procedure calls the event procedure cmdUpdate_Click, so that procedure will use the same error handler.

```
On Error GoTo cmdUpdate_Error
```

The first line of code identifies the name of the error handler (cmdUpdate_Error) for the procedure. When an error occurs, the statement following the label named cmdUpdate_Error: will be executed. Remember that run-time errors still occur, but the program is dealing with the errors.

```
Exit Sub
```

Notice the location of the Exit Sub statement. This causes the procedure to exit and return to the calling procedure or, in this case, wait for more events. Without this statement, Visual Basic would continue execution of the procedure. This would cause the statements in the error handler to be executed, even if there was no error.

```
cmdUpdate_Error:
```

This statement is the label for the error handler. Be careful not to confuse this with a Label object. A label is used to provide a reference for the GoTo statement. In this example, when an error occurs, Visual Basic will go to the label causing execution to continue at the statement following the label.

```
If txtFields(0) = "" Then
    MsgBox "Cannot insert record without Last Name", _
        vbExclamation
Else
    MsgBox "Cannot perform operation # " & Err.Number & _
        ": " & Err.Description, vbExclamation
End If
Resume Next
```

These statements are the essence of the error handler. First, the If statement tests whether text was entered into the field used to represent the last name. If the field is blank, a specific message box is displayed, the If statement terminates, and the Resume Next statement causes execution to continue at the statement following the one that caused the error. If a name was entered into the field, the error was caused by something else. You use another object provided by Visual Basic, the Err object, to describe the nature of the error to the user. In your program, the screen will display the first record after either error occurs.

This is a good time to see how the error handler works when the program is running. To test the error handler, you need to run the program and make an intentional error. Because the date added is stored as a Date data type in Microsoft Access, an invalid date will generate a run-time error.

To test the error handler:

1. Start the program.

2. Click the **Add** button, enter **Jones** as the Last Name, **Mary** as the First Name, leave the Telephone Number blank, and enter **Date** as the Date Added.

3. Click the **Update** button. The error handler displays a message box describing the error. See Figure 4-25.

Figure 4-25 ◀
Data type
conversion
run-time error

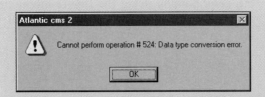

As you can see from Figure 4-25, a data type conversion error occurred. This happened when the system tried to convert the string "Date" to a valid date.

4. Click the **OK** button to close the message box and return to the first record.

5. End the program.

Trapping Deletion Errors

When a user tries to delete a record, but no record is current, an error will occur. Nina wants the program to display an error message while continuing to run. To accomplish this you can use the On Error statement.

To display a message when a user tries to delete a record with no record current:

1. Open the Code window for the **cmdDelete** object's **Click** event procedure.

2. Enter the following code in the window:

```
Private Sub cmdDelete_Click()
    On Error GoTo cmdDelete_Error

    datContact.Recordset.Delete
    datContact.Recordset.MoveNext

    Exit Sub

    cmdDelete_Error:

    MsgBox "Cannot perform operation # " & Err.Number _
        & ": " & Err.Description, vbExclamation

    Resume Next

End Sub
```

This error handler is nearly identical to the one you wrote from the cmdUpdate event procedure. However, this error handler will be called when an error occurs in the cmdDelete_Click event procedure (called by the Delete button or the Delete menu item). Remember, each event or general procedure you write must have its own error handler if you want the program to continue processing after an error occurs.

Now you need to test the error handler for cmdDelete_Click. This error handler will be activated when a user tries to delete a record when there is no current record. This would happen if the user deleted the record at the end of the Recordset object and then clicked the Delete button again.

To test the cmdDelete error handler using the Delete menu command:

1. Start the program.

2. Click the **Add** button.

3. Enter **Zyl** as the last name and then click the **Update** button.

4. Click the **Last Record** button ▶| in the Data control to display the record for Zyl.

5. Click the **Records** menu, then click **Delete** to delete the record from the database. All the text boxes on the form are now empty.

6. Click the **Delete** button again to cause the error. The error handler displays the message box shown in Figure 4-26.

Figure 4-26 ◀
No current
record run-time
error

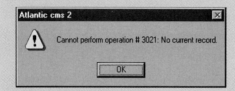

7. Click the **OK** button. The error handler displays the message box again because the MoveNext method caused an error after the Delete method.

8. Click the **OK** button. You return to the blank form.

9. End the program and then save it.

The contact management system is now complete. Nina is certain that the various objects on the form—Data control, text boxes, command buttons, menu, combo box, and list box—will make it easy for the Atlantic Marketing salespeople to enter, locate, and maintain information about contacts. The error handler will help users correct errors while running the program. Nina knows that the contact management system is a great improvement over the paper-based system, and will be well-received by the salespeople.

Quick Check

1 Describe the properties of a combo box and how they affect the appearance of the object.

2 What is the difference between a combo box and a list box?

3 What is the purpose of the FindFirst method of the Recordset object, and how would you use it in a Visual Basic statement?

4 What is the purpose of an input box?

5 What is the purpose of an error handler and what Visual Basic statements are used to create an error handler?

Figure 4-27 lists and defines the new terms presented in this tutorial.

Figure 4-27 ◀
New terms

Term	Description
Bound control	A bound control is a control that can provide access to a specific field in a database through a Data control by setting the DataSource and DataField properties.
Data control	The Data control is a control that is used to bind the data in an Access database to other controls in your Visual Basic program.
Database	A database is a collection of information organized in tables.
Field	A field is a column of data stored in a table.
Record	A record is a row of data stored in.a table. A record represents one database entry.
Recordset object	A Recordset object is created at run time by the Recordset property of the Data control. It provides a view of the data stored in the database.
Shortcut key	A key sequence like Alt+C or a function key that allows the user to execute a command using the keyboard. Also called a hot key.

Tutorial Assignments

Nina has asked you to design a program for Atlantic Marketing that can be used by each salesperson and the sales manager to navigate through the client database, select a specific salesperson from a list, and display all the client records for that salesperson along with the date each client record was added to the database. The Data control, which communicates with the database, will be invisible in this program because, although the program will use the functionality of the Data control, the user will never manipulate it directly. Users will navigate through the database using command buttons and Visual Basic code. Figure 4-28 shows the completed form for the program.

Figure 4-28 ◀

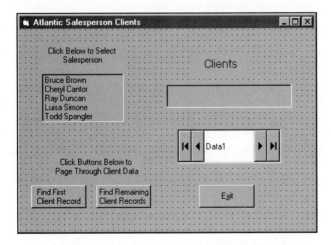

1. Make sure your Student Disk is in the disk drive, then start Visual Basic.
2. Change the form name to **frmClients**, and its Caption to **Atlantic Salesperson Clients**. Set the Width property to **6645**.

3. Open the general declarations section of the Code window and declare a string variable called **TmpSalesperson**. TmpSalesperson will be used to build a search string for record retrieval from the database.

4. Draw a list box on the form. Set the name to **lstSalesperson**, the font to **MS Sans Serif**, and the background color to **Light Gray**. Position the objects as shown in Figure 4-28.

5. Add the following names to the list box using the Properties window. Note that if you set the Sorted property to True the list will be sorted by first name.
   Ray Duncan
   Cheryl Cantor
   Todd Spangler
   Luisa Simone
   Bruce Brown

6. Draw a label identifying lstSalesperson and type as the caption **Click Below to Select Salesperson.** Center the caption.

7. Draw a Data control on the form. Set the Visible property so that the Data control will not be visible when the program is run. (Because it will be invisible when the program runs, it does not matter where you draw the Data control; you are just using its functionality). Set the properties of the Data control so that it will connect to the table named **tblContacts** in the database named **A:\Tutorial.04\TAssign\AMG_CMS.mdb**. The Recordset object created should be a **Dynaset** type recordset.

8. Draw a text box in which you will display the client's name and the date the record was added on the form. Set the Name to **txtClients** and remove the text from the object.

9. Draw a label identifying the txtClients object. Set the Caption to **Clients** and center the caption.

10. Create a command button on the form to exit the program. Set **Alt+X** as the hot key combination.

11. Create a command button that will be used to find the clients for a specific salesperson. Draw a command button as shown in Figure 4-28. Set the Caption to **Find First Client Record** and the Name to **cmdFindFirst**.

12. Below the command button you just created, draw another command button on the form. This will be used to find the remaining client records. Set the Caption to **Find Remaining Client Records** and the name to **cmdFindRest**.

13. Draw a label above the command buttons. Set the Caption to **Click Buttons Below to Page Through Client Data** and center it. Resize the object as necessary so that the text will fit inside the object.

14. Open the Code window for the lstSalesPerson_Click event and insert a line of code that will store the Text property of the ListBox into the form-level variable, TmpSalesperson, you declared.

15. In the Properties window, connect the text box to the Data control. In the DataField property, observe the field names that exist in the database table you are using. You will not bind the text box in the Properties window. Rather, you will use code that includes these field names to attach the database at run time. Delete the Data control name from the DataSource property.

16. Activate the Code window for the cmdFindFirst's Click event procedure. Type the following code, which uses the FindFirst method of the Recordset object to attempt to locate the first record matching the TmpSalesperson string:

```
Data1.Recordset.FindFirst "fldSalespersonName = " _
    & "'" & TmpSalesperson & "'"
txtClients.Text = Data1.Recordset("fldLastName") _
    & " " & Data1.Recordset("fldDateAdded")
```

17. Activate the Code window for the cmdFindRest's Click event and type:

```
Data1.Recordset.FindNext "fldSalespersonName = " _
    & "'" & TmpSalesperson & "'"
txtClients.Text = Data1.Recordset("fldLastName") _
    & " " & Data1.Recordset("fldDateAdded")
```

18. Explain exactly what the statements in the cmdFindFirst_Click event and the cmdFindRest_Click event do.
19. Close the Code window.
20. Test the program by clicking any salesperson's name in the list box. Click the **FindFirst Client Record** button to find the first record that matches the search string. Click on the **Find Remaining Client Records** button to search for more matches. For the selected salesperson, the clients' names and the dates they were added appear in the Client text box.

21. Explain why the FindNext method does not find the first matching string again? Use Visual Basic online Help for the FindNext method, if needed.
22. Exit the program by using the hot key combination.
23. Print the form image and code. Save the project as **Atlantic Salespersons' Contacts** in the TAssign folder of the Tutorial.04 folder on your Student Disk.
24. Exit Visual Basic.

Case Problems

1. Galaxy Graphics Galaxy Graphics is a small, high-tech graphics design firm that creates printed and on-line advertising. The firm specializes in creating attractive, eye-catching ads that blend text and images into pleasing and effective advertisements. Often, graphic patterns from different vendors do not show well together. Angela Burns, president of Galaxy Graphics, would like to be able to view different computer graphic patterns before including them in an ad. She has asked you to create a Visual Basic program that will allow her to compare two different patterns side-by-side. You will set the Stretch property so that every graphic opened fills the Image object. Figure 4-29 shows the completed form.

Figure 4-29 ◀

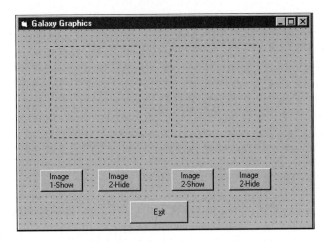

1. Start Visual Basic.
2. Change the form Caption to **Galaxy Graphics** and the Name to **frmGalaxy**.
3. Open the general declarations section of the Code window and create two string variables named **Image1Name** and **Image2Name**, respectively.

4. Draw an Image object on the left side of the form as shown in Figure 4-29. Set the Name to **imgDesign**. Set the properties so that the graphics you open will be sized to fill the Image objects.

5. Create a control array from the first Image object and position it on the screen as shown in Figure 4-29.

6. Draw the Image 1-Show and Image 1-Hide command buttons side-by-side below the first Image object and set the Names to **cmdImage1Show** and **cmdImage1Hide**, and Captions to **Image 1-Show** and **Image 1-Hide**, respectively.

7. Repeat Step 6 to draw the Image 2-Show and Image 2-Hide command buttons. Change the names and captions accordingly.

8. Draw a working Exit command button with a hot key combination of Alt+X on the bottom of the form.

9. Create a public general procedure called **GetFirstImage** and write the statement that will call the InputBox function with appropriate prompts to the user. The input box will be used to get the file name of the image from the user as shown in Figure 4-30. *Hint:* The user's response should be stored in the variable Image1Name, which you already declared.

Figure 4-30 ◀

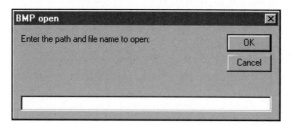

10. Repeat Step 9 to create a general procedure, **GetSecondImage**, that will use an input box to query the use for the second image name.

11. Activate the Code window for the cmdImage1Show_Click event procedure. Make sure you are entering the code in the Click event procedure. Write the statement to call the GetFirstImage function. Write another statement that will load the image file stored in Image1Name and place the result in the Picture property of the first element of the imgDesign control array. *Hint:* To load a picture at run time, you can call the LoadPicture function with one argument (a string variable containing the picture name you want to load). Refer to the Help system for the LoadPicture function.

12. Activate the Code window for the cmdImage1Hide_Click event procedure. Write a statement that will set the Picture property of the first element of the imgDesign control array to blank. *Hint:* The LoadPicture function will accept a null argument. Refer to the Help system for the LoadPicture function.

13. Repeat Steps 11 and 12 for the cmdImage2Show_Click and cmdImage2Hide_Click event procedures. Use the second element in the imgDesign control array and call the GetSecondImage general procedure.

14. Save your project as **Galaxy Graphics** in the Cases folder of the Tutorial.04 folder on your Student Disk.

15. Minimize Visual Basic in the Windows Explorer program on the Windows desktop. Open the Windows folder and examine the files listed for bitmap files. If the bmp type of file is not shown, click on Details in the View menu. Write down the names of at least six bitmap files to use to test the Galaxy Graphics program. Close the Explorer and maximize your Visual Basic program.

16. Test the program by clicking on the Image1-Show button. When prompted, enter the path and filename of one of the bitmap images.

17. Repeat Step 16 for the Image2-Show button inserting another path and filename.

18. Click on either of the Image Hide buttons to remove one of the images from the screen.

19. Insert the remainder of the bitmap file names that you wrote down in the input boxes. Be sure to type in the full file name, which includes the path name.
20. Print the form image and code of your program and exit Visual Basic.

2. Neptune Warehouse Neptune Warehouse stores a variety of goods for the auto parts industry. Lou Ortiz is in charge of creating a simple system that will allow an employee to select the name of an item and find out how many of that item are on hand. Eventually this system will be expanded to look up more information on items in the Neptune database. As a member of Lou's team, it is your responsibility to begin the program. When complete the form will look like Figure 4-31.

Figure 4-31 ◀

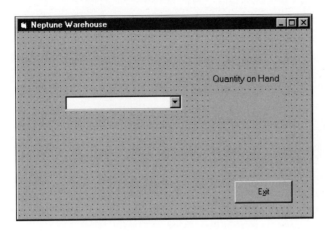

1. Start Visual Basic.
2. Change the form's Caption to **Neptune Warehouse** and the Name to **frmNeptune**.
3. Draw a combo box that will allow the employee to click a particular item in the inventory on the form. Set the Name to **cboParts** and clear the initial text. Position the objects as shown in Figure 4-31.
4. Draw a label that will display the inventory quantity of the selected item on the form. Remove the text from the Caption and set the Name to **lblQuantity**.
5. Draw a **Quantity on Hand** label above lblQuantity that will identify the inventory quantity.
6. Create a working Exit button with a hot key combination of Alt + X.
7. Minimize Visual Basic and open the file **Neptune.txt** in Notepad or your word processor. The file Neptune.txt is in the Cases folder of the Tutorial.04 folder on your Student Disk. Print the text file. Select the text and copy it to the Windows clipboard. Exit Notepad and maximize Visual Basic.
8. Open the Code window for the Form_Load event procedure. Paste the text you copied into the Code window between the Private Sub and End Sub statements.

9. On the printed copy of the text file, write what the AddItem method and the Item Data property do.
10. Open Visual Basic online Help. Search for the ItemData property of the ComboBox object. Print the topic.
11. In the Code window for the object cboParts's Click event procedure, type the code that will set the Caption for the lblQuantity object to the ItemData property of the cboParts object. *Hint:* Use the ListIndex property of cboParts as the argument for the ItemData property of cboParts. Close the Code window.
12. Test the program by clicking on any item in the combo box. The quantity on hand appears below the Quantity on Hand Label.
13. Print the form image and code. Save the project as **Neptune Warehouse** in the Cases folder of the Tutorial.04 folder on your Student Disk.
14. Exit Visual Basic.

3. Ramey Associates TOE Chart Generator You have been asked to build a tool in Visual Basic for Ramey Associates that will help programmers write TOE charts for their programs. Ramey Associates requires complete documentation for each program. The program you create will allow the programmers at Ramey Associates to type in a task and then select an object and an event. The program will then allow the programmer to print a line of the TOE chart on the printer. When complete your form will look like Figure 4-32.

Figure 4-32 ◀

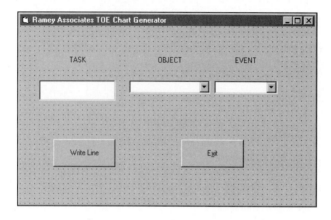

1. Start Visual Basic.
2. Change the form's Caption to **Ramey Associates TOE Chart Generator**. Change the Name to **frmTOEGenerator**.
3. Draw a text box that will allow the programmer to input the specific task to be accomplished. Set the name to **txtTask** and remove the initial text. Position the objects as shown in Figure 4-32.
4. Draw a combo box that will allow the programmer to select an object from the list or input a specific object on the form. Set the name to **cboObject** and remove the initial text from the list.
5. Draw a combo box that will allow the programmer to select an event from the list. Set the name to **cboEvent** and remove the initial text from the list.
6. Draw labels to identify the text box and combo boxes. Give them the following centered captions: **TASK**, **OBJECT**, and **EVENT**, respectively.
7. Draw a command button on the form. Set the caption to **Write Line** and the name to **cmdWrite**.

8. Create a working Exit command button with the hot key combination Alt + X that will also print everything in your printer buffer when you click Exit. *Hint:* The EndDoc method of the Printer object will send output to the printer. Refer to Visual Basic online Help for the EndDoc method. Make sure you empty the printer buffer *before* you end the program.

9. Open the Code window for the Form_Load event procedure. Write the AddItem statements to add the following items to the cboObject object at run time. *Hint:* To save type by typing the first AddItem statement, copy it, and paste seven more just like it. Then you only need to change the text string for each copied line.
   Label
   TextBox
   Frame
   CommandButton
   OptionButton
   CheckBox
   ComboBox
   ScrollBar

10. Repeat Step 9 to add the following items to the cboEvent object at run time.
    None
    Click
    LostFocus
    GotFocus
    Change
11. Open the Code window for the cmdWrite object's Click event procedure. Type the following between the Private Sub and End Sub statements.
    ```
    Printer.Print txtTask.Text, Spc(5); cboObject.Text, _
         Spc(5); cboEvent.Text
    txtTask.Text = ""
    txtTask.SetFocus
    ```

12. Explain what each statement in the cmdWrite_Click event procedure does?
13. Close the Code window.
14. Test the program by typing any TOE chart text in the Task text box. Click on the ComboBox object and select the object that you will use to perform the task. Finally, click on the ComboBox event and select the appropriate event to trigger the task.
15. Write each line of your TOE chart to your printer's buffer by clicking the Write Line button.
16. When you are finished, click Exit to send the contents of the printer buffer to the printer and exit the program.
17. Test the program again and complete a TOE chart for this program. Print the TOE chart. Exit the program

18. Print the Form image and the code. Save the project as **Ramey Associates TOE Calculator** in the Cases folder of the Tutorial.04 folder on your Student Disk.
19. Exit Visual Basic.

4. Henderson's Music Store Henderson's Music Store wants a program to display items from its music collection database. The music collection database was created using Microsoft Access. The three items to be displayed are Music Categories, Recording Artists, and Recordings. Valerie Henderson, the store's owner, has asked you to create a test program with the title, **Henderson's Music Database**. She wants the program to contain three text boxes and three Data controls. Each text box will be bound to one of the three Data controls so that when a user clicks a Data control, one of the categories will be displayed in the matching bound text box. You do not have to write any code for the Data controls to access the database in this program, but you should provide descriptive labels for the objects. You will write only one line of code for the working Exit button. Make sure you use valid names for the objects on the form. Each of the three Data objects will connect to **Music.mdb**, which is located in the Cases folder of the Tutorial.04 folder on your Student Disk. Be sure to use the Properties button that appears when you click the DatabaseName property value to select the proper filename and path. The RecordSource for each Data control should be set to **Music Categories**, **Recording Artists**, and **Recordings**, respectively. The DataSource property for the bound text boxes should be set to the name of the appropriate Data control, and the DataField property should be set to **MusicCategory**, **RecordingArtistName**, and **RecordingTitle**, respectively. When your form and code are complete, test the program and save the form as **frmHendersons** and the project as **Henderson's Music Store** in the Cases folder of the Tutorial.04 folder on your Student Disk. Print the form image and the form as text.

Designing a Report and Improving a User Interface

Creating a Sales Report and Menu Bar for Pacific Electronics

OBJECTIVES

In this tutorial you will:

- Use the Printer object and its methods to generate a report

- Create object variables

- Use a Do loop to move sequentially through each record in a Recordset object

- Add a menu system to a program

- Write a program that has multiple forms

- Write code for the different events that occur when a form is loaded and unloaded

Pacific Electronics

CASE

Pacific Electronics is an electronic parts distributor that has been doing business in Seattle, Washington, since 1991. In addition to selling transistors, wiring, and other parts used by the electronics industry in the area, the company has recently expanded to serve all of Washington and Oregon and has increased its inventory to include selected computer chips. As part of this expansion, the management wants to develop a sales reporting system. A Microsoft Access database of parts inventory and sales records has already been created for use by the inventory control department. Now the company wants a Visual Basic program that, together with the databases, will allow the salespeople to print reports of their sales. This information will be used by the salespeople to identify which items are selling well and which items are not. Also, the sales manager will use the sales reports to determine the commission for each salesperson.

Mary Deems, an analyst for the company for many years, has been working on the project since its inception and has developed several components already. You will help Mary complete the project by using the Data control to connect to the database and to print a sales report from the information contained in the database.

For every product, the salespeople need to be able to print the Product ID number, a description of the product, the quantity of the product sold so far this year, the sales price of the product, and the extended price. Also, the salespeople need to know the total number of orders, the total items sold, and the total sales in dollars so far this year. The salespeople work in small regional offices and will access the program from the main sales office in Seattle via their computer modems.

The program must also have a menu system like other Windows 95 programs and an introductory screen for the program. The menu system needs to have commands to open and close the database; use the cut, copy, and paste features of Windows 95; and print a sales and inventory report. While you will create the menu system, Mary will add the code later to perform these functions. Mary wants you to develop the sales report, the menu system, and the introductory screen for the program.

SESSION

5.1

In this session, you will design a sales report of sales records contained in a database. You will connect to the database using the Data control, write code to print each record by enclosing the statements in a loop, write code to interact directly with the fields in the Recordset object, and use a counter and an accumulator to compute total orders and sales totals.

Specifying the Information for the Sales Report

In Tutorial 4, you used the Data control to create a Recordset object based on the information you specified for the DatabaseName and RecordSource properties. In this tutorial, you will again use the Data control to create a Recordset object at run time. However, this Recordset object will be based on information from two tables instead of one, as in the previous tutorial.

You can combine information from two or more tables by creating a **query**. Mary has already created the query in Access. The standard prefix for a query is "qry." Figure 5-1 shows the records and fields in the query. You can create queries in Access or by using the Data Manager supplied with the Standard and Professional editions of Visual Basic. Refer to Visual Basic Help for more information on the Data Manager.

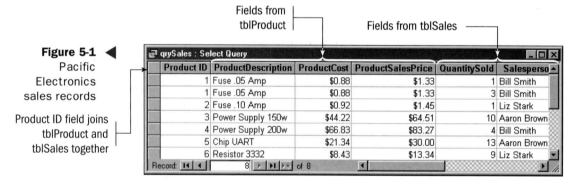

Figure 5-1
Pacific
Electronics
sales records

Product ID field joins
tblProduct and
tblSales together

As shown in Figure 5-1, a query named qrySales was created by Mary. The query contains information from the table named tblProduct and tblSales. The table tblProduct contains the product description, product cost, and product sales price. The table tblSales contains the quantity sold and salesperson name. The Product ID is contained in both tables and is used to join them together in the query. Notice that Product ID contains a space. Field names in Microsoft Access can contain spaces.

The pseudocode and TOE chart for the sales reporting program are stored in the file PE_TOE.txt on your Student Disk. Mary suggests that you review them before you begin to work on the program.

To view and print the pseudocode and TOE chart:

1. Start Notepad or any word processing program and make sure your Student Disk is in the disk drive.

2. Open the file named **PE_TOE.txt** located in the Tutorial.05 folder on your Student Disk.

3. Print the file and exit Notepad or the word processing program.

The pseudocode shows that the page and column titles for the sales report will be printed first. But before you can print anything, you must connect the program to the database. Keep the pseudocode and TOE chart next to you as you complete the program.

Before you can print any sales reports, you must connect the project to the database, Pacific.mdb in the Tutorial.05 folder of your Student Disk.

To create the Recordset object using the Data control:

1. Start Visual Basic and open the project file named **Pacific.vbp** in the Tutorial.05 folder on your Student Disk. If necessary, click the **View Form** button in the Project window to display the form.

2. Save the form as **Pacific Sales.frm** and the project as **Pacific Sales.vbp.**

3. Click the **Data** control ▦ on the toolbox and draw an instance of the Data control across the bottom of the form. See Figure 5-2.

4. Set the DatabaseName property of the Data control to **A:\Tutorial.05\Pacific.mdb**, and set the RecordSource property to **qrySales**.

5. Set the Name property of the Data control to **datSales,** and set the Caption property to **Sales database**. Your form should look like Figure 5-2.

Figure 5-2 ◀
Pacific
Electronics
form with Data
control

command button

Data control

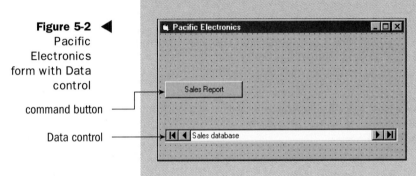

You can use the Recordset object created with the Data control to access the information in the sales database. In the form you opened, Mary has already created the Sales Report command button, which you will use to print the sales report.

Now you can begin to design and create the sales report based on the information in the sales database.

Designing a Report

Just as a well-designed form makes the user interface of a program easy to use, a well-designed report makes the report easy to read and understand. A report should have a page title that describes the report. Reports are often organized into columns. Each column should have a title that describes the information contained in the column, and the columns should be printed evenly on the page. That is, the left and right margins should be the same, and the spacing between the columns should be uniform. Figure 5-3 illustrates the sales report you will create in this session.

Figure 5-3 ◀
Sales report
layout

page title

column titles

detail lines

report totals

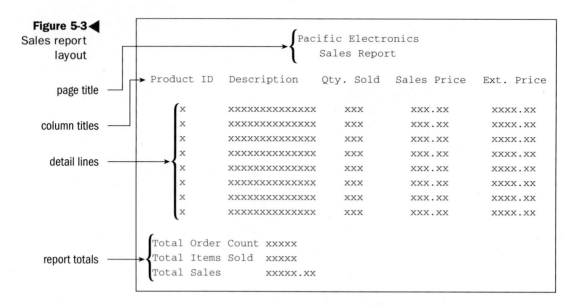

In addition to the page title and column titles, the report includes detail lines. When you print the detail lines of your report, you print a line for each record in the Recordset. To do this, you use a loop to execute the same statements repeatedly for each record printed in the report. (Loops are discussed later in this session). When you print the detail records, you use variables to count the number of orders and accumulate the number of items ordered and total sales. After all the records have been processed, the report prints the totals below the detail lines.

Refer to your pseudocode. The page and column titles need to be printed first. Then a loop is created to print each detail line. When each record has been processed, the report totals are printed. All these activities will occur when the user clicks the Sales Report command button.

Some reports are more complicated than the one you will create, but the basic logic of printing a report, as shown in the pseudocode, is useful for beginning nearly every report you will print. Although you could write all of the code to print the report in a single event procedure, you will instead divide the code into different general procedures, as you did in Tutorial 3 when you created a general procedure to compute the order totals in the cash register program. This process of dividing a task into multiple sub-tasks is called **modularization**. Dividing your programs into multiple procedures, also called **component modules**, simplifies the debugging process, because you can identify the procedure containing an error and focus on only those few lines of code. As your program grows, you can use component modules in other sections of the program. This will save time in the development process. The program you will create for Mary will include one general procedure to print the titles, one to print the detail lines, and one to print the report totals.

Printing a Report with the Printer Object

There are several ways of printing text and graphics. In this session you will learn how to print using the **Printer** object, which is initially set to the default printer from the Printers collection. A **collection** is an object that contains similar objects. It is simply a way of grouping like objects together. Although you have not worked with them explicitly, the Controls collection lists all the controls on a form and the Recordsets collection identifies the open Recordset objects in a database. The Printers collection contains each of the printers defined on your system. Visual Basic sets the Printer object to the default printer on your system. Just as the Recordset object supports several methods to manipulate data in a database, the Printer object supports different methods to control how your output will be printed on the page. In this tutorial you will use the Print, NewPage, and EndDoc methods of the Printer object.

You will use the **Print method** of the Printer object more than any other method. The Print method prints text to the printer. It accepts optional arguments that define the text to be printed and the format of the text. The Print method has the following syntax:

Printer.Print *outputlist*

- The *outputlist* is the text to be printed, and it has the following syntax:

[**Spc***(number)* | **Tab***(number)*] *expression* [*character-position*]

- If the optional **Spc** argument is included, space characters will be inserted in the output before the *expression* is printed. The number of space characters inserted is specified by the *number* argument. The Spc argument is useful for inserting a fixed number of spaces between the column titles in a report.

- If the optional **Tab** argument is included, the *expression* will be inserted at the absolute column number specified by the *number* argument. The Tab argument is useful for aligning all the detail lines to the correct column. Using Spc or Tab is often a matter of personal preference.

- The *expression* represents the data to print. It can be a text string enclosed in quotation marks, a variable, or a reference to a property of an object.

- The optional *character-position* specifies the insertion point for the next expression. If you place a semicolon here, the insertion point of the next expression immediately follows the last character displayed. The default character-position is the first absolute column on a new line.

In this tutorial, you will use the Print method within your general procedures to send all the titles, detail lines, and totals to the Printer object.

The **NewPage method** ends the current page and advances to the next page on the Printer object. To call the NewPage method, use the following syntax:

Printer.NewPage

- The NewPage method advances to the next printer page and resets the print position to the upper-left corner of the new page. If you have printed only a partial page when the NewPage method is called, the partial page is printed and any other text you send with the Print method appears on the next page. When called, the NewPage method increases the Printer object's Page property by 1.

The **EndDoc method** ends a print operation sent to the Printer object. To call the EndDoc method, use the following syntax:

Printer.EndDoc

- When the EndDoc method is called, any unprinted text sent to the Printer object with the Print method is printed. If you have printed only a partial page when the EndDoc method is called, the partial page is printed.

You will use the EndDoc method to send all the information in the printer buffer to the printer after the titles, detail lines, and report totals have been printed. In this session, you will print text on the page in columns using the Tab and Spc arguments to position the insertion point at the correct position on a line.

Printing a Page Title on a Report

The first step in printing the report is to print a title across the top of the page and to print the column titles. You will create a general procedure to print the page title centered on the top of the page and to print the column titles so that they are spaced evenly across the page. Remember you should name a general procedure so that you can recognize what it does. In this case, Mary suggests that you name this general procedure PrintTitles. As with any general procedure, you must explicitly call this one from an event procedure or another general procedure. Because your program has only one module, a form module, the procedure should be Private. Also, because it will not return any information to the calling procedure, it should be declared a Sub procedure.

You need to print the report titles in the PrintTitles general procedure, as shown in Figure 5-4. Notice that the page titles are positioned using the Tab() argument and the column titles are positioned relative to each other using the Spc() argument.

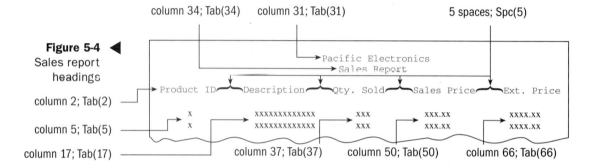

Figure 5-4
Sales report headings

To print the page and column titles on the sales report:

1. Open the Code window by pressing the **F7** key. Because you are creating a new general procedure, it does not matter which object and event procedure are currently active in the Code window.

2. Click **Insert** on the menu bar, then click **Procedure**. The Insert Procedure dialog box opens.

3. In the Name text box, type **PrintTitles**.

4. In the Type section, click the **Sub** radio button.

5. In the Scope section, click the **Private** radio button.

6. Click the **OK** button. The Code window displays the procedure you just created.

7. Enter the following bold-faced code into the procedure:

```
Private Sub PrintTitles()
    Printer.Print Tab(31); "Pacific Electronics"
    Printer.Print Tab(34); "Sales Report"
    Printer.Print ""

    Printer.Print Tab(2); "Product ID";
    Printer.Print Spc(5); "Description";
    Printer.Print Spc(5); "Qty. Sold";
    Printer.Print Spc(5); "Sales Price";
    Printer.Print Spc(5); "Ext. Price"
    Printer.Print ""

End Sub
```

When the statements in the PrintTitles general procedure are executed, they will print page and column titles to the printer, as shown in Figure 5-4. Remember, nothing will actually be sent to the printer until the Printer.EndDoc method is called. You want the page and column titles, the detail lines, and the totals to all go to the printer together, so you will not call the EndDoc method until all of the information in the report has been printed.

The first three statements use the Print method of the Printer object to print a title on the report containing the company name (Pacific Electronics) and report name (Sales Report), respectively. The third line is blank so that the page title will be visually separated from the column titles by a blank line. The Tab argument is used to position the text on the line. The first line is indented 31 characters and the second line is indented 34 characters, because the page title should be centered on the line.

Notice that each Tab argument is followed by a semi-colon (;). This character tells the Print method to print the next argument on the same line, immediately following this argument.

The next five statements print the column titles. You could have called the Print method once to print the line of column titles; however, if you placed all these titles on the same line of code, the line would not fit in one screen and you would have to use the scroll bars in the Code window to view the entire line. In these statements the Spc argument prints five spaces between each of the columns. The first four lines end with a semicolon, which causes the following text to be printed in the next character position on the same line. Because you want to print each of the five column titles on the same line, all but the Print method for the last column title end with a semicolon. After printing the last column title (Ext. Price), the Printer object moves to the next line. The final statement prints a blank line to separate the column titles from the detail records that will be printed. Remember, the output is not sent to the printer until the EndDoc method is called.

Printing the Data on a Report

Now that you have written the code to print the page and column titles in the sales report, you must write the code to print each of the sales records. To access the sales data contained in the database Mary created, you will again use a Recordset object. Remember the Data control creates a Recordset object at run time.

Creating an Object Variable

You could use the Recordset property of the Data control (the Recordset object) to call methods like MoveNext, but you can also create an **object variable** that will reference the Recordset object. Using this variable will save typing, because you will be able to use a short variable name in place of datSales.Recordset. Just as you use the Dim statement to declare variables that contain numbers and text, you can use it to create variables that point to existing objects and to create instances of new objects. To create an object variable you use the following syntax:

Dim *varname* **As [New]** *Object*

- The name of the object variable is specified with *varname* and must follow the standard naming conventions for variables.
- The **New** keyword is used to create new objects. In this session you will use the object variable to reference an existing object, the Recordset object, so you will not use the New keyword.
- *Object* is a placeholder for the kind of object you want to reference.

After you create an object variable, the variable must be set to point to an existing object or to create a new instance of an object. You accomplish this using the **Set** statement, which has the following syntax:

Set *varname* = [[**New**] *objectexpression* | **Nothing**]

- The *varname* can be any valid object variable name.

- The **New** keyword creates a new instance of the object.

- The *objectexpression* can be any existing instance of an object, such as a Recordset, a form, or an instance of a control, when the New keyword is not used.

- The **Nothing** keyword is used to disassociate an object variable from an actual object. When you assign Nothing to an object variable, the variable will no longer refer to an actual object. If there are multiple object variables that reference the same object, setting all of them to Nothing will free the memory and system resources used by the object.

You will declare the object variable in the general declarations section of the Code window, because the variable will be used by several procedures in your program. The cmdSalesReport_Click event procedure performs all the tasks to print the sales report. This includes initializing the object variable, calling the general procedure to print the report titles, printing the sales information, printing the report totals, and, finally, sending the output to the printer by calling the EndDoc method. You will set the value of the object variable in this event procedure.

The first step is to create the object variable that will reference the Recordset object created by the Data control at run time. The prefix "rst" is the standard prefix for a Recordset object.

To create an object variable that points to the datSales.Recordset object:

1. Activate the general declarations section of the Code window.

2. Append the following statements to the general declarations:

```
Option Explicit
Dim rstSales as Recordset
```

3. Activate the Code window for the **cmdSalesReport** object's **Click** event procedure.

4. Enter the following code in the window:

```
Set rstSales = datSales.Recordset
```

The two statements in the general declarations section create a new Recordset object variable named rstSales, which can be used wherever you would use datSales.Recordset. This will help reduce typing and make your program easier to read. At run time, you can use the variable rstSales to set properties and call methods that apply to the Recordset object, just as you have done for other Recordset objects you have used. The Dim statement you wrote only creates an object variable. You still need to use a Set statement to point the object variable to an instance of a Recordset object.

```
Set rstSales = datSales.Recordset
```

This statement sets the variable rstSales in the cmdSalesReport_Click event to point to an existing Recordset object, which was created for you by the Data control. The Recordset object variable can be used by different procedures in your program, because you delared it in the general declarations section of the Code window.

Now you have created the rstSales object variable and set it to the Recordset property of the Data control. So, rstSales references a valid instance of a Recordset object. You can use this variable to reference the contents of the current record and send the different fields of the record to the printer buffer. To do this, you need to use this object variable in a set of statements that will print each record of the database in turn.

Creating a Do Loop

Because the program must examine, compute totals for, and print each record from the sales table, you need a way to execute the same statements repeatedly. In addition to allowing you to execute statements conditionally, using **If** and **Select Case**, you use a Visual Basic Do loop. A **Do loop** repeats a block of statements while a condition is True or until a condition becomes True. The Do loop has the following syntax:

Do [[**While|Until**] *condition*]

  statements

Loop

- This code evaluates the *condition* before any of the *statements* are executed. If you use the **While** keyword, the *statements* are executed while the *condition* is True, the *condition* is tested again and, if it is still True, the *statements* are executed again. Whenever the *condition* becomes False, the loop exits, and the statement after the Loop statement is executed. If you use the **Until** keyword, the statements are executed until the *condition* is True.

You will use the Do loop to move one by one through each sales record in the new Recordset object you created, until there are no more records in the Recordset. Every Recordset object has an EOF (End Of File) property that is False whenever there are more records in the Recordset object and True when the end of the file has been reached. You will use the EOF property of the rstSales object variable to determine when there are no more sales records to process. You will also use the MoveNext method of the Recordset object to move one by one through each sales record in a Do Until loop with the following syntax:

```
Do Until rstSales.EOF = True
    statements
    rstSales.MoveNext
Loop
```

This syntax shows only a prototype for moving through any Recordset object. You will insert multiple *statements* to print each of the sales records contained in the current Recordset object. You will test the Do loop and Print method statements for the detail lines of your report as you develop them. In this way, you can locate and correct errors by looking at small pieces of code rather than having to debug a large procedure. First, you will test the loop structure by printing a test string to the Debug window. (You used the Debug.Print method in Tutorial 3.) Remember that you want the command button to initialize the object variable before it does anything, so you will add the Do loop after the Set statement in the button's Click event procedure.

To create the Do loop structure for the sales report:

1. Activate the Code window for the **cmdSalesReport** object's Click event procedure.

2. Append the following statements to the end of the procedure, just before the End Sub line:

```
Do Until rstSales.EOF = True
    Debug.Print "RecordFound"
    rstSales.MoveNext
Loop
```

This loop first checks the EOF property of the Recordset object. If the EOF property is not True, it executes the statements and tests the condition again.

```
Do Until rstSales.EOF = True
```

The Do Until statement looks at each record of the Recordset object rstSales until the end of the Recordset object is reached (EOF = True). If EOF = True, there are no more records in the Recordset object and the loop exits; otherwise, the statements are executed.

```
Debug.Print "RecordFound"
```

This statement uses the Print method of the Debug object. Just as you have typed statements into the Debug window to look at information about a program while it is in break mode, you can print information in the Debug window by using the Print method of the Debug object.

The Print method of the Debug object works just like the Print method of the Printer object, except that you do not need to call the EndDoc method to send the text to the Debug window. Remember the Print method of the Debug object can be called only at run time.

The text string RecordFound is the argument to the Debug.Print method. It will be printed in the Debug window every time the loop executes. In addition to text strings, you can print variables and object properties to the Debug window at run time. If your program is not working properly, you can include Debug.Print statements inside any general or event procedure to trace the execution of the program and look at the values of variables and objects. Refer to Appendix A for more information on debugging.

```
    rstSales.MoveNext
Loop
```

After the text string is printed to the Debug window, the MoveNext method positions the current record pointer at the next sales record in the Recordset object. When the Loop keyword is reached, the Do Until statement is executed again and the EOF property of the Recordset object variable is tested to determine if there are more records to process.

You have written enough code at this point to test the program and determine if the loop is accessing each of the records in the Recordset object and terminating correctly.

To test that the Do Until loop is working properly:

1. Start the program.

2. Click **View** on the menu bar, then click **Debug Window** to open the Debug window. Position and size the Debug window so that you can see it and the form at the same time.

3. Click the **Sales Report** command button. As the program runs, it will print the text "RecordFound" in the Debug window seven times, once for each sales record.

   TROUBLE? If your program displays the line of text without stopping after the seventh time, you have created an error called an infinite loop. This is a common problem with Do loops. In this case it would happen if the Recordset object never reached the end of the file. End the program and check to make sure that the Do loop is correct and that the MoveNext method is being called inside the Do loop.

4. End the program and then save it.

Mary is satisfied that the Do loop works correctly and finds each record. She observes that because the Do loop and the Debug.Print method work, you can continue to develop the program with the Printer.Print method, which will print the detail lines for the report.

Printing the Detail Lines

The next general procedure you will create will be called from inside of the Do loop you just wrote, and will print each record in the sales report each time the loop is executed. For each record, you need to print the Product ID, Description, and other fields in columns so that each field appears under its corresponding column title. So, you will use the Tab() argument of the Print method to align each field to an exact position. The information you need to print will come from the fields of the Recordset object.

Before you can print a field inside a Recordset object, you need to learn how to write the syntax to reference the field in Visual Basic. The fields that constitute a Recordset object are considered members of the Recordsets collection. Referencing a collection member is similar to referencing the different properties of an object. When you refer to an object's properties, you use the following syntax:

object-name.property-name

When you reference a particular object in a collection, you use an exclamation point (!) instead of a period (.). So, to reference a specific member (field) in a Recordset object, you use the following syntax:

recordset-name!field-name

- Unlike Visual Basic variable and object names, field names in Access databases can contain spaces. So that the Microsoft Jet database engine knows that you are using a field with an embedded space, you must put the field name in brackets. When field names do not contain spaces, the brackets are optional. However using them will help the reader of your program know that you are referring to a field name.

To reference the Product ID field in the Recordset object rstSales, you would use the following statement:

```
rstSales![Product ID]
```

The statements to print each record in the Recordset object will be enclosed in a general procedure, just as the titles were. The Click event procedure for the Sales Report command button will call each general procedure once for each record to print the report. Therefore, the code in the Click event procedure will be much shorter and simpler to comprehend. Before you can write the procedure, you need to know the different fields in the Recordset object. Figure 5-5 shows the fields you need to print the sales report.

Figure 5-5 ◀
Fields in the
Recordset
object

Field name	Description
Product ID	Product identification number
ProductDescription	Description of the product
QuantitySold	Quantity sold of the product
ProductSalesPrice	Sales price of the product

The extended price is not a field stored in the database. Rather, you will compute this value by multiplying the quantity sold by the sales price.

You will create a general procedure to print the current record's fields. In this general procedure you will use a variable to calculate and hold the temporary value of the extended price. Again, this procedure should be Private because it will only be used by this module. It should also be declared as a Sub procedure because it does not return any information to the calling procedure.

To write the statements to print the current record's fields:

1. Activate the Code window by pressing the **F7** key.

2. Click **Insert** on the menu bar, then click **Procedure** to open the Insert Procedure dialog box.

3. In the Name text box, type **PrintDetail**.

4. In the Type section, click the **Sub** radio button.

5. In the Scope section, click the **Private** radio button.

6. Click the **OK** button. The Code window activates the procedure you just created.

7. Enter the following code into the procedure:

```
Private Sub PrintDetail()

    Dim TmpExtPrice As Currency

    TmpExtPrice = rstSales![QuantitySold] * _
        rstSales![ProductSalesPrice]


    Printer.Print Tab(3); rstSales![Product ID];
    Printer.Print Tab(17); rstSales![ProductDescription];
    Printer.Print Tab(37); rstSales![QuantitySold];
    Printer.Print Tab(50); Format(rstSales![ProductSalesPrice],
        "fixed");
    Printer.Print Tab(66); Format(TmpExtPrice,"fixed")

End Sub
```

When the statements in the PrintDetail general procedure are executed, they will print the contents of each field in the current record to the printer buffer. Remember, nothing will actually be sent to the printer until the Printer.EndDoc method is called. You want the page and column titles, the detail lines, and the totals to be printed together, so you will not call the EndDoc method until you have printed all the information by calling the general procedures.

```
Dim TmpExtPrice As Currency
```

This statement defines the variable TmpExtPrice, which will hold the value of the extended price for the current record. The Currency data type is used to store variables representing dollars and cents.

```
TmpExtPrice = rstSales![QuantitySold] * _
    rstSales![ProductSalesPrice]
```

This statement computes the total sales amount for an item (the extended price) by multiplying the QuantitySold by the ProductSalesPrice and storing the result in the local variable TmpExtPrice.

```
Printer.Print Tab(3); rstSales![Product ID];
Printer.Print Tab(17); rstSales![ProductDescription];
Printer.Print Tab(37); rstSales![QuantitySold];
Printer.Print Tab(50); Format(rstSales![ProductSalesPrice],
    _"fixed");
Printer.Print Tab(66); Format(TmpExtPrice, "fixed")
```

These Printer.Print statements look similar to the statements you wrote to create the page title. However, instead of simply printing text strings enclosed in quotation marks, these statements print information from the rstSales object. Each Printer.Print statement moves to the appropriate column, as specified by the Tab function, and prints the contents of that field for the current record. The ProductSalesPrice value will be formatted with two decimal places (fixed). Because the Tab and field name arguments end with a semicolon, each argument is printed on the same line. The final Printer.Print statement moves to the final column and prints the value of the temporary variable, formatted with two decimal places (fixed).

Now you can modify the command button's Click event procedure to print the report. All you need to do is call the general procedure PrintTitles to print the report titles and the general procedure PrintDetail to print the detail lines when the button is clicked.

To modify the Click event procedure to call the print procedures:

1. Activate the Code window for the **cmdSalesReport** object's **Click** event procedure.

2. Change the contents of the event procedure as shown; new or changed lines appear in bold:

```
Private Sub cmdSalesReport_Click()

    Set rstSales = datSales.Recordset

    'Print the report title and column titles
    PrintTitles

    Do Until rstSales.EOF = True
        'Print a detail line on the report
        PrintDetail
        rstSales.MoveNext
    Loop

    'Send the contents of the printer buffer to the printer
    Printer.EndDoc

End Sub
```

The first statement in this procedure calls the PrintTitles general procedure only once, because this statement is outside of the Do loop. The titles should appear only once on the report, so the PrintTitles general procedure needs to be called only once.

Next, the Do loop prints the contents of each record by calling the PrintDetail general procedure, and steps through each record in the Recordset object by calling the MoveNext method. The MoveNext method must be called after the PrintDetail general procedure is called. If the program called the MoveNext method first, it would skip over the first record in the Recordset object before printing, and the first record would never be printed.

```
Printer.EndDoc
```

This statement calls the EndDoc method. All the information sent to the printer is stored in the printer buffer until the EndDoc method is called. Then all the information stored in the printer buffer is sent to the Printer object—your default printer.

Mary suggests that you test the program at this point to verify that the sales report is working properly.

To test the sales report:

1. Start the program.

2. Click the **Sales Report** command button. Your sales report should look like Figure 5-6.

Figure 5-6 ◄
Sales report
with detail lines

```
                        Pacific Electronics
                           Sales Report

Product ID      Description      Qty. Sold      Sales Price      Ext. Price

   1            Fuse .05 Amp       1              1.33             1.33
   1            Fuse .05 Amp       3              1.33             3.99
   2            Fuse .10 Amp       1              1.45             1.45
   3            Power Supply 150w  10             64.51            645.10
   4            Power Supply 200w  4              83.27            333.08
   5            Chip UART          13             30.00            390.00
   6            Resistor 3332      9              13.34            120.06
```

Notice that the Product ID number 1 is printed twice. This is because there were two sales records for the item.

TROUBLE? If the detail lines on the report are not formatted correctly, check the PrintDetail general procedure. If the alignment is not correct, verify that the tab positions are correct. If you receive a run-time error telling you that an item is not found in the collection, make sure the field names are spelled correctly.

3. End the program.

4. Click the Save Project button 🖫 to save your work.

Mary viewed the report and is satisfied that it will print the page title, the column titles, and the detail lines for each record in the Recordset object. Now she would like you to print the order count, the number of items sold, and the total sales below the detail lines.

Computing Totals with Counters and Accumulators

To compute the order count, the number of items sold, and the total sales, you will create variables to hold these three values. Each time a record is printed, the program must add 1 to the order count and update the items sold and total sales by the value of the respective field in the current record. You can do this using variables that work as counters and accumulators.

A **counter** is a variable that increases by 1 each time some activity occurs. When you work with a counter, you first initialize the value of the counter to 0. Each time an activity occurs, such as a record being printed, the counter describing the number of records is increased, or incremented, by 1. Incrementing a program counter has the following syntax:

MyCounter = MyCounter + 1

- Each time the program executes this statement, the existing value of MyCounter is replaced by its previous value plus 1. In your program, each time a sales record is printed, the counter representing the total orders should increment by 1.

An **accumulator** is like a counter but instead of increasing by 1, accumulators are used to tally values. Updating an accumulator has the following syntax:

MyAccumulator = MyAccumulator + TotalQuantitySold

In this session you will use two accumulators to tally the quantity sold and the cumulative extended prices of each item (the total sales). To do this you will initialize the accumulators to 0 when the report begins, add to the proper accumulator when each record is printed, and ultimately print the value of the accumulators at the end of the report. Figure 5-7 shows how the counter and accumulators will work in your program.

Figure 5-7 ◀
Counters and
accumulators

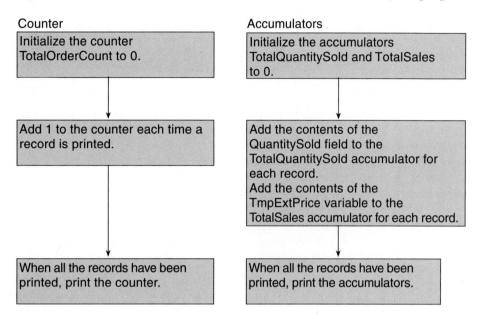

You need to create the counter, TotalOrderCount, and the first accumulator, TotalQuantitySold, as Integer data types. The second accumulator, TotalSales, will be a Single data type to hold the two decimal places needed for dollar amounts. Because the counter and accumulators will be used by multiple procedures in your program, you need to declare them as form-level variables.

To declare and initialize the counters and accumulators:

1. Activate the general declarations section of the Code window and append the following declarations to the end of the existing declarations:

```
Dim TotalOrderCount As Integer
Dim TotalQuantitySold As Integer
Dim TotalSales As Single
```

2. Activate the Code window for the **cmdSalesReport** object's **Click** event procedure.

3. Enter the following code immediately below the Set statement:

```
TotalOrderCount = 0
TotalQuantitySold = 0
TotalSales = 0
```

The first three statements create the form-level variables. The TotalOrderCount variable is a counter that will count the total number of orders. The TotalQuantitySold and TotalSales variables are the two accumulators. After processing each of the sales records and updating the counter and accumulators, the program needs to print the contents of these variables.

Whenever a user clicks the Sales Report command button at run time, the second three statements will set the value of the counter and accumulators to 0. You initialize these values in the command button's Click event procedure so that they will be reset and the report will produce the correct values every time it is printed. If you initialized these values in the Form_Load procedure, the report would be correct the first time it was printed. However, if you printed the report again without reloading the form, the values would not reset, and the report totals would be incorrect.

Now you can write the statements to update the counter and accumulators each time a detail line is printed. Because the incrementing must take place each time a record is printed, it makes sense to place this code inside the PrintDetail procedure you already wrote.

To update the PrintDetail procedure to increment the values of the counter and accumulators:

1. Activate the Code window for the general object and the PrintDetail procedure.

2. Insert the following lines to update the counter and accumulators; the lines you need to add appear in bold:

```
Private Sub PrintDetail()

    Dim TmpExtPrice As Currency

    TmpExtPrice = rstSales![QuantitySold] * _
        rstSales![ProductSalesPrice]

    Printer.Print Tab(3); rstSales![Product ID];
    Printer.Print Tab(17); rstSales![ProductDescription];
    Printer.Print Tab(37); rstSales![QuantitySold];
    Printer.Print Tab(50); Format (rstSales![ProductSalesPrice],
        "fixed");
        Printer.Print Tab(66); Format(TmpExtPrice,"fixed")

    TotalOrderCount = TotalOrderCount + 1
    TotalQuantitySold = TotalQuantitySold + _
        rstSales![QuantitySold]
    TotalSales = TotalSales + TmpExtPrice

End Sub
```

Each time a detail record is printed, the order count is incremented by 1. The quantity sold accumulator is incremented by the contents of the QuantitySold field of the current record, and the total sales accumulator is incremented by the contents of the TmpExtPrice variable for the current record.

You now need to print the totals after all the sales records have been processed. You can place the statements for printing the counter and accumulators in a general procedure and then call them with one simple statement in the command button's Click event procedure. This will keep the Click event procedure small and easy to read.

To create the procedure to print the counter and accumulators:

1. Be sure the Code window is open.

2. Click **Insert** on the menu bar, then click **Procedure** to open the Insert Procedure dialog box.

3. In the Name text box, type **PrintTotals**.

4. In the Type section, click the **Sub** radio button.

5. In the Scope section, click the **Private** radio button.

6. Click the **OK** button. The Code window activates the procedure you just created.

7. Enter the following code into the procedure:

```
Private Sub PrintTotals()

    Printer.Print ""
    Printer.Print " Total Order Count "; Tab(20);_
        TotalOrderCount
    Printer.Print " Total Items Sold "; Tab(20);_
        TotalQuantitySold
    Printer.Print " Total Sales "; Tab(20); TotalSales

End Sub
```

As with any other general procedure, you need to explicitly call the PrintTotals procedure. When called, it will first print a blank line as specified by the double quotation marks, to visually separate the totals from the detail lines. Then the procedure will print the Total Order Count prompt and value. The Printer object will then move to a new line, print the Total Items Sold prompt and value, move to a new line, and print the Total Sales prompt and value.

You will call the PrintTotals procedure before the Printer.EndDoc statement, and after the Loop statement so that the totals will be sent to the printer after all the records have been read.

To call the PrintTotals general procedure:

1. Activate the Code window for the **cmdSalesReport** object's **Click** event procedure.

2. Append the following line of code to the event procedure, just before the Printer.EndDoc statement:

```
PrintTotals
```

You have now completed all of the components of the sales report for Pacific Electronics. Because you divided the tasks of printing the report into several different general procedures, Mary can make changes to the report titles, the formatting of the detail lines, or the report totals without having to look at unrelated code. Now Mary asks you to test the completed program to see if the report prints correctly. You have already tested the code to print the report titles and detail lines, so any problems that might exist would be due to errors in the code for the counter and accumulators.

To test the completed sales report:

1. Start the program.

2. Click the **Sales Report** command button. Your report should look like Figure 5-8.

Figure 5-8 ◄
Completed
sales report

```
                        Pacific Electronics
                           Sales Report

    Product ID      Description      Qty. Sold    Sales Price    Ext. Price

        1           Fuse .05 Amp         1            1.33          1.33
        1           Fuse .05 Amp         3            1.33          3.99
        2           Fuse .10 Amp         1            1.45          1.45
        3           Power Supply 150w   10           64.51         645.10
        4           Power Supply 200w    4           83.27         333.08
        5           Chip UART           13           30.00         390.00
        6           Resistor 3332        9           13.34         120.06

    Total Order Count   7
    Total Items Sold   41
    Total Sales      1495.01
```

TROUBLE? If the counter and accumulators do not appear on the report, be sure the program calls the PrintTotals procedure in the cmdSalesReport_Click event procedure *before* the EndDoc method is called. If the values of the counter or accumulators are not correct, be sure that they are being updated correctly in the PrintDetail general procedure. If the output is not formatted correctly, verify that the PrintTotals general procedure is correct.

3. End the program and then save it.

The prototype for the Pacific Electronics sales report is now complete. Salespeople can click the Sales Report command button to print a report based on the underlying database. The report contains the page title required by Pacific Electronics, which includes the company name and the report title. It also includes the Product ID, Description, Quantity Sold, Price, and Extended Price value for each record in the Recordset object. Finally, the report counts the number of orders and accumulates the total items sold and the total sales.

Mary will distribute the prototype sales reporting program to the sales managers for testing so that they can verify that the information in the sales report is correct and that the report is organized and formatted in a way that is most useful to them.

Quick Check

1 Identify and describe two methods of the Printer object.

2 What is the difference between the Tab and Spc arguments of the Print method?

3 How do you declare an object variable?

4 What is the difference between a Do Until Loop and a Do While Loop?

5 Write the Visual Basic statements for the following pseudocode:
Execute the following two statements while there are more records in the Recordset object named rstPacific:
Print the field named fldProductID to the Debug window
Move to the next record

6 What is the purpose of a counter and an accumulator?

Now that you have completed Session 5.1, you can exit Visual Basic or you can continue to the next session.

SESSION 5.2

In this session, you will create a menu system containing items that will allow users to print a sales report and exit the program. You will add several other menu items that will not be active, because the code for these items does not yet exist. You will also create a form that acts as a startup (splash) screen to provide information about the program and give the program time to load all its files before the user can do anything.

Adding Menus to a Program

Although you could use command buttons to execute all the code in a program, you will find that as programs become larger, the number of command buttons can become excessive. In fact, a form with eight or ten command buttons would cause the form to appear cluttered or messy. Menus can be an integral part of the user interface of a Visual Basic program and provide users with another way to complete tasks. Menus you create in Visual Basic function in the same way as menus in any Windows 95 program.

Because the program you are writing will ultimately perform many tasks, it would require many command buttons. Mary believes that instead of creating several command buttons, a menu system will improve the user interface. These menus will allow the user to open and close the database, use the cut, copy, and paste features of Windows 95, and print the sales and inventory reports. Mary will write the code for all of the functions, except for the sales report, later.

Windows 95 and Visual Basic menus support shortcut keys and access keys. A shortcut key or hot key, is a function key (such as F5) or key combination (such as Ctrl+A) that executes a command. An **access key** is a key you press while holding down the Alt key to open a menu or carry out a command. For example, Alt+F opens the File menu in most Windows 95 applications. When you are finished with this session, your form and its menus will look like Figure 5-9.

Figure 5-9 ◀
Completed form with menus

menu bar

command button

Data control

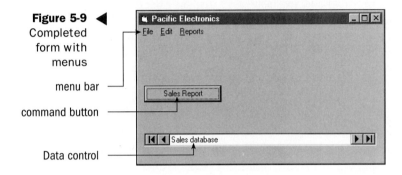

The menus you create consist of several parts. Figure 5-10 shows the anatomy of a menu.

Figure 5-10 ◀
Anatomy of a menu

menu title

menu item

separator bar

menu

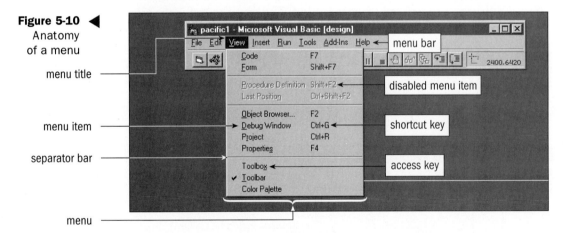

You will use the **Menu Editor** in Visual Basic to create the menu bar and menu items, as Mary requested, but you will not program all the menu items. You are responsible for programming only the Exit menu item on the File menu and the Sales Report menu item on the Reports menu; Mary will program the rest of the menu items. Menu items work in a similar way as command buttons. Each menu item has a name that responds to a Click event procedure, and each item also has a caption.

Creating the Menu Titles for the Sales Reporting System

The first step in creating a menu bar is to create the menu titles that appear on the menu bar. Each menu title has a Caption property that contains the text the user sees on the screen. The first letter of a menu caption should be capitalized. You can create an access key for a menu title by inserting the ampersand character (&) in the caption immediately to the left of the character you want to use as the access key. Menu titles are objects and, as such, they use the standard prefix "mnu" in the Name property.

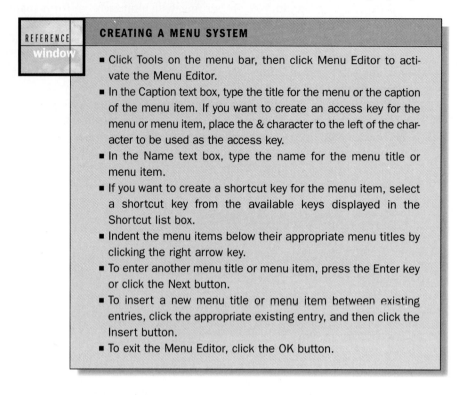

REFERENCE window

CREATING A MENU SYSTEM

- Click Tools on the menu bar, then click Menu Editor to activate the Menu Editor.
- In the Caption text box, type the title for the menu or the caption of the menu item. If you want to create an access key for the menu or menu item, place the & character to the left of the character to be used as the access key.
- In the Name text box, type the name for the menu title or menu item.
- If you want to create a shortcut key for the menu item, select a shortcut key from the available keys displayed in the Shortcut list box.
- Indent the menu items below their appropriate menu titles by clicking the right arrow key.
- To enter another menu title or menu item, press the Enter key or click the Next button.
- To insert a new menu title or menu item between existing entries, click the appropriate existing entry, and then click the Insert button.
- To exit the Menu Editor, click the OK button.

Mary wants you to create the menu titles for all the menus, even though you do not have to program all the menu items. The menu titles for the sales reporting program are File, Edit, and Reports.

To create the menu titles for the program:

1. Make sure the sales reporting form is displayed on your screen, and is active.

2. Click the Menu Editor button 🗐 on the toolbar to open the Menu Editor. See Figure 5-11.

Figure 5-11 ◀
Menu Editor components

Menu control properties

Menu control list box

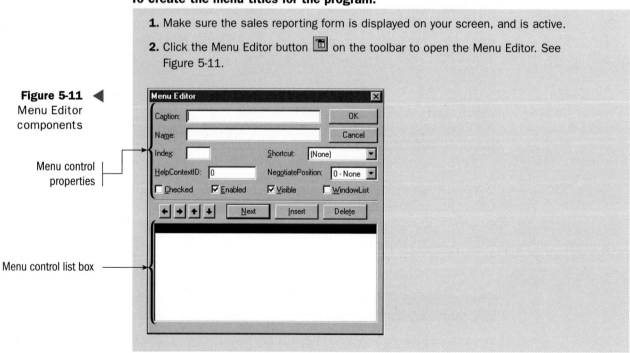

TROUBLE? If the Menu Editor button is disabled, click the form and then repeat Step 2. Because menus are bound to a form, the form must be active before you can use the Menu Editor. Also the Menu Editor is available only at design time; make sure the Visual Basic title bar says [design].

3. In the Caption text box, type **&File**. The & character to the left of the letter "F" identifies Alt+F as the access key combination for the File menu.

4. In the Name text box, type **mnuFile**.

5. Click the **Next** button. Your screen should look like Figure 5-12.

Figure 5-12 ◀
Menu title
defined

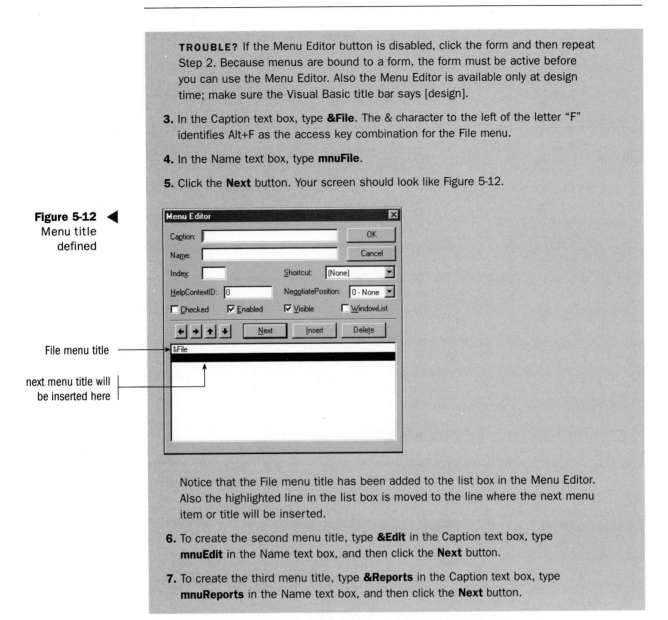

Notice that the File menu title has been added to the list box in the Menu Editor. Also the highlighted line in the list box is moved to the line where the next menu item or title will be inserted.

6. To create the second menu title, type **&Edit** in the Caption text box, type **mnuEdit** in the Name text box, and then click the **Next** button.

7. To create the third menu title, type **&Reports** in the Caption text box, type **mnuReports** in the Name text box, and then click the **Next** button.

You have created the three menu titles for the sales reporting program. Your next task is to add the menu items to each menu. Although you will add all the necessary menu items, you need to write the code for only two of them (Exit and Sales Report); Mary will program the rest.

Creating Menu Items

The menu titles you have created are just the first step in creating a useful menu system for your program. In the program, the File menu will ultimately allow users to open and close a database file and exit the sales reporting program. Now you must create the actual menu items—Open, Close, and Exit. When clicked, each menu item will generate a Click event and call the corresponding event procedure. This is just like clicking a command button to generate a Click event procedure. Although the menu titles also generate a Click event displaying the menu items, you do not have to write any code to activate the menu when a menu title is clicked; Visual Basic does this for you.

Several style guidelines will help you create menus that have a similar look and feel to menus in other Windows 95 programs. A menu item's Caption property should be short enough to appear on one line, but it can contain multiple words to convey its purpose. The first letter of a menu item's caption should be capitalized. If a menu item displays a dialog box or requires the user to complete other information, the item's name should be followed by an ellipsis (...). You can create an access key for a menu item with the & character, as you did for the menu titles. Menu items are also Menu objects and, as such, their names should begin with the prefix "mnu." To indicate that an object is a menu item, not a menu title, its name should be followed by the suffix "Item." For example, the Open menu item would have the Name property, mnuOpenItem.

Most Windows 95 programs separate certain menu items with a separator bar. A **separator bar** is a horizontal line that visually groups related menu items together to make the interface easier to use. Like all components of a menu, a separator bar must have a unique name or be a member of a control array. You create a separator bar by setting its Caption property to a hyphen (-).

Now you will create the Open, Close, and Exit menu items for the File menu. Because exiting the program is an operation that is not related to the other operations, Mary wants the Exit menu item to be separated from the other menu items with a separator bar.

To create the File menu items and the separator bar:

1. In the Menu control list box, click &Edit to select the Edit menu, and then click the **Insert** button to insert the menu item before the Edit menu.

2. Type **&Open...** in the Caption text box, and then type **mnuOpenItem** in the Name text box. This sets the access key combination to Alt+O for the Open menu item. Remember, the ellipsis (...) indicates that when a user clicks the menu item a dialog box will open (in this case, the Open dialog box). Mary will program this menu item later, so you do not need to worry about writing the code for displaying the dialog box. You will disable the menu item in the next set of steps; it will remain disabled until Mary writes the code for it.

3. Click the **right arrow** button to change the indent level of the menu item. This causes the Open menu item to be an item on the File menu. Notice that when a menu item is indented, it appears with four leading dots (....). See Figure 5-13.

Figure 5-13 ◀
Adding a
menu item

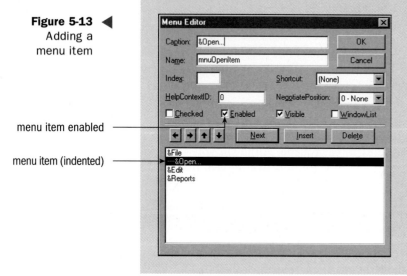

menu item enabled

menu item (indented)

You are responsible for creating the menu structure and for coding only two menu items. As Mary writes the specific code to perform the actions for the other menu items, the code will be added to the menu's event procedure. Until that time, the users of the program should not be able to click a menu item when the code for it has not been written. To prevent a user from clicking a menu item, you need to disable the item.

Disabling a Menu Item

Visual Basic allows you to **disable** a menu item when letting a user choose the item would make no sense in the program. For example, a Close menu item is not relevant if no files are open.

You can enable and disable different menu items at design time by clicking the Enabled check box for the menu item in the Menu Editor. When a menu item is enabled, the user can click it and generate an event. When a menu item is disabled, it will appear shaded on the menu, and the user cannot click it.

You can also set the Enabled property of a menu item at run time. For example, although you might want the Close menu item disabled when the program first starts, after a user opens a file, the Close menu item should be enabled. You can enable and disable a menu item by writing code to set the Enabled property using the menu name in any event or general procedure. The Enabled property accepts the Boolean values of True or False. The Enabled property applies not only to menu items, but also to command buttons, text boxes, and most other objects than can receive the focus.

Mary will write the code for the Open and Close procedures for the File menu; therefore, you should disable these menu items when you create them so a user cannot try to access them. When Mary completes the procedures, she will enable these items.

To disable the Open menu item and finish creating the File menu:

1. Be sure **&Open...** is highlighted in the Menu control list box of the Menu Editor.

2. Click the **Enabled** check box to clear it.

3. Click the **Next** button to move down to the next line, and then click the **Insert** button.

4. Type **&Close** in the Caption text box and then type **mnuCloseItem** in the Name text box.

5. Click the **right arrow** button ⬛ to change the indent level of the menu item.

   You have now created the Close menu item with the access key "C." Because Mary will program the Close menu item, you need to disable it.

6. Click the **Enabled** check box to clear it.

7. Click the **Next** button to move down to the next item line, and then click the **Insert** button.

   Recall that Mary wants the Open and Close menu items to be separated from the Exit menu item. So, you need to create a separator bar as the next item by typing a hyphen in the Caption text box.

8. Type - (a hyphen) in the Caption text box, type **mnuSep1** in the Name text box, and then click the **right arrow** button ⬛ to indent the item. You need to indent the separator bar to include it as an item on the File menu, just as you would any menu item.

9. Click the **Next** button to move down to the next line, and then click the **Insert** button.

10. Type **E&xit** in the Caption text box, type **mnuExitItem** in the Name text box, and then click the **right arrow** button ⬛. Your screen should look like Figure 5-14.

Figure 5-14 ◀
Completed File
menu items

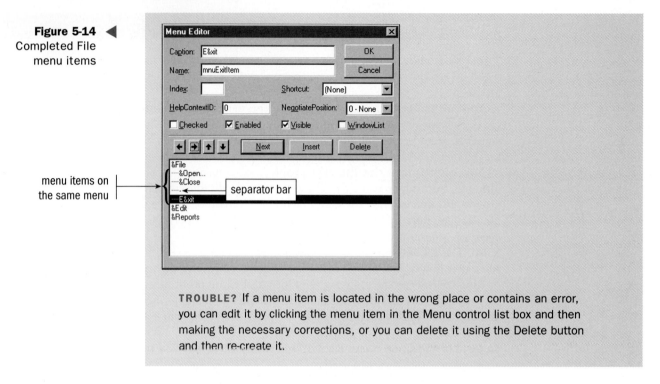

menu items on
the same menu

separator bar

TROUBLE? If a menu item is located in the wrong place or contains an error, you can edit it by clicking the menu item in the Menu control list box and then making the necessary corrections, or you can delete it using the Delete button and then re-create it.

The File menu contains all its menu items. Now you need to exit the Menu Editor so that you can write the necessary code.

Creating an Event Procedure for a Menu Item

The only File menu item you need to program is the Exit menu item. The Click event of the mnuExitItem object must end the program.

To write the code for the Exit menu item:

1. Click the **OK** button to close the Menu Editor.

TROUBLE? If you receive an error message indicating that a menu item must have a name, click the OK button to close the message box. The menu item in question will be highlighted. Be sure you entered a valid name in the Name text box. This error will occur if you neglect to assign a menu a name. If you assign the same name to two menu items, Visual Basic will display the error message "Menu control array must have an index." Like other objects you have created, menu items can be created as a control array, each sharing the same event procedure. This means you need to assign an index to the menu using the Index text box in the Menu Editor or assign a unique name to each item. Visual Basic will not create a control array of menu items for you.

The menu titles now appear at the top of the form. You can see all the File menu items and access keys by displaying the menu. You can also click the Exit menu item at design time to open the Code window and write the code for the item's Click event procedure.

To view the File menu items and write the code for the Exit menu item:

1. Click the **File** menu on your form. The menu items are displayed.

Figure 5-15 ◀
File menu
displayed

disabled menu items ───

separator bar ───

enabled menu item ───

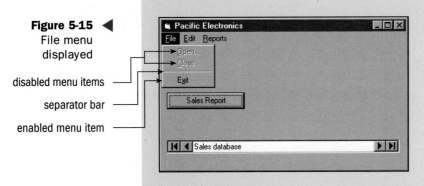

Notice that the Open and Close menu items appear shaded, because they are disabled. Also notice that the separator bar appears above the Exit menu item, which is enabled. See Figure 5-15.

2. Click the **Exit** menu item. The Code window for the mnuExitItem_Click event appears on your screen.

3. Enter the following code in the window:

```
End
```

4. Close the Code window.

The Exit menu item is now operational. Next, you need to add the menu items to the Edit and Reports menus.

Creating a Shortcut Key for a Menu Item

Mary wants the Edit menu to include the menu items Cut, Copy, and Paste. You will create these three items, and Mary will add the code for them later to implement the Cut, Copy, and Paste features of the Windows Clipboard. Mary wants these items to include Shortcut Key definitions, so that users can choose the items using both the keyboard and the mouse. You can create a shortcut only for a menu item, not for a menu title. You can specify the shortcut key you want to use for a menu item by selecting it from the Shortcut list box in the Menu Editor. You cannot create shortcut keys that are not listed in the Shortcut list box.

The Edit menu items should also have access keys. By allowing both mouse and keyboard input for the menus, the interface will appeal to the broadest number of users.

To create the menu items for the Edit menu:

1. Make sure the form is active. Click the **Menu Editor** button 🖼 on the toolbar to open the Menu Editor.

2. In the Menu control list box, click **&Reports** and then click the **Insert** button.

3. Type **Cu&t** in the Caption text box, and then type **mnuCutItem** in the Name text box. This sets the access key combination to Alt+T for the Cut menu item.

4. Click the **right arrow** button ➡ to indent the Cut menu item, indicating that it is on the Edit menu.

5. Click the **Shortcut** list arrow, and then click **Ctrl+X**.

Notice that the list box for the Cut item now contains the shortcut key Ctrl+X. Thus, whenever the user presses Ctrl+X, the code for this menu item will be executed.

Because Mary will program all the Edit menu items, you need to disable the Cut menu item.

6. Click the **Enabled** check box to clear it. Your Menu Editor should look like Figure 5-16.

Figure 5-16 ◀
Creating the
Cut menu item

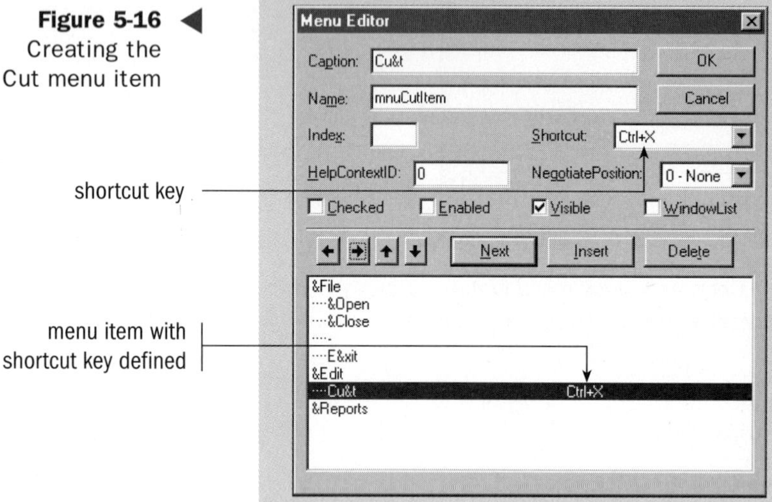

shortcut key ────

menu item with
shortcut key defined ─

7. Click the **Next** button.

8. Repeat Steps 2 through 7 to create the Copy menu item with the caption **&Copy**, the name **mnuCopyItem**, and the shortcut **Ctrl+C**.

9. Repeat Steps 2 through 7 to create the Paste menu item with the caption **&Paste**, the name **mnuPasteItem**, and the shortcut **Ctrl+V**.

The Edit menu now contains all its items. Later, Mary will write the code for these items in the appropriate event procedures.

Now you need to create the menu items for the Reports menu. The Sales Report menu item will perform the same task as the Sales Report command button does when clicked.

To create the Reports menu items:

1. Click the blank line below &Reports in the Menu control list box.

   TROUBLE? Depending on the resolution of your computer's monitor, scroll bars will appear when the list of menu items no longer fits in the Menu control list box.

2. Type **&Sales Report** in the Caption text box, type **mnuSalesItem** in the Name text box, and then click the **right arrow** button 🔁.

3. Click the **Next** button. Notice that the menu level stays indented for the next entry.

4. Type **&Inventory Report** in the Caption text box, and then type **mnuInventoryItem** in the Name text box. Mary will write the code for the Inventory Report item later.

5. Click the **Enabled** check box to clear it.

6. Click the **OK** button to close the Menu Editor.

Mary asks you to look at the Edit and Reports menus to make sure that each menu item is in the correct place and that the proper menu items are disabled. If you forgot to indent a menu item, it might appear on the menu bar rather than within the menu. You also need to verify that the access keys and shortcut keys appear, and that only the Sales Report menu item is enabled. You can view all the menu items, access keys, and shortcut keys at design time, so there is no need to run the program.

To view the Edit and Reports menus:

1. Click the **Edit** menu on your form. The menu items are displayed. See Figure 5-17.

Figure 5-17 ◀
Edit menu
displayed

menu items disabled

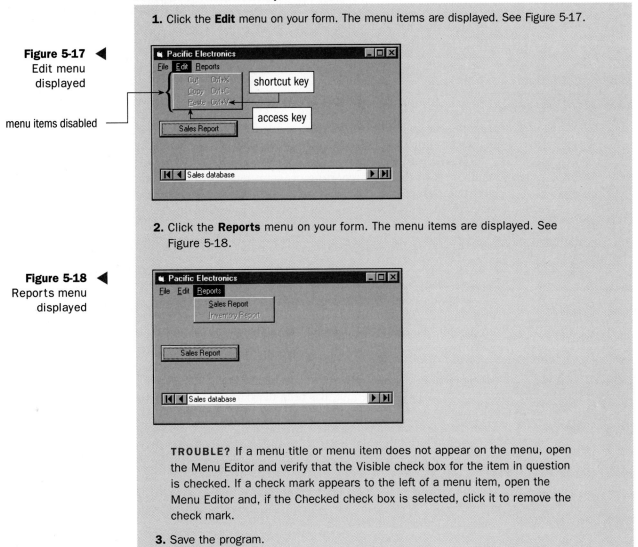

2. Click the **Reports** menu on your form. The menu items are displayed. See Figure 5-18.

Figure 5-18 ◀
Reports menu
displayed

TROUBLE? If a menu title or menu item does not appear on the menu, open the Menu Editor and verify that the Visible check box for the item in question is checked. If a check mark appears to the left of a menu item, open the Menu Editor and, if the Checked check box is selected, click it to remove the check mark.

3. Save the program.

The menu system now contains all the necessary items. The final menu-related task you need to complete is to program the Sales Report menu item. To do this, you can copy the code from the Sales Report command button's Click event procedure and paste the code in the menu item's Click event procedure.

To program the mnuSalesItem object:

1. Activate the Code window for the **cmdSalesReport** object's **Click** event procedure.

2. Highlight all the code *except* the Private Sub and End Sub statements, then press **Ctrl+C** to copy the code.

3. Activate the Code window for the **mnuSalesItem** object's **Click** event procedure.

4. Press **Ctrl+V** to paste the code into the event procedure, then close the Code window.

Now Mary asks you to run and test the program to make sure the Exit and Sales Report items work correctly.

To run and test the program:

1. Start the program.

2. Click the **Reports** menu, then click **Sales Report** to test the Sales Report item. The program processes and prints the same sales report you printed in Session 5.1.

3. Click the **File** menu, then click **Exit** to test the Exit menu item. Your program ends and you return to design mode.

4. Save the program.

The menu system is now complete. As Mary completes the different components of the program, she will add the necessary code to the proper event procedures and then enable all the currently disabled menu items.

However, before the main form containing the menus appears on the screen, another requirement of the sales reporting program must be met. Mary tells you that all Pacific Electronics programs must have a startup screen, called a splash screen, to display the company name, the company logo, and the program name.

Creating a Splash Screen for a Program

Your next task is to create an initial screen that will appear when the program is run. The initial screen, commonly called a **splash screen**, will display the company name, the company logo, and the program name each time the program starts. Also, because the main form for the sales reporting program will ultimately be quite large, displaying a splash screen while the rest of the program is loading will reassure the user that the computer has not frozen. You see the Visual Basic splash screen each time you start Visual Basic. When Visual Basic runs a program, it loads a form and displays it on the screen. This is called the **startup form**. In the programs you have worked with to this point, you have used only a single form, which, by default, has been the startup form. However, the splash screen you will create must be the startup form so that it will be loaded first when the project is run. After the splash screen is loaded, it will open the main form in your program.

The purpose of the splash screen form is different from the other forms you have created. The splash screen only provides a visual message to the user while the rest of the program loads and then it disappears without any input from the user. So, there is no need for many of the form elements you've created in the past—a title bar, a border, or any input objects—because the user will not need to do anything to the form. When complete, your splash screen will look like Figure 5-19.

Figure 5-19 ◀
Splash screen

company logo image
fills the region
of the form

program name

no title bar

company name

no borders

The BorderStyle property of the Form object works differently from the BorderStyle property of the Shape object. By default, the BorderStyle property of the form is set to 2-Sizable. This setting creates a border around the form and displays a title bar, allowing the user to resize the form while the program is running. When the BorderStyle property is set to 0-None, the form will not display a border or title bar at run time. There are other BorderStyle property settings you can use in your program. Look at the Help screen for the BorderStyle property of the Form object for further information.

Mary has received a directive from management that the splash screen for all the programs in the company should contain the company name, the program name, and the company logo, so that users of all the different programs are sure they are running the correct program. You are now ready to add this second form to your program to function as a splash screen.

Like an Image control, a form also supports a Picture property. So, you can display an image directly on a form without having to create an Image object. However, there are limitations when you set the Picture property of the form. First, the form does not support the Stretch property, so, you cannot resize the image. Also, the image is displayed in the upper-left corner of the form and it cannot be moved elsewhere. Setting the Picture property of the form is useful when the picture and the form are of the same size and you want the picture to cover the entire region of the form. You will do this for the splash Screen form.

To add a second form to your program:

1. Click the **Form** button 🖻 on the toolbar. A second form named Form1 appears on your screen. Remember, Visual Basic assigns a default name to each object you create.

2. Set the BorderStyle property of the form to **0 - None**. The title bar and border will not be displayed at run time but continues to appear at design time.

3. Set the Caption property to **Start**. This caption will not be displayed at run time, but it will help you know which form you are working on while you are designing forms.

4. Set the Name property to **frmStart**.

5. Set the Picture property to **A:\Tutorial.05\logo.bmp**. This file contains the picture of the company logo for Pacific Electronics.

6. Resize the form so that the logo fills the form.

7. Move the form to the center of the screen. This is where the form will appear at run time.

8. Click **File** on the menu bar, then click **Save File As** and save the form as **Start.frm** in the Tutorial.05 folder on your Student Disk.

By creating the new form, you have added another form module to your project. The new form module is displayed in the Project window, as shown in Figure 5-20.

Figure 5-20 ◀
Project with
two form
modules

new form module ⎯

When you work with programs that have multiple forms, be careful that you are setting properties and writing code for the correct form module. Both the Properties window and the Code window display the form name in the title bar.

You can use Label controls to display the company and program names. Usually a Label control is displayed with a border, which would obscure the picture. To avoid this, you can hide the border surrounding the label by setting its BackStyle property to 0-Transparent, so that only the caption of the label is visible.

To create the objects for the splash screen:

1. Create a label on the startup form where "Pacific Electronics" appears in Figure 5-19.

2. Set the Caption property of the label to **Pacific Electronics**.

3. Set the Alignment property to **2 - Center**.

4. Open the Font dialog box and set the size to **18 point** and the typeface to **Bold Italic**.

5. Set the ForeColor property to **Yellow**. This sets the color for the text in the caption.

6. Set the BackStyle property to **0 - Transparent**. This setting hides the border of the Label object.

7. Create the second label on the startup form just below the first.

8. Set the Caption property of the second label to **Sales Reporting**.

9. Repeat Steps 3 through 6 to set the remaining properties. Your startup form should look like Figure 5-21.

Figure 5-21 ◀
Startup form at
design time

title bar appears
with caption at
design time

borders appear
at design time

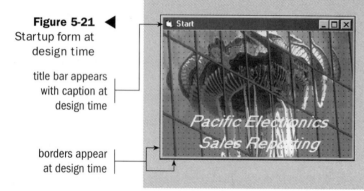

The splash screen contains all the objects and properties it needs in the final program, but it will not appear in your program if you run it now. You need to change the startup form for your project from frmMain to frmStart. After frmStart is loaded, it can then open frmMain in your program.

To set the startup form in your program:

1. Click **Tools** on the menu bar, then click **Options**. The Options dialog box opens.

2. Click the **Project** tab to display the options pertaining to projects.

3. Click the **Startup Form** list arrow. The Options dialog box should look like Figure 5-22.

   By default, the startup form is the first form in your project. However, you want the splash screen, frmStart, to be the startup form.

Figure 5-22 ◀
Setting the
startup form

frmMain was the
default startup form

frmStart is the
desired startup form

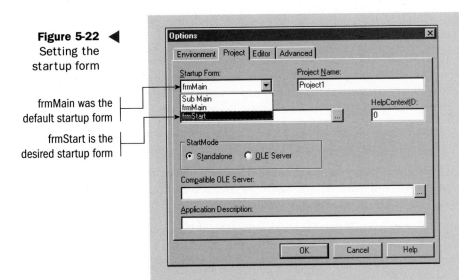

TROUBLE? If the form named frmStart does not appear in the Startup Form list, you probably did not set the Name property of the new form when you created it. Activate the startup form you created, activate its Properties window, and then set the Name property to frmStart.

4. Click **frmStart** in the Startup Form list.

5. Click the **OK** button to close the Options dialog box.

Mary suggests you run the program at this point to see if the splash screen works correctly.

6. Start the program. Notice that the splash screen shown in Figure 5-19 is displayed when the program starts. However, the main form is no longer displayed on the screen. You still need to write the code to display the main form.

TROUBLE? If the frmStart form does not appear on your screen, end the program and then open the Options dialog box. Click the Project tab and be sure the Startup Form is set to frmStart.

7. End the program. Both forms are now displayed on the screen again.

Note: If you are using the Visual Basic Working Model rather than the Standard or Professional edition, you cannot load multiple forms into the project file with the Open Project command from the File menu or the Open Project button. If you take a break and save the project so that you can open it later, you must start from a new project file. Click Remove File on the File menu to delete the new blank form created with the new project. Click Add File on the File menu and load the first form (.frm, not the project .vbp) directly. Click Add File on the File menu again and load the second form. Change the Startup Form setting in the Options dialog box to the form you want to use as your initial form. Your program will then work correctly.

When your program starts, the splash screen (frmStart) should receive the focus and display its contents. Then it should wait for about five seconds before calling the Form_Load event procedure for frmMain. Before you proceed, you must better understand the different events that occur when a form is loaded and unloaded.

As you know, you can write Visual Basic code that will execute when a form is loaded by placing the code in the Form_Load procedure. However, this is only one of the event procedures that occurs when a form is loaded. The following steps describe what happens when the splash screen, or any form, becomes the active object, and how control is transferred to the main form.

1. When Visual Basic creates the instance of the Form object at run time, the Initialize event occurs first.

2. The Load event occurs next as Visual Basic begins to make the form the active object. When the form is a startup form, this occurs when a program starts. Loading the form merely places the form and its objects into the computer's memory; it does not display the form on the screen.

3. The Activate event occurs for the form after the form is loaded. A startup form is automatically activated after it is loaded.

4. After the form is activated, it becomes the active object and the GotFocus event occurs. A form can also become active by user action, such as clicking the form, or by using the Show or SetFocus methods in code.

5. Finally, the object with the TabIndex property of 0 becomes the active object—that is, the GotFocus event occurs for that object. An object can also become active by user action, such as clicking the object, or by using the Show or SetFocus methods in code.

These individual events are generated when any form loads, activates, and gets the focus. You now need to load and set the focus from the splash screen to the main sales reporting form.

Displaying the Main Form

All of the code you have written in previous sessions was contained in a single form. Your project now contains two form modules, each of which is stored as a separate file on your Student Disk. Each form is a separate instance of a Form object, so each form can respond to events such as Load and GotFocus. The Load event for frmStart occurs when that form is loaded, and the Load event for frmMain occurs when that form is loaded. These are different event procedures. When you write code to respond to event procedures in programs with multiple forms, you must be sure that you write the code for the correct form. You can do so by verifying that the title bar of the Code window displays the correct form. Because you use the Code window to edit the code for a form or other module, you can open a separate Code window for each of the different forms or other modules in your program at the same time. However, you can open only one Properties window at a time. So, you must make sure that the code you are writing is for the correct form module and that the Properties window displays the properties for the correct object.

For the sales reporting program, you must first make sure that frmStart stays on the screen for the entire time required for frmMain to load. You need to write the code in the startup form that will ensure that frmStart is displayed, waits for five seconds, and then shows the form frmMain and all of its objects. Just as you have called the different methods of the Recordset object, you can call different methods of the Form object. The **Refresh method** of the Form object forces the Form object to be completely repainted, which allows you to display all the objects on one form completely while another form loads. The **Show method** can be used to load if necessary, and display another form. You can call the Show method of the main form in the startup form to load, and display the main form and its objects.

There are two ways to make your program wait for five seconds before executing the next statement. You can use the **Sleep function** supplied with Windows 95, or you can use a control called a Timer. The Sleep function is easier to use, because it requires less code. More information on the Sleep function is available in Visual Basic online Help under

Sleep API. (API is the Windows Applications Programming Interface that allows various Windows 95 applications to use the same functions.) To call functions that are part of Windows 95, but not part of Visual Basic, you must make the function known to Visual Basic using the Declare statement. The Sleep function uses the following syntax:

Private Declare Sub Sleep Lib "kernel32" (ByVal dwMilliseconds As Long)

Sleep(n)

- The **Declare** statement declares a reference to a function supplied by Windows 95. Once declared, you can call the function just as you can call any other Visual Basic procedure. This statement declares the function named **Sleep** contained in the Windows API library named **kernel32**. Whenever, you declare a function that is contained elsewhere it must be declared outside of a specific procedure, so you should add the declaration in the general declarations section of the Code window.

- When called, the Sleep function takes one argument—the number of milliseconds you want the program to wait.

You will add code to the frmStart_GotFocus event that will refresh the startup form, cause the program to wait for five seconds, and then load the main form. The Sleep function is called in the GotFocus event because you want the computer to wait five seconds after the startup form is displayed on the screen.

To cause frmStart to load frmMain:

1. Click **frmStart** in the Project window.

2. Click the **View Code** button to open the Code window for frmStart. Note that frmStart will appear in the title bar of the Code window.

3. Open the general declarations section of the Code window and enter the following code:

```
Private Declare Sub Sleep Lib "kernel32" _
    (ByVal dwMilliseconds As Long)
```

4. Activate the **GotFocus** event for the **Form** object.

5. Enter the following code:

```
Private Sub Form_GotFocus()

    frmStart.Refresh
    Sleep (5000)
    frmMain.Show

End Sub
```

6. Close the Code window.

Examine the statements you entered in the general declarations section of the Code window.

```
Private Declare Sub Sleep Lib "kernel32" _
    (ByVal dwMilliseconds As Long)
```

The Declare statement is used to identify to your Visual Basic program the Sleep function supplied by Windows 95 and its location. You can then call the procedure just as you can call any other Visual Basic procedure or function.

The code in the GotFocus event contains three different statements to cause the splash screen to be displayed, and to then display frmMain.

```
frmStart.Refresh
```

First, the Refresh method is called for frmStart. If the Refresh method is not called, it is possible that frmMain would begin loading before the contents of the labels on the splash screen were completely displayed. The Refresh method redraws all of the objects created on the startup form.

```
Sleep (5000)
```

This procedure causes the program to wait for five seconds (5000 milliseconds) before executing the next statement. This function is not part of Visual Basic but is accessible because you used a Declare statement to make the Windows 95 Sleep function available to your program.

```
frmMain.Show
```

Finally, the Show method of the main form is called. This causes the Initialize, Load, Activate, and GotFocus events to occur for frmMain.

Your program is now equipped with a functional startup form that calls the main form. After this code is executed, frmMain will have the focus, but the splash screen will still appear on the screen.

There are two ways to remove the startup form from the screen. Form objects support the **Hide method**, which makes a form invisible. When hidden, the form is still loaded in the computer's memory but is not visible on the screen. Because you will not be using the splash screen again in your program, it would be better to remove the form completely from the computer's memory so that the memory is available for other uses.

Unloading the Startup Form

To remove an object from the computer's memory, you use the **Unload** statement, which has the following syntax:

Unload *formname*

- The **Unload** statement takes one argument: the *object* to unload.

When you unload a form, an Unload event is generated so that the program can take care of any necessary tasks, such as closing files, in the same way as you have performed initialization tasks in the Load event procedure in previous tutorials. When a form is unloaded, the form and all its objects are no longer visible or accessible. All run-time changes to properties of the form and its objects are also lost.

You will use the last event that occurred, the GotFocus event of frmMain, in your program to close the splash screen with the Unload statement.

To cause the main form to unload the startup form:

1. Click **frmMain** in the Project window.

2. Click the **View Code** button to open the Code window for frmMain.

3. Activate the **Form_GotFocus** event procedure for frmMain. "Form" will appear in the object pull-down menu; "frmMain" will appear in the title bar of the Code window.

4. Enter the following code:

```
Private Sub Form_GotFocus()

     Unload frmStart

End Sub
```

Now when the Show method of the main form is called, and the Initialize, Load, Activate, and GotFocus events occur for frmMain, the GotFocus event for the main form will unload the startup form.

The menu system and the splash screen are now complete. Mary asks you to test the program a final time to be sure that the splash screen appears, the main form is loaded, and the splash screen disappears.

To test the completed program:

1. Start the program. The splash screen appears for five seconds, then opens the main form and disappears.

   TROUBLE? If the splash screen appears and disappears immediately, be sure you called the Sleep function with the correct argument, 5000 milliseconds, in the GotFocus event procedure for frmStart. If the splash screen does not disappear, be sure you used the Unload statement in the GotFocus event procedure for frmMain.

2. End the program and then save it.

The command button, menu system, and splash screen for the sales reporting program are now working correctly. As she completes different pieces of code for the menu items, Mary will insert the code in the proper event procedures and enable all the menu items. The splash screen will communicate the name of the program to the user and display the Pacific Electronics logo, then bring up the main form. With minor modifications this splash screen can be used in all Pacific Electronics programs.

Quick Check

1 What is the difference between a menu title and a menu item?

2 What is the difference between an access key and a shortcut key?

3 What is the purpose of a separator bar?

4 What is the difference between the Initialize, Load, Activate, and GotFocus events?

5 What is the purpose of the Refresh and Show methods of the Form object?

6 What does the Unload statement do and how does it differ from the Hide method?

7 What is a splash screen?

Figure 5-23 lists and defines the new terms presented in this tutorial.

Figure 5-23 ◀
New terms

Term	Description
Access key	The underlined character of a menu title or menu item that allows the title or item by pressing the Alt key and the access key at the same time.
Accumulator	An accumulator is a variable that is incremented by the value of some other variable.
Collection	A collection is an object that contains similar objects.
Counter	A counter is a variable that is incremented by a constant value, usually 1, each time some activity occurs. Counters are usually declared as integer variables.
Do loop	A Do loop is a set of statements including a Do While or Do Until statement that will be executed while or until a condition is true.
Modularization	Modularization is the process of dividing a task into multiple sub-tasks.
Object variable	An object variable is a variable that points to an instance of an existing object.
Printer object	A Printer object is an object that has methods to format information and send it to a printer.
Set statement	A Set statement is a statement used to assign object variables to existing objects. If the New keyword is used, the Set statement will create a new object.

Tutorial Assignments

Pacific Electronics requires a product report describing the items it sells. The report must contain the Product ID, the Product Description, the Product Cost, and the Product Sales Price for each item. The report must also total the number of items sold and allow the user to specify whether the report will be printed to the screen or printed on the printer. This report is a prototype for a more complex report, so it will not have a large number of items in the underlying database. You do not have to consider page or screen breaks. You need to create a menu item to generate the report. The report will contain a final line stating that you tested the program. You will enter your name into the program using an input box. The finished form will look like Figure 5-24.

Figure 5-24 ◀

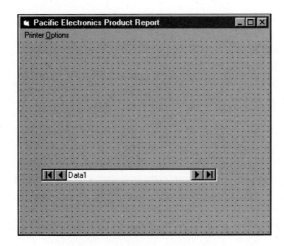

1. Make sure your Student Disk is in the disk drive, and then start Visual Basic.
2. Change the form name to **frmProductReport** and change its caption to **Pacific Electronics Product Report.**
3. Display the Menu Editor for the form.
4. Create a menu title with the caption **Printer &Options** and the name **mnuPrinterOptions.**
5. Create a menu item on the Printer Options menu with the caption **Print to &Printer** and the name **mnuPrinterItem.** Refer to the tutorial for help on creating a menu item.
6. Create another menu item on the Printer Options menu with the caption **Print to &Screen** and the name **mnuScreenItem.**
7. Create another menu item on the Printer Options menu with the caption **E&xit** and the name **mnuExitItem.**
8. Exit the Menu Editor.

9. Draw a Data control on the form, as shown in Figure 5-24, and set the following properties: DatabaseName = **A:\Tutorial.05\TAssign\Pacific.mdb** and RecordSource = **tblProduct.** Make the Data control invisible at run time. Check Visual Basic online Help for information on the Visible property, if necessary.

10. Open the general declarations section of the Code window and declare the following variables: **ProgName, Message,** and **Title,** all as the String data type; and **ItemCnt** as the Integer data type. Declare **rstProduct** as the Recordset object variable. Remember to include the necessary statement to require that all variables be defined before they can be used.
11. In the Code window for the mnuExitItem_Click event, add the code that will end the program.
12. In the Form_Load event procedure, create two variables, **Message,** which will be set to "Type in Tester Name" and **Title,** which will be set to "Pacific Electronics Program Testing." Use these variables as arguments in an InputBox function. Assign the result of the function to the variable **ProgName.** Close the Code window.
13. Start Notepad or any word processing program and open the file **Pacific1.txt** located in the TAssign folder of the Tutorial.05 folder on your Student Disk. This file contains the code to open the Recordset object, print to the printer the headings for the product report, and page through the database, printing the required report fields. At EOF, the code prints the name of the person who tested the program, makes the menu item invisible, and closes the printer buffer. Copy the code in the Pacific1.txt file to the clipboard, return to Visual Basic, and paste it in the mnuPrintPrinter_Click event procedure.
14. Return to Notepad or the word processing program and open the file **Pacific2.txt,** located in the TAssign folder of Tutorial.05 folder on your Student Disk. This file contains the code to open the Recordset object, print to the screen the headings for the product report, and page through the database,

printing the required report fields. At EOF, the code prints the name of the person who tested the program, and makes the menu items invisible. Copy the code in the Pacific2.txt file to the clipboard and paste it in the mnuPrintScreen_Click event procedure.

15. Save the form as **frm Product Report** and the project as **Pacific Product Report** in the TAssign folder of the Tutorial.05 folder on your Student Disk.

16. Run the program. Click the Printer Options menu, then click Print to Screen and examine the report. If the report contains any errors, correct them, and print the report to the screen again.

17. Click the Printer Options menu, then click Print to Printer. The report prints on your printer. If the report contains any errors, correct them, and print the report to the printer again.

18. Click the Printer Options menu, then click Exit.

19. Print the program code. On the printout of the code, write down the function of each statement in the mnuPrinterPrint procedure. Consult Visual Basic online Help if you have any questions about the code.

20. Exit Visual Basic.

Case Problems

1. Helping Hand Incorporated Helping Hand Incorporated organizes and solicits contributions for various charities in the northern United States and Canada. As part of their business activities, Helping Hand staff members often write letters to possible donors. These letters are written to a large number of donors, and Helping Hand would like to have a program to speed up this process. The program will allow staff members to compose a letter, and add the closing and a volunteer name on one form, and use another form to capture the donor name and address information, and print the letter. You will create the program for Helping Hand.

Figure 5-25 shows the completed form for composing the letter.

Figure 5-25 ◀

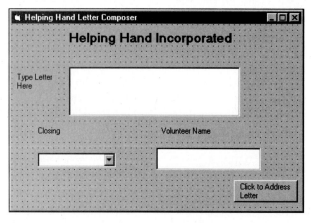

1. Make sure your Student Disk is in the disk drive, then start Visual Basic.

2. Change the form name to **frmHHLetter** and change its caption to **Helping Hand Letter Composer**.

3. Draw a label in the top middle of the form for the title, **Helping Hand Incorporated**. Change the font size to **14-Bold**.

4. Look up the AutoSize property for the Label object in Visual Basic online Help. Change the AutoSize of the label you just created to **True**.

5. Draw a large text box in the middle of the form with the name **txtLetter**. Remove the initial text from the object. Set the Multiline property of the text box so that it can be used to store multiple lines of text. Draw an identifying label with the caption **Type Letter Here**.

6. Draw a combo box in the lower left of the form; the combo box will be used to add a standard closing to a letter. Change the Text property of the combo box to **blank** and the Name property to **cboClosing**. Open the Code window for the

cboClosing_Click event. Make sure the event is the Click event, and set the focus to txtVolunteer. Refer to Visual Basic online Help for the SetFocus event, if necessary. Draw an identifying label above the combo box with the caption **Closing**.

7. Draw a text box next to the combo box. Change the Text property of the text box to **blank** and the Name property to **txtVolunteer**. Draw an identifying label above the text box with the caption **Volunteer Name**.

8. Draw a command button in the lower right of the form with the caption **Click to Address Letter** and the name **cmdGoToAddress**.

9. Open the Code window for the Form_Load event. Use the AddItem method of the cboClosing object to add each of the following closings: **Sincerely, Regretfully, Kindest Regards,** and **Yours Faithfully**.

10. Open the Code window for the cmdGoToAddress_Click event and add code to call the Hide method for the frmHHLetter object and the Show method for the frmHHAddress object.

11. Save the form as **frmHHLetter** in the Cases folder of the Tutorial.05 folder on your Student Disk.

12. Create a second form with the name **frmHHAddress** and the caption **Helping Hand Letter Address**.

13. Use the Project window to return to frmHHLetter.

14. Select the title label and copy it, return to frmHHAddress using the Project window, and then paste the title on the frmHHAddress form in the location shown in Figure 5-26.

Figure 5-26 ◀

```
Helping Hand Letter Address                    _ □ ×

         Helping Hand Incorporated

Donor Name:     [_____]      Go Back to
                                         Letter

Address1        [_____]

                                         Click to Print
Address2        [_____]       Letter

Address3        [_____]
                                            Exit
```

15. Draw four identifying labels down the left side of the form with the captions **Donor Name, Address1, Address2,** and **Address3**, respectively.

16. Draw four text boxes to the right of the labels. Change the Text property of all the text boxes to **blank** and the Name property to **txtDonor, txtAddress1, txtAddress2,** and **txtAddress3**, respectively.

17. Draw a command button in the upper right of the form (refer to Figure 5-26). Change its Caption property to **Go Back to Letter** and its Name property to **cmdGoToLetter**. Open the Code window for the cmdGoToLetter_Click event and type the code that will show the letter form and hide the address form.

18. Draw a command button in the middle right of the form (refer to Figure 5-26). Change its Caption property to **Click to Print Letter** and its Name property to **cmdPrint**.

19. Start Notepad or any word processing program and open the file **HHPrint.txt**, located in the Cases folder of Tutorial.05 folder on your Student Disk. Copy the code contained in the HHPrint.txt file, return to Visual Basic, and paste it in the Click event procedure for cmdPrint. Examine the code so that you understand what it accomplishes. Note that the form name has now been included in some print lines. Why?

20. Add the necessary statements to clear the contents of the input text boxes on the frmHHAddress form just after the information is printed.

21. Draw a working Exit command button on the bottom right side of the form (refer to Figure 5-26) with the hot key combination Alt+X.
22. Save the form as **frmHHAddress** in the Cases folder of the Tutorial.05 folder on your Student Disk.
23. Run the program. The first form displayed should be the frmHHLetter form. Type a thank you letter in the letter text box, then use the combo box to add a closing. Type your name in the Volunteer Name text box.
24. Click the appropriate button to display the address form. Type information of your choice in the Donor Name, Address1, Address2, and Address3 text boxes.
25. Click the button to print the letter. Check that all the fields correctly print what you entered in each form.
26. Enter another address and generate another letter, or go back to the first form and then change the letter you already wrote. When you have finished testing the program, exit it by clicking the Exit button.
27. Print the form image and code for both forms. Save the project as **Helping Hand Letter Generator** in the Cases folder of the Tutorial.05 folder on your Student Disk. (Remember, to open a two-form project in Visual Basic 4.0 Working Model, refer to the Note on page 209 in the tutorial.)
28. Exit Visual Basic.

2. Toys, Toys, Toys, and More Toys Toys, Toys, Toys, and More Toys is a toy manufacturer operating in western Europe. The company has decided to begin work on a comprehensive stock control application. The anticipated system will use an Access database to store information about the toys currently being manufactured, how many toys of each type are in stock, and delivery estimates for toy orders currently in production. Because this is a new application, you will design the startup screen, create a second screen, and then test the links between the two screens. You will use a Data control to retrieve the toy names from a test database.

Figure 5-27 shows the startup (splash) screen for the program.

Figure 5-27 ◀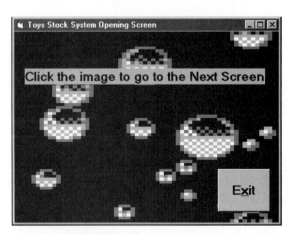

1. Make sure your Student Disk is in the disk drive, then start Visual Basic.
2. Change the form name to **frmToyOpenScreen** and change its caption to **Toys Stock System Opening Screen**.
3. Draw an image that completely covers the form, then set the following properties: Stretch = **True**, Picture = **Bubbles** (or any other bmp file from the Windows folder), and Name = **imgOpenImg**.
4. Open the Code window for the imgOpenImg_Click event and write the code to hide the opening screen and show a form named frmToysStockScreen.
5. Draw a label in the top middle of the image (refer to Figure 5-27), and set the following properties: AutoSize = **True**, Caption = **Click the Image to go to the Next Screen**, and Font Size = **14 Bold**.
6. Draw a working Exit command button on the lower right of the image (refer to Figure 5-27) with the hot key combination Alt+X.

7. Save the form as **frmToysOpenScreen** in the Cases folder of the Tutorial.05 folder on your Student Disk.

8. Add a new blank form named **frmToysStockScreen** with the caption **Toys Stock Screen** to your project. Change the WindowState property to **Maximized**. Check Visual Basic online Help for more information on the WindowState property if necessary. Figure 5-28 shows the main form for the program.

Figure 5-28 ◀

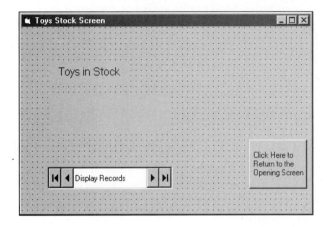

9. Draw a Data control at the bottom of the form (refer to Figure 5-28), and set the following properties: Caption = **Display Records**, DatabaseName = **A:\Tutorial.05\Cases\Toys.mdb**, Name = **datProduct**, and RecordSource = **tblToyProducts**. Make sure that the RecordsetType shows **1 - Dynaset**.

10. Draw a label in the middle of the screen (refer to Figure 5-28), and set the following properties: Name = **lblToys**, DataSource = **datProduct**, DataField = **ProductName**, and Caption = **blank**.

11. Draw an identifying label above lblToys and change its caption to **Toys in Stock**.

12. Draw a command button named **cmdOpenScreen** with the caption **Click Here to Return to the Opening Screen** in the lower right of the form (refer to Figure 5-28). Size the command button so that the caption fits. Write the code to hide the stock screen and show the opening screen.

13. Save the form as **frmToysStockScreen** in the Cases folder of the Tutorial.05 folder on your Student Disk.

14. Run the program. Click the image to go to the stock screen. Click the Data control arrows to view the stock information in the label. Click the command button to return to the opening screen. Click the Exit button to end the program.

15. Print the form image and code for both forms. Save the project as **Toys Stock Application** in the Cases folder of the Tutorial.05 folder on your Student Disk. (Remember, to open a two-form project in Visual Basic 4.0 Working Model, refer to Note on page 209 in the tutorial.)

16. Exit Visual Basic.

3. Jill Jones Phone Log Jill Jones is your neighbor and she has been watching your progress learning Visual Basic. Over a cup of coffee one morning, she wondered if you could create a program that would allow her to look up a friend's name and have the phone number displayed. She would like to be able to load her existing phone list and add and delete names and numbers, change numbers, and print the list. You tell Jill that you could create a program that will function usefully but not have the capability to permanently record additions, changes, or deletions to database records.

Jill has given you a list of four names for testing. You have created the pseudocode for the program. Figure 5-29 shows the completed form for the program.

Figure 5-29 ◀

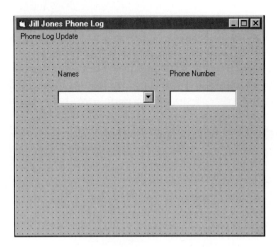

1. Open Notepad or any word processing program, and open the file **JJ_Pcode.txt** located in the Cases folder of the Tutorial.05 folder on your Student Disk. Print and examine the pseudocode and keep it next to you while you work on the program. Exit Notepad or the word processing program.
2. Start Visual Basic.
3. Change the form caption to **Jill Jones Phone Log** and change its name to **frmJill**.
4. Draw a combo box in the middle of the form (refer to Figure 5-29) and set the following properties: Left = **2400**, Name = **cboPerson**, Sorted = **True**, Text = **blank**, Top = **1080**, and Width = **2295**.
5. Draw a text box to the right of the combo box, (refer to Figure 5-29) and set the following properties: Name = **txtPhone** and Text = **blank**.
6. Draw an identifying label above the combo box and change its caption to **Names**. Draw another identifying label above the text box and change its caption to **Phone Number**.
7. In the Menu Editor create one menu title with five menu items, as shown in Figure 5-30.

Figure 5-30 ◀

mnuUpdate

mnuAddItem

mnuExitItem

mnuDeleteItem

mnuPhoneItem

mnuPrintItem

8. Close the Menu Editor.
9. Open the Code window for Form_Load and type the code shown below. The ItemData property works like a combo box's List property. For each entry in the combo box or list box, a long integer field is set up to correspond to that entry. You can use this field to store numbers that can be retrieved when the user clicks an item. The NewIndex property returns the index of the most recently added item in a combo box.

```
'Add name to cboPerson
cboPerson.AddItem "Tom Jones"
cboPerson.ItemData(cboPerson.NewIndex) = 5551264
```

10. Add the names of the rest of Jill's friends to the combo box and ItemData property. Their names and phone numbers are: **Joy Fegusson, 4253647; William Thomson, 9673967;** and **Kim Evans, 2234547**.

11. Open the Code window for the cboPerson_Click event and type the code to set the Text property of the txtPhone object to the currently selected person in the cboPerson combo box. You can look up the phone number by using the ItemData property. Remember the active item can be referenced using the ListIndex property.
12. Open the Code window for the mnuAddItem_Click event and type the following code:

```
cboPerson.AddItem cboPerson.Text
cboPerson.ItemData(cboPerson.NewIndex) _
    = Val(txtPhone.Text)
```

13. Open the Code window for the mnuDeleteItem_Click event and write the code to remove the current item from the cboPerson combo box. You need to call the RemoveItem method. The active item in the combo box is stored in the ListIndex property. Also, write the statement to remove the text from the txtPhone text box.
14. Open the Code window for the mnuPhoneItem_Click event and type the following code:

```
cboPerson.ItemData(cboPerson.ListIndex) _
    = Val(txtPhone.Text)
```

15. Open the Code window for the mnuPrintItem_Click event and write the code to print the contents of the cboPerson combo box. You need to write a Do loop that increments a counter from 0 to the number of items in the combo box. The variable you use as a counter should be named Counter and declared as an integer. The number of items is stored in the ListCount property. Each time through the loop, you need to increment the counter by 1. For each item in the list, print the contents of both the List and ItemData properties on a single line. These properties take an argument, the index of the item in the combo box you want. Use the Counter variable to step through each item in the combo box.
16. Open the Code window for the mnuExitItem_Click event and create a working Exit menu item.
17. Run the program. Click the list arrow for the combo box and select any of Jill's friends to see the corresponding phone number. Add, change, and delete records and then view the results by clicking the list. To add a record, click the text portion of the combo box and delete the entry. Then type a new name, click on the phone number text box (or press the Tab key) and type a number containing fewer than the maximum number of characters for a long integer data type (you might want to look this up in Help). Click Phone Log Update and click Add to add a record. Change a phone number by selecting a name, clicking and changing the number, and then clicking the Change Phone menu item. To delete a record, select a name and click the Delete menu item. To print the log, click the Print Log menu item. To exit, click the Exit menu item. Any changes you make will only be valid while the program is running. Remember that any changes you make will not be saved from one program run to the next.
18. Print the form image and code. Save the form as **frmJill** and the project as **Jill Jones Phone Log** in the Cases folder of the Tutorial.05 folder on your Student Disk.
19. Exit Visual Basic.

4. Jill Jones Phone Log Database Jill thought your phone log program was a great idea. Because you have begun working with databases, you would like to try to modify the phone log program to load the data from a database rather than from within the program as you did in Case Problem 3. You have converted the names and phone numbers of Jill's friends to a table in an Access database. A copy of the database is stored as **dbJill.mdb** in the Cases folder of the Tutorial.05 folder on your Student Disk. Read Case Problem 3 to review the specifics of the phone log interface.

Load the combo box with the names of the friends in the database and the ItemData box with the phone numbers. You can use a Do loop containing statements to read the database table and insert the fields into the combo box and ItemData box. Use the Form_Activate event to hold this code and remove the AddItem code from the Form_Load event. This will allow you to test the program's add, change, and delete capabilities during run time, but not to actually modify the database. The table in the database is called **tblJill** and the fields are **FriendsName** and **Telephone**.

Hint: Review the tutorial and Tutorial Assignments carefully to determine the statements that will be required for your program.

Print the form image and code. Save the form as **frmJillDatabase** and the project as **Jill Jones Phone Log Database** in the Cases folder of the Tutorial.05 folder on your Student Disk.

Reading and Writing Text Files into List Boxes and Arrays

Creating a Quotation System for Star Plant Supply

OBJECTIVES

In this tutorial you will:

■ Read information from a text file and load it into a list box at run time

■ Create an array to store a series of variables

■ Add and remove all the items or individual items in a list box

■ Create a For loop that will execute statements a fixed number of times

■ Create a multi-dimensional array made up of rows and columns

■ Write information to a text file

CASE

Star Plant Supply

Rose Blain is the owner of Star Plant Supply, a company that has been supplying plants to landscaping firms in Naples, Florida, since 1986. Currently Rose employs nine people. Eight of the staff members perform deliveries, unload shipments, and keep track of inventory. Rose also has an assistant to help her manage the business.

Before Rose's customers place an order, they require a verbal or written price estimate, or quotation. Her customers want to make sure they are getting the best price for each item they buy, so they shop around. They also need to meet deadlines for their landscaping projects, so they must obtain quotations quickly. Rose currently maintains a price list and uses a quotation form and calculator to write quotations for her customers. Her business is growing so rapidly that she often cannot write all the quotations that have been requested. This means she loses the sale. Also, because Rose needs to look up the price of each item by hand when she writes quotations, the current system is prone to errors. Furthermore, she has noticed that she makes errors occasionally when computing the extended prices for items and adding the extended prices together to compute the quotation total. Rose wants a computerized system that will help her keep up with the volume of quotations she has to write and compute the pricing information for her automatically.

Rose's friend, Mack Woolard, has been helping her to develop the quotation system in Visual Basic. Mack has been creating a program for her, but he does not have time to complete it, and they have asked you to finish it. Rose is not very familiar with computers and she is a poor typist, so she wants to be able to select an item from a list of the products she carries, enter the quantity requested, then have the program compute the extended price of the item. Most customers want a running total of the items they have requested, so she also wants the program to add together the extended prices of all the items and compute a quotation total each time an item is added to the quotation.

Rose's assistant, Joan Grayson, used Notepad to create a price list of all Star Plant Supply's products. Each product is listed on a separate line followed by the corresponding price for the item. Joan updates this file when the prices change or new items are added to the inventory. Rose currently uses a printed copy of the price list to manually prepare the quotations. Mack explains that the quotation program can read this text file and use the information to produce the quotations for the customers.

SESSION

6.1

In this session you will learn how to read information from a text file into a series of variables stored as one unit called an array. You will also insert items into a list box using code and access the items of a list box using the List and ListIndex properties. Also, you will write a For loop to step through the items in a list box.

Analyzing the Program

Mack has already written the pseudocode and TOE chart, and he has designed the screen for the quotation program. Also, he has created a form with all the objects he plans to use. However, he has not written any code yet or set many of the properties for the objects he created. Before you begin working on the program, you should review the design specifications.

To look at the design specifications for the quotation program:

1. Start Notepad or any word processing program and make sure your Student Disk is in the disk drive.

2. Open the file named **Star_TOE.txt** located in the **Tutorial.06** folder on your Student Disk.

3. Print the file and then exit Notepad or the word processing program.

Examine the pseudocode and TOE chart. All of the product descriptions will be stored in a list that Rose can use to choose products. Rose will be able to add a product to the quotation by clicking the product in the list, typing the quantity requested, and then clicking a button to add the item to the output section of the price quotation. The program will include four list boxes for output: Product Description, Quantity, Price Each, and Extended Price. Keep the printed pseudocode and TOE chart next to you while you complete the program.

Rose's customers work with tight budgets, so she wants to be able to give customers immediate feedback about the quotation total so they can make their purchasing decisions. Therefore, she would like the extended price of an item and the quotation total to be computed each time an item is added to the quotation. Mack has completed the screen design for the program, as shown in Figure 6-1.

Figure 6-1 ◀
Screen design
of the quotation
form

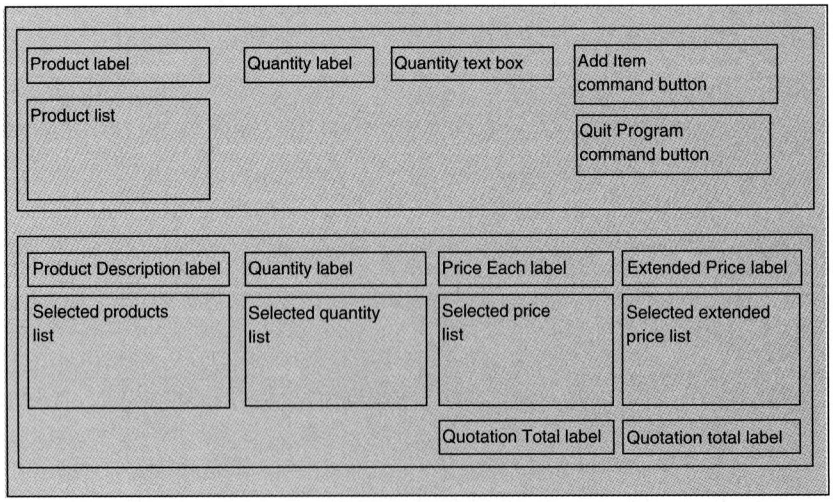

Following good user-interface design principles, Mack divided the screen into two sections—the upper section for input and the lower section for output. Each section is bordered by a frame for visual identification. In this case, the frames are not being used as containers for option buttons. Rather, they are used only to visually separate the input and output sections of the program. Because Rose is a poor typist, Mack used a list box for the product list so that Rose can use scroll bars and the mouse to select a product instead of typing the product description.

The output section of the form contains four list boxes, four labels that describe the contents of the list boxes, and two labels that identify and display the quotation total. Each item in the quotation will appear on its own line in the list boxes.

When Rose clicks the Add Item command button, the program will look up the price of the selected item, then multiply it by the quantity requested to compute the extended price. Then, the item, quantity ordered, price, and extended price will be displayed in the lists used for output. Finally, the quotation total will be computed.

You will begin by opening the project file that Mack already created.

To open the partially completed quotation program:

1. Start Visual Basic and open the project file named **Star1.vbp** in the **Tutorial.06** folder on your Student Disk. If necessary, click the **View Form** button in the Project window to display the form. See Figure 6-2.

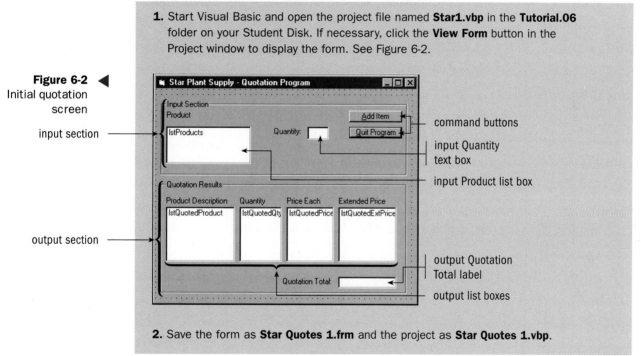

Figure 6-2 ◀
Initial quotation screen

input section

output section

command buttons

input Quantity text box

input Product list box

output Quotation Total label

output list boxes

2. Save the form as **Star Quotes 1.frm** and the project as **Star Quotes 1.vbp**.

The price list, which Joan created in Notepad, lists each of Star Plant Supply's products on a separate line followed by the corresponding price for each product. Joan updates this list when the prices change or new items are added to the inventory. Figure 6-3 shows the contents of the Notepad text file.

Figure 6-3 ◀
Price list for Star Plant Supply

Flower - Iris	4.37
Flower - Lilac	5.22
Herb - Mint	1.88
Shrub - Boxwood	9.22
Shrub - Juniper	4.18
Tree - Ash	43.80
Tree - Pine	28.60
Tree - Oak	33.84
Tree - Olive	19.20

The quotation program you are creating can read this text file and use the information in it. However, Joan needs to make some changes to the formatting so that Visual Basic can read the file. To use the text file with Visual Basic, Joan must remove the tabs and enter commas, with no spaces, to separate the products from the prices. Also, the product names must be enclosed in quotation marks.

Loading a Text File into a Program

When the quotation program starts, the first thing it must do is load all the products into the Product list box. There are two options available for loading the product and price list. You could store the product information in a database and use a Data control and its Recordset property with a Do loop to add each item, or you could load the product and pricing information into the computer's memory from a text file when the program first starts.

The decision to use a text file or a database to store the data is based on several factors. When the number of items to be used is relatively small, they can be read effectively from a text file and stored in the computer's memory using list boxes and combo boxes, without slowing down your system. Reading the information from a database each time a product is accessed would take longer than finding the information in a list or a variable. The information in your input list is read-only; that is, once the information is loaded into the program, it will not be changed. So, there is no need to write individual records back to a database. Also, Rose wants to continue using the text file containing the price list. In this way, if the computer is not available because of a disk failure, or if she is preparing a quotation outside the office, she can refer to a printout of the price list to prepare quotations manually. So, your program will read the product information from the Notepad text file that Joan created.

In Tutorials 4 and 5, you accessed a table in a database by creating an instance of a Data control and using the methods of the Data control and the Recordset object to navigate through the records. Unlike a database, a text file is not an object. Instead of calling the methods of an object that works with databases, you use a Visual Basic statement to open a text file. Once a text file is open, you can read the file from beginning to end. This method of accessing a text file is called **sequential access**. A program cannot explicitly locate a specific line in a text file without reading all the lines preceding it.

Opening a Text File

When you open a text file, you must explicitly open the file and tell Visual Basic what operations you want to perform on it. You open the file with the **Open** statement, which has the following syntax:

Open *pathname* **For [Input | Output | Append] As #***filenumber*

- The *pathname* contains a string describing the name and location of the file you want to open.

- One of three options—Input, Output, or Append—must be included in the Open statement or Visual Basic will generate a syntax error. If the file is opened **For Input**, it must already exist. You can read information contained in the file but you cannot write to the file when it is opened For Input. This is the method you will use to read the file for the Star Plant Supply quotation program.

- If the file is opened **For Output**, you can write to the file but you cannot read it. If the file does not exist, Visual Basic will create it for you. If the file does exist, the existing contents will be deleted. The user will not see a dialog box asking to confirm the deletion. You can create a message box to ask for confirmation from the user with the MsgBox function. The For Output option is useful if you want to rewrite an existing file entirely.

- If the file is opened **For Append**, information you write to the file will be appended to the end of the file, but you cannot read from it. If the file does not exist, Visual Basic will create it for you. Unlike opening a file For Output, the existing contents of a file opened For Append will not be deleted.

- The *filenumber* is an arbitrary number you assign as a reference to the file while it is open. Starting the filenumber at #1 for the first open file and #2 for the second open file will make your program more understandable, but you can use any number. If you do not specify a filenumber, Visual Basic will generate a syntax error.

Although you can have several files open at once, you cannot open an infinite number of files. Windows 95 determines how many total files you can have open at once, which varies from system to system.

REFERENCE window	**OPENING A TEXT FILE**
	■ To open a file for reading, type the Open statement followed by the filename and the For Input clause after the filename.
	■ To assign a filenumber to the file, type As #*n* at the end of the Open statement, where *n* is an integer number not already assigned to a file. To make your programs more readable, the first file you open should have a filenumber of 1.

Because the information contained in the text file must be loaded before Rose can begin preparing any quotations, the program should read the text file when the form is loaded. So, the program should read the information into a list box and variable in the Form_Load event procedure.

To write the code for opening the text file into the program:

1. Open the Code window for the **Form_Load** event procedure.

2. Enter the following code in the window:

```
Open "A:\Tutorial.06\Product.txt" For Input As #1
```

This statement opens the Price list file, Product.txt, in the Tutorial.06 folder located on your Student Disk. Because you will be reading information into the program, you opened the file For Input. It is the first open file, so its filenumber is #1.

Reading a Text File

After opening the file For Input, the program can read each of the products from the file into the Product list box. You could enter all the items at design time by setting the list box's List property, but if you did so, any changes to the list of products would have to be made by changing the properties using the Properties window. Because Rose is not very familiar with computers, she does not want to have to modify the program. Reading the products from a file is the best solution, because Joan can update the text file in Notepad when products are added and removed or the prices change. As long as Joan keeps the price list current, every time Rose runs the program it will contain the current information from the text file.

The **Input #** statement is used when each line of the file contains information separated by commas, and any text strings in the file are enclosed in quotation marks. The Input # statement has the following syntax:

Input #*filenumber*, *variablelist*

- The *filenumber* can be any valid filenumber assigned by the Open statement.

- The *variablelist* is a list of variables, separated by commas, that are assigned values read from the file. When an input file has information separated by commas, each item of information can be thought of as a field, like in a database. The data type of each variable should correspond to the data type in the respective field.

REFERENCE window	**READING A TEXT FILE**
	■ To read information from a file into different variables, use the Input # statement followed by the filenumber describing the open file. ■ Append a variable name for each field in the record. ■ To close the file, execute a Close statement followed by the filenumber.

Visual Basic can read text files using an Input # statement when each field in a line is separated, or delimited, by a comma, and string information is enclosed in quotation marks. This type of file is called an **ASCII delimited file** and is supported by most word processing, spreadsheet, and database programs. Joan has converted the Notepad text file into a form suitable for reading by your Visual Basic program. Figure 6-4 shows part of the ASCII delimited file for the quotation program.

Figure 6-4 ◀
ASCII delimited
file with two
fields

text field ———

comma separator ———

numeric field ———

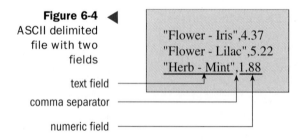

"Flower - Iris",4.37
"Flower - Lilac",5.22
"Herb - Mint",1.88

As shown in Figure 6-4, the input file contains two items of information separated by a comma. Each of these items can be thought of as a field. The first field contains text enclosed in quotation marks. The second field is numeric; it is not enclosed in quotations. Each line in the file can be thought of as a record. In this figure there are three records.

Generally you want the text to be read just after the file is opened, so the program should read the file immediately after opening it in the Form_Load event procedure. To do this, you will create a variable that will temporarily store the information before adding it to the Product list box. Remember, you should declare all variables before executing any statements in a procedure to improve program readability.

To read the text file, you will create a Do loop that calls the Input# statement repeatedly until the end of the file has been reached. To determine when the end of the file has been read you will use the EOF function. The EOF function takes one argument—the filenumber assigned to the file. The function returns the value True when the end of the input file has been reached, otherwise, it returns the value False.

To read the text file into the Product list box:

1. Make sure the Code window for the **Form_Load** event procedure is still active.

2. Enter the following code in the window; the statements you need to enter appear in bold (be sure to include the Dim statements before the Open statement you typed earlier):

```
Dim TmpProduct As String
Dim TmpPrice As Single
Open "A:\Tutorial.06\Product.txt" For Input As #1
Do Until EOF(1) = True
    Input #1, TmpProduct, TmpPrice
        lstProducts.AddItem TmpProduct
Loop
```

These statements read the input from the text file and load the items into the list box used for input.

```
Dim TmpProduct As String
Dim TmpPrice As Single
```

These statements declare two variables. The variable TmpProduct will store the name of each product. The variable TmpPrice will store the price of each product; you will use this variable later in the session.

```
Do Until EOF(1) = True
    Input #1, TmpProduct, TmpPrice
    lstProducts.AddItem TmpProduct
Loop
```

The EOF function works with a text file in the same way that the EOF property works with Recordset objects. The EOF function determines when the end of a file is reached. This is used to exit the Do loop. The EOF function returns the value False unless the end of the file has been reached; then it returns the value True. The argument 1 is the filenumber corresponding to the open file.

In the Input statement, the filenumber #1 is associated with the file you opened when you executed the Open statement. Each time the program reads a line from the file, the values it reads are stored in the variables TmpProduct and TmpPrice. If the input file included more than two fields on a line, you would have stored the fields in additional variables separated by commas. Because the number of variables in the Input statement must correspond to the number of fields in the file, the variable TmpPrice must be included here, even though the program is not using this information at this point.

The third statement adds the contents of the variable TmpProduct to the lstProducts list box with the AddItem method.

The Loop statement sends the program back to the Do statement to determine if the end of the file has been reached.

You should now test the Do loop you just wrote to see if the products in the text file are being read into the Product list box.

To test the Do loop:

1. Start the program. When the form is displayed, your screen should look like Figure 6-5.

Figure 6-5
Input list box
with data

list box with data —

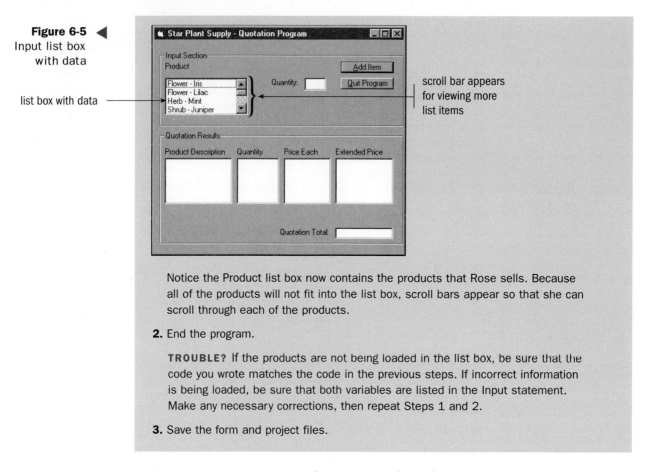

scroll bar appears
for viewing more
list items

Notice the Product list box now contains the products that Rose sells. Because all of the products will not fit into the list box, scroll bars appear so that she can scroll through each of the products.

2. End the program.

TROUBLE? If the products are not being loaded in the list box, be sure that the code you wrote matches the code in the previous steps. If incorrect information is being loaded, be sure that both variables are listed in the Input statement. Make any necessary corrections, then repeat Steps 1 and 2.

3. Save the form and project files.

Now, every time you run the program, the information in the first field of the Product.txt file will be stored in the Product list box.

Closing the File

Whenever a program finishes reading a file, the program should close the file explicitly using the **Close** statement. Because Windows 95 limits the number of files you can have open at one time, closing files that are not being used will ensure that there are adequate filenumbers remaining. Also, each open file consumes some memory. So, too many open files can slow down your computer, depending on the amount of memory it has.

The syntax of the Close statement is:

Close [*filenumberlist*]

- The *filenumberlist* argument can be one or more filenumbers separated by commas. So, to close file #1 and #2 you would write the following statement:

```
Close #1, #2
```

- If you do not specify a filenumberlist, any files opened with the Open statement are closed. If you are working with several files, including such a Close statement just before the program exits will guarantee that all files have been closed.

You currently have one file open, Product.txt, which is associated with the filenumber #1. You now need to write the code for closing this file.

To close the open text file:

1. Open the Code window for the **Form_Load** event procedure.

2. Enter the following line of code, just before the End Sub statement:

```
Close #1
```

When the running program reaches this statement, the program will close the Product.txt file. The filenumber #1 will no longer be associated with the file. If the program needs to read the file again, the program must open the file again with the Open statement.

Creating an Array to Store Information

In each program you have written until this point, you have declared variables that can store only a single item of information, such as a price. In the quotation program, you need to store the prices for each product sold by Star Plant Supply. When Rose selects an item from the list box of products, the program needs to look up the corresponding price. The company sells nine different products, so you would need nine different variables to store the information. Although creating nine variables does not present a problem, consider a company that sells 50 or 500 products. The problem becomes more complicated when you need to add new products, because you would need to create new variables.

You have seen how several objects of the same type can be grouped together in a control array. Each object in a control array has the same name and is referenced with its Index property value, which is unique. You can group variables together in the same way using an array. An **array** is a list of several items of the same data type. Each item in an array is called an **element**. Each individual element is referenced by a unique index number, called a **subscript**. You can declare variables that can store several pieces of similar information in a column using an array. When you want to access an individual element in an array, you use the array name and the subscript to reference the element.

You can create an array to store the prices of each item in one variable, just as you can store many items in one list box. Figure 6-6 shows the relationship between the information stored in the array and the list box.

Figure 6-6 ◀
Relationship
between an
array and a
list box

first array item

fourth array item

array containing
four prices

corresponding list box
with four product
descriptions

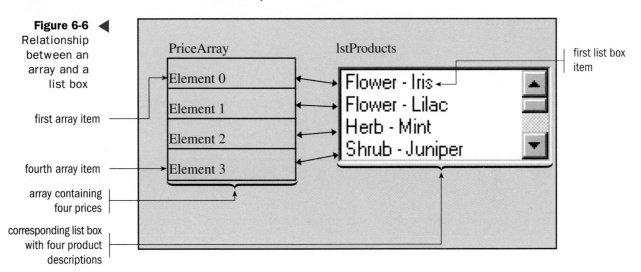

As shown in Figure 6-6, the array PriceArray contains four elements, numbered 0 through 3, that correspond to the product descriptions stored in the lstProducts list box. Thus, the price for the final product, Flower - Iris, is stored in the first element of PriceArray, which is element 0.

When you create an array, you use the Dim statement, just as you do when you declare any variable. An array is simply a variable that contains many elements of the same data type.

To declare an array, you use a Dim statement with the following syntax:

Dim *array-name(lower-bound* **To** *upper-bound)* **As** *datatype*

- The *array-name* can be any valid variable name.

- The *lower-bound* defines the first element of the array. If you do not specify a lower-bound, it will be set to 0 by default.

- The *upper-bound* defines the last element of the array.

- The *datatype* can be any valid Visual Basic data type.

You need to create an array to store the price for each of the products loaded into the Product list box. Like any variable, an array declared in the general declarations section of a form is available to all procedures in the form module. If you declare an array inside a procedure, the array is considered local to the procedure and can be referenced inside that procedure only. Because the array you create will be used by the cmdAdd_Click event procedure to look up the prices and add them to the Price Each output list box, and also used by the Form_Load event procedure to load the prices into the array, you must declare the array in the general declarations section.

Like variables, arrays consume memory. If you make an array too large, memory will be wasted because Visual Basic allocates memory for each element in the array whether or not the program stores values in each element. So, you should try to accurately estimate the number of elements in the array. Rose estimates that she will sell at most 100 different products, so the array should be declared to hold 100 items. However, you do not need to store a value in each element of an array right away. You can add values later. Running the program with some empty array elements will not cause an error.

To declare an array to contain the prices of the products:

1. Activate the general declarations section of the Code window.

The Option Explicit statement is already included to make sure that all variables in your program are declared before you use them.

2. Enter the following statement in the Code window, just after the Option Explicit statement:

```
Dim PriceArray(0 To 99) As Single
```

The array PriceArray contains 100 elements. The first element is 0 and the last element is 99. Each element in the array is defined as a Single data type, which is the appropriate data type because the prices will contain decimal places.

Storing Information in an Array

Once the array has been declared, you need to store the information in it. This information will consist of the price for each item. Each price will correspond to an item in the Product list box, as shown in Figure 6-6, but the array will include 100 elements instead of four.

When you store information in an array and retrieve information from an array, you are interested in a specific element rather than the contents of the entire array. In this case the array stores the price for each product in the inventory. When you need to look up a price in the array, you are looking for the price of a particular item, rather than all of the prices.

Next, you need to load the prices into the array. The price of each product must be stored in the array in such a way that the first item in the Product list box will correspond to the price contained in the first element of the array.

The procedure for loading the prices into the array is similar to the procedure you used to load the products into the list box. Because all the products and corresponding prices must be loaded into the computer's memory before Rose can begin writing a quotation, the array should be loaded at the same time that the products are loaded into the list box. So, you can modify the Form_Load event procedure you already wrote to add the necessary statements for loading prices into the array. In fact, you can expand the Do loop that reads the products into the Product list box so that it also loads the prices into the array.

To write the code for loading the prices into the array:

1. Activate the Code window for the **Form_Load** event procedure.

2. Add the following statements shown in bold to the event procedure:

```
Private Sub Form_Load()
    Dim TmpProduct As String
    Dim TmpPrice As Single
    Dim CurrentItem As Integer

    CurrentItem = 0
    Open "A:\Tutorial.06\Product.txt" For Input As #1
    Do Until EOF(1)
        Input #1, TmpProduct, TmpPrice
        lstProducts.AddItem TmpProduct
        PriceArray(CurrentItem) = TmpPrice
        CurrentItem = CurrentItem + 1
    Loop
    Close #1
End Sub
```

The code you just entered will load the prices from the text file into the array.

```
Dim CurrentItem As Integer
CurrentItem = 0
```

The CurrentItem variable is used as an array subscript, which is always a whole number. Because you want the program to load the first line of the text file into the first element of the array, you initialized the CurrentItem variable to 0.

```
PriceArray(CurrentItem) = TmpPrice
CurrentItem = CurrentItem + 1
```

Each time a line is read from the file, a variable used in the Input statement, TmpPrice, is assigned to the element in PriceArray corresponding to the product contained in the Product list box. Whenever you reference an array, you use the subscript to identify which member of the array you are referring to. Because the variable CurrentItem was initialized to 0, the first value of TmpPrice will be stored at element position 0. This is the lower bound, or first element, of the array. Next, CurrentItem is explicitly incremented by 1 so that the next time through the loop, the value of TmpPrice will be stored in the next element.

All the products and prices will be loaded into the program when it starts. Now, when Rose clicks a product in the list box, the program must determine which item she selected so that it can find the corresponding price from PriceArray. The program also needs to copy this information into the ListBox objects used for output when the Add Item command button is clicked. The ListIndex property of the ListBox object solves this problem.

The **ListIndex** property is an integer value that identifies the currently selected item in a list box. The first item in the list has a ListIndex property value of 0, the second item has a value of 1, and so on. If no item has been selected, the ListIndex property has a value of -1. The expression List1.ListIndex returns the integer index for the currently selected item in the List Box object named List 1. This is similar to the way you reference an element in an array with a subscript, but with an array you are not using a property.

You can assign a value to the ListIndex property. When you do, you set the active item for the list. For example, if you wanted to make the currently selected item the first item of a list box, you would set its ListIndex property to 0. If you wanted to deselect all items in the list, you would set the ListIndex property to -1.

Adding an item to the quotation is the most common event that Rose will trigger in this program. To allow Rose to press the Enter key to add an item to the quotation, Mack set the Default property of the Add Item command button to True in the Properties window. You now need to program the Add Item command button to look up the price for each selected product and store the product and price information in the output list boxes.

To program the Add Item command button to look up prices and add both product and price information to the output ListBox objects:

1. Activate the Code window for the **cmdAdd_Click** event procedure.

2. Enter the following code in the window:

```
Private Sub cmdAdd_Click()
    lstQuotedProduct.AddItem lstProducts.Text
    lstQuotedPrice.AddItem _
        Format(PriceArray(lstProducts.ListIndex), "fixed")
    lstProducts.ListIndex = -1
End Sub
```

Each time Rose clicks a product in the Product list box and then clicks the Add Item command button, the code you just wrote will add the information into the Product Description and Price Each output list boxes.

```
lstQuotedProduct.AddItem lstProducts.Text
```

This statement adds the text of the currently selected item in estProducts to the output list box lstQuotedProduct.

```
lstQuotedPrice.AddItem _
        Format(PriceArray(lstProducts.ListIndex), "fixed")
```

This statement uses the array you created to locate the price for the selected product. To do this, the value of the ListIndex property of the currently selected product in the lstProducts list box is referenced, and that value becomes the subscript referenced in the PriceArray. Figure 6-7 shows how this process works. To display the prices with two decimal places, you used the Format function with the fixed argument.

Figure 6-7 ◀
Adding the
product and
price to the
output list
boxes

third item
(Herb - Mint) is
selected; this is
lstProducts.Text

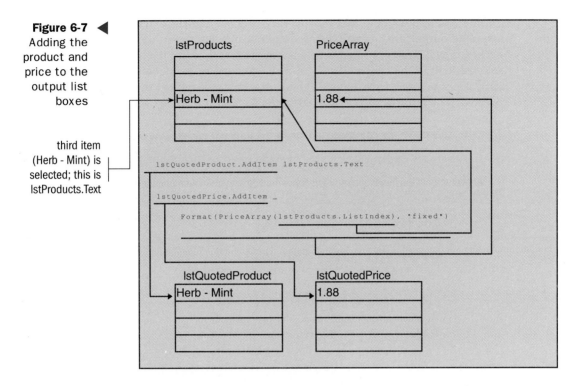

```
lstProducts.ListIndex = -1
```

This statement sets the ListIndex property of the list box to -1, which deselects the item in the Product list box so it is clear for the next product selection.

You should now test the program to determine if the Add Item command button is working properly. When clicked, this button should add the selected product and its corresponding price to the quotation, and then deselect the active item in the Product list box.

To test the Add Item command button:

1. Start the program.
2. Click the product **Herb - Mint** in the Product list box.
3. Click the **Add Item** command button. Your screen should look like Figure 6-8.

Figure 6-8 ◀
Testing the
Add Item
command
button

no active item after
clicking the Add Item
command button

output product
description

output price

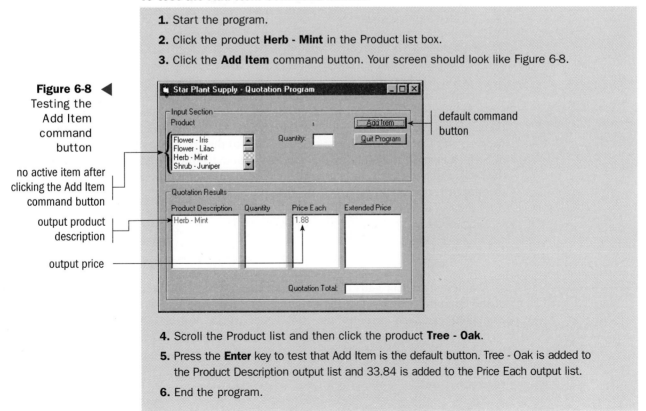

4. Scroll the Product list and then click the product **Tree - Oak**.
5. Press the **Enter** key to test that Add Item is the default button. Tree - Oak is added to the Product Description output list and 33.84 is added to the Price Each output list.
6. End the program.

Now you are ready to add the quantity ordered and the extended prices to the corresponding output list boxes. This needs to occur when the Add Item command button is clicked. The quantity ordered was typed in the text box and the product description is the selected item in the Product list box. The extended price is computed by looking up the correct price in the array named PriceArray, and multiplying that value by the quantity ordered. The result is then displayed in the Extended Price list box.

To write the code for the quantity ordered and extended price output:

1. Activate the Code window for the **cmdAdd** object's **Click** event procedure.

2. Add the following statements (shown in bold) to the event procedure:

```
Private Sub cmdAdd_Click()
    Dim TmpExtPrice As Single

    TmpExtPrice = (txtQty.Text * _
        PriceArray(lstProducts.ListIndex))

    lstQuotedProduct.AddItem lstProducts.Text
    lstQuotedQty.AddItem txtQty.Text
    lstQuotedPrice.AddItem _
        Format(PriceArray(lstProducts.ListIndex), "fixed")
    lstQuotedExtPrice.AddItem Format(TmpExtPrice, "fixed")
    lstProducts.ListIndex = -1
    txtQty.Text = ""

End Sub
```

The code you added will move the quantity from the Quantity text box in the input section to the Quantity list box in the output section. It will also compute the extended price and place it in the Extended Price list box.

```
Dim TmpExtPrice As Single

TmpExtPrice = (txtQty.Text * _
    PriceArray(lstProducts.ListIndex))
```

The first statement creates a local variable, TmpExtPrice, to store the temporary extended price used in this procedure. The local variable you declared is then used to store the extended price of the product. To produce the extended price, you use the ListIndex property of the Product list box as the subscript of the array, and multiply the value stored in each element of the array by the quantity ordered value stored in the Text property of the txtQty object. After computing the extended price, the program can add the items to the output list boxes.

```
lstQuotedQty.AddItem txtQty.Text

lstQuotedExtPrice.AddItem Format(TmpExtPrice, "fixed")
```

The first statement adds the quantity of the specific item (stored in the Text property of the Quantity text box) to the lstQuotedQty list box. The second statement adds the computed extended price to the lstQuotedExtPrice list box by calling the AddItem method. To display the extended price with two decimal places, you called the Format function with the fixed argument.

```
txtQty.Text = ""
```

This statement sets the Text property of the txtQty text box to a blank value, which clears the Quantity text box and makes the form ready for the next product and quantity to be added.

Now you should test the program to verify that the output is being added to the correct ListBox objects, that the extended prices are being computed properly, and that the input list box and text box are being reset.

To test the extended price and quantity output:

1. Start the program.

2. Click the product **Herb - Mint** in the Product list box.

3. Type **2** in for the Quantity text box.

4. Click the **Add Item** command button.

   The product description, quantity, and price each are displayed in the Quotation Results section on the form. Also, the extended price is computed and displayed in the Quotation Results section.

   TROUBLE? If you do not enter a valid number in the Quantity text box, the program will generate a run-time error when it tries to multiply the quantity requested by the price. End the program and then repeat Steps 1 through 4, making sure you enter the number "2" in the Quantity text box.

5. Scroll the product list and then click the product **Tree - Oak**.

6. Type **1** in the Quantity text box.

7. Press the **Enter** key to execute the Add Item command button. Your screen should look like Figure 6-9.

Figure 6-9 ◀
Completed output list boxes

input section cleared for next selection

output list boxes completed

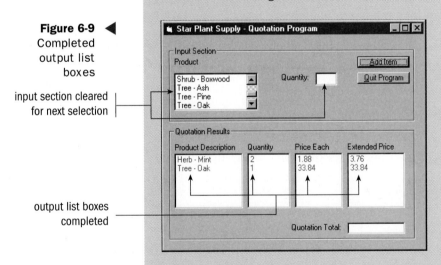

Just like the first item you added, the product description, quantity, price each, and extended price are displayed in the Quotation Results section of the form. Notice the quotation total contains no information because you have not yet written the code to compute the total.

8. End the program.

You have completed the statements to store the product description, quantity, price each, and extended price in the output list boxes. Your next task is to update the quotation total each time an item is added.

Looping Through the Items in a List Box

In previous tutorials, you used the Change event of an object to call a general procedure that calculates totals each time the value of the object changed. In this case, unlike a TextBox object, the ListBox object does not support the Change event. So, the program must update the total when the Add Item command button is clicked.

You have seen how to use a Do loop with the EOF function to examine each line of a text file repetitively until the end-of-file condition is reached. In that situation, the program does not know how many lines are in the text file. Rather, the loop terminates when the end-of-file condition is true.

You could use a Do loop to step through each item in the Extended Price list box as well, by creating a variable used as an index. Another ListBox property, the **ListCount property**, determines the number of items in a list. This property is an integer that contains the number of items in a list box. If the list box is empty, the ListCount is 0; otherwise, the value of ListCount is the number of items in the list.

Your Do loop would use a variable to represent the ListIndex property. It would contain a statement to increment the variable each time through the loop. Before executing the loop again, the condition in the Do loop would test that the variable representing the current ListIndex property is less than the number of items in the list box (represented by the ListCount property), and exit the loop when it has examined all of the items.

However, Visual Basic provides another kind of looping structure that works like a counter. Each time the statements in the loop are executed, a counter is incremented until the counter is the same as some value you assign. This type of looping structure is called a **For loop** and it uses the For statement.

You can use a For statement when you know in advance how many times the statements in the loop need to be executed. Because your program includes items in a list box and elements in an array, the number of items (represented by the ListCount property) and the number of elements (represented by the array subscript) are known at any given time. So, a For loop is appropriate for stepping through each item in the list box. When you use a For loop, you do not have to write any statements to increment the variable you are using as a counter. Instead, the For statement does this for you. The For loop has the following syntax:

```
For counter = start To end [Step increment]
    [statement-block]
    [Exit For]
    [statement-block]
Next [counter]
```

Consider the For loop as a structure that works with counters, as illustrated in Figure 6-10.

Figure 6-10 ◄
The For loop

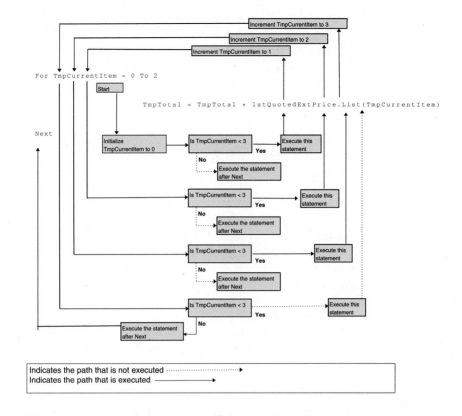

Indicates the path that is not executed ································►
Indicates the path that is executed ─────────►

When you execute a For loop, the following happens:

1. The *counter* is initialized to the value of *start* the first time the For loop is executed. The counter is a variable of the Integer data type that you already declared using a Dim statement. To look at the first item in a list box, *start* should have a value of 0, the lower bound of the list box.

2. Every time through the loop, the value of the counter is increased by the *increment*. If the increment is not specified, the default value is 1. So, after the statements in the loop are executed, the counter must be incremented by 1 to look at every item in the list box.

3. When the value of the counter is greater than *end,* the For loop exits and the *statement-block* in the loop is not executed again. This will happen after all the items in the list box have been examined.

4. If the counter is less than *end,* the first *statement-block* is executed; *end* would be the number of items in the list box.

5. If an Exit For statement is reached, usually enclosed in an If statement as the result of an abnormal condition, the For loop will exit. Otherwise the next *statement-block* is executed. A For loop does not require an Exit For statement. For example, if you are adding to the contents of the list boxes and wanted to make sure each list box contained numbers, you could use an Exit For statement to stop the loop if one of the list boxes contained invalid data. Because the prices are taken from a text file and the extended prices are computed by the program, rather than entered by the user, you do not need to check for valid data. So, an Exit For statement is not necessary.

6. When the Next statement is reached, the *counter* is incremented and the For loop is tested again.

The List property of the ListBox object, used with an index, acts like an array. You can use the List property to reference the text in each item of the Extended Price list box. The first list item has an index of 0. You use the List property with an index of the item just as you use the subscript for an array. The List property has the following syntax:

*object.**List***(*index*)

- For example, if you wanted to reference the text of the second item (remember, its ListIndex property is 1) to the list box named lstMyList, you would use the following statement:

```
lstMyList.List(1)
```

For the quotation program, you want to create a loop that will step through all of the items in the Extended Price list box, so that the program can compute the quotation total. The first item in the list box has an index of 0. The ListCount property tells you how many items are in the list. You can compute the index value of the last item in the list by subtracting 1 from the ListCount property. So, you have the information for the start and end conditions of the For loop. You can use the List property with the index to reference the item you want the program to look at. This index should be the *counter* from the For loop. The index of the first item in a list box is always 0, so the For loop should start at 0 and end when all the items have been examined (ListCount - 1).

Using a For loop and the properties of the list box, you can compute the quotation total by adding together each extended price in the Extended Price list box. You need to declare a variable to be used as an accumulator that will store the quotation total. Each time through the loop, the program must add the extended price to the accumulator. When the loop is complete (each item has been examined), the result should be formatted and displayed in the lblTotal label.

Because the program must also compute the quotation total when products are removed, you can write the necessary code once in a general procedure and call the general procedure whenever the total needs to be recomputed. So, you need to use the Insert Procedure dialog box to write this code.

To compute the quotation total using a For loop:

1. Open the Code window. Because you are going to create a new general procedure, it does not matter which object and event procedure are currently active in the Code window.

2. Click **Insert** on the menu bar, then click **Procedure** to open the Insert Procedure dialog box.

3. In the Name text box, type **ComputeTotal.**

   You will create a Sub procedure because it will not return a value.

4. In the Type section, click the **Sub** radio button.

   You will declare the procedure as Private because it will only be used by this form.

5. In the Scope section, click the **Private** radio button.

6. Click the **OK** button.

7. Enter the following statements in the Code window:

```
Private Sub ComputeTotal()
    Dim TmpTotal As Single
    Dim TmpCurrentItem As Integer
    TmpTotal = 0
    For TmpCurrentItem = 0 To _
        lstQuotedExtPrice.ListCount - 1
        TmpTotal = TmpTotal + _
            lstQuotedExtPrice.List(TmpCurrentItem)
    Next
    lblTotal.Caption = Format(TmpTotal, "currency")
End Sub
```

With the For loop, these statements use a counter (TmpCurrentItem) to look at each value in the Extended Price list box and add the value to an accumulator (TmpTotal).

```
Dim TmpTotal As Single
Dim TmpCurrentItem As Integer

TmpTotal = 0
```

These statements declare two local variables, which exist only while the procedure is running. TmpTotal is used as an accumulator. Each time the program steps through an item in the Extended Price list box, it adds the extended price to TmpTotal. The variable TmpCurrentItem is used as the counter in the For loop.

It is a good practice to initialize variables, so you set the value of TmpTotal to 0 before the program begins processing. This gives the reader of your program a clear indication of what the value of the variable should be when the procedure starts. However, it is not necessary to initialize the value of the counter TmpCurrentItem, because the For loop itself initializes this value.

```
For TmpCurrentItem = 0 To _
    lstQuotedExtPrice.ListCount - 1
    TmpTotal = TmpTotal + _
        lstQuotedExtPrice.List(TmpCurrentItem)
Next
```

The For loop steps through each item in the lstQuotedExtPrice list box by starting at item 0. This is the start value of the For loop.

The List property of the list box retrieves the contents of the list box, in this case the extended prices, and adds them to the variable for the total. Remember, the List property is like an array. It requires an index of the element to use. In this case, the index is the loop's counter, TmpCurrentItem.

When the Next statement is reached, the value of the counter TmpCurrentItem is increased by 1. If the new value of the counter is less than or equal to ListCount - 1, then the statements in the loop are executed again. This process continues until there are no more items in the list box, which means that the counter has reached the end value, ListCount - 1, and the For loop will exit. Recall that no Exit statements are needed to exit a For loop—it exits automatically when the end value of the counter is reached.

```
lblTotal.Caption = Format(TmpTotal, "currency")
```

This statement formats the quotation total with two decimal places and a leading dollar sign.

Now that you have written the ComputeTotal general procedure, you need to call it explicitly. The cmdAdd_Click procedure controls what occurs when a product is added to the quotation. If you want the quotation total to be updated whenever a product is added to the quotation, you need to call the general procedure from the cmdAdd_Click event procedure.

To call the ComputeTotal general procedure:

1. Activate the Code window for the **cmdAdd_Click** event procedure.

2. Add the following statement to the procedure, just before the End Sub statement:

```
ComputeTotal
```

You have completed the first phase of the quotation program. Rose can now add products, quantities, and prices to a quotation and see the new total of the quotation each time she adds a product. You should run the program to verify that the quotation total is being computed correctly.

To test the quotation total:

1. Start the program.

2. Enter the products and quantities shown in Figure 6-11.

Figure 6-11 ◀
Testing the quotation total

select these products

enter these quantities

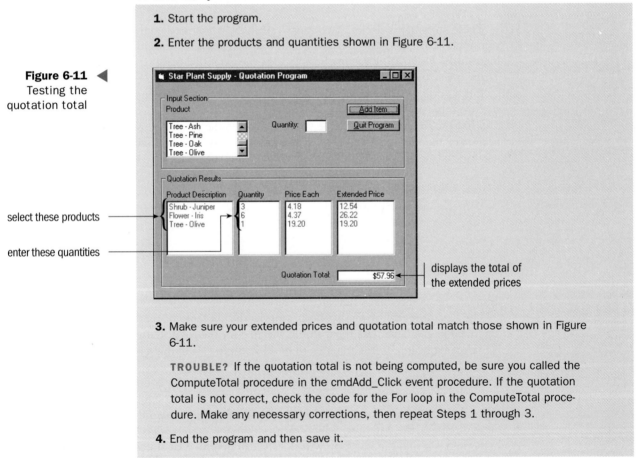

displays the total of
the extended prices

3. Make sure your extended prices and quotation total match those shown in Figure 6-11.

   TROUBLE? If the quotation total is not being computed, be sure you called the ComputeTotal procedure in the cmdAdd_Click event procedure. If the quotation total is not correct, check the code for the For loop in the ComputeTotal procedure. Make any necessary corrections, then repeat Steps 1 through 3.

4. End the program and then save it.

Rose can now create her quotations electronically, with a minimal amount of typing. By preserving the contents of the text file containing the product and price information, she can still print a copy of the file for use out of the office.

Quick Check

1. Describe the difference between using a database and a sequential file for processing, and describe the advantages and disadvantages of each method.

2. What is the purpose of the Open statement, the Input # statement, and the Close statement?

3. What is the EOF function used for?

4. Declare an array named Prices with 20 elements and a lower bound of 1.

5. Describe the purpose of the List, ListCount, and ListIndex properties of a list box.

6. Write a For loop that will count from 20 to 100 and print the value of the counter.

7. What is the purpose of the Exit For statement?

SESSION 6.2

In this session you will learn how to remove a specific item from a list box and how to remove all the items in a list box at once. You will also create a two-dimensional array, use the Variant data type for storing any kind of data, display pictures at run time in a PictureBox control, and write program results to a text file.

Modifying the Program

Rose spent some time testing the program with Mack. They have some suggestions to improve the program so that it more closely models her business activities. First, Rose needs to be able to clear all of the list boxes used for output so that she can prepare a new quotation. Also, when she is preparing a quotation, she needs the ability to delete specific products from the quotation if the customer decides to omit items to maintain the budget for a project. Rose would like the program to include a Remove button that would delete a quoted product from the output and recompute the total whenever an item is removed. Also, Rose often gives customers a discount depending on their annual purchasing volume, so she wants the program to be able to apply the discount. She would also like to display pictures of the different products on the form for those times when the customer is in the office. In this way, customers can see the products that they are ordering. Finally, Rose wants a way to write the program results to a file she can format and print the quotation using her word processing program.

Mack has revised the pseudocode and TOE chart for the program, and he suggests that you review them.

To view the changes Mack made to the pseudocode and TOE chart:

1. Use Notepad or any word processing program to open and print the pseudocode and TOE chart in the file **StarTOE2.txt** located in the **Tutorial.06** folder on your Student Disk.

2. Exit Notepad or the word processing program.

As indicated in the TOE chart, new objects have been added to reset the form for a new quotation, remove an item from the output section, apply a discount to a quotation, display a picture, and write a quotation to a disk file. Mack has already modified the form to implement some of these changes.

To view the changes Mack made to the form:

1. Open the project file named **Star2.vbp** in the **Tutorial.06** folder on your Student Disk.

2. If necessary, click the **View Form** button in the Project window to display the form. Your screen should look like Figure 6-12.

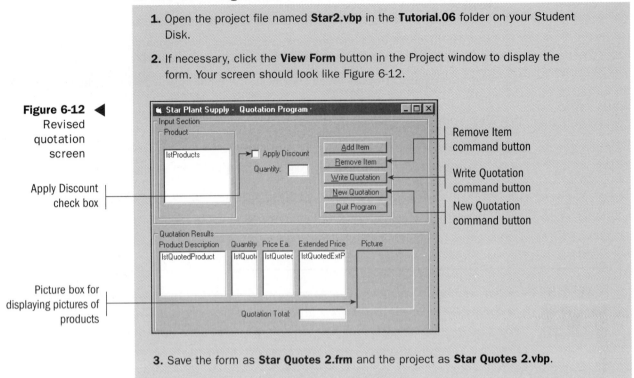

Figure 6-12 ◀
Revised quotation screen

Apply Discount check box

Remove Item command button

Write Quotation command button

New Quotation command button

Picture box for displaying pictures of products

3. Save the form as **Star Quotes 2.frm** and the project as **Star Quotes 2.vbp**.

The input and output list boxes, Quantity text box, Add Item command button, and Quotation Total labels are all the same. The program now includes a Remove Item command button, which will delete a product from the output lists and recompute the quotation total whenever an item is deleted. The new Write Quotation command button will allow Rose to print the quotation to a text file. Then Rose can use the text file in her word processing program to format and print quotations for customers. The New Quotation command button will clear the contents of the output list boxes and quotation total so that Rose can enter a new quotation. The new Apply Discount check box will enable Rose to apply a discount to the prices she charges, when appropriate. Next to the output list boxes, the program now includes a picture box, which will display pictures of the different products. You need to complete the programming for these new objects to perform their functions.

Clearing the Contents of a List Box

After Rose completes a quotation, she needs to reset all the output list boxes and the quotation total to begin a new quotation for another customer. The New Quotation command button will reset the list boxes used for output in preparation for another quotation. You need to delete all of the items from the ListBox objects and set the quotation total to 0 again. This can be accomplished using the Clear method for each of the four ListBox objects. The Clear method has the following syntax:

object.**Clear**

- Objects like list boxes and combo boxes support the **Clear method**. When called, this method removes all items from the *object*.

You can now write the code for the New Quotation command button.

To program the New Quotation command button:

1. Open the Code window for the **cmdNewQuotation_ Click** event procedure.

2. Enter the following code in the window:

```
Private Sub cmdNewQuotation_Click()
    lstQuotedProduct.Clear
    lstQuotedQty.Clear
    lstQuotedPrice.Clear
    lstQuotedExtPrice.Clear
    lblTotal.Caption = ""
    txtQty.Text = ""
    lstProducts.ListIndex = -1
    chkDiscount.Value = vbUnchecked
End Sub
```

These statements clear the input and output objects in preparation for another quotation.

```
lstQuotedProduct.Clear
lstQuotedQty.Clear
lstQuotedPrice.Clear
lstQuotedExtPrice.Clear
```

The Clear method deletes all the items in a list box, and is called in these four statements for each of the four output list boxes.

```
lblTotal.Caption = ""
txtQty.Text = ""
lstProducts.ListIndex = -1
chkDiscount.Value = vbUnchecked
```

These statements erase the value of the Caption property of the Label object used for the quotation total, clear the contents of the Quantity text box, deselect all the items in the Product list box, and clear the Apply Discount check box. You need to clear the Quantity text box and the Product list box because if Rose selects a new product or enters a new quantity, but does not click the Add Item button to add those selections to the output, they would still be selected.

Now you should run and test the program to be sure the code for the New Quotation command button is working properly.

To test the New Quotation command button:

1. Start the program.

2. Enter the products and quantities shown in Figure 6-13.

Figure 6-13 ◀
Testing the
New Quotation
command
button

add these products
to the quotation

use these quantities

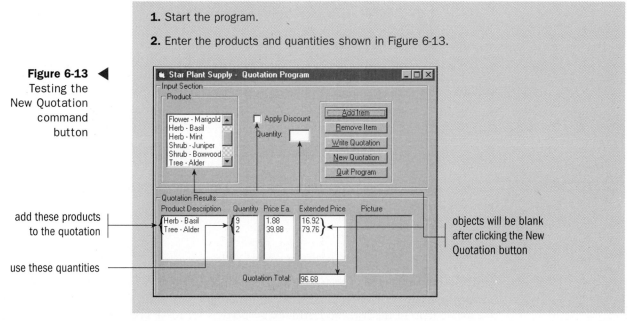

objects will be blank
after clicking the New
Quotation button

> **3.** Click the **New Quotation** command button. Each line in the output list boxes is erased. The Quotation Total label is blank. No product is selected in the Product list box, the Quantity text box, and the Apply Discount check box are blank.
>
> **TROUBLE?** If the output lists and quotation total did not clear, check the code for the New Quotation command button and be sure you called the Clear method for each of the output ListBox objects and set the label's Caption property to an empty string. Make any necessary corrections, then repeat Steps 1 through 3.
>
> **4.** End the program and then save it.

Now that you have used the Clear method to remove all the items from a list box, you can proceed to write the statements that will allow Rose to remove an individual item from one of the output list boxes in case she makes a mistake or a customer decides not to order a product.

Removing a Specific Item from a List Box

Just as you used the AddItem method to add an item to a list box, you can use the **RemoveItem method** to delete an item from a list box. The RemoveItem method has the following syntax:

*object.***RemoveItem** *index*

- The RemoveItem method takes one argument—the index of the item you want to delete. If you want to remove the first item, the index would be 0; if you want to remove the second item, the index would be 1, and so on.

The program needs to call the RemoveItem method for each output list box when the Remove Item command button is clicked. You will use a temporary variable representing the ListIndex property as the argument to each call to the RemoveItem method.

To write the code to delete an item from the quotation output list boxes:

> **1.** Activate the Code window for the **cmdRemove_Click** event procedure.
>
> **2.** Enter the following code in the window:

```
Private Sub cmdRemove_Click()
    Dim TmpIndex As Integer
    TmpIndex = lstQuotedProduct.ListIndex
    If TmpIndex > -1 Then
        lstQuotedProduct.RemoveItem TmpIndex
        lstQuotedQty.RemoveItem TmpIndex
        lstQuotedPrice.RemoveItem TmpIndex
        lstQuotedExtPrice.RemoveItem TmpIndex
        ComputeTotal
    End If
End Sub
```

These statements remove a selected item from the output ListBox objects and recompute the quotation total.

```
Dim TmpIndex As Integer
TmpIndex = lstQuotedProduct.ListIndex
```

These two statements declare the variable TmpIndex and store into that variable the index of the currently selected item. When the program calls the RemoveItem method on the active item in the list, the ListIndex property is set to -1 because the active item no longer exists. If you try to use the ListIndex property, rather than the temporary variable, as the argument to the RemoveItem method when its value is -1, the program would generate a run-time error.

```
If TmpIndex > -1 Then
    lstQuotedProduct.RemoveItem TmpIndex
    lstQuotedQty.RemoveItem TmpIndex
    lstQuotedPrice.RemoveItem TmpIndex
    lstQuotedExtPrice.RemoveItem TmpIndex
    ComputeTotal
End If
```

This code uses an If statement to determine if an item is selected in the lstQuotedProduct list box. If no item is selected, the value of the ListIndex property and of TmpIndex is -1, so no attempt will be made to remove an item when none has been selected. Next the RemoveItem method is called for each of the four output list boxes. Then, because the program removed an item, it computes the quotation total again by calling the ComputeTotal general procedure.

You should now test your program to determine if the cmdRemove_Click event works properly.

To test the Remove Item command button:

1. Start the program.

2. Enter the products and corresponding quantities into the quotation, as shown in Figure 6-14.

Figure 6-14 ◀
Testing the
Remove Item
command
button

enter these two
products and
quantities

select this item to be
removed

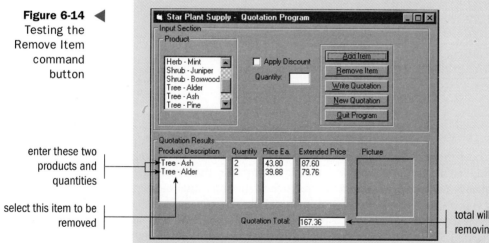

total will update after
removing item

3. Click the product **Tree - Alder** in the output list, as shown in Figure 6-14.

4. Click the **Remove Item** command button. The program removes the item Tree - Alder from the output lists and recomputes the quotation total.

> **TROUBLE?** If you receive a run-time error or if the item Tree - Alder was not deleted from the list and the quotation total was not recalculated, make sure your code for the cmdRemove_Click event procedure is the same as the code in the previous steps. Make any necessary corrections, then repeat Steps 1 through 4.

5. Make sure no product is selected in the Product Description list box.

6. Click the **Remove Item** command button. No item is removed from the lists.

7. End the program and then save it.

Rose has looked at the program and thinks it is very easy to use. She can quickly look up each of the products she sells and see a quotation without worrying about looking up the wrong prices or making computational errors. And, with the Remove Item command button, she can delete items from the quotation without starting over. She would also like the program to compute a discount for customers with a large annual sales volume. To do this, you need to create a multi-dimensional array.

Creating a Multi-dimensional Array

Rose sometimes gives a discount to customers based on their annual sales volume and she would like the program to apply the discount when computing the extended price. One way to achieve this is to include a second price list that contains the discounted prices. To do this you can create an array with two columns. One column will contain the regular price for each product and the other column will contain the discounted price for each product. Mack has already created the Apply Discount check box, which Rose can click to indicate whether the discounted price or the regular price should be used for a quotation.

The array you need to create, with one column for the regular prices and another for the discounted prices, is called a **two-dimensional array**. Two-dimensional refers to rows and columns. The one-column array you created in the previous session to contain the prices for the products is a **one-dimensional array** because it contains only rows. In the two-dimensional array for regular and discounted prices, one dimension, the rows, will hold the information for each element in the array, and the other dimension, the columns, will hold the regular prices in one column and the discounted prices in the second column. Figure 6-15 shows part of the two-dimensional array for the regular and discounted prices.

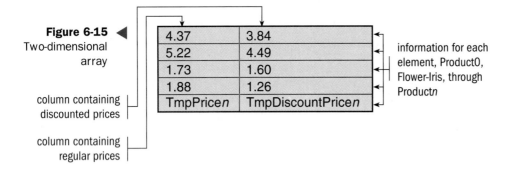

Figure 6-15
Two-dimensional array

column containing discounted prices

column containing regular prices

4.37	3.84
5.22	4.49
1.73	1.60
1.88	1.26
TmpPrice*n*	TmpDiscountPrice*n*

information for each element, Product0, Flower-Iris, through Product*n*

Like the one-dimensional array you created in the first session, a multi-dimensional array is not an object. Rather it is a variable that contains elements. In a multi-dimensional array, you make a reference to an individual element using a subscript, just as you do in a one-dimensional array. However, you must supply a subscript for each dimension of the array. So, a two-dimensional array has two subscripts. One subscript describes the row number and the other describes the column number. The syntax to create a two-dimensional array is similar to the syntax to create a one-dimensional array:

Dim *array-name(lower-bound* **To** *upper-bound, lower-bound* **To** *upper-bound)* **As** *datatype*

- This statement declares an array with the name *array-name*, which can be any valid variable name. This array has two subscripts instead of just one.

- The first subscript is the range of rows and the second is the range of columns. The first *lower-bound* defines the element in the first row of the array. The second *lower-bound* defines the element in the first column of the array. If you do not specify a lower-bound, it will be set to 0 by default.

- The first *upper-bound* defines the element in the last row of the array. The second *upper-bound* defines the element in the last column of the array.

- The *datatype* can be any valid Visual Basic data type.

You need to change the price array so that it has two columns. The first column will store the regular prices and the second column will store the discounted prices.

To declare the two-dimensional array:

1. Open the general declarations section of the Code window.

2. Change the declaration of the PriceArray as shown; the text you need to change appears in bold:

```
Dim PriceArray(0 To 99,0 To 1) As Single
```

This statement declares a two-dimensional array made up of 100 rows and two columns. There are 100 products that can be stored in the rows for each of the two different prices.

Now you need to write the statements to load the array. Joan has already changed the contents of the Notepad file to contain the discounted prices. Mack has created a variable named TmpDiscountPrice, which is needed to store the discount prices, and modified the Input statement in the Form_Load event procedure so that it reads all the contents of the new file. The first subscript refers to the rows, as in the original array. The second subscript refers to the columns. The first column can be referenced using a subscript of 0. The second column has a subscript of 1.

To load the discounted prices into the array:

1. Activate the Code window for the **Form_Load** event procedure.

2. Change the existing PriceArray statement in the event procedure, and add the new PriceArray statement to match the following code; the changed and new lines appear in bold:

```
PriceArray(CurrentItem, 0) = TmpPrice
PriceArray(CurrentItem, 1) = TmpDiscountPrice
```

The changes you just made to the Form_Load event procedure will load the price information into a two-dimensional array.

```
PriceArray(CurrentItem, 0) = TmpPrice
PriceArray(CurrentItem, 1) = TmpDiscountPrice
```

These statements store the values of the variables into each column of the PriceArray. The first statement stores the regular prices into the first column (column 0), and the second statement stores the discounted prices into the second column (column 1). The row is defined by the variable CurrentItem and is set by the For loop.

Now you can make the necessary modifications to the Add Item command button so that the correct price will be used depending on whether or not the Apply Discount check box is checked. To do so you need to write an If statement to determine the value of the check box. You will use this information to determine whether to use the regular or discounted price.

To code the Add Item command button to assign the appropriate price:

1. Activate the Code window for the **cmdAdd** object's **Click** event procedure.

2. Modify the code to included the TmpExtPrice statement and its AddItem statement in an If statement so that it looks like the following code; be sure to add the column subscripts to the PriceArray:

```
If chkDiscount.Value = vbChecked Then
    TmpExtPrice = (txtQty.Text * _
        PriceArray(lstProducts.ListIndex, 1))
    lstQuotedPrice.AddItem _
        Format(PriceArray(lstProducts.ListIndex, 1),"fixed")
Else
    TmpExtPrice = (txtQty.Text * _
        PriceArray(lstProducts.ListIndex, 0))
    lstQuotedPrice.AddItem _
        Format(PriceArray(lstProducts.ListIndex, 0),"fixed")
End If
```

This code uses an If statement to apply a discount if the Apply Discount CheckBox object is checked. If the object is not checked, the regular prices are used. You can now test the program to determine if the regular and discounted prices are being computed correctly.

To test the discount prices:

1. Start the program.

2. Click the **Apply Discount** check box to select it.

3. Enter the products and corresponding quantities into the quotation, as shown in Figure 6-16.

Figure 6-16 ◀
Testing the
discount prices

indicates discount
prices are used

enter these products

enter these quantities

verify the prices are
the same

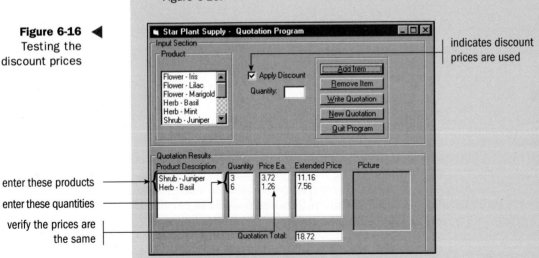

The program applies to the discount and displays the discount price for each selected product.

4. Be sure the discount prices are the same as those in Figure 6-16

   TROUBLE? If you receive a run-time error, be sure you changed the number of dimensions of the array in the general declarations section. Also be sure you changed the dimensions of the array in the Form_Load event procedure and added the statement to load the discount price. And, check to make sure that the If statement in the cmdAdd_Click procedure is correct. Make any necessary corrections, then repeat Steps 1 through 4.

5. End the program and then save it.

Now the program can calculate the quotations at the regular price or at the discount price. Rose would also like to display pictures of the products to her customers when they are in the office as she prepares their quotations. At some point, she will have pictures of all the products, but currently she has only a few images that were supplied as samples by different vendors.

Adding Pictures to a Form

You can use either a PictureBox object or an Image object to display pictures on a form. The **PictureBox object** supports more events and properties than the Image object. For example, a picture box can respond to a Change event in addition to a Click event.

Unlike the Image control, the PictureBox control cannot resize pictures with the Stretch property. The pictures Rose intends to use will all be the same size, so you can create a PictureBox control that is the same size as the pictures. There is no need to resize a picture.

As with the Image control, you could assign the pictures to the picture box by setting the Picture property in the Properties window at design time. But then your program would contain only one picture. You want the picture displayed to depend on the active product; therefore, you should set the Picture property with code, rather than in the Properties window.

Joan has changed the price list file, Product2.txt, so that it includes a field containing the filename of the picture. The program must be able to load the file containing the picture when an item in the Product list box is selected. You could create another array of the String data type. When you load the price, you could write another statement to load the filename of the picture using the filename contained in the other array. In this case, the other array would be a one-dimensional array.

You have learned that all of the elements in an array must be of the same data type. However, you want to store numbers with a decimal point— regular prices in one column and discounted prices in another—and strings (picture filenames), in the third column. On the surface, this seems to break the Visual Basic "rule" of using variables of the same data type. However, another option will allow you to include prices and filenames in the same array.

Arrays of Variant Data

Visual Basic supports a data type called **Variant**, which can store all of the other data types such as Integer, Single, and String. For example, Var1 declared as a Variant data type could contain the values 1, 1.05, TRUE, "Hello", or "c:\windows\waves.bmp". Visual Basic accomplishes this by storing the data type of the variable in the variable itself. If you store an integer into a variant array or variable, the variable is an Integer Variant. If you later store a string in the variant, the variable becomes a String Variant. Variant variables, and members of variant arrays, can change their data type while a program is running.

So, to hold both the prices and the picture filenames, you can create a two-dimensional variant array and use the first and second columns as Single Variant data types for the product prices and discount prices, and the third column as a String Variant data type for the picture filenames.

To declare an array of the Variant data type you use the Dim statement, as you have done before.

To develop the code to work with the pictures as well as the prices, you need to change the two-dimensional PriceArray, which contains prices (Single data type), to a two-dimensional array of variants (Single and String data types). You also need to specify a third column to hold the picture filenames from the text file.

To change the PriceArray to a Variant Array:

1. Open the general declarations section of the Code window.

2. Change the declaration for PriceArray as shown; the changes you need to make are shown in bold:

```
Dim PriceArray(0 To 99,0 To 2) As Variant
```

Now that you have declared the three-column array of Variant data type, you can write the code to load the picture filenames into the third column of the array. The specific picture should be loaded when Rose clicks a product so that a customer in the office can see the product being quoted. So, you need to modify the Form_Load event procedure. In your array, the first subscript still represents the rows. The second subscript represents the columns. The regular prices are represented by the column subscript 0; the discount prices are represented by the column subscript 1; and the picture filenames are represented by the column subscript 2.

To load the filenames into the Variant Array:

1. Activate the Code window for the **Form_Load** event procedure.

2. Add the following line of code immediately after the Input statement and the first two PriceArray statements to store the filename of the picture into PriceArray:

```
PriceArray(CurrentItem, 2) = TmpPicture
```

This statement stores the picture filenames into the third column of the array. Now you can write the code for displaying a picture in the picture box when an item in the Product list box is clicked. When Rose clicks a product in the Product list box, the program must load the corresponding picture using its filename. You can do this by calling the **LoadPicture function** at run time. The LoadPicture function supports one argument, the filename of a picture, and has the following syntax:

object.pictureproperty = **LoadPicture**(*filename*)

■ The *pictureproperty* must be the Picture property of a valid *object* that supports the Picture property.

■ The *filename* can be any filename containing a picture.

The third column of the array contains the filenames of the pictures you want to show in the quotation program. You will use the ListIndex property of the lstProducts ListBox object as a subscript of the array to look up the correct filename.

To load the pictures into the picture box:

1. Activate the Code window for the **lstProducts_Click** event procedure.

2. Enter the following code in the window:

```
Private Sub lstProducts_Click()
    If lstProducts.ListIndex > -1 Then
        Picture1.Picture = _
            LoadPicture(PriceArray _
            (lstProducts.ListIndex, 2))
    End If
End Sub
```

When an item in the Product list box is clicked, the code you just wrote will display the corresponding picture in the picture box.

```
If lstProducts.ListIndex > -1 Then
    Picture1.Picture = _
        LoadPicture(PriceArray _
          (lstProducts.ListIndex, 2))
End If
```

The first statement determines if an item is selected in the Product list box. The subsequent statements are called only if an item is selected (ListIndex > -1). The second statement calls the LoadPicture function with one argument, the filename of the picture to load. The filenames are stored in the third column of the PriceArray. The current row is determined by using the current index (ListIndex property) of lstProducts.

Now you should test the new picture box and the code you added to the lstProducts_Click event procedure.

To test the picture box:

1. Start the program.

2. Click **Flower - Iris** in the Product list box. The picture of the selected product appears in the PictureBox object, as shown in Figure 6-17.

Figure 6-17 ◀
Testing the picture box

selected product

picture appears in PictureBox object

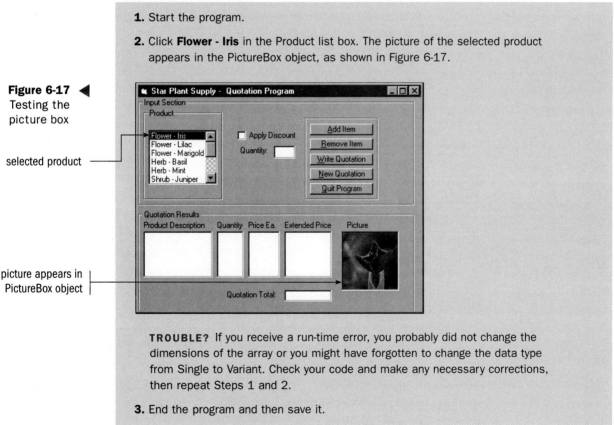

TROUBLE? If you receive a run-time error, you probably did not change the dimensions of the array or you might have forgotten to change the data type from Single to Variant. Check your code and make any necessary corrections, then repeat Steps 1 and 2.

3. End the program and then save it.

Your program will now display pictures for those items that have pictures available by setting the Picture property of the PictureBox object at run time.

Writing a Text File

Some of Rose's customers want a printed copy of a quotation. Rose currently uses a word processing application to format the information. She likes the layout she has created and sometimes customizes the printout for an individual customer's needs. She wants to use the information produced by this quotation program in her word processed documents.

Visual Basic supports a **Write #** statement that will write text to ASCII delimited files, which can then be read by most word processing, spreadsheet, and database programs. This is the same type of file you used to read text into the quotation program when you called the Input # statement.

When you write a text file, just as when you read one, you must first open the file using the Open statement. You used the Open statement For Input in the previous session to read the text file containing the product and price information. This time you need to use the Open statement For Output so that you can write a file. Then, you can use the Write statement to write information from the program to the text file. Remember that if the file already exists when you open it For Output, it will be overwritten. As with other files you open, you must close a text file when you are finished writing to it. The syntax of the Write statement is:

Write #*filenumber*, [*outputlist*]

- The Write # statement writes to a file that has already been opened For Output or For Append. It also inserts commas between each item in the *outputlist* and places quotation marks around strings as they are written to the file. Numeric data is always written using the period (.) as the decimal separator. Files written with the Write # statement can be easily read with the Input # statement.

- The *filenumber* is a valid filenumber created by an Open statement.

- Each item in the *outputlist* is usually a variable or object property in your program separated by a comma. The *outputlist* is similar to the *inputlist* of the Input # statement.

- In the file, Visual Basic will insert commas between the fields and surround string variables with quotation marks.

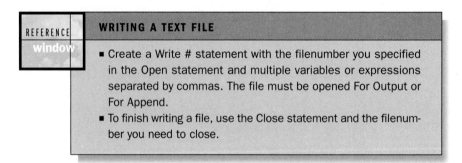

REFERENCE window	**WRITING A TEXT FILE**
	■ Create a Write # statement with the filenumber you specified in the Open statement and multiple variables or expressions separated by commas. The file must be opened For Output or For Append. ■ To finish writing a file, use the Close statement and the filenumber you need to close.

You need to add the statements to the Write Quotation command button so that clicking this button will create a text file of the quotation output. Rose will then be able to read the file into her word processing program so that she can format it. To do this you need to open the file For Output and create a For loop to examine every item in the output list boxes, just as you did to include every item in the ComputeTotal general procedure. Inside the For loop, you need to use the Write # statement to write the contents of each output list box—Product Description, Quantity, Price Each, and Extended Price—to the text file.

To write the code to create a text file of the current quotation output:

1. Open the Code window for the **cmdWriteQuotation_Click** event procedure.

2. Enter the following code in the window:

```
Private Sub cmdWriteQuotation_Click()
     Dim TmpCurrentItem As Integer

     Open "A:\Tutorial.06\quote.txt" For Output As #1
```

```
      For TmpCurrentItem = 0 To _
          lstQuotedExtPrice.ListCount - 1
          Write #1, lstQuotedProduct.List(TmpCurrentItem), _
              Val(lstQuotedQty.List(TmpCurrentItem)), _
              Val(lstQuotedPrice.List(TmpCurrentItem)), _
              Val(lstQuotedExtPrice.List(TmpCurrentItem))
      Next


      Close #1
End Sub
```

The code to write an ascii delimited file is similar to the code to read one. You open the file, use a loop to write each line in the file, and close the file once all the lines have been written.

```
Open "A:\Tutorial.06\quote.txt" For Output As #1
```

This statement opens the file using the Open statement, which specifies the filename and a number to represent the active filenumber. In this case you are writing the program output to a file named "quote.txt." However, instead of opening the file For Input (reading the file) you need to open the file For Output (writing the file). When opened For Output, the contents of the file are overwritten if the file already exists. If you want to append information to a file, you use the For Append option.

```
For TmpCurrentItem = 0 To _
    lstQuotedExtPrice.ListCount - 1
    Write #1, lstQuotedProduct.List(TmpCurrentItem), _
        Val(lstQuotedQty.List(TmpCurrentItem)), _
        Val(lstQuotedPrice.List(TmpCurrentItem)), _
        Val(lstQuotedExtPrice.List(TmpCurrentItem))
Next
```

The For loop steps through each item in the output list box lstQuotedExtPrice, starting at 0 and ending at the end of the list (ListCount -1). A line is written for each of the items quoted. Each line written contains the four items from the output list boxes. Visual Basic will insert a comma between each item. Because list boxes are treated as strings, these statements call the Val function on the quantity price, and extended price fields so that they are converted to numbers and written without quotation marks.

Now you need to test the program one more time to make sure the Write Quotation command button works correctly.

To test the Write Quotation command button:

1. Start the program.

2. Enter the products and corresponding quantities, as shown in Figure 6-18.

Figure 6-18 ◀
Testing the
Write Quotation
command
button

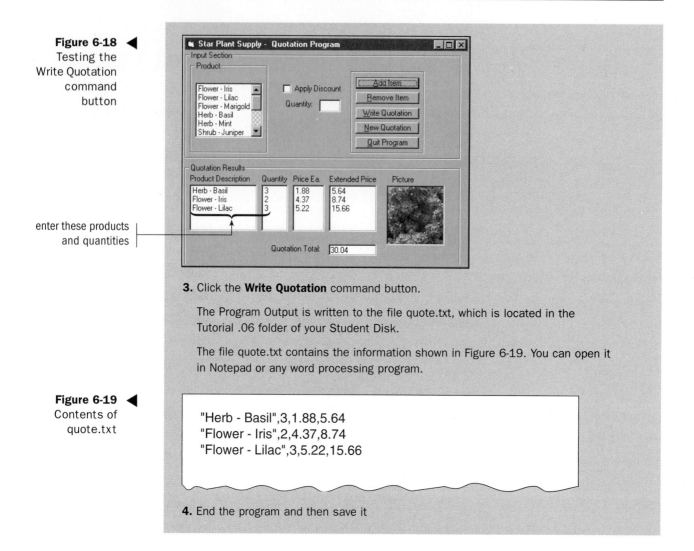

enter these products
and quantities

3. Click the **Write Quotation** command button.

The Program Output is written to the file quote.txt, which is located in the Tutorial .06 folder of your Student Disk.

The file quote.txt contains the information shown in Figure 6-19. You can open it in Notepad or any word processing program.

Figure 6-19 ◀
Contents of
quote.txt

```
"Herb - Basil",3,1.88,5.64
"Flower - Iris",2,4.37,8.74
"Flower - Lilac",3,5.22,15.66
```

4. End the program and then save it

The quotation program is now complete. When Rose starts the program, the textfile containing the price list will be loaded into the computer's memory. When she selects a product in the Product list box, a picture of the product (if one exists) will be displayed in the picture box. Rose can enter a quantity and click the Add Item command button to display the product description, the quantity, the price per product, and the extended price in the output section of the form. The price per product can be either the regular price or the discount price, based on the customer's volume of sales. All Rose needs to do to determine which price to use is click the Apply Discount check box. Rose can clear one or all products from the output section of the quotation program. The quotation total will be updated with every change to the output section of the form. Finally, Rose can write the quotation to a text file, which she can use to format the quotation in her word processing program and print a copy for the customer.

Quick Check

1 What is the purpose of the RemoveItem method and the Clear method of a ListBox object?

2 What is the difference between a one-dimensional array and a two-dimensional array?

3 How does the procedure to open a file for reading differ from the procedure to open a file for writing?

4 What is the Variant data type?

5 What is the purpose of the Write # statement?

Figure 6-20 lists and defines the new terms presented in this tutorial.

Figure 6-20 ◄
New terms

Term	Description
Array	An array is a list of items having the same data type. You create an array using the Dim statement. The number of items in an array is determined by the array's lower and upper bounds.
ASCII delimited file	An ASCII delimited file is a text file that contains one or more fields separated by commas. Text fields are enclosed in double quotation marks. The period (.) is used as the decimal separator.
Element	An element is a specific item in an array.
For loop	A For loop is a statement that works with a counter variable that increments each time the loop is executed. When the counter does not meet some condition, the For loop exits. The loop increments the counter for you.
Sequential access	Sequential access is the process of reading a text file from beginning to end using the Open, Input # and Close statements.
Subscript	A subscript is an integer value that is used to reference a specific element in an array.
Two-dimensional array	A two-dimensional array is an array made up of rows and columns. Two-dimensional arrays use two subscripts to reference an element. One subscript defines the row; the other defines the column.
Variant	The Variant data type is a data type that can contain any of the other Visual Basic data types. The type of data contained in a variant variable can be changed at run time.

Tutorial Assignments

One of Star Plant Supply's customers, Maria Cepada, works for a large software company. She suggested that Rose provide an information display computer in her store so customers could use it to find out about the many varieties of flowers and plants that Star Plant Supply carries. Rose is somewhat hesitant to purchase such a computer, and she asks you to create a sample program that will initially show pictures of three types of roses and supply both background and planting information to the customer. Rose will evaluate the sample program to determine if she wants to provide an information display computer.

Figure 6-21 shows the final interface design for the program. Eventually, this program could be expanded to include hundreds of graphic and text files for Star Plant Supply, which Rose hopes will attract a large number of new customers. The program will use a PictureBox object to display the pictures of the roses, a frame containing option buttons to select the rose types, and a multiline text box to display a description of the flowers.

Figure 6-21 ◄

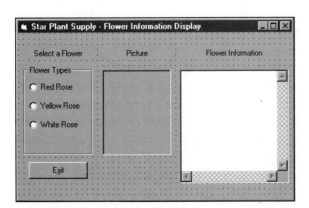

1. Make sure your Student Disk is in the disk drive, and then start Visual Basic.
2. Change the form name to **frmStarLandscaping** and change its caption to **Star Plant Supply - Flower Information Display**.
3. Create a frame on the form with the caption **Flower Types**. See Figure 6-21 for object positions and sizes.
4. Create a control array of three OptionButton objects in the frame. Name the first option button **optFlowers**. Set the Caption of the three option buttons to Red Rose, Yellow Rose, and White Rose, respectively.
5. Create a working Exit command button with Alt+X as the shortcut key combination.
6. Draw a PictureBox object on the form and set its Name to **picFlowers**.
7. Draw a multiline text box with vertical and horizontal scroll bars to hold the flower information on the form. Set the Name property of the text box to **txtInfo** and clear the Text property.
8. Draw three identifying labels above the three objects you just created, and set the Alignment property of the labels to **2 - Center**. From left to right, set the captions of the labels to **Select a Flower**, **Picture**, and **Flower Information**.
9. Open the general declarations section of the Code window and create an array with three elements named **FlowerInfo**. The array should be of the String data type. Create three other string variables named **RoseInfo**, **OutInfo**, and **NL**.
10. To load the array when the form is loaded, write the necessary code in the Form_Load event procedure. The array named FlowerInfo must contain the names of the three different roses. Store the filename **A:\Tutorial.06\TAssign\RedR.bmp** into the first element of the array, **A:\Tutorial.06\TAssign\YellowR.bmp** into the second element, and **A:\Tutorial.06\TAssign\WhiteR.bmp** into the third element.
11. When the form is loaded, the program must load the description of the flowers into the Flower Information text box. This information is stored in the file **Rose.txt** in the **TAssign** folder of the **Tutorial.06** folder on your Student Disk. Add to the end of the Form_Load procedure the statement to open the file for input. Because this is the only file open, use filenumber 1.

12. Now you can read the records into the string OutInfo. You need to append a carriage return character and a new line character to the end of each line so the message box will display the text correctly. Append the following code to the Form_Load procedure.
```
NL = Chr(13) & Chr(10)
Do While Not EOF(1)
     Input #1, RoseInfo
     OutInfo = OutInfo & RoseInfo & NL
Loop
```

13. The String variable OutInfo now contains the text describing the flowers and giving planting instructions. You now need to store this text in the Text property of the txtInfo text box. Write this statement just after the loop you just created.
14. Now you can write the code to load the pictures of the different roses. A picture will be loaded into the picture box when a user clicks one of the option buttons. So, the code should be executed when an option button is clicked. Because the option buttons belong to a control array, the same code will execute when any one of the option buttons is clicked. You need to call the LoadPicture function. The argument to LoadPicture is a filename containing a picture. This is stored in the array FlowerInfo(*subscript*) where *subscript* is 0, 1, or 2. You should store the result in picFlowers.Picture. Refer to Adding Pictures to a Form in this tutorial.
15. Save the project as **Star Plant** in the **TAssign** folder of the **Tutorial.06** folder on your Student Disk.

16. Run your program. Click any option button to see the corresponding picture of the roses that were copied using the Copy facilities of the Microsoft Encarta software package and the Paste and Cut facilities of Paint. Scroll through the Flower Information text box to read the roses text that was loaded from Encarta as a text file. Note that the picture display would be much faster if the .bmp files were stored on the hard disk. Click the Exit command button to exit the program.
17. Print the form image and code.
18. Exit Visual Basic.

Case Problems

1. Valley Computer Supply Valley Computer Supply carries a wide variety of computers and computer accessories. Joe Kent, the business manager, keeps a list of all the different laptop computers in a sequential file, with each computer listed on a separate line. This file is used for a variety of reports and to answer customer questions about what vendors Valley Computer Supply does business with. Joe would like to use this file for a report, but the list is not sorted alphabetically by laptop name, as required. You will write a program to sort the list using the Sorted property of an invisible list box. Figure 6-22 shows the completed form.

Figure 6-22 ◀

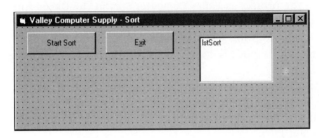

1. Start Notepad or any word processing program and examine the file **Laptops.txt** located in the **Cases** folder of the **Tutorial.06** folder on your Student Disk. This file contains the unsorted list of laptop computer names. Exit Notepad or the word processing program without saving the file.
2. Start Visual Basic.
3. Change the form name to **frmValleySort** and change its caption to **Valley Computer Supply - Sort.**
4. Draw a command button, with the name **cmdStart** and the caption **Start Sort.** Make this the default button for the form. Position and size all objects as shown in Figure 6-22.
5. Create a working Exit command button with Alt+X as the shortcut key combination.
6. Draw a list box on the form. Set its name to lstSort, and make it invisible at run time. Set the Sorted property so that the list box will be sorted at run time.
7. All the processing will occur when the cmdStart button is clicked, so you need to write all your code and declare all your variables in its Click event procedure. Open the Code window for the cmdStart_Click event and declare three local String variables: **ComputerName, InputFileName, OutputFileName.** Declare a local Integer variable named **Count.**
8. Using the InputBox function with the prompt: **"Enter Input File Name"**, store the user's response in the variable called **InputFileName.**
9. Using the InputBox function with the prompt: **"Enter Output File Name"**, store the user's response in the variable called **OutputFileName.**
10. Open InputFileName for input using the results of the InputBox function. Open the file as filenumber 1.

11. Create a Do loop to read each computer name and add it to the list box you already created. Because there is one computer name on a line, the Input # statement should store the field in the variable **ComputerName**. To store the computer names in the list box, you need another statement that will add an item to the lstSort list box. The text of the item you want to add is in the variable ComputerName.

12. Open OutputFileName for output using the results of the InputBox function. Open the file as filenumber 2.

13. Write a For loop that will loop through all the items in the list box and write the items to the output file. Remember, the first item in a list box is 0. You can use the ListCount property to find out how many items are in the list box. Inside the For loop, create a Write # statement that will write the correct item to the output file. Remember, you can use the List property with the Count variable as its argument, which is set by the For loop to do this.

14. Close all the files.

15. Change the caption of the Start Sort command button to contain the number of records sorted followed by the string **Records Sorted**. You will need to concatenate the two strings to do this. Remember, the ListCount property of the lstSort object contains the number of items in the list box. This is the number of items sorted.

16. Save the project as **Valley Computer Sort** in the **Cases** folder of the **Tutorial.06** folder on your Student Disk.

17. Run the program. Click the **Start Sort** command button. The program will request an input file name. Type **A:\Tutorial.06\Cases\Laptops.txt** in the input box.

18. The program will request an output file name. Type **A:\Tutorial.06\Cases\Sorted Laptops.txt** in the second input box. The program will sort the Laptops text file and create the Sorted Laptops file on your Student Disk.

19. Open Notepad or any word processing program and look at the **Sorted Laptops.txt** file in the **Cases** folder of the **Tutorial.06** folder on your Student Disk. Note that the names of the laptops have been sorted by the invisible list box's Sorted property.

20. Print the list, then return to Visual Basic and print the program code and form image.

21. Exit Visual Basic.

2. Sundown Hospital Sundown Hospital is a small regional hospital that serves as a primary care center. Sundown Hospital admits approximately 20 individuals per day and would like a method of storing and recalling admitted patient information. The program will display previous patient information and accept new patient information. The program will also store the information in a sequential file for later use and be able to quickly call up the information for an admitted patient at any time by storing the sequential file as a two-dimensional array. Occasionally the hospital loses power to the admitting station, so the staff would like to be able to start the program and recover all the admitted patient data so that after each new patient is added, the program will append that information to the sequential file. The admitting interface form has already been completed. You now have to add the code that will perform the tasks. Figure 6-23 shows the completed form.

Figure 6-23 ◀

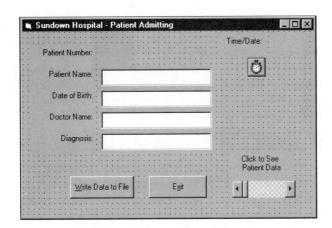

1. Make sure your Student Disk is in the disk drive, and then start Visual Basic.
2. Click **File** then click **Remove File** to clear the default Form1. Click **File**, then **Add File**. Load the form **frmSunDN.frm** from the **Cases** folder of the **Tutorial.06** folder on your Student Disk. Change the startup form to this new form.

3. Draw a Timer object anywhere on the form. Set its Interval property to **1000**. Refer to Visual Basic Help for more information on the Timer control.
4. Write the Code for the Timer1_Timer event and type the following code, which will display the system's time on the form.

   ```
   lblTime.Caption = Now
   ```

5. Save the form as **frmSundownHospital** and the project as **Sundown Hospital Admitting** in the **Cases** folder of the **Tutorial.06** folder on your Student Disk.

6. Open the general declarations section of the Code window. Declare a two-dimensional string array of 50 rows and 6 columns named **PatientTbl**. The first element of the array should be 1, not 0. Refer to Visual Basic online Help for information on the Option Base statement, which allows you to start array subscripts at 1 rather than 0. Declare an Integer variable named **Row** and another Integer variable named **Column**.
7. Open the Code window for the Form_Load event procedure and open the file named **A:\Tutorial.06\Cases\Patient.txt** for input using filenumber 1. Write a Do loop to load the information in the file into the two-dimensional array you just created. Use the variable Row as a counter that will be incremented by 1 each time through the loop. This variable also needs to be used as the row subscript in the two dimensional array. The Do loop should end when the end of file is reached.
8. Inside the Do loop, write an Input # statement to read the file into the different rows and columns of the array PatientTbl. The file **Patient.txt** has 6 fields, so there will be six arguments to the Input # statement. The first argument will be PatientTbl(Row,1). Remember, the lower bound of the array is 1, not 0. Close the text file.

9. As the final part of loading the form, use the Value property of the scroll bar to store the patient information into the text boxes and labels on the form. The names of the objects corresponds to the columns, as follows:

lblPatientNumb	Value of the scroll bar or Column 1
txtPatientName	Column 2
txtDOB	Column 3
txtDoctor	Column 4
txtDiagnosis	Column 5
lblTime	Time when patient was admitted or Column 6

10. Write the code for the Write Data to File command button so that when it is clicked it appends the information for the patient shown on the screen to the file named **A:\Tutorial.06\Cases\Patient.txt**. *Hint*: Open the file For Append. Write the contents of the 6 fields to the file you just opened. Be sure you write them in the same order. Close the File.

11. Write the code for the scroll bar so that when the user changes the value of the scroll bar the current patient information will be displayed in the TextBox and Label objects. When the scroll bar changes, the value of the scroll bar can be used as the subscript of the array(row). Using the scroll bar's value as the row subscript and specifying the column, write the six statements to copy the six columns into the objects displayed on the screen. The object names and columns numbers are shown in Step 9.

12. Enter the following code:

```
lblPatatientNumb.Caption = hsbPNumber.Value
txtPatientName.Text = PatientTbl(hsbPNumber.Value, 2)
txtDOB.Text = PatientTbl(hsbPNumber.Value, 3)
txtDoctor.Text = PatientTbl(hsbPNumber.Value, 4)
txtDiagnosis.Text = PatientTbl(hsbPNumber.Value, 5)
```

13. Set the focus to txtPatientName. Save your form and project.

14. Run the program. The sequential file Patient.txt already includes some sample patient data. Clicking the scroll bar will advance you through the existing patient data to a blank screen. Type in patient data of your choice for five patients. After you type in the information for each patient, click the **Write Data to File** command button. Review the patient data by clicking the scroll bar. Exit the program.

15. Run the program again and observe, by clicking the scroll bar, that the data you entered has been appended to the file and loaded into the data array in the program for use by Sundown Hospital's admitting staff. Print the form image, code, and form as text.

16. Add a command button to the form with **&Print Data** as the caption. Name the button cmdPrint. In the cmdPrint_click event write a nested For loop using the Print method that will print the two-dimensional patient array to the printer. The external part of the nested For loop will vary the row of the array from 1 to the number of records you have in the file (check using the scroll bar if you do not remember). The internal part of the For loop will vary the column from 1 to 6. The print statement in the nested For Next statement will take the form of **Printer.Print PatientTbl(Row, Column);**. The ";" turns off automatic line feeds. And, a Printer.EndDoc statement after the last Next statement will send the output to the printer.

17. Run the program. Click the **Print Data** command button and examine your output. There is no line feed after the six patient fields are printed. Add a line containing **Printer.Print** only between the two Next statements, click the command button again, and observe the results. Make sure you understand the code you have written.

18. Save the changed form as **frmSundownHospital 1** and the project as **Sundown Hospital Admitting 1** in the **Cases** folder of the **Tutorial.06** folder on your Student Disk. Print the form image and code.

19. Exit Visual Basic.

3. Super Office Super Office sells small office supplies to the general public. Super Office would like a program that would read a data file containing item names and prices. Place the item names in a list box and the prices in a one-dimensional array that can contain up to ten Single data type items. The program should load a ListBox with the item name and the matching ItemData property of the ListBox object with an integer subscript that references where in the one-dimensional array the price is stored. Allow the clerk to click a ListBox item, enter the quantity, and calculate the extended price by retrieving the ItemData property as a subscript and retrieving the price using that subscript from the array. Also, calculate any tax, and total the order. Create a PictureBox object to display a logo using a graphic file of your choice. Use Notepad or any word processing program to create a sequential data file with at least five items and prices, and save the file as **Office.txt** in the **Cases** folder of the **Tutorial.06** folder of your Student Disk. Look at any of the sequential files used in this tutorial to see how records and fields are stored. Run the program and correct any errors. Save the form as **frmSuperProject** and the project as **Super Office** in the **Cases** folder of the **Tutorial.06** folder on your Student Disk. Print the form image, form as text, and the code.

4. Consumers Catalog Sales Consumers Catalog Sales sells specialty items directly to its customers around the world. The company would like to have a program that both displays customer address data (Customer Name, Address 1, Address 2, City, State or Province, Zip Code or Postal Code, and Country) and allows for adding new customer data to the file. The data is stored in a sequential file and is read into a two-dimensional array with 50 rows and 7 columns. The existing customer names should be loaded into a combo box so that they can be selected by the user. The ItemData property of the ComboBox object will be used to store the row location of the customer information stored in the array. This is necessary because the combo box will sort the names in the box, and the sorted combo box list will not reflect the sequence of the array information. Each time a new record is added, it is written to both the array and the sequential file. *Hint:* Use the ListIndex property of the ComboBox object with the ItemData property to directly reference information in the array. Additionally, the program should provide a way to print out a mailing label for the customer displayed on the screen.

Create the sequential data file with at least five records using addresses of your choice in Notepad or any word processing program. Make sure that you have seven fields in each record, separated by the comma delimiter, and that you press the Enter key after each line. Save the file as **Consumer.txt** in the **Cases** folder of the **Tutorial.06** folder on your Student Disk. Run the program and correct any errors. When finished, save the form as **frmComsumers** and the project as **Consumers Mailing** in the **Cases** folder of the **Tutorial.06** folder on your Student Disk. Print the form image, form as text, and code.

Debugging

OBJECTIVES

In this appendix you will:

■ Locate and fix run-time errors

■ Set breakpoints in code

■ Set watch expressions in code

■ Inspect the value of variables and objects using the immediate pane of the Debug window

■ Look at the active procedures in a program

Types of Programming Errors

Programming errors can occur in your program when you are writing code or when you are running the program. A **programming error** is any error in a program that causes it to end abnormally or produce incorrect results.

Errors can be categorized into three different types: syntax errors, run-time errors, and logic errors. **Syntax** is a set of rules that specifies the proper way to use the statements that make up a programming language. A **syntax error** occurs when you write statements that Visual Basic cannot understand. If you misspell a word such as Dim when declaring a variable, Visual Basic will detect a syntax error. Syntax errors are found either when you enter statements in the Code window or when you compile a program. **Compiling** your program is the process of translating the Visual Basic statements you wrote into statements the computer can understand. When you encounter a syntax error, look closely at the Help system describing the statement or expression, and make sure you have typed it correctly.

A **run-time error** occurs when your program is running. A run-time error results from a statement that attempts an invalid operation such as dividing a number by 0 or trying to store a letter in a variable that is declared as Single or Integer.

A **logic error** occurs when the program does not perform as intended and produces incorrect results. You generally notice logic errors at run-time. For example, if you intend to compute the area of a rectangle, you would multiply the length by the width. If your program added the numbers rather than multiplying them, the program would not generate the right answer and you would have created a logic error. Using the debugging tools described in this appendix will help you fix run-time and logic errors.

The distinction between logic and run-time errors is not always clear. You might have incorrectly coded an expression, which would be a logic error. For example, if you intended to add two numbers together but wrote statements to multiply them instead. When the program is run, the multiplication could generate a number that is too big for the system to deal with. In this example, the logic error, in turn, causes a run-time error. Run-time errors can also occur when a user types a value your program does not expect.

To find and fix run-time and logic errors in program code, you use a process called **debugging**. Visual Basic provides built-in tools that help you debug your programs.

Visual Basic Debugging Tools

The Visual Basic debugging analysis tools consist of commands that allow you to temporarily suspend the execution of your program by entering break mode and follow each statement as it is being executed. You can execute each statement in the program line by line and have your program stop executing when a specific statement is reached or when the value of a variable or object changes.

Whenever you suspend the execution of your program, you do so to try to identify a particular problem. This involves looking at the values of the variables and object properties in your program to see if they contain correct data. You can look at the contents of variables and objects using a window called the **Debug window**. Figure A-1 shows the Debug window and its components.

Figure A-1 ◀
The Debug
window

immediate pane ──→

── Calls button

You can click the Calls button while a program is in break mode to look at each procedure that is active in the program and the order in which the procedures were called. In the immediate pane, you can type statements to look at and set the values of variables and objects.

You use the debugging commands in conjunction with the Debug window as tools to help you locate and fix errors in your program. Before you can use the debugging tools, you need to check the settings in your environment that define what Visual Basic will do when it encounters errors.

Preparing a Program for Debugging

Visual Basic checks for syntax errors when a program compiles, or translates the code you write into executable code. How a program is compiled, and how errors are handled, depend on settings in the Options dialog box. These settings are saved to your environment, so you should verify that they are correct before you begin to debug your program.

To set the Compile and Error Trapping settings in the Options dialog box:

1. Start Visual Basic and make sure your Student Disk is in the disk drive.

2. Click the **Open Project** button 🖼 on the toolbar and open the project named **RunTime.vbp** located in the **Appendix.A** folder on your Student Disk.

3. Click **Tools** on the menu bar, then click **Options** to open the Options dialog box.

4. Click the **Advanced** tab. See Figure A-2.

Figure A-2 ◀
Compile and
Error Trapping
settings

compiles procedures
when executed for the
first time

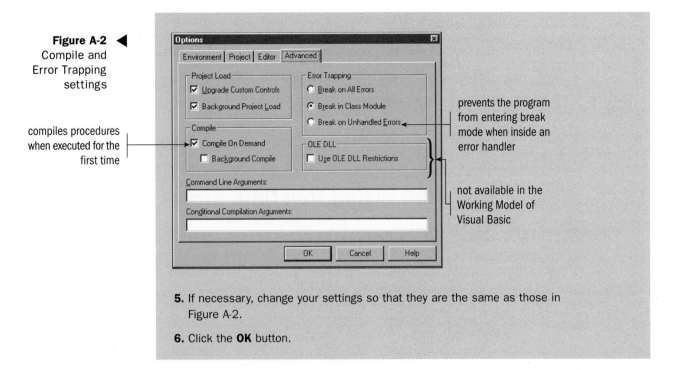

prevents the program
from entering break
mode when inside an
error handler

not available in the
Working Model of
Visual Basic

5. If necessary, change your settings so that they are the same as those in Figure A-2.

6. Click the **OK** button.

The Compile section of the Advanced tab contains two check boxes:

- If the **Compile On Demand** box is checked, Visual Basic will compile the current project and analyze it for syntax errors as you run it. For example, a procedure will only be compiled when it is called for the first time. When the Compile On Demand option is selected, you will not find all the syntax errors until you execute all the procedures in your program. While you are writing and testing programs, checking this box will cause your programs to start much faster. If the Compile On Demand box is not checked, the syntax of an entire program is checked before the program begins executing. As you write the programs in this book, you can turn off Compile On Demand and then run your program to check for any syntax errors you might have created in different procedures.

- The **Background Compile** option allows a program to be compiled while the computer is idle during run-time. Background Compile can improve run-time execution speed the first time procedures are executed. This option is available only when Compile On Demand is checked. Leaving the Background Compile option off will ensure that you get the same results described in this text.

As with syntax errors, how Visual Basic handles run-time errors depends on settings in the Options dialog box. The Advanced tab on the Options dialog box contains a section named Error Trapping. The three options in this section control the behavior of Visual Basic when a run-time error occurs:

- When the **Break on All Errors** radio button is selected, any run-time error will cause Visual Basic to enter break mode, open a dialog box allowing you to activate the Code window, and display the line that caused the error.

- When the **Break in Class Module** radio button is selected, errors in class modules that are not handled by an On Error statement cause Visual Basic to enter break mode, allowing you to fix the error. Refer to Visual Basic online Help for more information on the ClassModule object and the On Error statement.

- When the **Break on Unhandled Errors** radio button is selected, Visual Basic enters break mode when a run-time error occurs that is not handled by an On Error statement. The On Error statement allows you to continue processing when a run-time error occurs.

When you debug a program, you might have several windows open at a time, which might cause windows to obscure each other. Consider making the Debug window and the Code window as small as possible so that you can see each window on the screen. Also, try to keep windows from obscuring the toolbar. You will use these toolbar buttons often, and they might be hard to find if obscured by another window.

Locating and Fixing Run-time Errors

Run-time errors can occur for many reasons, but unlike syntax errors, they cannot be found when a program is being compiled. Rather, these errors occur while a program is running and are caused by performing an operation such as calling an intrinsic procedure with an invalid number of arguments, storing data of the incorrect type into a variable or object property, or performing invalid run-time operations on a database object like a Recordset. Because this information is not known until the program is running, the statements will not actually cause an error until they are executed.

When a run-time error occurs one of two dialog boxes can open. One contains an OK button that, when clicked, activates the Code window and highlights the statement that caused the error. The other dialog box contains two items of information—an error number and a description. Error numbers are typically used by an error handling routine, or **error handler**, in your code to determine whether or not it is reasonable for the program to continue processing. A well-designed program should alert the user to the problem, but continue to run, even when the program encounters an error or the user gives the program erroneous input.

For debugging purposes, always read the description of the error carefully to determine the nature of the error. You can choose from four actions in this dialog box:

- Click the **Continue** button to try to run your program. Depending on the nature of the error, this option is sometimes disabled, indicating that you cannot continue execution until the problem is fixed.

- You can click the **End** button to end your program. This will cause Visual Basic to return to design mode.

- You can attempt to fix the program by clicking the **Debug** button. The Code window will be activated and the statement causing the error will be surrounded by a border. After fixing the statement or statements that caused the error, you can click the Start button on the toolbar to continue execution at the statement that caused the error. However, if the corrections require that you change variable declarations or add new variables or procedures, you generally must end and restart the program explicitly.

- If you do not understand the meaning of the run-time error, clicking the **Help** button will give you more information about the nature of the problem.

Run-time errors come from many sources. They can be caused by using an incorrect number of arguments when calling functions, referencing invalid object properties, or storing data of the wrong type into a property or variable. The underlying cause of a run-time error might stem from other statements in your program. In most cases, you should consider ending the program and starting it again.

To look at errors caused by intrinsic function and object references:

1. Click the **Start** button on the toolbar to run the program.

2. Enter **.10** for the Interest Rate, **10** for the Periods, and **1000** for the Amount.

3. Click the **Intrinsic Function** button. The Run-time error dialog box opens as shown in Figure A-3.

Figure A-3 ◄
Run-time error
dialog box (1)

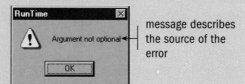

message describes
the source of the
error

4. Click the **OK** button to look at the error in the Code window in break mode.

Notice that the Pmt function is highlighted; it was the reason for the error. The error was caused by passing an incorrect number of arguments to the intrinsic function named Pmt. This function requires three arguments, but there only two are in the function call.

5. Read the comments in the event procedure and fix the program.

6. Click the **Start** button ▣ on the toolbar to continue executing the program where you left off. Click the **Intrinsic Function** button again to verify that your changes corrected the problem.

7. Click the **Object Reference** button. When the dialog box opens, notice the error message, "Method or data member not found." This error was caused by using an incorrect object property, Caption. Click the **OK** button to look at the error in the Code window in break mode.

8. Read the comments in the event procedure and fix the program. Click the **End** button ▣ on the toolbar to end the program and then run it again and repeat Step 7, to verify that the program works with the changes you made.

9. Click the **End** button ▣ on the toolbar.

When you perform arithmetic operations in a program, you must be careful to use the correct data type for the operation you are trying to perform. If you use an Integer data type, the variable cannot store a number larger than 32767. If you try to store a number larger than that into an integer, you will get an **overflow run-time error**. Generally, the solution to an overflow problem is to use a data type that can store a larger number.

However, there might be times when a user enters numbers that are too large for the computer to process. In such a case, you can write an error handler that will advise users of the problem so that they can try to correct their input values.

Another error is caused when you try to store a character string into a numeric data type like Integer or Single. This error is called a **type mismatch error**. A type mismatch error can happen when a user enters invalid data into a text box that you intend to use as a number. To prepare for this kind of invalid data entry, you can call the IsNumeric function or the Val function on the user input. If the input is valid then call the function; otherwise you could display a message box.

To find and fix overflow and type mismatch errors:

1. Click the **Start** button ▣ on the toolbar.

2. Enter **.25** for the Interest Rate, **15000** for the Periods, and **1000000** for the Amount and then click the **Numeric Overflow** button. The run-time error dialog box opens, as shown in Figure A-4.

Figure A-4 ◀
Run-time error
dialog box (2)

error number ———

error description ———

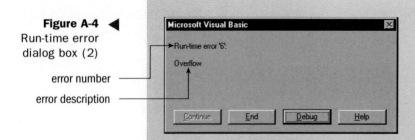

3. Click the **Debug** button to look at the error.

Note that the line containing the error is the Pmt function. One way to allow the program to continue after it encounters this error is to write an error handler that displays a message box describing the problem to the user. Although the program can continue to run, the results will not be accurate.

4. Read the comments in the event procedure to create an error handler and call the MsgBox function to fix the program. Repeat Steps 1 and 2 to verify that the message box opens and the run-time error is handled by the event procedure.

5. Click the **End** button in the message box to end the program, and then start it again.

6. Enter the text **abc** in the Interest Rate text box and then click the **Type Mismatch** button. When the run-time error occurs, click the **Debug** button.

This error is caused by trying to store text into an argument of the Pmt function that can contain only numbers.

7. Read the comments and fix the program then repeat Steps 5 and 6 to verify that the If statement validates the user input before calling the Pmt function.

8. End the program.

In all cases, the statement that caused the error could be only a symptom of the underlying problem. You found the cause of the previous errors by debugging the statement that caused a run-time error. However, a program will sometimes produce incorrect results, but will not generate a run-time error, or you may want to look at the statements that led up to the run-time error. For example, if you called the Pmt function and the argument values were incorrect, the function call would generate a run-time error. You will need to first determine the argument that is incorrect, then locate the statement that set the value of the argument.

Tracing Program Execution

Often a program contains logic errors—that is, it produces incorrect results, but does not necessarily generate a run-time error. This is when the debugging tools are most useful. When a program is producing incorrect results, but you are not sure why, it might be helpful to step through the program one statement at a time by clicking the Step Into button or pressing the F8 key. When you use the Step Into command, the procedure declaration that will be executed next is highlighted with a border in the Code window.

To use the Step Into statements and procedures:

1. Click the **Start** button ▶ on the toolbar.

2. Click the **Exit** command button on the form. Notice that the word "program" in the message box is misspelled.

3. Click **No** in the message box.

4. Click the **End** button ■ on the toolbar.

5. Because you are not sure where the message box function is called or where the prompt is being set, click the **Step Into** button ⬚ on the toolbar to execute the first statement in your program. The first statement to execute is in the Form_Load event procedure, so this procedure is highlighted in the Code window and the Code window becomes the active window. The next time you click the Step Into button the first statement in the procedure will be executed.

6. Click the **Step Into** button ⬚ again.

7. Before executing the procedure, correct the spelling for the word **program**. Add a **?** to the end of the prompt.

8. Continue clicking the **Step Into** button ⬚ until the form appears.

9. Click the **Exit** command button. The Code window is activated. Continue to click the **Step Into** button ⬚ until the message box appears.

10. Click the **Yes** button in the message box.

In addition to stepping through every statement in every procedure in a program, you can step through parts of a program or pause the program and continue executing statements one at a time. When you are debugging a procedure that calls other procedures, you do not have to trace through the statements in a procedure when you know it works correctly. You can use the Step Over button to execute all the statements in a procedure and suspend execution at the statement following that procedure.

To step over a general procedure:

1. Press the **F8** key to begin stepping through your program.

Because you have corrected the spelling errors in the message box, you do not need to step through these statements again.

2. Click the **Start** button ⬚ on the toolbar. Your program is in run mode and will execute the statements without displaying them in the Code window.

3. Click the **Break** button ⬚ on the toolbar. The Debug window opens.

4. Press the **F8** key to begin stepping through each statement in the program.

At this time, no statement is executing. The form has been loaded and Visual Basic is waiting for an event to occur. When you generate an event, the Code window will again become active and you can continue to click the Step Into button to trace the execution of your program.

5. Activate the form and click the **Exit** command button. The Click event procedure is activated in the Code window.

6. Press the **F8** key again. The ExitProgram general procedure is highlighted.

7. Click the **Step Over** button ⬚ on the toolbar. You have already verified that the ExitProgram procedure is working correctly. Notice that the procedure will execute and the message box will appear.

8. Click the **No** button to continue running the program.

9. When the ExitProgram procedure is finished, Visual Basic will suspend execution and enter break mode on the statement after ExitProgram. You can continue to examine the code statement by statement.

10. Click the **End** button ⬚ on the toolbar.

As you debug your programs, you will find it useful to pause the program and then step through each statement that you suspect is in error. When general procedures appear to be working correctly, you should step over them.

Setting Breakpoints

When you suspect a problem is occurring in a particular procedure or that a particular statement is not correct, you can suspend execution of your program at any executable statement by setting a breakpoint. A **breakpoint** is a program line you specify where the program will stop execution and enter break mode. Setting a breakpoint can be accomplished by locating a statement in the Code window and clicking the Toggle Breakpoint button or pressing the F9 key. The Toggle Breakpoint button is available only when the Code window is active.

When a breakpoint is set on a line, the line will appear in a highlighted color. To clear a breakpoint, move the cursor to the line in the program where a breakpoint is set and click the Toggle Breakpoint button. When you run the program and the statement containing the breakpoint is reached, Visual Basic will suspend execution of the program and enter break mode just before executing the statement containing the breakpoint. The line will appear highlighted.

Once in break mode, you can use the Debug window and the Step Into or Step Over buttons to find problems in your code. You can also look at the values of variables and objects in the Debug window. For example, if you have determined that a function such as Pmt is producing incorrect results, you might want to set a breakpoint just before the function is called, and then look at the values of the arguments to determine which one is not correct.

To set a breakpoint in your program:

1. Be sure the program is in design mode. Activate the Code window for the general procedure named **ExitProgram**. Move the cursor to the beginning of the following line:

   ```
   ReturnValue = MsgBox(Prompt, Buttons, Title)
   ```

2. Click the **Toggle Breakpoint** button on the toolbar. The line appears highlighted in a different color.

3. Click the **Start** button on the toolbar to run the program.

4. Click the **Exit** command button. The program enters break mode just before executing the MsgBox statement where you set the breakpoint. You can now examine the statement.

After you have set a breakpoint, you will often want to look at the values of variables or the properties of objects. You do this using the immediate pane of the Debug window.

Using the Immediate Pane

You use the **immediate pane** of the Debug window to look at the values of variables and object properties and to change those values. There are two ways to use the immediate pane of the Debug window:

- You can use the **Debug.** statement in a program. When this method is called, the values of its arguments are printed in the immediate pane of the Debug window.

- You can also type Print statements directly in the immediate pane to look at values in the program. You can type statements in the immediate pane only while a program is in break mode or design mode. Most statements are valid only in break mode.

To look at program values using the immediate pane of the Debug window:

1. Make sure the Debug window is active and the program is in break mode. You may want to resize or move the Debug window and the Form window so that they do not obscure each other.

2. Type the following statements (shown in bold) into the Debug window:

   print Prompt

   Do you really want to exit the program?

   print Label1.Visible

   True

   print Label1.Caption

   Infinite Events

In addition to looking at the values of properties and variables, you can use the immediate pane to set properties and the values of variables. When you change the values of variables using the immediate pane, the changes take effect only while the program is running.

To set properties and values from the Debug window:

1. Be sure Visual Basic is still in break mode.

2. Enter the following statements in the Debug window:

   ```
   Label1.Caption = "New Caption"
   Prompt = "New prompt for the MessageBox"
   ```

3. Click the **Start** button on the toolbar to run the program. Notice that the Infinite Events label now says "New Caption".

4. Click the **Exit** command button. The message box displays the new prompt.

5. Click the **Yes** button to exit the program.

You can now explicitly set breakpoints at specific statements in your program. You can set as many breakpoints as you want throughout a program. When you close the project or exit Visual Basic, all breakpoints disappear. The Toggle Breakpoint button works like a switch. If you want to remove an existing breakpoint, highlight the line containing the breakpoint, and then click the Toggle Breakpoint button.

In addition to setting breakpoints, Visual Basic also allows you to stop a program based on the status or value of an object or variable by watching an expression.

Adding Watch Expressions

Watch expressions are similar to breakpoints, but **watch expressions** allow you to suspend execution when a condition is True or when the value of an object or variable changes. Like breakpoints, watch expressions can be created, changed, or deleted while a program is in design mode or break mode. Watch expressions are not preserved after you save and close a project or exit Visual Basic. The more watch expressions you define, the longer it will take your program to execute, because Visual Basic must check each watch expression for every statement that is executed. When you debug a program, use watch expressions sparingly.

Visual Basic uses the Add Watch dialog box to add a watch expression to the project. Figure A-5 shows the Add Watch dialog box.

Figure A-5 ◀
Adding a watch
expression

enter expression
to watch

define where to
watch the expression

define what to do
when something
happens to the
expression

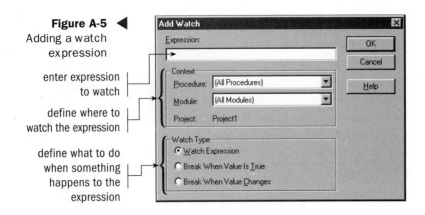

The Add Watch dialog box contains three sections:

■ The **Expression** text box is where you enter the expression you want Visual Basic to evaluate. If you want to watch the value of a variable, enter the variable name. You can copy the expression or variable from the Code window to the Add Watch dialog box using the Copy and Paste commands to avoid typographical errors.

■ The **Context** section sets the procedure name to watch. This is useful if you have variables of the same name in different procedures. **Module** refers to the form in your project that should be watched.

■ The **Watch Type** section tells Visual Basic how to respond to the watch expression. If the **Watch Expression** option is selected, Visual Basic will display the value of the expression in the Debug window. The program will not enter break mode when the expression becomes True or changes. You should consider selecting the Watch Expression option if you print the value of a variable frequently when you reach a breakpoint. This option is also useful for tracing the value of a variable when you are using the Step Into button to watch the contents of a variable in detail. If the **Break When Value Is True** option is selected, Visual Basic will enter break mode whenever the expression is True. If the **Break When Value Changes** option is selected, Visual Basic will enter break mode whenever a statement changes the value of the watch expression.

The watch expressions you create appear in the watch pane of the Debug window. As their values change, the contents of the corresponding variables or expressions will also be shown. Figure A-6 shows the Debug window with the three watch expressions you will create next.

Figure A-6 ◀
Setting watch
expressions

watch expression but
do not suspend
execution

break when
expression is true

break when
expression has
changed

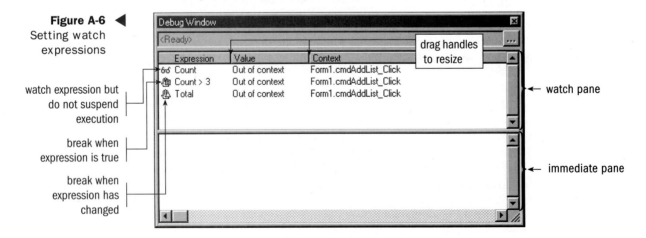

The watch pane contains three columns. The **Expression column** describes the watch expression and its type. The **Value column** displays the current value of the watch expression. Remember that local variables exist only while an event or local procedure is running. When your program is not running, the value "Out of context" is displayed. You will also see the Out of context message when you are not running a procedure in which the watch expression is declared. The **Context column** defines the context of the watch expression—in other words, the form name followed by the procedure.

When you create a watch expression, the Add Watch dialog box tries to anticipate the context based on the active procedure in the Code window. If you are watching a variable that is local to a specific procedure on a specific form, activate that procedure before setting the watch expression and Visual Basic will set the context for you.

To set a watch expression:

1. Activate the Code window for the **cmdAddList** procedure's **Click** event.

2. Click **Tools** on the menu bar, then click **Add Watch**.

3. In the Expression box, type **Count**.

4. In the Context section, make sure **Form1** is the module and **cmdAddList_Click** is the procedure.

5. In the Watch Type section, make sure the **Watch Expression** radio button is selected.

6. Click the **OK** button to add the watch expression.

A more complex expression that breaks the program when an expression is True is useful to find why a For loop is not working correctly or an array is exceeding its bounds.

To set a watch expression that will enter break mode when the expression is True:

1. Click **Tools** on the menu bar, then click **Add Watch**.

2. In the Expression text box, type **Count > 3**.

3. In the Context section, make sure **Form1** is the module and **cmdAddList_Click** is the procedure.

4. In the Watch Type section, click the **Break When Value Is True** radio button to select it.

5. Click the **OK** button to add the watch expression.

In some circumstances, you might want to generate a breakpoint when a value changes. For example, if you are working with a payroll program and the gross wages are not being computed correctly, you could write a watch expression to break whenever the value of the variable GrossPayroll changes. This would save time in locating the statement causing the error.

To set a watch expression that will enter break mode when an expression changes:

1. Click **Tools** on the menu bar, then click **Add Watch**.

2. In the Expression text box, type **Total**.

3. Make sure **Form1** is the module, and **cmdAddList_Click** is the procedure.

4. In the Watch Type section, click the **Break When Value Changes** radio button to select it.

5. Click the **OK** button to add the expression.

6. Activate the Debug window. The top section of the Debug window should look like Figure A-6.

Now that you have set the watch expressions, you can use them to debug the program.

To test the watch expressions you have set:

1. Click the **Start** button ▣ on the toolbar.

2. Click the **Add List** command button. The event procedure begins to execute. Visual Basic enters break mode when the values of the variables change. Each time the Debug window becomes active, notice the values of the watch expressions you created.

3. Continue to click the **Start** button until a run-time error occurs. This error happens because one of the list items contains invalid data. Type the Print statements you used in previous steps to find the item that contains invalid data. To correct the error you could add the necessary statements to verify the data contains a valid number by using a function like IsNumeric.

Editing a Watch Expression

You can edit a watch expressions when a program is in design mode or break mode. To edit a watch expression, click the watch expression in the watch pane of the Debug window, then click the right mouse button and click Edit Watch. This will activate the Edit Watch dialog box, which allows you to change any of the settings in the watch expression.

Deleting a Watch Expression

You can delete a watch expressions when a program is in design mode or break mode. To delete a watch expression, click the watch expression in the watch pane of the Debug window, and then press the Delete key.

Tracing the Events in a Program

Another problem with event-driven programs is that improper logic can cause events to trigger each other indefinitely. This problem happens when a statement causes a Change event in one object. That object, in turn, causes a Change event in a second object, and so on. If an object down the line causes a Change event in the first object, this program becomes circular—that is, the events will continue calling themselves indefinitely.

Consider this problem in a simple example with two text boxes. When each text box receives the focus, it sets the focus to the other text box, and focus shifts back and forth between the two text boxes indefinitely. The program seems to lock up, and you cannot click any other object on the form while the text boxes are updating each other. Whenever a program seems to lock up, you should press the Ctrl+Break keys and then check the relationship between the events in your program. Setting breakpoints and watch expressions might be the only way to determine the sequence of events that is happening.

To see events call other events infinitely:

1. Click the **Start** button �) on the toolbar.

2. Click the text box containing the text **Text2**. The contents of the text boxes are updated each time a text box receives the focus. You cannot click the End button or the Exit command button to end the program.

3. Press the **Ctrl+Break** keys to stop the program and enter design mode.

4. Set a breakpoint in the line that reads **times = times + 1** for the Text1_GotFocus and Text2_GotFocus events.

5. Click the **Start** button ▶ on the toolbar.

6. Click the **Text2** text box. The program breaks and shows you the Code window each time the variable times is updated in the GotFocus events of the text boxes.

7. Continue to click the **Start** button ▶ several times to see the event procedures being called indefinitely.

8. Delete one of the SetFocus statements to end this infinite loop.

9. Click the **End** button ■ on the toolbar.

Identifying the exact cause of a problem like this can be difficult. You might need to set breakpoints or use the Step Into button in each event procedure that might be causing the problem, in order to see which events are being called. The best solution to the problem is prevention. Good design and well-written pseudocode and TOE charts will help avoid such problems.

You should use the Visual Basic debugging tools to diagnose errors interactively in your program. As your programs become larger, be sure to write small pieces of code, and then thoroughly test the code and fix any problems. Then, as you continue developing a program, you can step over those procedures that you know are working.

When you notice that a variable has a value you do not expect it to have, set a watch expression that will cause the program to enter break mode whenever the value of the variable changes. If a procedure seems to be incorrect, set a breakpoint just before the first statement of the procedure executes and then trace each statement in the procedure, if necessary.

Answers to Quick Check Questions

SESSION 1.1

1 Creating a program can be divided into four steps. First you create the interface by drawing the controls on the form. Then you write the necessary Visual Basic statements to accomplish the tasks the program needs to perform. You can then run the program and test for errors. The fourth and final step is to correct any errors and continue testing.

2 A Project contains all of the information about the files that make up a Visual Basic program. This information includes the forms used in the program, and other files containing Visual Basic statements. You can change the files used by a project with the Project window.

3 A form is an object that contain other objects that use will to interact with the program. For example, the use can interact with text boxes and see descriptive information in labels on a form. A form has several properties that describes its appearance. These properties include the background color, and border style. Just like other objects, a form can respond to events.

4 The Index tab is used to search for information directly using key words. As you type characters, the subjects matching your characters will appear in a window. You can click on the desired topic to display help for that item. Using the Contents tab is much like looking through a table of contents.

5 Run the current project. This has the effect of switching Visual Basic from design mode to run mode. End the current project. This has the effect of switching Visual Basic from run mode to design mode. Open an existing Project.

6 Click the File Print commands and select the Form Image option.

SESSION 1.2

1 The Properties window is used to change the properties of the active object while Visual Basic is in design mode. Each object, including forms and controls created from the toolbox have a fixed set of properties you can set with the Properties window. Different objects have different properties.

2 The Label control is used to display output from your program. This output is controlled by the Caption property. The property can be set using the Properties window while in design mode or using Visual Basic code while in run mode.

3 You can move an object by clicking on the object and holding down the left mouse button while moving the mouse on the screen. An outline of the object will be displayed while it is being moved. To position the object, release the mouse button. To resize an object, click on the object. Then, hold down the left mouse button of one of the sizing handles. Move the mouse until the object is of the desired size and release the mouse button. To delete an object, click on the object and press the delete key.

4 The Command Button is typically used when you want to execute code in response to the user clicking the mouse over the object. When the user clicks on the object at run time, a Click event will be generated. If there are Visual Basic statements in the Click event procedure, they will be executed. If the button is disabled, no events will be generated. You can set the Caption property to change the text displayed inside the button.

5 The Image control is used to display a picture inside the region of the object. The picture that is displayed is controlled by the Picture property. You can cause the picture to be resized to fill the region of the Image by setting the Stretch property to True.

6 You write all Visual Basic statements in a window called the Code window. It allows you to select the object and procedure for which you want to write statements.

7 You can save a project by using the Menu Bar commands File Save Project.

SESSION 2.1

1 Well planned and designed programs will take less time to code and have fewer errors. The user interface will also tend to be improved and more consistent. A program that is well documented can be maintained more easily.

2 The steps of design consist of
 • The IPO model
 • Pseudocode
 • Screen layout
 • TOE chart

3 IPO is an acronym for INPUT-PROCCESSING-OUTPUT. It is a methodology for describing the input values to a program, the operations to be performed on those inputs, and finally the results of the program and how they are to be displayed.

4 Pseudocode is a way of expressing a computer problem using English-like statements to describe the problem's solution.

> Pseudocode to balance a checkbook.
>
> INPUT SECTION
> Get ending balance shown in the bank statement
> Get all deposits not shown in the statement
> Get all checks not shown in the statement
>
> PROCESSING SECTION
> Add to the ending balance the deposits not shown on the statement and subtract
> the check not shown in the statement
>
> OUTPUT SECTION
> Display the result which should be the ending balance in your checkbook

5 A TOE chart is a way of expressing the tasks a program needs to perform, the objects used to perform those tasks, and the events that will cause the tasks to be performed.

6 A Label control can only display output from your program or descriptive text by storing a value into the Caption property. A user cannot type values into a Label. A TextBox can both receive input and display output. The contents of a text box are displayed in the Text property.

7 The line control can help visually identify to the user the different parts of a form or provide emphasis to parts of the form.

SESSION 2.2

1 The Dim statement is used to explicitly declare variables. Variables have a data type that describe the kind of information the variable can store. Some of the Visual Basic data types include Integer and Single.

2 When a user clicks on an object it is set to receive focus. At this time, the GotFocus event occurs for the object. When the user clicks or presses the Tab key to move to another object, the LostFocus event occurs. The Click event occurs when the user clicks on an object. This happens after the GotFocus event occurs for an object. If the contents of an object like a TextBox changes, a Change event will occur.

3 ^ is performed first
Multiplication (*) and division (/) are performed next in the order of their appearance in the expression
Integer division is performed next (\)
Modulo arithmetic is performed next (Mod)
Addition (+) and subtraction (-) are performed at the same time
Strings are concatenated (&) last

4 Syntax errors are caused when you incorrectly use Visual Basic statements or write other statements that have no meaning to Visual Basic. The Visual Basic Code window will detect syntax errors for you as you write your program. Run-time errors occur while your program is running and are the result of an error that could not be detected when the code was being written. Run-time errors can be caused by trying to perform arithmetic operations on variables that do not contain numbers or calling intrinsic functions with incorrect arguments. Logic errors happen when you write Visual Basic statements that are correct, but the statements do not correctly solve the problem.

5 Clicking the Print command on the File menu will activate the Print Dialog Box. You can print the code in your program using the code option. If you want to print the different objects created on the form, the properties and their settings, use the Form As Text option. Finally, the Form As Image will print an image of the form to the printer.

SESSION 3.1

1 The Min and Max properties describe the valid range of values for a ScrollBar. The value cannot be less than Min or greater than Max. LargeChange and SmallChange describe how must the value of the ScrollBar will be changed. When you click on the scroll arrows, the value will be increased or decreased by SmallChange. When you click in the region of the ScrollBar the value will be changed by LargeChange. The Value property is an integer that defines the current value of the ScrollBar.

2 Boolean values are a Visual Basic data type that can only contain the values of True or False. You cannot store any other value in a Boolean variable.

3 A CheckBox is a control that allows the user to place a check mark in the object.

4 A CheckBox can have three values. It can be checked, unchecked or dimmed. You can find out the status of a CheckBox by looking at the value property at run time.

5 If lblTaxes.Visible = True then
     lblTaxes.Caption = 33
  End If
  If lblTaxes.Visible <> False then
     lblTaxes.Caption = 0
  End If
  if lblJan > lblFeb Then
     lblJan.Caption = Val(lblJan.Caption) + 1
  End If
  If yesterday < today Then
     End
  End If

6 The Change event occurs when the contents of an object changes. The Change event applies to scroll bars and text boxes. The Click event occurs when the user clicks the mouse on object. The Click event is useful with the CommandButton and Image objects.

7 When an event procedure for an object changes the value of another object, a change event will occur for that object. If the changed object changes the value of another object, a Change event will occur for that object.

SESSION 3.2

1 A Frame is used to contain other objects like option buttons so that they will operate as a group. A Frame can also be used to visually identify parts of a form.

2 When you create option buttons inside a Frame, they are said to be contained by the Frame. Thus, only one OptionButton in the Frame can be active at any one time. You can create several frames on a form.

3 The Debug window is used to print out the values of variables and object properties in your program while in break mode. It can help you locate and fix errors in your program.

4 A control array allows you to create several objects that have the same name and share event procedure. You reference individual elements (objects) in a control array using the Index property and the object name.

5 By holding down the Shift key and clicking on different objects, you can select multiple objects. Each selected object will appear with grayed handles. After selecting multiple objects, you can click and drag the options as a group by holding down the mouse button inside a selected object and moving the mouse. When the objects are in the desired location, release the mouse button.

6 Message boxes are useful to confirm a user action like exiting the program. Message boxes are displayed by calling the MsgBox function. A Message box window will be displayed when the MsgBox function is called. The window has a title bar, descriptive text, and a button the user can click. You can take different actions depending upon which button the user clicked.

SESSION 4.1

1 The Data control uses the Connect property to determine the type of database to be used. By default, the value of this property is Access. The DatabaseName property is used to identify the actual database that is used. After setting the DatabaseName, the RecordSource property is used to specify the individual table that the Data Control will reference. Finally, the RecordsetType property determines the kind of Recordset that will be created by the Data control at run time.

2 When a control is used to display data from a database or save data to a database, it is referred to as a bound control. You can bind controls to a database by setting the DataSource property to the name of an existing Data control and the DataField property to a field in the table identified by the Data control. You should always set these properties after creating and setting the properties for the Data control.

3 A Recordset is an object that exists at run time that works a table into a database like a window. When you set the properties of the Data control, it will create a Recordset object at run time. You can access the Recordset using the Recordset property of the Data control. A Recordset has properties to determine the position of the current record pointer in the Recordset, and methods to navigate through the records. A Recordset object does not support any events.

4 A TextBox that can display multiple lines of text is called a multi-line TextBox. To create a multi-line TextBox you need to set the MultiLine property to True. If the text will not fit in the region of the TextBox, you should set the ScrollBars property to 1-Horizontal to display a horizontal scroll bar across the bottom of the Text Box, or 2-Vertical to display a vertical scroll bar across the right side of the TextBox. If you want both horizontal and vertical scroll bars to appear, set the ScrollBars property to 3-Both.

5 The UpdateRecord method is supported by the Data control to record changes to the database. The Refresh method is supported by both the Data Control and the Recordset object to reload the contents of the Records. The AddNew method will create a new record in the Recordset. The Update method will record changes to the Recordset, and the Delete method will remove the current record. These three methods are supported by the Recordset object only.

SESSION 4.2

1 The Style property of the ComboBox controls its appearance. If it is set to 0-Dropdown Combo, a list of choices will appear when the user clicks on the list arrow on the right side of the ComboBox. The user can select an item from the list or type in a different value. If the Style is set to 2-Dropdown List, it behaves like a Dropdown Combo but the user must select a value from the list. A Simple combo box does not have a list or arrows and displays several items at once. If the items will not fit in the ComboBox, scroll bars will appear. The user must select from the list of values.

2 A ListBox is almost identical to a Simple ComboBox. However, it is possible to select multiple items from a ListBox.

3 The FindFirst method of the Recordset object will locate the first record in a Recordset that satisfies some criteria. If a record matching the criteria cannot be located, the current record pointer is positioned to the first record in the Recordset. If the Recordset contains more than one record that satisfies the criteria, FindFirst locates the first occurrence. The following statement would locate the first occurrence of the name "Smith" in the field fldLastName.
```
datContact.Recordset.FindFirst "fldLastName = " & "'" & "Smith" & "'"
```

4 An Input Box is a window that is opened when the InputBox function is called. It is used to obtain a text string from the user. An Input Box has two buttons. If the user clicks the OK button, the test string will be returned from the function. If the user clicks the Cancel button, the text string will be empty.

5 An error handler is used so that your program will not end as a result of a run-time error. The On Error statement is used to set up an error handler in a procedure. Usually the statement is followed by a GoTo label statement. When an error occurs, the statement after the label will be executed. The Resume Next statement is used inside the error handler to execute the statement following the one that caused the error.

SESSION 5.1

1 An object variable is declared using the Dim statement just like an ordinary variable. However, instead of using a clause like As Integer, the As clause is used with a type of object like Recordset.

2 A Do Until loop executes statements until some condition is True. A Do While loop executes statements while some condition is True.

3
```
Do While rstPacific.EOF = False
    Debug.Print rstPacific![fldProductID]
    rstPacific.MoveNext
Loop
```

4 A counter is used to increment a variable by a fixed value, usually one, each time some activity occurs like printing a record. An accumulator is used to store totals. Each time some activity occurs, you will generally add the contents of a variable to an accumulator. Both counters and accumulators are usually initialized to zero.

5 The print method of the printer object is used to send output to the printer buffer. You can specify the Tab and Spc arguments to position text. The EndDoc method is used to send the contents of the printer buffer to the printer.

6 The Tab argument is used to position the next argument at an absolute column on the page. The Spc argument is used to move some number of spaces from the current position on the page.

SESSION 5.2

1 A menu title appears on the menu bar across the top of the form. When a menu title is clicked, a menu is opened containing menu items. When a menu item is clicked, a Click event is generated for which you generally write code to perform some action.

2   An access key is the underlined character that appears on a menu title or menu item. It allows the user to hold down the ALT key and press the access key to navigate through the menu. Access keys provide the user the ability to use keyboard input to execute menu commands. A shortcut key can be a function key or control key sequence that will allow a user to execute a menu item directly without navigating through the menus. Shortcut keys should be supplied for frequently used commands.

3   Separator bars are used to visually separate similar items on a menu. You can have as many separator bars on a menu as you need.

4   When a form becomes an active object, several events occur. The Load event occurs just after the Initialize event and occurs the first time the form is loaded. When a program has multiple forms, the activate event occurs each time the user switches from one form to another. After the Activate event occurs, the GotFocus event occurs. This is the final event that occurs for the form.

5   The Refresh method is used to redraw all of the controls on the form. The Show method is used to display a form on the screen. If it has not already been loaded, a Load event will occur.

6   The Unload statement will unload a form or control from memory. If a form was unloaded, calling the Show method will cause the form to be reloaded and a Load event will occur. The Hide method is used to make the form invisible although it continues to be loaded into memory.

SESSION 6.1

1   When you are reading and writing information that needs to be kept sorted, or you are working with a large amount of data, you should consider using a database. However, when the amount of data you are reading is quite small, you can often use a text file. While you use the methods of the Recordset object to read, write and locate records in a Recordset, you use the Visual Basic statements Open, Close, Input and Write to read and write text files. You cannot locate a specific record in a text file without reading all of the records before it.

2   The Open statement is used to Open text files. If the For Input clause is used, the file will be opended for reading. If the For Output clause is used, the file will be opened for writing, and any existing contents will be deleted from the file. If the For Append clause is used, data written to the file will be appended to any existing contents. The Input statement is used to read a file. When you are finished reading or writing a file, it should be explicitly closed using the Close statement.

3   The EOF function is used to determine the end of a text file. It returns True when the end of file has been reached and False otherwise.

4   Dim Prices(1 to 20) as Single

5   Each of these properties applies to a ListBox object. The List property takes one argument; an integer index. It will return the text contained in the corresponding list item. The ListCount property is an integer value that defines how many items are in a list. The ListIndex property is an integer value that defines the active item in a list. If the value is -1, then no item is selected.

6   For Count = 20 to 100
       print Count
    Next

7   The Exit For statement is used to exit a For loop before the counter no longer meets the specified condition. It is useful to exit the loop as a result of some error condition like invalid data.

SESSION 6.2

1   The RemoveItem method takes one argument, the index of the item to remove. When called with a ListBox object the specified item will be removed. The Clear method is used to Remove all the items from a list box at once. It takes no arguments. Both methods set the ListIndex property to -1 after they are called since there is no longer an active item.

2   A one-dimensional array consists of rows whereas a two-dimensional array is made up of rows and columns. You use one subscript with a one-dimensional array and two subscripts with a two-dimensional array.

3   When you open a file you use the For Input clause on the Open statement. When you open it for writing, you use the For Output or For Append clause. You use the Input statement to read a file and the Write statement to write a file.

4   The Variant data type can contain data from any of the other Visual Basic data types. In addition to storing the variable, Visual Basic stores the current data type of a variable.

Index

Visual Basic Task Reference

TASK	PAGE #	RECOMMENDED METHOD	NOTES
Accumulator, using	VB 190	Declare a variable to be used as an accumulator and set the initial value to 0. Add to the accumulator each time through a Do loop or a For loop.	
Array, creating	VB 229	Use the Dim statement followed by the array name. Enclose the subscript(s) in parentheses. Use the As clause followed by the data type.	**Dim** *array-name(lower-bound* **To** *upper-bound)* **As** *datatype*
Array, referencing	VB 230	Use the array name followed by an integer subscript enclosed in parentheses.	Use two subscripts with a two-dimensional array.
Change event, coding	VB 4	Write code for the Change event when you want statements to execute when the contents of an object change.	
CheckBox control, creating	VB 95	Set the Caption property to display a prompt for the object. Use the Value property at run time to determine if the box is checked or not.	See Reference Window, "Adding a CheckBox Object to a Form."
Code window, inserting a procedure into	VB 99	Click Insert then click Procedure to open the dialog box. Specify the procedure name.	When using multiple forms, be sure the Code window is set to the correct form module.
Code window, setting the active procedure in	VB 32	Click the correct module in the Project window and click View Code. Select the object then select the event or general procedure in the object and proc list boxes at the top of the window.	
Code, printing	VB 51	Click File, then click Print. Click Code. Use the Range section of the dialog box to print the current module or the project.	
ComboBox control, creating and programming	VB 156	Set the Style property to control the appearance of the object. Set the List property at design time, or call the AddItem method at run time to fill the list with the items.	*Object.***AddItem** *"Text"*
CommandButton control, creating and programming	VB 30	Set the Caption property to display text in the button. Write statements for the Click event procedure that are executed when the button is clicked at run time.	See Reference Window "Creating a Command Button."
Constants, using	VB 105	Create user-defined constants to store information that will not change at run time. Use intrinsic constants to improve program readability.	**[Public	Private] Const** *constantname* **[As** *type]* = *expression*
Control array, creating	VB 118	Select a control instance. Copy and paste the object. Respond "Yes" to the prompt for creating a control array. Position the object on the form. Use the Index argument for the event procedure to reference the specific object in a control array.	See Reference Window "Creating a Control Array."

Task Reference

TASK	PAGE #	RECOMMENDED METHOD	NOTES
Controls, binding	VB 145	Set the DataSource property to an existing Data control, then set the DataField property to the correct field in the table.	Be sure to create the Data control and set its properties before binding other controls like text boxes.
Controls, deleting	VB 26	Select the object(s) and press the Delete key.	You can use the Delete Undo command from the edit menu to undo accidental deletions.
Controls, moving	VB 120	Select the object(s) to move. With the cursor inside one of the selected objects, drag the objects to their new position.	See Reference Window "Setting the Size and Position of a Form."
Controls, resizing	VB 27	Select the object(s) to resize. Drag one of the sizing handles to resize the object.	See Reference Window "Setting the Size and Position of a Form."
Controls, selecting a group of	VB 120	Hold down the Shift key and click the controls to activate them, or use the mouse to draw a rectangle around the objects you want to activate.	Selected controls appear with grayed handles.
Counter, using	VB 190	Declare a variable to be used as a counter and set the initial value to 0. Add 1 to the counter each time through a Do loop. A For loop increments a counter automatically.	
Data control, creating and programming	VB 140	Set the DatabaseName property to the database file, then set the RecordSource property to the name of the table or query you want to use. The database and table must already exist.	See Reference Window "Using a Data Control to Connect to an Existing Database"
Data type, choosing	VB 72	Create an Integer or Long variable for numbers without a decimal point. Use a Single variable for numbers with a decimal point. Character strings should have the String type.	
Debugging, creating watch expressions	VB 272	Click Tools, then click Add Watch to open the Add Watch dialog box. Enter the expression and the context. Depending on the action you want to take when something happens to the expression, set the Watch Type.	Use watch expressions sparingly in large or long-running programs. They can significantly slow down your program.
Debugging, deleting watch expressions	VB 272	Click the watch expression in the Debug window, then press the Delete key.	
Debugging, examining each statement	VB 274	Click the Step Into button. The Code window will display each statement with a border just before it is executed.	
Debugging, looking at variables in break mode	VB 270	Activate the immediate pane of the Debug window. Type a Print statement followed by the object property you want to look at.	Set watch expressions for variables you look at frequently.

Task Reference

Task Reference

TASK	PAGE #	RECOMMENDED METHOD	NOTES
Form, defining a startup	VB 204	Click Tools, then click Options. Click the Project tab and select the startup form from the list box.	
Form, unloading	VB 207	Use the Unload statement followed by the object to unload. Any properties set at run time for the object are lost when the object is reloaded.	**Unload** *formname*
Format function, using	VB 79	Use the fixed format to display data with two decimal places. Use the currency format to display data with a leading dollar sign.	**Format**(*expression*[,*format*])
Frame control, creating	VB 114	Set the Caption property to display a prompt in the frame. Draw option buttons inside the frame so that they will work as an option group.	See Reference Window "Adding a Frame Object to a Form."
GotFocus event, coding	VB 68	Write code for the GotFocus event procedure for a form or object. The code will execute when the object becomes the active object.	
HScrollBar control, creating	VB 97	Set the Max, Min, LargeChange and SmallChange properties to define how the object will behave at run time. Use the Change event to check the Value property at run time.	See Reference Window "Adding a ScrollBar Object to a Form."
Image control, creating	VB 34	Set the Stretch property to True to size the picture to the size of the object. Set the Picture property to the file containing the picture. The image can respond to a Click event.	See Reference Window "Adding an Image Control to a Form."
InputBox function, using	VB 161	Set the prompt to display a prompt in the box, and set the title to display information in the title bar. Set the default to define is the default button.	**InputBox**(*prompt*[,*title*] [,*default*])
Label control, creating	VB 26	Set the Caption property to display text in the label. Set other properties to justify and change the appearance of the text.	See Reference Window "Adding a Label Contol to a form."
Line control, creating	VB 66	Set the BorderWidth property to change the thickness of the line or the ForeColor property to change the color.	See Reference Window "Creating a Line Object."
ListBox control, clearing the contents of	VB 242	Use the Clear method on a ListBox object to remove all the items in the object.	The ListIndex property is set to -1 after this method is called because no active item is.
ListBox control, filling with data	VB 160	Set the List property at design time, or call the AddItem method at run time to fill the list with the items you want.	

Task Reference

TASK	PAGE #	RECOMMENDED METHOD	NOTES
ListBox control, referencing items	VB 243	Use the List property with an index as an argument to reference the contents of an item in the list. Use the ListCount property to determine the number of items in a list, and the ListIndex property to identify the active item.	The ListIndex property begins at 0. If there is no active item, this property is set to -1.
ListBox control, removing a single item from	VB 244	Use the RemoveItem method on a ListBox object to remove an item. The method takes one argument—an index representing the item to remove.	
LostFocus event, coding	VB 68	Write code for the LostFocus event procedure for a form or object. The code will execute just before the active object becomes inactive.	
Menu item, creating a shortcut key for	VB 201	For a menu item, select the desired shortcut key you want.	You cannot define a short cut key for a menu title.
Menu, creating	VB 197	Open the Menu Editor for a form. Set the Name and Caption properties. The Caption will be displayed on the menu. The Name is used to reference the event procedure. Indent the menu to the desired level.	See Reference Window "Creating a Menu System."
Menu, creating an access key for	VB 201	Place the & character to the left of the character to be used as an access key.	Be careful not to use the same access key for a menu item as for the menu title.
MsgBox function, using	VB 126	Set the prompt to display a prompt in the box, the title to display information in the title bar, and the buttons to specify the number and caption of the buttons in the message box.	**MsgBox**(*prompt*[, *buttons*] [, *title*])
Object properties, printing	VB 84	Click File, then click print. Click Form As Text. The non-default properties of an object are printed.	
Object variables, creating	VB 183	Use the Dim statement to create the object variable then the Set statement to point the variable to an existing object. Use the New keyword to create an instance of the object.	**Dim** *varname* **As [New]** *object* **Set object = [[New]** *object expression* | **Nothing**]
OptionButton control, creating	VB 46	Set the Caption property to display a prompt in the option button. Draw buttons inside a frame so that they will work as an option group.	See Reference Window Object "Adding an OptionButton Object to a Frame."
Program, breaking	VB 18	Click the Break button ▯.	Program will be in break mode. You can type statements into the Debug window.
Program, ending	VB 19	Click the End button ▪.	The program will be in design mode after clicking the button.

Task Reference

Task Reference

TASK	PAGE #	RECOMMENDED METHOD	NOTES
Shape control, creating	VB 93	Set the BorderWidth property to change the thickness of the line around the shape. Set the BackColor and BackStyle properties to control the background of the shape. Set the FillStyle and FillColor properties to control the fore-ground of the shape.	See Reference Window "Adding a Shape Object to a Form."
Statements, executing a fixed number of times	VB 32	The counter will be initialized to start. If it is less than or equal to end, the statements in the loop will execute; otherwise, the statement after Next will execute. Each time through the loop, the counter is incremented by increment.	**For** *counter* = *start* **To** *end* [**Step** *increment*] [*statement-block*] [**Exit For**] [*statement-block*] **Next** [*counter*]
Statements, executing until a condition is True	VB 188	Create a Do While loop to execute statements while a condition is True or a Do Until loop until a condition is True.	**Do** [[**While|Until**] *condition*] *statements* **Loop**
Tab order, setting	VB 65	Change the TabIndex property of objects that receive the focus. The first object to receive the focus has a TabIndex of 0, and the second a TabIndex of 1.	
Text file, closing	VB 228	Use the Close statement followed by the file-number(s) to close, Filenumbers should be separated by commas. If you do not specify a filenumber, all open files will be closed.	**Close** [*filenumberlist*]
Text file, opening	VB 224	Use the Open statement followed by the name of the file. Add the For Input, For Output, or For Append clause depending on whether you are reading or writing the file. Add the As clause followed by an unassigned filenumber.	**Open** *pathname* **For** [**Input | Output | Append**] **As** #*filenumber* See Reference Window "Opening a Text File."
Text file, reading	VB 225	Use the Input statement followed by the filenum-ber of a file opened with the Open statement. Append variable names separated by commas that correspond to the fields in the input file.	**Input** #*filenumber*, *variablelist* See Reference Window "Reading a Text File."
Text file, writing	VB 252	Use the Write statement followed by the filenum-ber of a file opened with the Open statement. Append variable names separated by commas as necessary	**Write** #*filenumber, variablelist* See Reference Window "Writing a Text File."
TextBox control, creating	VB 62	Set the Text property at run time to display text in the text box. Set other properties to justify and change the appearance of the text.	See Reference Window "Creating a TextBox Object."
TextBox control, specifying multiple lines in	VB 161	Set the MultiLine property to True. Set the MaxLength property to the maximum number of characters to store in the object. Set the ScrollBars property to display vertical and/or horizontal scroll bars in the object.	The MultiLine property must be set to True to display scroll bars.

Task Reference

TASK	PAGE #	RECOMMENDED METHOD	NOTES
Variable, creating	VB 71	Write a Dim statement and specify the data or object type. Local variables are declared inside a procedure. Module-level variables are declared in the general declarations section of the module.	See Figure 2-23 for the valid data types. **Dim** [*Varname* [**As** *Type*]]
VScrollBar control, creating	VB 97	Set the Max, Min, LargeChange, and Small Change properties to define how the object will behave at run time. Use the Change event to check the Value property at run time.	See Reference Window "Adding a ScrollBar Object to a Form."